Measurement and Evaluation of Learning

Measurement and Evaluation of Learning

Fourth Edition

Arnold J. Lien
University of Wisconsin/Whitewater

in collaboration with
Harriet S. Lien

wcb

Wm. C. Brown Company Publishers
Dubuque, Iowa

Contents

PART 2
Classroom Techniques and Procedures of Measurement and Evaluation

Preface

Measurement and Evaluation of Learning, the fourth edition, like the first three editions, is a basic textbook for undergraduate measurement and evaluation courses. It may also be used by experienced teachers as they study together in the in-service program or individually as there is a need for a reference book of specific ideas or techniques in measurement and evaluation.

Ways in which this edition is similar to the first three editions include the organization into parts: *Foundations of Educational Measurement and Evaluation, Classroom Techniques and Procedures of Measurement and Evaluation, Describing Educational Data and Standardized Testing,* and *Application of Measurement and Evaluation;* a question-and-answer approach; a fast transfer from theory to the use and application of measurement principles; summary statements, discussion questions, student activities, selected readings at the end of each chapter; and an extended appendix for reference purposes.

The objectives of Part One, *Foundations of Educational Measurement and Evaluation,* include the following.

To acquaint the student with the relationship between evaluation and the teaching process. Here, the student learns that measurement and evaluation are an integral part of the teaching process. The three main steps or tasks in the teaching process are introduced and discussed.

To acquaint the student with the essential characteristics of a good measuring instrument. This topic continues to be divided into two chapters. Prior to the third edition, everything was included in one chapter. In this, the fourth edition, Chapter Two will deal with the main criteria of a good measuring instrument; namely, validity, reliability, and usability. Later in this book, Chapter 8 will deal with interpretation of test scores, norms, and derived scores. It is placed there because it relates best to standardized test scores.

Part Two covers *Classroom Techniques and Procedures of Measurement and Evaluation*. The main objectives here are as follows.

To assist the student in planning for measurement and evaluation in a lesson or unit. The first step in planning for measurement and evaluation is to develop a clear statement of objectives. Chapter 3 takes the student step-by-step through this process, culminating in a chart showing a complete plan for measurement of a unit. It emphasizes the domains of educational objectives and gives examples of objectives in each. Minimum competency testing has been added here.

To enable the student to write test items of various kinds and to organize them into a test. Chapter 4 is devoted to the construction and use of classroom tests. Here, the student will learn the functions of teacher-made tests, how to ask questions to develop diversity of thinking, the difference between criterion- and norm-referenced testing, basic types of items, general principles of test construction, and steps in building a test. In addition, there is a page or more devoted to each of nine different types of test items which tells the student how to construct and use each one. Oral questioning and interpretation of situational-type items have been included. A very important final topic is evaluation of a classroom test through the technique of item analysis.

To assist the student in understanding how to measure and evaluate the more affective and/or performance type of student learning. Chapter 5 covers observational tools while Chapter 6 is devoted to judging procedures, products, and performances. In Chapter 5, the student is exposed to the concepts and techniques of observational tools including techniques to measure personal-social adjustment. Chapter 6 describes how to measure and evaluate procedures, products, and performances. These outcomes are extremely important in the fields of art, music, physical education, home economics, industrial arts, business education, and the like. They are also useful in many performances in regular subjects. Work-sample tests, identification tests, simulated conditions tests, and assignments and projects are explained in Chapter 6.

Part Three includes *Describing Educational Data and Standardized Testing*. The main objectives include the following.

To help the student describe educational data. The specific purposes of Chapter 7 are to help students present data properly, analyze it accurately, and apply the results to better understand student growth toward the objectives. It will also help the teacher to read educational journals with greater comprehension.

To enable the student to have an understanding of norms and derived scores. Here, the student will learn how to read norm tables and will learn to compute and interpret such derived scores as percentiles, stanines, z-scores, T-scores, and deviation IQs, among others.

To help the student understand and to enable him/her to use standardized tests. Chapter 9 introduces standardized tests and acquaints the student with their purposes, programs, selection, sources of information about them, and how to administer and score them. Chapter 10 describes ability and aptitude tests. Stress is placed on understanding the different types of ability and aptitude tests, an annotated listing of common ones, and how to interpret and use ability and aptitude tests. There are also examples of profiles of these two kinds of tests. Chapter 11 discusses achievement tests. In addition to describing how a standardized achievement test is built, the chapter tells how standardized tests are classified into diagnostic, single-subject, and batteries of achievement tests. There is an annotated listing of individual and/or referral tests as well. Emphasis is placed on how to interpret an achievement test. Test profiles are also presented of some of the common ones. Finally, there is a discussion of uses of achievement tests.

Part Four relates to *Application of Measurement and Evaluation.* The objectives of this part are as follows.

To help the student interpret measurement data to pupils and parents. In Chapter 12, an attempt is made to provide a rationale for interpreting measurement and evaluation data to pupils and parents. Once this is established, the student is aided with principles and techniques of interpretation. Expectancy tables are described as a means of determining student progress in relation to ability. Since many states now have legislation on student records, a sample piece of legislation on the maintenance and confidentiality of student records is reproduced.

To acquaint the student with current thinking on grading, marking, and reporting practices. Chapter 13 helps the student deal with one of the very difficult procedures in teaching. This is an exhaustive discussion on scoring, grading, marking, and reporting practices. New topics on assignment of grades and course marks are introduced; how to assign marks to classes having different levels of academic ability is described. The problem of how to assign weights to different performances of the students and combine them into a final mark is presented. Examples of various reporting forms are reproduced and described.

To assist the reader in understanding the evaluation implication of Public Law 94-142; to help the student understand the principles of individually guided education and how one assesses pupil growth in this program. The first part of this chapter is devoted to how evaluation fits into an IEP, the Individual Educational Program required under Public Law 94-142. The latter part of the chapter is a condensed version of one of the best dissertations on the topic of individually guided education, with emphasis on assessment. This is a must, whether the teacher is in a multi-unit school or tries to meet individual differences in a self-contained classroom.

The appendixes contain the many sources that a teacher needs to use. It includes such topics as: condensed versions of the cognitive and affective domains of the Taxonomy of Educational Objectives, illustrative verbs to use in behavioral objectives, computation of the Pearson Product-Moment coefficient of Correlation, statistical symbols and formulas commonly used in measurement, how to compute the square root of a number, table of squares and square roots, computation of stanines, selected test publishers directory, examples of profiles of early childhood tests, percent of cases falling below selected values on the normal curve, marking and report forms of special types of schools, a directory of test scoring services, and a glossary of common measurement terms.

The author becomes indebted to many people during the course of a revision such as this. It is not possible to list all the persons who have contributed to it, but special thanks should be given to my colleagues in the College of Education at the University of Wisconsin-Whitewater, who have contributed valuable suggestions. Sharon Easley of Wm. C. Brown Company Publishers helped by providing me with valuable comments from users and reviewers. I had the great advantage of having a copy editor in my home—my wife, Harriet S. Lien, who not only edited copy, but did all of the necessary technical and office tasks; without her help, the revision could not have been completed. A number of publishers and individuals, cited in the text, generously permitted me to reproduce their tabular or graphic matter.

Arnold J. Lien
Professor of Education
University of Wisconsin-Whitewater

Foundations of Educational Measurement and Evaluation

1

1

Evaluation and the Teaching Process

What are the main tasks in the teaching process?
What is the language of measurement?
What are the types of measurement techniques and procedures?
What are the requisites for a teacher to be competent in measurement and evaluation?
What are the principal functions or purposes of measurement and evaluation?
What are the main developments in the history of measurement?

A. What Are the Main Tasks in the Teaching Process?

When a teacher thinks about the teaching process, a number of detailed steps or tasks may come to mind. In condensing these steps to the main essentials, however, three main tasks seem to come into focus. Thomas describes these tasks briefly as follows:[1]

Teacher Terms	Pupil Terms
What is worth teaching?	What is worth learning?
How can it best be taught?	How can it best be learned?
How well has it been taught?	How well has it been learned?

At this point, it is not significant whether one thinks of these steps in teacher terms or in pupil terms. In Chapter 3, when one starts planning definitely for measurement in a unit, it will be shown that it is desirable to think of these steps in terms of the pupil.

However, two things must be remembered about these basic steps. First of all, they should be considered a CYCLE. From the listing above, it would appear that the job is done when these three steps are completed; this is not

1. R. Murray Thomas, *Judging Student Progress,* 2nd ed. (New York: David McKay Co., Inc.), p. 5. © Longmans, Green & Co., Inc., New York, 1960. Reprinted with permission of the publisher.

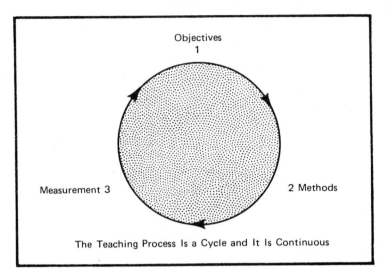

Figure 1.1   The Teaching Process.

the case. From Figure 1.1, one notes that Step 1 (objectives) assists in giving directions to Step 2 (methods); Step 2 then aids in determining Step 3 (measurement and evaluation); Step 3 gives further direction to Step 1. Second, this cycle should be regarded as CONTINUOUS. The teaching process is never completed; rather, it is only changed as new goals, new methods, and measurement modify the process.

So that each of these steps may be more clearly understood, one must look further at each one, filling in a little more detail.

1. What Is Worth Teaching—What Is Worth Learning?

   a. What does this mean?

   This refers to the objectives, aims, ends, outcomes, or goals of instruction.

   b. What is the purpose of this step?

   The purpose of this step is to plan, from the beginning, the outcomes toward which the pupil should be striving and to aid the teacher in instruction.

   c. But aren't the objectives already stated?

   Yes, many objectives already have been stated by education authorities, but these are general objectives that are stated for all schools on all levels. In 1918, the Seven Cardinal Principles of Education stressed such things as Health, Command of Fundamental Processes, Vocation, Ethical Character, Worthy Home Membership, Citizenship, and Worthy Use of Leisure Time.

In 1938, the Educational Policies Commission presented four main objectives of education, which are Self-Realization, Human Relationships, Economic Efficiency, and Civic Responsibility.

More recently, in 1961, the NEA through it Educational Policies Commission, stated the general objective of the public schools in America as follows:

> The central purpose of American Schools is the development of every student's rational powers; the ability to think. The kind of education that will make this possible is that which frees the mind and enables it to contribute to a full and worthy life. The school must be guided, in pursuing its central purpose or any other purposes, by certain conditions which are known to be basic to significant mental development. The school has responsibility to establish and maintain these conditions. These conditions are [paraphrased]: physical health; mental health; rapport with each pupil; recognition of human individuality; and meeting the needs of those who are handicapped in their rational powers by cultural deprivation, low levels of family aspiration, or severely limited endowment.[2]

Another source of objectives is the publications of the National Assessment of Educational Progress (NAEP),[3] which has published separate booklets of objectives for ten subject-matter areas: art, career and occupational development, citizenship, literature, mathematics, music, reading, science, social studies, and writing.

Objectives in each of these areas had to meet three criteria: They had to be ones that (1) the schools were currently seeking to attain, (2) scholars in the field considered authentic to their discipline, and (3) thoughtful laymen considered important. The third criterion was the most unique aspect of the National Assessment approach to developing objectives. Most published lists of objectives meet the first two criteria, but few, if any, other lists received so much scrutiny by laymen prior to publication. Eleven different lay panels reviewed the objectives in each of the subject-matter areas and, following these panel meetings, the eleven panel chairmen met and pooled the recommendations.

A further source of objectives is the Instructional Objective Exchange Center.[4] The center has different collections of behavioral objectives covering a range of subject matter. Most objectives are accompanied by six test items which may be used to assess whether the objective has been achieved.

2. Educational Policies Commission, *Central Purpose of American Education* (National Education Association, 1961), pp. 12-16.

3. National Assessment of Educational Progress, *Objectives in Ten Subject Matter Areas,* Denver, Colorado.

4. A current description of available objectives can be obtained from the Exchange, Box 24095, Los Angeles, California 90024.

In determining objectives for specific courses, major textbooks designed for those courses can be quite useful. However, it is possible to be too dependent on a textbook when developing objectives. These sources are often inadequate guides for developing affective objectives (attitudes and appreciations). Other specific aids would be publications (where they exist) of curriculum guides and course outlines.

d. *With these general objectives, why should teachers be able to state their own goals of instruction?*

The above objectives are general objectives which certainly should be of help to teachers, but there are several reasons why teachers should have skill in stating their own specific objectives:

So they can restate the general objectives for their own uses;

So they can state specific objectives for the pupils in their classrooms;

So they can continually evaluate and improve their present objectives;

Because objectives reflect upon the methods of instruction (Step 2);

Because objectives give direction to the proper measurement and evaluation (Step 3).

2. How Can It Best Be Taught? How Can It Best Be Learned?

a. *What does this mean?*

In the teaching process, the second step means that one must think through the methods, techniques, procedures, experiences, and activities to be used.

b. *What is the purpose of this step?*

Providing opportunities by which the pupils can grow toward the goals of instruction determined in Step 1 is the purpose of this step.

c. *What is the problem in this step?*

Here the real problem is not what methods or experiences can be used, since there is a storehouse of methods and experiences from which to choose. The problem is to select the most appropriate methods and experiences which will help the pupil grow toward the objectives.

For example, suppose one has the following general objective for a unit on safety. Objective: The pupil understands the rules of safety and practices them consistently in daily living.

What methods can be used? It would not take very long to think of several methods and experiences which might be used. Some of them are:

Read a bulletin on basic safety practices.
Write a paper on safe bicycle habits.
Listen to a local police official talk about community safety rules.
Give an informal talk on how to keep a bicycle in good repair.
Demonstrate proper street crossing practices.
Illustrate safety practices in and about school.

Then the job is to decide on the best methods and experiences to use with this class based on the time available, the facilities, and the abilities of the pupils. Sometimes, the answer will not be known definitely until the third step of the teaching process is completed and evaluation is made as to how well the pupils have grown toward the goals of instruction.

3. How Well Has It Been Taught? How Well Has It Been Learned?

a. What does this mean?

This is the measurement and evaluation phase of the teaching process.

b. What is the purpose of this step?

Determining by measuring and evaluating pupil progress how well the pupil has grown toward the goals of instruction is the basic aim of this step.

c. Do the terms measurement and evaluation mean the same thing?

No; in fact, like the teaching process, measurement and evaluation has its own process of three steps. One can see each of these phases by defining three key terms in order:

Measurement: Collection of data, by both objective and subjective means, to provide evidence for analysis and interpretation (Collection Phase).

Analysis: Presentation and analysis of data (collected through measurement), preparing it for interpretation (Analysis Phase).

Evaluation: Including measurement and statistics in the broad sense, but, in and of itself, interpretation of the results to determine how well the pupil has grown toward the goals of instruction (Interpretation Phase).

A Glossary of Common Measurement Terms is found in Appendix N.
TenBrink describes an evaluation model in three stages and ten steps.[5]
First, he defines evaluation as the process of obtaining information and us-
ing it to make judgments. The three stages and ten steps are as follows:

1. Preparation: Getting set to evaluate.
    a. *Specify the judgments and decisions to be made.* Unless we specify
        the decisions which are to be made, it is difficult to determine accu-
        rately what kind of information is needed.
    b. *Describe the information needed.* The more accurately you can de-
        scribe the information needed, the better you will be able to select
        the method best suited.
    c. *Locate information already available.* When some information is
        available, and it is the kind of information you need, and it is likely
        to be fairly accurate, use it.
    d. *Decide when and how to obtain needed information.* It is often use-
        ful to set up a schedule for obtaining information. This schedule
        would specify both when and how the information is to be ob-
        tained.
    e. *Construct (or select) the information-gathering instruments to be
        used.* There are many types of information-gathering techniques
        available to the teacher. (See next section for a listing.)
2. Data Collection: Obtaining the needed information.
    f. *Obtain the needed information.* No matter how well you plan your
        evaluation activities, the information you obtain will be grossly in
        error unless you use the various information-gathering techniques
        carefully.
    g. *Analyze and record information.* After the information has been ob-
        tained, it must be analyzed to obtain evidence of its accuracy and
        then recorded so that it can be used in forming judgments.
3. Evaluation: Forming judgments and making decisions.
    h. *Form judgments.* Forming judgments which can be used in decision-
        making is a relatively simple process. One begins by comparing the
        information he has (e.g., test scores) with some referent. On the
        basis of this comparison, estimative judgments and/or predictive
        judgments are formed.
    i. *Make decisions.* A teacher should have some guidelines by which to
        make decisions. The guidelines should have the characteristics of
        simplicity, flexibility, and objectivity.
    j. *Summarize and report the results.* Very often, teachers are asked to
        report their evaluation to others. These include parents, other teach-
        ers, administrators, and the students.

5. Terry D. TenBrink, *Evaluation: A Practical Guide for Teachers* (New York: Mc-
Graw-Hill Book Company, 1974), pp. 2-18.

B.   What Is the Language of Measurement?

To understand measurement, one must consider the nature of the scale on which the characteristic is being measured. These scales are hierarchical in that the higher level scales meet all the assumptions of the lower order scales plus additional ones characteristic of their particular level.

Characteristics of types of measurement scales are shown in Table 1.1.

The *nominal scale* includes such broad categories as male or female; Republican, Democrat, or independent; college majors of art, history, elementary education, or some other emphasis. This scale is of limited usefulness in teaching or psychology since it allows for only broad classification without any indication of magnitude, while, in most instances, we are interested in some idea of magnitude. However, there can be the assignment of numerals to objects or events according to rules, so we shall consider nominal scales as an example of measurement.

The next level of measurement, the *ordinal scale,* not only allows for grouping by category, as in a nominal scale, but also for an indication of magnitude. It allows us to rank people in order of magnitude on some decision (height, weight, intelligence, achievement). However, we cannot say *how much* one child is over another, we can only say he is higher or lower in rank. The ordinal scale allows for computation of some useful statistics. We can compute the *median* (the score that divides the distribution into halves), *percentiles* (the percent of people scoring below a given individual or score point), and *rank order* correlations. What we cannot do is to say

TABLE 1.1

Characteristics of Types of Measurement Scales

Scale	Operation	Description
Nominal	Equality	Mutually exclusive categories; objects or events fall into one class only; all members of same class considered equal; categories differ qualitatively, not quantitatively.
Ordinal	Equality Ranking	Idea of magnitude enters; object is larger or smaller than another (but not both); any monotonic transformation permissible.
Interval	Equality Ranking Equal-sized units	Additivity; all units of equal size; can establish equivalent distances along scale; any linear transformation permissible.
Ratio	Equality Ranking Equal-sized units True (absolute) zero	True or absolute zero point can be defined; meaningful ratios can be derived.

that a difference of a certain magnitude means the same thing at all points along the scale.

The *interval scale* is one in which the score units can be shown to be equivalent at all points on a scale. All that is lacking is a true zero point, i.e., an absolute zero. On an interval scale, scores can be transformed in any linear manner. That is, we can add, subtract, multiply, or divide scores.

Ratio scales are basically nonexistent in educational or psychological testing since they must have true zero points. Measurements of ability and achievement do not meet this criterion.

Most measurements in education then are of the ordinal or interval type. Because an interval scale possesses distinct advantages over an ordinal scale when analysis of scores is to be made, most educators prefer that test scores be expressed on an interval scale.

C. What Are the Types of Measurement Techniques and Procedures?

Following the definition of measurement (that is, the collection of data by both objective and subjective means), main headings of the common types of data-gathering devices can be specified.

1. Standardized Tests
    a. Ability and Aptitude
    b. Achievement and Diagnostic
    c. Interest, Attitude, and Personality
2. Classroom Tests
    a. Essay or Free Response
    b. Objective
        1. Recall or Supply
            a. Simple Recall
            b. Completion
        2. Recognition or Select
            a. Alternative Response
            b. Multiple Choice
            c. Matching
        3. Analogies
        4. Rearrangement
3. Observational Tools
    a. Participation Charts
    b. Checklists
    c. Rating Scales
    d. Anecdotal Records
    e. Interview
    f. Time Sampling

4. Sociometric and Related Techniques
   a. Sociogram
   b. Social Distance Scale
   c. "Guess Who" Questionnaires
5. Self-Report Inventories
   a. Attitude Scales and Questionnaires
   b. Autobiography
   c. Biographical Data Blank
6. Routine Measurement
   a. Assignments
   b. Oral Reports
   c. Laboratory Exercises
   d. Projects
   e. Performances

Each of these techniques will be discussed in the appropriate chapter further on in the text.

D. What Are the Requisites for a Teacher to Be Competent in Measurement and Evaluation?

In order to measure and evaluate effectively, there are certain requirements or qualifications which a teacher must meet. Some of these are developed in psychology courses, some in methods and student teaching, some in a measurements course, and all of them are further developed in actual experience. John Dobbin, Director, Cooperative Test Division, Educational Testing Service, lists five prerequisites which he believes are essential for teachers so that they will measure and evaluate pupils effectively.[6]

1. A Rather Complete Knowledge of the Typical Behaviors of Youngsters in the Age Group He Is Teaching.

If one of the teacher's goals, for example, is that of better rapport and greater cooperation between the individual student and the class in which he participates, the behavior he expects to see among eight- and nine-year-olds will be quite different from that which he expects to see among twelve- and thirteen-year-olds. The content and method of instruction have been quite different from that which he might use on another age group; similarly, the behaviors he observes as outcomes of instruction will vary considerably depending on the age level of the group with which he works. A first requisite for this skill in pupil observation, then, is a considerable knowledge of what behavioral characteristics are at various age levels.

---

6. National Education Association, National Commission on Teacher Education and Professional Standards, *The Improvement and Use of Tests by Teachers: Implications for Teacher Education.* Washington, D.C.: The Commission, 1955, p. 13.

2. A Rather Complete Knowledge of the Atypical or the Behavior Symptomatic of Individual Aberration from "Normality."

For example, a teacher looking for signs of growth toward better adjustment to the class group will know that the symptoms of growth will be different in a boy who began as a gregarious and outgoing individual than they will be in a youngster who, for a variety of reasons, is an introvert. In many of these kinds of growth, there is no "norm" or average behavior—only a range of different behaviors which, together, may be regarded as within the limits of normality.

3. A Third Body of Knowledge Which the Teacher Needs to Bring to His Observation of Pupil Progress Stems from His Knowledge and Experience in the Methodology of the Field He Is Teaching.

In addition to the training needed in child psychology and child development, a teacher must have specific knowledge of the developmental patterns of growth in certain kinds of learning. Thus, the teacher who is aiming toward certain specified proficiencies in multiplication of whole numbers knows that youngsters who are progressing satisfactorily toward the goal ordinarily will make certain kinds of errors before they establish, as habitual, successful behavior.

Furthermore, he knows that students who are not learning the material properly or adequately will make other kinds of errors, and the teacher can spot them immediately. So some of the teacher's preparation for his work in pupil observation proceeds from educational research as well as from research in child psychology and child development.

4. A Fourth Skill Necessary for Efficient and Useful Observation of Students Is the Skill in Organizing the Observations.

That is, few teachers will accomplish their goals by simply standing around and observing youngsters, nodding approval at those who exhibit the desired behavior and clucking their tongues at those who do not. The teacher needs to be trained and experienced in organizing these observations so that, together, they become meaningful and thereby useful. The organization of the observation is a whole special technique in itself and one which is of immeasurable value to the teacher and to the school when it has been learned and accomplished effectively. When the organization of observation has not been learned, the teacher may do his observation with insight and considerable skill, but, at the end of his observation, he has a disorganized mass of impressions and observations which are of little aid to him in deciding where he has succeeded and where he has failed and what he should do next.

5. The Fifth Skill Required in the Observation of Pupil Behavior Is That of Interpreting the Observations After They Have Been Made and Organized.

It is necessary for the teacher to understand the data and to be able to use the results for better instruction and pupil guidance. Usually, a teacher will have to interpret his results in three ways. First of all is interpretation to himself; this requires a very specific and detailed interpretation. Second is interpretation to the administrators, who usually are more interested in class summary reports than in particulars on an individual. Third is interpretation to the pupils and parents, who can best understand the results of pupil observation by an interpretation which is general and descriptive in nature.

E. What Are the Principal Functions or Purposes of Measurement and Evaluation?

When one measures and evaluates, one does so with a specific objective or purpose in mind. Objectives for which the teacher measures may be generally classified under one of several functions or purposes of measurement and evaluation. In the study of the specific measuring tools in Chapters 4-6 and 9-11, it can be noted that each one has specific functions or purposes to perform; however, they will be within one of these seven functions as proposed by Remmers and Gage.[7] Each function will be followed by a specific example to indicate how a measurement situation may serve that function. Following are the seven functions:

1. To Assist in the Guidance of Pupils
    Example: The teacher analyzes the cumulative record or background data of the individual pupils in his class to obtain helpful information for guidance purposes.
2. To Select Pupils
    Example: A placement test is administered in the ninth grade, which, together with other data, will assist in the grouping of pupils for instruction in basic fields. Pupils in this grade, then, will be grouped according to apparent ability as indicated by the test.
3. To Maintain Standards
    Example: (a) Group Standards. An analysis is made of the mental maturity test results of the total class to determine the general capacity of the group for learning. (b) Individual Standards. The results of an individual's achievement test are compared with his mental maturity test results to determine how well this student is reaching his standard of attainment.
4. To Motivate Pupils
    Example: A pretest is administered during the introduction to a new lesson or unit to make the pupils aware of the material to be studied, of what they already know to a degree, and of what material needs to be learned.
5. To Guide Teaching
    Example: The teacher analyzes the results of a checklist on study habits to determine strong and weak areas of pupil growth.

7. H. H. Remmers and N. L. Gage, *Educational Measurement and Evaluation* (New York: Harper & Row Publishers, Inc., 1955), p. 10.

6. To Furnish Instruction to the Pupils
   Example: Material is assigned covering multiplication of fractions, and students are asked to check their answers with those given at the back of the textbook.
7. To Evaluate Educational Methods, Facilities, or Procedures
   Example: Two groups, only one of which has had instruction in typing, are given a spelling achievement test to determine whether teaching spelling with typing is superior to teaching spelling by itself.

F. What Are the Main Developments in the History of Measurement?

Period of Development	Key Persons	New Developments
I. Early informal measurement approaches (ancient times to 1850)		Chinese essay examination 2200 B. C.
	Socrates	Socrates oral examination
	Quintilian	Individual difference studies
		University of Paris oral thesis examination, 1215
		Prussian "leaving exam" 1787
	Thomas Campbell	A university to examine and grant degrees, 1836
	Horace Mann	Replacement of oral by written examinations, 1845
II. Growth of psychological measurement and experimentation (1850 to 1930's)	George Fisher	Scale book standards for evaluation
	Regents of New York	State testing program
	Sir Francis Galton	Hereditary Genius, 1869
	Karl Pearson	Product-moment correlation
	Wilhelm Wundt	Experimental psychological laboratory, 1879
	Francis Galton and James Cattell	Study of intelligence through individual differences in sensory-motor performance
	Joseph Rice	School reform via survey testing, 1894
	Charles W. Eliot	College Entrance Examination Board, 1899
	E. L. Thorndike	Textbook in educational measurement, 1903
	Alfred Binet	First individual mental test, 1905
	C. W. Stone	Standard tests of arithmetic, 1908
	E. L. Thorndike	Handwriting quality scale, 1910
	Daniel Starch	Reliability of essay grades, 1912
	Charles Spearman	Factors of intelligence, 1914
	Lewis Terman	Stanford-Binet Intelligence Test, 1916

Figure 1.2   Milestones of Educational Measurement.

Figure 1.2 Continued

Period of Development	*Key Persons*	*New Developments*
	Arthur Otis	Army Alpha group intelligence test, 1917
	William McCall	Teacher-made classroom tests, 1920
	Terman, Kelley, and Ruch	First battery of standardized achievement tests, the *Stanford Achievement* Tests, 1923
	E. K. Strong	Measurement of vocational interest, 1925
III. Many standardized tests developed and used widely in education. Large scale evaluation	Charles Taylor	Educational Records Bureau, 1927
	Ben Wood	Pennsylvania study of educational achievement, 1928
	L. L. Thurstone	Scale for attitude measurement, 1929
	E. F. Lindquist	Every-pupil testing program, 1929
	Ben Wood	Cooperative Test Service, 1930
	Ralph Tyler	Eight-year study of secondary schools, 1932-40
	Jacob Moreno	Beginning of sociometry, 1935
	Reynold Johnson	Test scoring machine, 1935
	O. K. Buros	First Mental Measurement Yearbook, 1936
	William Learned	Graduate Record Examination, 1936
	State testing leaders	Invitational Conference on Testing Problems
	L. L. Thurstone	Tests of primary mental abilities, 1938
	Hermann Rorschach	Projective Techniques
	Ben Wood	National Teacher Examination, 1940
		National Council on Measurement in Education
	David Wechsler	Wechsler-Bellevue Intelligence Scale, 1939
		First issue of Educational and Psychological Measurement, 1941
	E. F. Lindquist	Tests of educational development, 1943
	James Conant	Educational Testing Service, 1947
	David Wechsler	Wechsler Intelligence Scale for Children, 1949
IV. Continued development of cognitive development, but start of affective objectives	E. F. Lindquist	Electronic test processing, 1953
	John Stalnaker	Scholarship examinations, 1955
		Publication of Technical Standards for Achievement Tests AERA-NCME, 1955
	Benjamin Bloom	Taxonomy of Educational Objectives: Cognitive Domain, 1956
	John C. Flanagan	Project TALENT, 1959
	Terman and Merrill	Revision of Stanford-Binet Test, 1960

Figure 1.2 Continued

Period of Development	*Key Persons*	*New Developments*
	Torsten Husen	International evaluation of achievement, 1961
	D. Krathwohl	Taxonomy of Educational Objectives: Affective Domain, 1964
V. Emphasis on Accountability in Education and Assessment Programs	Frances Keppel	National assessment of educational progress, 1964
	David Wechsler	Wechsler Intelligence Scale for Children (WPPSI), 1968
		Criterion-Referenced Testing
		Computer Assisted Testing
		Assessment in Individualized Instruction
		State Assessment Programs

1. Early Informal Measurement Approaches (Ancient Times to 1850)

The lengthy era might be termed the era of formal discipline. Emphasis in school learning was on mental growth only. The main objective of education seemed to be to train or discipline the mind. In order to do this, the curriculum and methods must promote this purpose. The curriculum contained what was termed discipline subjects. Depending on the grade level, it might include reading, arithmetic, foreign language, spelling, and the like. The methodology was drill and memorization. With this purpose and methodology, measurement would be very restrictive. It was limited basically to oral recitation and long, difficult essay-type examinations. It wasn't until Horace Mann questioned the equality of learning in the Boston schools that short written tests came into being.

2. Growth of Psychological Measurement and Experimentation (1850 to 1930's)

This period has to be considered the renaissance in the development of measurement and evaluation. Until this time, there was practically no real growth and, in this period, a tremendous surge laid the groundwork for our current programs. Study, experimentation, and development of objective measurement might characterize this era. The work of Galton and Cattell in individual differences laid the foundation for acceptance of the concept of individual differences in our schools since that time. Their lack of success in relating results of sensory-motor tests to school learning was disheartening to them, but the concept of individual differences was initiated nevertheless.

Father of achievement testing is a name generally given to Joseph Rice. Through his surveys of pupil learning in spelling, arithmetic, and language, he was able to survey the status of pupil learning through objective type of measurement. At the same time, Alfred Binet should be credited with the real beginning of intelligence measurement. Binet was commissioned by the

French government to develop a measure to identify children who could profit from special instruction. After much study, Binet and his assistant, Theodore Simon, published an article in 1905 in which they presented a series of tests to measure the level of mental development in children. Subsequent tests in 1908 and 1911 improve the original version. In the U.S., the original version of the Stanford-Binet was developed by Terman in 1916; revisions in 1937 and 1960 have played major roles in mental testing.

Thus, the standardized testing movement had begun. Even though Rice had initiated the idea of achievement testing 10-15 years previously, it wasn't until about 1908 that the real development started. The work of Stone in arithmetic reasoning, Courtis in arithmetic computation, Thorndike in handwriting, and Hillegas in composition promoted the movement in standardized achievement testing. World War I brought a very pressing need for the development of group tests to classify recruits according to mental ability. A Committee of the American Psychological Association, headed by Robert Yerkes, was asked to devise a method to do this. Fortunately, Arthur Otis, a student of Lewis Terman (author of the original Stanford-Binet) at Stanford University, had developed his doctoral dissertation on group intelligence testing following the ideas of the Stanford-Binet. Yerkes, Otis, and others then produced the first group test of intelligence; it was called the Army Alpha Test. The Alpha was the regular or verbal test. Subsequently, the Army Beta was developed for those who could not read sufficiently to take the Alpha Test. The tests proved to be remarkably successful in classifying recruits according to different levels of ability.

About 1920, teachers began to see the need for locally constructed tests and, through the efforts of McCall and Ruch among others, guidelines were established for the construction of written objective tests of recognition and recall. Thus, the tests known today as true-false, multiple-choice, matching, simple recall, and completion were begun. The first battery of achievement tests started in 1923 with the production of the Stanford Achievement Test. The first standardized inventory in the area of vocational interest was developed by E. K. Strong in 1925.

3. Continued Development of Standardized Tests, Large Scale Evaluation, and Development of Conferences and Measurement Agencies

In addition to the continual development of measuring instruments, this period was one of study, application, and professional growth of measurement as a field. As to instruments, the key ones of Learned's Graduate Record Examination, Thurstone's Primary Mental Abilities, Rorschach's Projective Techniques, and Wechsler's Adult and Children's Scales of Intelligence must be mentioned.

In the area of studies, there was the desire to measure more than facts, that is, to measure the ability to gather information and draw conclusions. There are some landmarks. These include the Pennsylvania Study in the late 1920's which was supported by the Carnegie Foundation for the Advancement of Teaching; the Eight-Year Study of the 1930's, supported by the Progressive Education Association; and the Study of General Education of the 1940's sponsored by the American Council on Education. These studies attempted to develop the rationale for education and measurement which might be characterized as follows:[8]

> The purpose of schools is to educate each young person in such a way that he will be able, to the limits of his natural ability, to contribute to the welfare and strength of American society and to realize a full development of his own potential as a human being. In order to do this, the school teaches each child certain subject matter content, such as English and history and mathematics, so that he may have the knowledge with which to solve his problems; the learning of this content is the immediate goal of instruction. When he has learned some subject matter and mastered some skills, the school teaches the student to apply them in a variety of new situations, so that he will be able to use them when they are needed in non-textbook circumstances; learning to use school-learned knowledge in a variety of ways is the intermediate goal of instruction. When he knows the subject matter and how to apply it, the ultimate goal of the school is that he will apply his learning, bettering his own life and the lives of his fellows.

The area of professional growth of measurement as a field of study had a great development during this era. The Cooperative Test Service was established in 1930. Test scoring machines were first introduced in 1935. The first of Oscar Buros' Mental Measurement Yearbooks was introduced in 1936. (The current edition is the Eighth Yearbook.) The first Invitational Conference on Testing Problems was started at this time. James Conant was instrumental in establishing the Educational Testing Service in 1947.

4. Continued Development of Cognitive Measurement and Start of Affective and Psychomotor Objectives and Measurement

In 1955, the American Educational Research Association and the National Council on Measurement in Education joined forces to produce the *Publication of Technical Standards for Achievement Tests*. Benjamin Bloom and associates produced the landmark publication, *Taxonomy of Educational Objectives: Part I, Cognitive Domain*, in 1956. In 1964, *Part II, Taxonomy of Educational Objectives, Affective Domain* was published. In the early 70s, Kibler, Harrow, and others started writing about the Psychomotor Domain.

---

8. Henry Chauncey and John E. Dobbin, *Testing: Its Place in Education Today*. Copyright © 1963 by Henry Chauncey. Reprinted by permission of Harper & Row Publishers, Inc., New York, p. 16.

5. Emphasis on Accountability in Education and Assessment Programs

Large scale testing programs have taken on significance over the years. One of the earliest of such programs is the Regents' examinations in New York. Of long standing is the work of the College Entrance Examination Board. More recent programs of this nature are the National Teachers Examinations, the National Merit Scholarship Program, and the American College Testing Program. State legislatures in many states have enacted laws requiring annual mental and/or achievement testing in certain grades in all public schools, both elementary and secondary. Minimum competency testing has been started in many states.

A nationwide testing program is that of National Assessment. Its purpose is to determine what children are learning in school and the progress they are making. Tests in ten areas (literature, science, writing, citizenship, music, social studies, reading, mathematics, art, and vocational education) are being given to 120,000-140,000 individuals in four age groups (9-13-17-young adults between 26-35) in a carefully chosen sample to represent different geographical regions, types of schools, types of communities, races, and socio-economic levels. Testing was done in three subject areas in 1969, three or four in 1970, and the remainder in 1971. The cycle then was repeated. No individual takes more than a few tests and no comparisons are made between individual school systems, communities, regions, and the like. The emphasis throughout is on "criterion referenced" testing, i.e., on the measured proficiency of defined groups on specified tasks and not on comparison of performance with that of others or with norms. Reports are made in terms of groups, such as: of girls of lower economic status from large cities in the northeast region, 32 percent of nine-year-olds knew or could do, 48 percent of seventeen-year-olds knew or could do, and the like.

Many states have gone into a similar assessment program. The areas of reading and mathematics seem to be the areas most are starting with. With the advent of individually guided education, there has been assessment in individualized instruction. A contract or goal charts are agreed upon between teacher and student. Pre- and post-testing takes place to determine degree and quality of growth toward the agreed upon goals.

Summary Statements

1. Measurement and evaluation is an integral part of the teaching process.
2. Measurement and evaluation should reveal how well the pupils have progressed toward the goals of instruction and how well the teacher has aided them in achieving these goals.
3. Measurement and evaluation serves teaching, administrative, and guidance functions.

4. A teacher must have skill in organizing and interpreting data as well as knowledge in the fields of child development and methodology of teaching.
5. Measurement and evaluation today must determine the total growth of the child, since the objectives of education are wide in scope and extremely diverse.

Discussion Questions

1. Explain why evaluation must be considered an integral part of the teaching process.
2. Describe the interrelationship which exists among the three steps of the teaching process—objectives, methods, and measurement.
3. Give examples of why the teaching process must be considered a *continuous cycle*.
4. How can teachers use the general objectives of education in our society to aid in planning their specific objectives?
5. What is the real problem a teacher faces in Step Two of the teaching process: How can it best be taught?
6. Are the terms *measurement* and *evaluation* synonymous? Give examples to illustrate your viewpoint.
7. Discuss how you would interpret the results of an achievement test differently to pupils, to parents, to the administration, and to yourself?
8. Summarize the salient points in the history of measurement during the five periods.

Student Activities

1. State a general objective you might have for a specific subject and grade level and, in five minutes, list all the various methods you might use to aid the pupils in growing toward this objective. Having done this, which ones might you choose to use if you were to teach toward this objective within the next week?
2. Assuming you will be administering a standardized achievement test at the end of the year, think through each step from beginning to end in using this instrument; then classify each step into one of the three phases of the measurement and evaluation process.
3. For a specific subject and grade level of your interest, illustrate measurement situations which depict each of the seven functions of measurement and evaluation.
4. Using the word *orange* as an example, tell how a first grader, a seventh grader, and a twelfth grader would define this word to show the *typical mental behavior* at each of these levels.

5. Select a concept or a skill to be taught and illustrate how the pattern of teaching it would affect your plans for its measurement and evaluation.
6. Dream a little in terms of the great explosion of knowledge today and indicate some areas of measurement which must be refined or developed to cope with this phenomenon.

Selected Readings

Ahmann, J. Stanley, and Glock, Marvin D. *Evaluating Pupil Growth,* 5th ed. Boston: Allyn and Bacon, Inc., 1975, Chapter 1.

———. *Measuring and Evaluating Educational Achievement,* 2nd ed. Boston: Allyn and Bacon, Inc., 1975, Chapter 1.

Anastasi, Anne. *Psychological Testing,* 4th ed. New York: The Macmillan Company, 1976, Chapter 1.

Brown, Frederick G. *Principles of Educational and Psychological Testing,* 2nd ed. New York: Holt, Rinehart and Winston, 1976. Chapters 1 and 2.

Cronbach, Lee J. *Essentials of Psychological Testing,* 3rd ed. New York: Harper & Row Publishers, Inc., 1970. Chapters 1 and 2.

Ebel, Robert L. *Essentials of Educational Measurement,* 3rd ed. Englewood Cliffs, NJ: Prentice-Hall, Inc., 1970. Chapter 1 and 2.

Gronlund, Norman E. *Measurement and Evaluation in Teaching,* 3rd ed. New York: The Macmillan Company, 1976. Chapter 1.

———. *Readings in Measurement and Evaluation.* New York: The Macmillan Company, 1968. Chapter 6.

Hopkins, Charles D., and Antes, Richard L. *Classroom Measurement and Evaluation.* Itasca, IL: F. E. Peacock Publishers, Inc., 1978. Chapter 1.

Linneman, Richard H., and Merenda, Peter F. *Educational Measurement,* 2nd ed. Glenview, IL: Scott, Foresman and Company, 1979. Chapter 1.

Mehrens, William A., and Lehman, Irvin J. *Measurement and Evaluation in Education and Psychology.* New York: Holt, Rinehart and Winston, 1973. Chapter 1.

National Assessment of Educational Progress. *Objectives in Ten Subject Matter Areas.* Pamphlet. Denver, Colorado. (No date.)

Noll, Victor H., Scannell, Dale P., and Noll, Rachel P. *Introductory Readings in tional Measurement,* 4th ed. Boston: Houghton Mifflin Company, 1979. Chapter 1.

Noll, Victor H., Scannell, Dale P., and Noll, Rachel P. *Introductory Readings in Educational Measurement.* Boston: Houghton Mifflin Company, 1972. Chapter 2.

Payne, David A., and McMorris, Robert F. *Educational and Psychological Measurement,* 2nd ed. Morristown, NJ: General Learning Press, 1974. Part I.

Sax, Gilbert. *Principles of Educational Measurement and Evaluation.* Belmont, California: Wadsworth Publishing Company, Inc., 1974. Chapter 1.

Stanley, Julian C., and Hopkins, Kenneth D. *Educational and Psychological Measurement and Evaluation.* Englewood Cliffs, NJ: Prentice-Hall, Inc., 1972. Chapters 1 and 7.

Thorndike, Robert L., and Hagen, Elizabeth. *Measurement and Evaluation in Psychology and Education,* 4th ed. New York: John Wiley & Sons, Inc., 1977. Chapter 1.

Tuckman, Bruce W. *Measuring Educational Outcomes: Fundamentals of Testing.* New York: Harcourt Brace Jovanovich, Inc., 1975. Chapter 1.

2

Essential Characteristics of a Good Measuring Instrument

What are the main qualities of a good measuring instrument?
What is meant by the technique of correlation?
What is meant by the validity of an instrument?
    Definition
    Methods of determining validity of an instrument
    General principles to improve the validity of an instrument
What is meant by the reliability of an instrument?
    Definition
    Methods of determining reliability of an instrument
    Factors affecting the reliability of an instrument
What is meant by the usability of an instrument?
    Definition
    Factors determining the usability of an instrument

A. What Are the Main Qualities of a Good Measuring Instrument?

Qualities of any measuring instrument might be compared to the purchase of an article in a store; there are certain qualities or characteristics for which one would look. Similarly, a teacher asks many questions about the use of a measuring instrument: How can I tell if this standardized test is a good one? How can I construct tests which will yield good results? How much confidence can I have in the results of a rating scale or other subjective instrument? How does cheating affect the results of an instrument? How do I interpret the coefficient of correlation? How do I interpret the different types of test norms?

Despite the vast differences between format and construction of varied measuring instruments, there are certain *common standards* or criteria which any measuring instrument should meet. It makes no differences whether one plans to use a true-false test, an essay test, or a rating scale; each should be selected carefully in terms of the criteria of:

Validity,
Reliability, and
Usability.

The teacher is justified in using a specific measuring instrument in working with pupils if it satisfies these criteria.

Before discussing the details of each of these three main criteria, it is advisable to have a working definition of a good measuring instrument. *Thus, a good measuring instrument measures what it is supposed to measure to a high degree, consistently, and with a minimum expenditure of time, energy, and money.* The first part of the definition concerns validity, the second concerns reliability, and the last part concerns usability.

B.   What Is Meant by the Technique of Correlation?

Definition

Correlation is the degree of relationship which exists between two sets of scores.

Purpose

The purpose is to reduce to a single number or index the relationship between two sets of scores. When this number or index is found, it is known as the *coefficient of correlation* and its symbol is *r*.

Uses of Correlation

The basic uses of simple correlation are to check for the validity and for the reliability of an instrument. It may be used in guidance work as a means of predicting student progress or ability.

Kinds of Correlation

There are basically two kinds of correlation.

Positive: When values or scores of one instrument go together *directly* with the values or scores of the other instrument, the correlation is positive. That is, the highs go with the highs, the middles with the middles, and the lows with the lows. The range of positive correlation is from +1.00 (perfect positive correlation) down through any fractional parts of positive 1 to zero.

Negative: When values or scores of one instrument go together *inversely* with the values or scores of the other instrument, the correlation is negative. That is, the highs of one go with the lows of the other. The range of negative correlation is from −1.00 (perfect negative correlation) down through any fractional parts of −1 to 0.

Range of Correlation Coefficients

−1.00	0	+1.00
	Negative Range Positive Range	

Formula for Figuring Correlation by the Rank-Difference Method

The Rank-Difference Method of determining the coefficient of correlation is probably the simplest to use and can be done easily by teachers. All that is necessary is to add, subtract, multiply, and divide accurately. One additional skill, the ranking of scores, needs to be understood, and this will be explained in the problem to follow.

$$r = 1.00 - \left(\frac{6 \times \Sigma D^2}{N(N^2 - 1)} \right) \text{ (also known as } \rho \text{ or rho formula)}$$

The r stands for the coefficient of correlation; the 1.00 is a perfect correlation from which any value in the quantity may be taken to reduce the coefficient; the number 6 is a constant value; the combination of symbols ΣD^2 stands for the sum of the difference in ranks squared. In the denominator, N stands for the number of cases; the subquantity then stands for the number of cases squared — (minus) one.

Running a Correlation

Suppose the teacher wanted to check the validity of a unit test (Column A) against a set of criterion scores which was an index of performance during the unit (Column B). In order to show the correlation in a simple way, one can use only ten cases; also the scores used will be in low figures. For the method to be used, see Table 2.1. Another formula for determining the coefficient of correlation, the Pearson r, or Product-Moment r, is found in Appendix D.

Some explanation of the steps in this problem may be necessary. After the score columns (A and B), there are two columns, each headed R_A and R_B respectively. In each column, the rank of each score is determined. When scores are ranked, this is nothing more than giving its position in the series of scores (such as rank of 1 to the highest, rank of 2 to the next highest). Some difficulty in ranking can occur when there are duplicate scores in a column. This can be illustrated by an example.

TABLE 2.1

Correlation Table

T-M Test	Past Performance				
A	B	R_A	R_B	D	D^2
20	14	1	4	3	9.00
18	16	2	3	1	1.00
16	18	3	2	1	1.00
14	20	4	1	3	9.00
12	6	5	8	3	9.00
10	8	6	7	1	1.00
8	10	7	6	1	1.00
6	12	8	5	3	9.00
4	2	9	10	1	1.00
2	4	10	9	1	1.00
	N-10				42.00

$$r = 1.00 - \left(\frac{6 \times \Sigma D^2}{N(N^2-1)} \right)$$

$$r = 1.00 - \left(\frac{6 \times 42}{10(99)} \right)$$

$$r = 1.00 - \left(\frac{252}{990} \right)$$

$$r = 1.00 - .25$$

$$r = .75$$

In Column A, if there were the following scores:

A	R_A	
20	1	Highest rank.
18	2.5	The score of 18 is obtained by two pupils. They are entitled to the same rank, yet they take up two positions. Thus, position 2 plus position 3
18	2.5	is 5; divided by 2 (two pupils) = 2.5.
16	4	Three positions have been used to this point; thus, this is a single score receiving the next rank which is 4.
14	6	There are three 14's. They take up positions 5-6-7.
14	6	When added, these total 18; 18 divided by 3 (three pupils)
14	6	equals a rank of 6.
12	8	The next position is 8 for a single score.
10	9	Next position.
8	10	Last position.
N=10		

Accuracy of the ranking can be checked by noting whether the last rank given equals N; that is, number of cases. In this example, the last score received a rank of 10; 10 is also the number of cases. The only exception here is that, if the last score were duplicated, the rank given would be an average of the positions taken up. The rank given would not equal the absolute value of N but would be incorporated into the rank.

Another point which should be clarified in the problem is that of rounding of numbers. Notice that in the progression from the formula down to the answer, two decimal places are retained. There are many ways of rounding numbers; the main idea is that one must be consistent. These chapters will follow the principle that when the third digit is above 5, raise the previous digit; when the third digit is exactly 5 (that is, no remainder), look to the previous digit. If it is an even number, leave it as it is; if it is an odd number, raise it to the next number above. Generalizing in this latter instance, when rounding from an exact 5, always round to the even.

Interpreting the Coefficient of Correlation

The correlation can vary from perfect positive $+1.00$ to -1.00, a perfect negative correlation. Normally, these extreme values are uncommon in practice although correlations may approach these extremes. As the coefficient increases from 0.00 to $+1.00$, the relationship becomes greater; as it approaches -1.00, it also becomes greater, but in the negative direction. Coefficients of equal size but in opposite zones, positive or negative, are of equal strength but the direction of the correlation is different; that is, one is a direct relationship and the other is inverse or negative.

How high should a correlation be in order to be regarded as "significant"? Garrett answers the question in the following way.

> It is difficult to answer this question categorically as the *level* of relationship indicated by r depends upon several factors: (1) the absolute size of the coefficient; (2) the purposes for which r is calculated; and (3) how our r compares with r's generally found for the variables studied.[1]

A common guide which will assist the beginner in interpreting a coefficient of correlation is as follows:

± .70 to ± 1.00	High to very high
± .40 to ± .70	Average to fairly high
± .20 to ± .40	Present, but low
± .00 to ± .20	Negligible or low

The difficulty with this table is that it does not hold up when we speak of comparing two *specific* variables. For example, a coefficient of .60 be-

1. Henry E. Garrett, *Elementary Statistics*, 2nd ed. (New York: David McKay Co., 1962), p. 100.

tween a general intelligence test administered at the beginning of the year and school marks recorded at the end of the year might be regarded as high, because the correlation between that particular predictor and criterion usually falls below .60. But a coefficient of .60 between scores on two forms of this intelligence test administered the same day to a typical school class would be unusually low. In other words, "high" and "low" have only *relative* meaning; before an interpretation can be made of a coefficient on this basis, the reader must at least know what the *central tendency* of such coefficients for similar data is. The following listing using *height* as the controlling variable may illustrate some antecedent correlations.

Identical twins reared together	.96
Identical twins reared apart	.94
Height at age 3 versus height at maturity	.75
Siblings	.50
Parent and child	.51
Grandparent and grandchild	.32
First cousins	.24
Height and IQ	.20

There is a relationship between the size of the sample and whether the correlation is significant. Since very high values for *r* are much more likely to occur by chance with small N's, very high values of *r* are required for statistical significance. The following table shows that correlation coefficients based on small samples are not very reliable and that very low relationships can be statistically significant with a very large N.

TABLE 2.2

Minimum Absolute Values of r Required to be Statistically Significant at the .05 Level for Various Sample Sizes (N)

N	Minimum r for Statistical Significance
5	.878
10	.632
25	.396
100	.197
1000	.062

The table can be interpreted in this way. For example, an N of 10 requires a minimum *r* for statistical significance of .632 at the .05 level. This is interpreted to mean that if a correlation of .632 is obtained with 10 cases, the correlation will be true 95 times out of 100 (.05 percent level). Stated another way, this correlation could occur by chance only 5 times out of 100.

Finally, there is the *Index of Forecasting Efficiency*. This indicates the percent of forecasting efficiency for a given *r*. Although it is correct to say that an *r* of 1.00 indicates a prediction of 100 percent accuracy, the decrease in prediction accuracy is not proportional to the decrease in the *r* value. Table 2.3 shows the percentage reduction in the margins of prediction error of scores on Test Y from scores derived from Test X as the correlation between the two sets of scores changes.

TABLE 2.3

Forecasting Efficiency of Product-Moment
Coefficients of Correlations of Various Sizes..

Coefficient of Correlation	Index of Forecasting Efficiency (percent)
1.00	100.0
0.99	85.9
0.97	75.7
0.95	68.8
0.90	56.4
0.80	40.0
0.70	28.6
0.60	20.0
0.50	13.4
0.40	8.4
0.30	4.6
0.20	2.0
0.10	0.5
0.00	0.0

Thus, a correlation of .60 does not have a forecasting efficiency of 60 percent, but rather 20 percent. The reduction in the margin of error is about 20 percent, which can be considered the percentage of improvement over chance. As the correlation increases, so does the reduction in the margin of error of prediction. Care must be used when using the index of forecasting efficiency to interpret correlation coefficients representing the predictive validity of a test. It is all too easy to underestimate the effectiveness of the prediction instrument. An example is the selection of reading groups for first grade. Here the reading readiness test score is far more useful than that suggested by the index of forecasting efficiency associated with its validity coefficient.

A final principle to remember in interpreting correlation is that it does not show causation. If one would obtain a correlation of +.90 between the heights of boys and basketball performance, the relationship is high, but it does not follow that either is the cause of the other. It may be that other factors of health, coordination, and the like, cause both. Correlation may suggest the possibility of causal relationship, but it does no more than this. Proof of such causation would have to be determined by means other than correlation.

Teachers should be acquainted with correlation for two reasons. One reason is that coefficients of correlation are used in standardized test manuals, and before a teacher selects and uses a standardized test, the correlation coefficients should be studied and interpreted. A second reason for a teacher's acquaintance with correlation is that a coefficient of validity and reliability might be obtained on teacher-made devices, especially if the results of such instruments will carry any great amount of weight in determining pupil progress and making important decisions about pupils. Considerable skill is required to interpret validity coefficients. Generally, the higher the correlation between the measuring instrument and the criterion, the better is the validity. There are some other factors, however, that should be considered in relation to this generalization.

The first of these is whether the test or instrument is adaptable to validation studies. Is there a good criterion with which the instrument may be validated? If a good criterion is available, one might expect higher validity coefficients than if a criterion were difficult to define. Second, one criterion might be more relevant for one specific purpose than for another. In selecting a clerical worker, an attitude inventory might correlate 0.70 with promptness records; a clerical aptitude test might correlate 0.20 with typing speed. Would it be advisable for the employer to use one or both criteria? The point is that one must consider to what degree a criterion is appropriate to the specific purpose. A third factor to consider is that an instrument which is appropriate on one level may not be appropriate on another. An instrument which differentiates between social characteristics of nursery school children may not be effective in senior high school because of the increased maturity of the latter group. Finally, validity coefficients will tend to be higher when the group being measured exhibits a wide range of scores. It might be simple for one to select the top student in a class on general merit, but it may be much more difficult to rank students who are in the middle of the class and who appear very similar in ability and performance. The more closely an instrument can differentiate among the subjects being measured, the higher the validity coefficient is likely to be. In summary, the higher the coefficient of validity, the better the instrument will be, if the above factors are considered.

C. What Is Meant by the Validity of an Instrument?

1. Definition: Validity Is the Degree to Which an Instrument Measures What It Is Supposed to Measure

Some synonyms for the word *validity* include *truthfulness, value,* and *worthwhileness.* Sometimes, it is easier to understand validity by describing it in relation to the use of certain instruments. Some of these statements might be: Validity refers to the care that is taken to include, in a test, items of prime importance and to exclude items of trivial nature; validity refers to the degree to which an instrument parallels the material which has been taught and the way in which it has been taught; validity refers to the degree to which an observational tool provides for objective appraisal of that which is observed; validity refers to the specificity of results obtained by means of a measuring device.

Summarizing these ideas, an instrument is considered valid only in terms of a specific group for a specific purpose at a specific time.

2. What Are the Methods of Determining the Validity of an Instrument?

For checking validity of an instrument, three basic methods with which a classroom teacher should be familiar are *curricular, criterion-related,* and *construct.*

The *curricular* method means checking validity through the *content* of the instrument. This can be accomplished before the instrument is used. It is, of course, subjective in the sense that each teacher will be checking the content in terms of the material which was taught and of how it was taught. The sources with which the teacher may check the content include his/her objectives; methods of instruction (such as lesson plans, teaching units); and textbooks, workbooks, and related materials.

When standardized tests are checked for validity, the curricular method is also used at times. The problem here is a little greater than that of a classroom teacher, since these tests must be checked so that they may be used throughout the entire country. For achievement tests, state-wide courses of study are sometimes used. Then an analysis is made of the common elements which are taught as one criterion of content which is to be included in the test.

In curricular validity, then, the teacher makes a judgment as to how well the instrument reflects the content of the material taught and the way in which it was taught.

When one examines the validity of an instrument by the *criterion-related* method, the validity is checked by the *results* obtained. In this method, the instrument must be administered to pupils to obtain the necessary results. It is a more objective method than the curricular method because an index of validity is obtained from which an interpretation is made. It usually involves correlating the results of an instrument of unknown validity against a set of criterion scores, the validity of which has been established or accepted. The higher the unknown set of scores correlates or relates to the known set, the greater is the validity.

Criterion-related validity may be considered as either concurrent or predictive. Sometimes, these are classified as separate types of validity. Actually, both are examples of criterion-related validity since they differ only as to time sequence of the criterion score. Concurrent validity relates a set of scores to an accepted present criterion of performance; predictive validity relates a set of scores to a criterion based on performance at some later time.

For example, a teacher may prepare an end-of-year achievement test. To determine whether the results are valid, they can be correlated with several possible criterion scores. The teacher may administer a recognized standardized test in this same area; he may correlate with the past performance of the student in the particular course throughout the year; or he may correlate with a rating which he/she would give each student based on his observation (concurrent validity). Or suppose a high school principal wishes to determine whether grades given in high school are a good predictor of grades in college. He or she would compare the grades which the students received in high school with an index of their college grades (predictive validity).

Any time one predicts a future performance of an individual from a test or other data, the *standard error of estimate* comes in (sometimes called the standard error of prediction). While validity indicates how free from error judgments are, the standard error of estimate estimates the amount of error made when a judgment is made. The basic idea is simple. It is a means of indicating where the true score probably lies in relation to the predicted score. If a student is predicted to score at the 80th percentile in achievement from an algebra aptitude test and the standard error of estimate was 5, his or her *true* predicted score would lie between the predicted score + and − 1 SE, or between 75-85 sixty-eight (68) times out of 100. If one would go out 2 SE, we would say that the true predicted score would be between 70 and 90 ninety-five (95) times out of a 100. For 3 SE his or her predicted score would be between 65 and 95 ninety-nine times out of 100. These probabilities are based on the normal probability curve and standard deviation.

The formula for the standard error of estimate is:

$$S_{y.x} = S_y \sqrt{1 - r^2_{xy}}$$

It reads: The standard error of estimate ($S_{y.x}$) is equal to the standard deviation of the test y (S_y) times the square root of 1 minus the square of the correlation betwen tests x and y. For example:

$$
\begin{aligned}
S_{y.x} &= 10\sqrt{1 - 0.60^2} \\
&= 10\sqrt{1 - 0.36} \\
&= 10\sqrt{0.64} \\
&= 10 \quad (0.8) \\
&= 8
\end{aligned}
$$

Formally, the method of checking the validity of a set of scores by the criterion-related method is through the technique of correlation. Correlation is the degree of relationships that exists between sets of scores.

A third method of checking the validity of an instrument is *construct validity. It is defined as the extent to which test performance can be interpreted in terms of certain psychological constructs.* The procedure for determining construct validity involves three steps: (1) Identifying the constructs presumed to account for test performance; (2) deriving hypothesis regarding test performance from the theory underlying the construct; and (3) verifying the hypothesis by logical and empirical means. On this last point, there is no adequate single method of establishing construct validity. It is a matter of accumulating evidence from many different sources. We may use both content validity and criterion-related validity as partial evidence to support construct validity, but neither of them alone is sufficient. Construct validation depends on logical inferences drawn from a variety of types of data.

Suppose, for example, we wish to check the claim that a newly constructed test measures creativity. From what is known about creativity, we might make the following predictions:

1. The test will discriminate between those who are vertical thinkers and those who are lateral thinkers.
2. The test scores will be influenced by atmosphere in the school and home.
3. The test scores will be related to such characteristics as imagination, seeking a new process, inventiveness, sometimes brashness.
4. The test scores are related to individuals who possess social courage and are willing to stand firm for their own beliefs.

Each of these predictions, and others, would then be tested, one by one. If positive results are obtained for each prediction, the combined evidence lends support to the claim that the test measures creativity. If a prediction is not confirmed, we must conclude that either the test is not a valid measure of creativity, or there is something wrong with the theory.

D. What Is Meant by the Reliability of an Instrument?

1. Definition: Reliability Is the Degree to Which an Instrument Consistently Measures What It Does Measure

Some synonyms for the word *reliability* include *dependability, stability,* and *confidence.* Many times, teachers confuse validity and reliability; that is, they discuss validity when they mean reliability, and vice versa. A few statements describing reliability might clarify these terms. One might say that an instrument may not measure what it is supposed to measure, but if it measures something consistently, it is reliable. This means that similar results might be obtained if an instrument is used a second time; the instrument would be reliable, but one could not be sure that it was measuring what it should measure (validity). Another statement might be that, although high reliability is not a guarantee that an instrument is completely good, low reliability would indicate that it was poor. This means that one cannot judge an instrument completely on high reliability. Thus, one must check both for validity and for reliability, in order to use the results with assurance.

2. What Are the Methods of Determining the Reliability of an Instrument?

All methods of determining reliability involve the technique of correlation. The closer the agreement between the two sets of scores, the greater is the reliability. There are three basic methods, and each will be discussed, beginning with the method used the least.

a. Test-retest method

The same instrument is used twice on the same group of pupils in this method, and the two sets of results are correlated to determine the degree of agreement.

There are definite limitations to this method. If the second administration is given too soon, immediate remembering or practice effect will modify the results. If too long a time elapses before the second administration, learning takes place, and the second results, of course, will be different from the first. A judgment must be made to determine the proper time for the retest so that the two factors operate at a minimum.

b. Alternate or parallel forms method

In this method, two or more forms of the instrument are prepared. The forms are equivalent as to content, difficulty, types of items, and the like. One form is administered, and the results are correlated with one or more of its equivalent forms. Again, the greater the agreement or correlation, the greater is the reliability.

The one limitation here is the extreme difficulty in making parallel or equivalent forms of the same instrument.

c. Split-halves or chance-halves method

This is the most practical method of the three because the instrument needs to be given only once. After the test is administered, it is scored in two parts; first, the odd-numbered items are scored to obtain a total for this half, then the even-numbered items are scored to obtain a total score for the other half. Thus, there are two columns of scores, the odd and the even. A correlation is run between the two scores.

It must be remembered that when this method is used, the initial coefficient of reliability obtained is for one-half of the test only and must be converted to the total reliability by a conversion formula. The formula most often used is the Spearman-Brown Formula of Conversion:

$$r = \frac{2 \times r \text{ of } \frac{1}{2} \text{ the test}}{1 + r \text{ of } \frac{1}{2} \text{ the test}}$$

This is a ratio type formula and thus will raise the correlation upwards toward 1.00, but of course it cannot go beyond this point.

Generally, the higher the reliability coefficient, the more reliable is the instrument; however, the Standard Error of Measurement must be considered, as should the factors presented in the next section.

3. What Are Some Factors Affecting the Reliability of an Instrument?

Although the factors may be listed under three headings, it is the responsibility of the teacher to control all factors as much as possible. Any one of them can distort the reliability of an instrument.

a. *General factors*

Length of the Instrument—Generally, the longer the instrument the greater is the reliability.

Objectivity—The greater the objectivity, the greater is the reliability.

b. *Teacher factors*

Classroom Environment—Generally, the better the classroom environment, the greater is the reliability.

Motivation—The more positive the motivation, the greater is the reliability.

Directions—The more consistent and complete the directions, the greater is the reliability.

Supervision—The better the supervision, the more reliable is the instrument.

c. *Pupil factors*

Physical Condition—The better the condition of the student physically, the more reliable, generally, are the results.

Emotional Condition—The more stable the pupil, the more stable, generally, are the results.

Pupil-Teacher Attitude—The better the pupil-teacher relationship, the better is the reliability of the results.

Desire to Learn—Generally, the greater the motivation of a pupil, the more consistent are the results.

4. Standard Error of Measurement

This concept is similar to that of the standard error of estimate except that the standard error of measurement is concerned with the reliability of a score. While reliability indicates *freedom* from error, the standard error of measurement estimates the amount of error which *does* exist. Whereas reliability is used as an estimate of the accuracy of the measurement results as a whole, the standard error of measurement is used as an estimate of the accuracy of the results for a given individual.

The basic idea behind the use of the standard error of measurement is very simple. Measurement error occurs when a person's obtained score differs from his or her true score. Saying it another way, a person's true score is found around the person's obtained score by the amount of standard error.

Supposing Rick obtained a grade equivalent of 7.5 in reading and the standard error of measurement for the test was 2 months. Where would his true score lie 68 times out of 100? It would be 7.5 ± 2 or between 7.3 and 7.7. Where would his true score lie 95 times out of 100? It would be 7.5 ± 2 SE or 7.5 ± 4 or between 7.1 and 7.9.

The formula for the Standard Error of Measurement follows:

$$SEM = S_X \sqrt{1 - r_{XX}}$$

Where SEM is the Standard Error of Measurement; S_X equals the standard deviation of the test; and r_{XX} is the reliability coefficient of the test. An example would be:

$$SEM = 10\sqrt{1 - 0.64}$$
$$SEM = 10\sqrt{0.36}$$
$$SEM = 10 \quad (0.6)$$
$$SEM = 6$$

The standard error of measurement, like the standard error of estimate, indicates that one should never state that a person's true score is exactly as obtained, but that it falls within a band of the standard errors. This will also allow flexibility within which to make decisions about the individual or the group.

E. What Is Meant by the Usability of an Instrument?

1. Definition: Usability Is the Degree to Which an Instrument Can Be Used with a Minimum Expenditure of Time, Energy, and Money

One other way to discuss usability is to ask the question: Is the instrument practical to use? There are some measuring instruments, such as the Stanford-Binet Test of Intelligence or the Wechsler Intelligence Scale for Children, which are highly valid and reliable. They generally are not usable by the classroom teacher since special training is required to administer and score the tests properly.

2. What Are the Main Factors Determining the Usability of an Instrument?

Ease of administration

The easier the instrument is to administer, the more usable it is. The two basic factors affecting administration of an instrument are directions and timing. If the directions are clear, curt, and complete for both the teacher and the pupil, the administration is simpler. If the timing is not too minute so that the teacher has to keep his eyes on the watch all of the time, it is not too difficult.

Ease of scoring

Scoring of an instrument can be difficult or simple, depending upon the directions for scoring, the objectivity of scoring, and an adequate key. Directions should be stated in such a manner that a teacher can proceed without any difficulty in understanding what to do. If the instrument can be scored objectively, the teacher can do it much more rapidly and will not have to make judgments on every item. The key accompanying the instrument should be one which can be aligned directly with the placement of the pupil responses. This accelerates the scoring process, and it reduces errors that could occur in scoring if the key were not arranged in this way.

Ease of interpretation and application

Basically, the nature of the score obtained from an instrument determines whether the results can be interpreted and applied easily. In standardized instruments, it is the norms accompanying the instrument that determine the ease of interpretation and application. Since norms sometimes are not understood to a great degree by teachers, some attention is devoted to them here. Chapter 8 is devoted to norms and derived scores.

Mechanical make-up

Sometimes the usability of an instrument can be affected by the way it is constructed, that is, its mechanical make-up. If the instrument cannot be followed easily by the pupil or if it does not call for all of the information that it necessary, it will not be very usable.

On the following page is a partial listing of the things which should be checked in a teacher-made instrument and in a standardized test instrument:

Teacher-Made	*Standardized Instrument*
Place for name	All items listed under teacher-made
Title of instrument	plus:
General directions	Place for personal data including
Specific directions	birthdate
Consistent answering system	Individual and class summary profile
Items spaced properly	Size of type
Like items placed together	Quality of printing and paper
Good duplicating	

Summary Statements

1. It is important for measuring instruments to be checked against certain standards or characteristics so that results obtained will be usable.
2. A good measuring instrument measures what it is supposed to measure to a high degree, consistently, and with a minimum expenditure of time, energy, and money.
3. Validity is the degree to which an instrument performs the task expected of it.
4. Reliability indicates dependability of the instrument for producing consistent results.
5. The Standard Error of Estimate estimates the amount of error surrounding a *predicted* score. The Standard Error of Measurement indicates the amount of error surrounding an *obtained* score. In each case, the true score will lie around the predicted or obtained score by the amount of standard error.
6. Usability tells how practical the instrument is to use from the standpoint of time, energy, and money.
7. Norms are aids or guides for the interpretation and application of results. They are not standards for all pupils to meet. The most common norms are age norms, grade norms, percentiles, and stanines.
8. Correlation is the degree of relationship which exists between two sets of scores. Among its uses are to check the validity and reliability of an instrument.

Discussion Questions

1. Define in your own words the factors which constitute a good measuring instrument.
2. Translate into your own words the meaning of correlation and its basic purpose. What advantage does the stated purpose have over a narrative description of the relationship between two columns of scores?

3. Explain the basic kinds of correlation as to what each means and its range of indices. When would we say that there is a zero correlation?
4. Discuss some factors which need to be considered in interpreting a correlation coefficient in addition to the general statement that the higher the correlation between the measuring instrument and the criterion, the better the validity.
5. Explain the following statements relative to validity:
   a. A test must contain items of prime importance and exclude trivial items.
   b. A measuring instrument must reflect the material which has been taught and the way in which it was taught.
   c. An observational tool must provide for objective appraisal.
   d. An instrument is valid only in terms of a specific group, at a specific time, and for a specific purpose.
6. Explain why the curricular method of checking validity is the most practical for the classroom teacher.
7. How does the criterion-related validity differ from curricular validity as to what is checked, when, and the degree of objectivity?
8. What, really, are we looking at when we check something by construct validity? How can we say that, in a way, construct validity includes curricular and criterion-related methods?
9. Explain the concept of standard error. Why does it exist? Of what value is it to us in test score interpretation?
10. Why will a unit test have greater validity if it is constructed while the unit is being taught?
11. Why will an achievement test have greater validity if the items proceed from the easier to the more difficult?
12. Generally speaking, will reliability coefficients be higher or lower than validity coefficients for a specific instrument? Why?
13. Distinguish between test-retest, parallel forms, and split-halves reliability by giving an illustration of each approach.
14. Suggest a few examples which show situations in which the classroom teacher may have to sacrifice the ideal of high validity and reliability somewhat for usability.

Student Activities

1. Construct a correlation table and run a correlation for the following sets of scores. The problem is to determine the degree of reliability of a test using the test-retest method. Interpret the correlation coefficient as to the reliability of this test.

A	99,	90,	95,	85,	75,	80,	65,	70,	55,	60
B	70,	75,	60,	65,	55,	50,	40,	35,	30,	45

2. Interpret the following coefficients of validity taking into consideration the factors on interpretation of validity coefficients which are discussed in this chapter.

   a. Teacher marks and test scores in arithmetic = .50.

   b. Standardized group intelligence test and individual standardized test = .80.

   c. Standardized personality tests and ratings of personality by peers = .45.

   d. Rank in high school graduating class and grade-point average in college = .60.

3. Assume that you wanted to develop a simple rating scale to measure growth toward the objective, *The student cooperates effectively with others*. List 5 or 6 traits you would seek to observe among pupils on a specific grade level toward this objective. Then indicate how you would check the validity of the instrument by the curricular method.

4. Convert the following coefficients to total reliability using the Spearman-Brown Formula:

   a. .75   c. .85

   b. .40   d. .95

What generalizations can be made? Why?

5. Determine the Standard Error of Estimate for the following data and apply it to the predicted percentile scores listed below interpreting the band for 1 $S_{y.x}$.

$$S_y = 5 \qquad r^2{}_{xy} = .80$$

   a. 80   c. 40

   b. 55   d. 28

6. Determine the Standard Error of Measurement for the following data and apply it to the obtained grade equivalents in reading listed below, interpreting the band for 1 SEM. Assume your SEM result is in months.

$$S_x = 4 \qquad r_{xx} = .75$$

   a. 6.4   c. 5.1

   b. 3.2   d. 6.9

7. Following are items of concern to criteria of a good instrument. Indicate for each whether it is primarily related to validity, reliability, or usability.

   a. Does the test contain items of the proper degree of difficulty?

   b. Was the instrument objective as to scoring?

   c. Does the instrument reflect what was taught?

d. Were the directions clear to the pupils?
e. Did the teacher introduce the test properly?
f. Did the test proceed from the easier to the more difficult items?
g. Can the measuring device be used within a normal class period?
h. Was the pupil-teacher attitude good?
i. Were there items which were passed by all and items failed by all?
j. Was the length of the test adequate?

Selected Readings

Adkins, Dorothy C. *Test Construction: Development and Interpretation of Achievement Tests,* 2nd ed. Columbus, Ohio: Charles E. Merrill Publishing Company, 1974. Chapter 3.

Ahmann, J. Stanley, and Glock, Marvin D. *Evaluating Pupil Growth,* 5th ed. Boston: Allyn and Bacon, Inc., 1975. Chapters 9 and 10.

———. *Measuring and Evaluating Educational Achievement,* 2nd ed. Boston: Allyn and Bacon, Inc., 1975. (Paperback) Chapters 9 and 10.

Aiken, Lewis R., Jr. *Readings in Psychological and Educational Testing.* Boston: Allyn and Bacon, Inc., 1973. Chapters 3 and 4.

Anastasi, Anne. *Psychological Testing,* 4th ed. New York: The Macmillan Company, 1976. Chapters 5-7.

Brown, Frederick G. *Principles of Educational and Psychological Testing,* 2nd ed. New York: Holt, Rinehart and Winston, 1976. Chapters 4-9.

Ebel, Robert L. *Essentials of Educational Measurement,* 3rd ed. Englewood Cliffs, New Jersey: Prentice-Hall, Inc., 1979. Chapters 14 and 15.

Green, John A. *Teacher-Made Tests.* 2nd ed. New York: Harper & Row Publishers, Inc., 1975. Chapter 8.

Gronlund, Norman E. *Measurement and Evaluation in Teaching,* 3rd ed. New York: The Macmillan Company, 1976. Chapters 4 and 5.

———. *Readings in Measurement and Evaluation.* New York: The Macmillan Company, 1968. Part IV.

Guilford, J. P., and Fruchter, Benjamin. *Fundamental Statistics in Psychology and Education,* 6th ed. New York: McGraw-Hill Book Co., 1978. Chapters 17 and 18.

Hopkins, Charles D., and Antes, Richard L. *Classroom Measurement and Evaluation.* Itasca, IL: F. E. Peacock Publishers, Inc., 1978. Chapters 9 and 10.

Linneman, Richard H., and Merenda, Peter F. *Educational Measurement,* 2nd ed. Glenview, IL: Scott, Foresman and Company, 1979. Chapter 3.

Mehrens, William A., and Lehmann, Irwin J. *Measurement and Evaluation in Education and Psychology.* New York: Holt, Rinehart and Winston, Inc., 1973. Chapter 5.

Noll, Victor H., Scannell, Dale P., and Craig, Robert C. *Introduction to Educational Measurement,* 4th ed. Boston: Houghton Mifflin Company, 1979. Chapter 4.

Noll, Victor H., Scannell, Dale P., and Noll, Rachel P. *Introductory Readings in Educational Measurement.* Boston: Houghton Mifflin Company, 1972. Chapters 7-11.

Payne, David A., and McMorris, Robert F. *Educational and Psychological Measurement.* Morristown, NJ: General Learning Press, 1974. Parts II and III.

Sax, Gilbert. *Principles of Educational Measurement and Evaluation.* Belmont, California: Wadsworth Publishing Company, Inc., 1974. Chapters 7 and 8.

Stanley, Julian C., and Hopkins, Kenneth D. *Educational and Psychological Measurement and Evaluation.* Englewood Cliffs, NJ: Prentice-Hall Inc., 1972. Chapters 4 and 5.

TenBrink, Terry D. *Evaluation. A Practical Guide for Teachers.* New York: McGraw-Hill Book Company, 1974. Chapter 2.

Thorndike, Robert L., and Hagen, Elizabeth. *Measurement and Evaluation in Psychology and Education,* 4th ed. New York: John Wiley & Sons, Inc., 1977. Chapter 3.

Tuckman, Bruce W. *Measuring Educational Outcomes: Fundamentals of Testing.* New York: Harcourt Brace Jovanovich, Inc., 1975. Chapters 8-10.

Wick, John W. *Educational Measurement. Where Are We Going and How Will We Get There?* Columbus, Ohio: Charles E. Merrill Publishing Company, 1973. Chapters 7 and 8.

Classroom Techniques and Procedures of Measurement and Evaluation

3

First Steps in Planning Measurement and Evaluation

"Would you tell me, please, which way I ought to go from here?"
"That depends a good deal on where you want to get to," said the Cat.
"I don't much care where—" said Alice.
"Then it doesn't matter which way you go," said the Cat.
"—so long as I get somewhere," Alice added as an explanation.
"Oh, you're sure to that," said the Cat, "if you would only walk long enough."[1]

How does one know whether measurement is good?
What is the core of the problem in planning for effective measurement?
What are the ways of classifying educational objectives?
How does one develop a clear statement of specific objectives?
How does one plan for measurement of a lesson or unit?
What are the limitations in the measurement and evaluation process?
What are the different levels of measurement and evaluation?
What is minimum competency testing?

In Chapter 1 it was stated that measurement and evaluation is the third step in the teaching process. As such, it is an integral part of the teacher's planning for effective teaching. So that this step may be done correctly, it is necessary for the teacher to know the proper procedures in planning for effective measurement and evaluation. This chapter will attempt to explain these procedures, starting at the beginning and proceeding until a measurement program is determined.

A. How Does One Know Whether Measurement Is Good?

Following are some examples of actual test items used at different grade levels. In examining each item, one must ask, Is the item good? If so, why? Is the item poor? If so, why?

1. Carroll, L., *Alice's Adventures in Wonderland* (Chicago: Rand McNally, 1916).

1. Situation: In Ricky's school, some children ride bicycles to school, some walk to school, and some ride the school bus. The pupils on the safety patrol must arrive at school early. Two children from each class in the school are members of the safety patrol. To find how many patrol members there are altogether, what other factor will be necessary for you to know?

   A. The number of children in the school
   B. The number of classes in the school
   C. The number of children in each class
   D. The number of school crossings

2. *True-False:* A box 4 in. $\times$ 6 in. $\times$ 10 in. contains the same number of cubic inches as a box 2 in. $\times$ 12 in. $\times$ 10 in.

3. In the story of Davey and Debbie: Who found the most eggs? Who chased the dog across the field? Why did Debbie's mother call her home?

4. What is needed for good health?

5. Toby saw an _____ in the nest.

There can be several reactions to these sample items. Some of the reactions might be: The first item is too long and involved; the second item is stated very clearly; there isn't much reasoning required in question 3; the fourth item is too indefinite; and the last item gives a clue by the use of the word "an."

These reactions are significant but are of secondary importance. If they are of secondary importance, how does one know, basically, whether measurement is good? *Basically, measurement is good if it measures appropriately behavior relevant to the goal of instruction.* If the type of item is appropriate to measure growth toward the goal of instruction, then the item can be improved in terms of the reactions given above. The same idea will hold true for any type of measuring device, not only for test items.

B. What Is the Core of the Problem in Planning for Effective Measurement?

Sometimes teachers are embarassed when they think of the way they judge their pupils. This is especially true after a parent-teacher conference if the teacher has not been able to explain the pupil's progress very effectively on the basis of the measurement data collected.

When teachers are not satisfied with their measurement approach, many of them begin to experiment with the measurement devices. After several trial-and-error approaches, which also may produce ineffective measurement, the teacher finds that he cannot correct the fault. He is not successful because he is starting to correct at the third step of the teaching process—measurement and evaluation—when the core of the problem lies in the first step— what is worth teaching? One cannot measure and evaluate effectively until the goals of instruction are clearly in mind. Thus, the basic step in planning for effective measurement and evaluation is a *clear statement of specific objectives at the very beginning of each instructional unit.*

C. What Are the Ways of Classifying Educational Objectives?

In developing a list of instructional objectives, a teacher must be concerned that his objectives cover a wide variety of types of learning. Instruction must be aimed at many goals in addition to a knowledge of facts. It must be concerned with the higher forms of knowledge, skills, interests, attitudes, and values.

At this juncture, the teacher might find it helpful to compare his list of objectives with some comprehensive list of most of the possible types of educational objectives. Two of these will be described here; namely, *The Taxonomy of Educational Objectives* and *The Taxonomy of Questions.*

The Taxonomy of Educational Objectives

One very useful list of this sort is the *Taxonomy of Educational Objectives* which has been prepared by a committee of college and university examiners who conceived the idea at a meeting of the American Psychological Association in 1948. The original purpose was to develop a theoretical framework which could be used to facilitate communication among examiners. After considerable discussion, there was agreement that such a theoretical framework might best be obtained through a system of classifying the goals of the educational process, since educational objectives provide the basis for building curricula and tests and represent the starting point for much of the educational research.

The *Taxonomy of Educational Objectives* classifies objectives into three domains; these are the cognitive domain, the affective domain, and the psychomotor domain. The cognitive domain includes those objectives which are related to the recall of knowledge and the development of intellectual abilities and skills. The affective domain includes those objectives concerning changes in pupil attitudes, interests, values, and appreciations. The psychomotor domain includes objectives related to the motor skills which pupils are to develop.

Following is an outline of the major divisions and sub-divisions in each of these domains. The author also strongly recommends that teachers read the complete references for each of these areas. The complete references are found at the end of this chapter. Condensed versions of the cognitive and affective domains are found in Appendixes A and B.

Outline of Major Categories of Cognitive Domain
Taxonomy of Educational Objectives[2]

1.00   Knowledge
    1.10   Knowledge of Specifics
        1.11   Knowledge of Terminology. Knowledge of the referents for specific symbols (verbal and nonverbal).
        1.12   Knowledge of Specific Facts. Knowledge of dates, events, persons, places, etc.
    1.20   Knowledge of Ways and Means of Dealing With Specifics
        1.21   Knowledge of Conventions. Knowledge of characteristic ways of treating and presenting ideas and phenomena.
        1.22   Knowledge of Trends and Sequences. Knowledge of the processes, directions, and movements of phenomena with respect to time.
        1.23   Knowledge of Classifications and Categories. Knowledge of the classes, sets, divisions, and arrangements which are regarded as fundamental for a given subject field, purpose, argument, or problem.
        1.24   Knowledge of Criteria. Knowledge of the criteria by which facts, principles, and conduct are tested or judged.
        1.25   Knowledge of Methodology. Knowledge of the methods of inquiry, techniques, and procedures employed in a particular subject field as well as those employed in investigating particular problems and phenomena.
    1.30   Knowledge of the Universals and Abstractions in a Field
        1.31   Knowledge of Principles and Generalizations. Knowledge of particular abstractions which summarize observations of phenomena.
        1.32   Knowledge of Theories and Structures. Knowledge of the body of principles and generalizations together with their interrelations which present a clear, rounded, and systematic view of a complex phenomena, problem, or field.

2.00   Comprehension
    2.10   Translation. Comprehension as evidenced by the care and accuracy with which the communication is paraphrased or rendered from one language or form of communication to another.

2. Benjamin S. Bloom and David Krathwohl, *Taxonomy of Educational Objectives, Handbook I: Cognitive Domain* (New York: David McKay Co., 1956), Part 2. Reprinted with permission of the publishers.

2.20   Interpretation. The explanation or summarization of a communication.

2.30   Extrapolation. The extension of trends or tendencies beyond the given data to determine implications, consequences, corollaries, effects, etc., which are in accordance with the conditions described in the original communication.

3.00   Application. The use of abstractions in particular and concrete situations. The abstractions may be in the form of general ideas, rules of procedure, or generalized methods.

4.00   Analysis
  4.10   Analysis of Elements. Identification of the elements included in a communication.
  4.20   Analysis of Relationships. The connections and interactions between elements and parts of a communication.
  4.30   Analysis of Organizational Principles. The organization, systematic arrangements, and structure which hold the communication together.

5.00   Synthesis
  5.10   Production of a Unique Communication. The development of a communication in which the writer or speaker attempts to convey ideas, feelings, and/or experiences to others.
  5.20   Production of a Plan, or Proposed Set of Operations. The development of a plan of work or the proposal of a plan of operations.
  5.30   Derivation of a Set of Abstract Relations. The development of a set of abstract relations either to classify or explain particular data or phenomena, or the deduction of propositions and relations from a set of basic propositions or symbolic representations.

6.00   Evaluation
  6.10   Judgments in Terms of Internal Evidence. Evaluation of the accuracy of a communication from such evidence as logical accuracy, consistency, and other internal criteria.
  6.20   Judgments in Terms of External Criteria. Evaluation of material with reference to selected or remembered criteria.

Some school systems will develop their own modifications of the taxonomy. An example of a school system's modification of the Cognitive Domain is shown on pages 50 and 51.

TABLE 3.1

Modification of the Cognitive Domain

Category Name	Expected Cognitive Activity	Key Terms	Sample Phrases and Questions
1. REMEMBERING (Knowledge)	The student recalls or recognizes information, ideas, and principles in the approximate form in which they were learned.	Memory, Knowledge, Repetition, Description, Recognition	1. "What did the book say about . . .?" 2. "Define . . ." 3. "List the three . . ." 4. "Who invented . . .?" 5. "In what year did . . .?"
2. UNDERSTANDING (Comprehension)	The student translates, comprehends, or interprets information based on prior learning.	Illustration, Comparison, Explanation, Translation, Interpretation	1. "Explain the . . ." 2. "What can you conclude . . .?" 3. "Tell in your own words . . ." 4. "What does the picture mean?" 5. "Write a summary of . . ." 6. "What are the similarities between . . .?" 7. "If it rains then what . . .?" 8. "What reasons or evidence . . .?"
3. SOLVING (Application)	The student selects, transfers, and uses data and principles to complete a problem task with a minimum of directions. Application requires transfer of training.	Solution, Application, Convergence, Incorporation, Construction, Organization	1. "If you know A & B, how could you determine C?" 2. "What might they do with . . .?" 3. "What other possible reasons . . .?" 4. "How might we organize . . .?" 5. "What do you suppose would happen if . . .?"

4. ANALYZING (Analysis)	The student distinguishes, classifies and relates the assumptions, hypotheses, evidence, conclusions, and structure of a statement or a question with an awareness of the thought processes he is using.	Logic, Induction and Deduction, Formal Reasoning	1. "What was the author's purpose, bias, or prejudice?" 2. "What must you know for that to be true?" 3. "Does that follow?" 4. "Which are facts and which are opinions?"
5. CREATING (Synthesis)	The student originates, integrates, and combines ideas into a product, plan, or proposal that is new to him.	Divergence, Productive Thinking, Creativity, Novelty	1. "If no one else knew, how could you find out?" 2. "Can you develop a new way?" 3. "Draw up a plan for . . ." 4. "Write a poem on . . ." 5. "Make up . . ." 6. "What would you do if . . ." 7. "How can we show . . .?"
6. JUDGING (Evaluation)	The student appraises, assesses, or criticizes on a basis of specific standards and criteria. Thus evaluation has two steps. The first is to set up appropriate standards and the second is to determine how closely the object or idea meets these standards.	Judgment, Selection, Qualification	1. "Which policy will result in the greatest good for the greatest number?" 2. "For what reason would you favor . . .?" 3. "Which of the books would you consider of greater value?" 4. "Evaluate that idea in terms of cost and community acceptance."

TABLE 3.2

Modification of the Affective Domain

Category	Description	Key Words	Sample Phrases or Questions
1. RECEIVING (Attending)	The first category is defined as sensitivity to the existence of certain phenomena and stimuli, that is, the willingness to receive or attend to them. A typical objective at this level would be: "The student develops a tolerance for a variety of types of music."	Sensitive Attention Conscious Tolerate Non-tension	1. Would you be presently interested in joining a club which meets frequently to discuss books? 2. Do you wish you had more time to read? 3. I have never had the wish to improve my understanding of music. 4. I have never had the desire to go to a concert.
2. RESPONDING	"Responding" refers to a behavior which goes beyond merely attending to the phenomena; it implies active attending, doing something with or about the phenomena, and not merely perceiving them. Here a typical objective would be: "The student voluntarily reads magazines and newspapers designed for young children."	Willingness Compliance Satisfaction Non-necessity "Interest"	1. Is it usually impossible for you to read for as long as an hour without being bored? 2. Do you have in mind one or two books you would like to read sometime soon? 3. Do you frequently use diagrams in presenting your thoughts? 4. Would you enjoy helping students to solve problems like this?
3. VALUING	Behavior which belongs to this level of the taxonomy goes beyond merely	Consistent Internalization	1. Do you ever spend time browsing in a library or bookstore?

	Description	Key words	Illustrative questions/statements
	doing something with or about certain phenomena. It implies perceiving them as having worth and consequently revealing consistency in behavior related to these phenomena. A typical objective at this level would be: "Writes letters to the press on issues he feels strongly about."	Commitment Belief Pursue	2. I like to listen to records which contain explanations of the music played. 3. Almost anyone can learn mathematics if he is willing to study. 4. Quite often I read articles on music with great interest.
4. ORGANIZATION	Organization is defined as the conceptualization of values and the employment of these concepts for determining the interrelationship among values. Here a typical objective might be: "Begins to form judgments as to the major directions in which American society should move."	System Interrelationships Quality Order Dynamic equilibrium.	1. Has your reading of books ever made you take up a hobby or interest? 2. When listening to music I often try to make judgments about the quality of the performance. 3. Have you ever thought about the meaning of "beauty in music?" 4. Have any books affected your choice of vocation?
5. CHARACTERIZATION	The organization of values, beliefs, ideas, and attitudes into an internally consistent system is called "characterization." This goes beyond merely determining interrelationships among various values; it implies their organization into a total philosophy. Typical example of objective: "Develops a consistent philosophy of life."	Philosophy Generalized set Inclusiveness World view Total	1. Do you revise judgments in the light of evidence? 2. Do you judge problems in terms of situations, issues, and purposes rather than a fixed notion? 3. Do you have a personal code of behavior based on ethical principles? 4. Have you developed a consistent philosophy of life?

Outline of Major Categories of Affective Domain
Taxonomy of Educational Objectives[3]

There are similar gradations for the Affective Domain. Five major categories have been identified, each of which has two or three subdivisions, as follows:

1.0   Receiving (Attending)
At this level the learner is recognizing phenomena and stimuli presented by the teacher.
1.1   Awareness
1.2   Willingness to receive
1.3   Controlled or selected attention

2.0   Responding
At this level, the learner is actively attending. He is becoming involved in or committed to the phenomena or stimuli.
2.1   Acquiescence in responding
2.2   Willingness to respond
2.3   Satisfaction in response

3.0   Valuing
The learner recognizes a thing, behavior, or phenomenon as having worth. He displays this behavior consistently enough to be considered to be holding a value.
3.1   Acceptance of a value
3.2   Preference for a value
3.3   Commitment

4.0   Organization
The learner begins to organize his values into a system, determines their interrelationships, and establishes the dominant and pervasive ones.
4.1   Conceptualization of a value
4.2   Organization of a value system

5.0   Characterization by a Value or Value Complex
The learner is described and characterized as a person in terms of the controlling influence of his value hierarchy, and these beliefs and attitudes are integrated into a total philosophy or world view for him.
5.1   Generalized set
5.2   Characterization

An example of a modification of the Affective Domain by a school system is illustrated in Table 3.2 on pages 52 and 53.

3. David R. Krathwohl, Benjamin S. Bloom, and Bertram B. Masia, *Taxonomy of Educational Objectives, Handbook II: Affective Domain* (New York: Longmans-McKay Co., 1964), Part II. Reprinted with permission of the publishers.

Outline of Major Categories of the Psychomotor Domain of Educational Objectives

An outline of the major categories of the Psychomotor Domain has not been developed by the authors of the previous domains. Harrow makes a comparison of three models and then develops her own taxonomy.

Ragsdale	Simpson	Kibler, et al.
NON-TAXONOMIC	TAXONOMIC	NON-TAXONOMIC
1. Object Motor (manipulating or acting with direct reference to an object)	1. Perception (interpreting)	1. Gross Body Movements (locomotor and axile)
	2. Set (preparing)	
2. Language Motor (movements of speech, sight, handwriting)	3. Guided Response (learning)	2. Finely Coordinated (manipulation and visual motor coordination)
	4. Mechanism (habituating)	
3. Feeling Motor (movements communicating feelings and attitudes)	5. Complex Overt Response (performing)	3. Nonverbal (communicating feelings and attitudes)
	6. Adaptation (modifying)	4. Speech Behaviors
	7. Origination (creating)	

Figure 3.1 A Comparative View of Three Models for Classifying Psychomotor Behaviors. (Anita J. Harrow, *A Taxonomy of the Psychomotor Domain* (New York: David McKay Company, Inc., 1972), p. 27. Reprinted with permission of the publishers).

Harrow then produces her own taxonomy of the Psychomotor Domain. The classification levels are intended to be hierarchial in order, arranged along a continuum from the lowest level of observable movement behavior to highest level. Harrow's taxonomy can be found on pages 56 and 57.

Kibler, Barker, and Miles have developed a classification of behaviors in the Psychomotor Domain. They say their classifications are *not* intended to represent a taxonomy. That is, they do not necessarily represent a hierarchy of skills in the Psychomotor Domain. The authors prefer to subdivide the Psychomotor Domain into behaviors involving (1) gross bodily movements, (2) finely coordinated bodily movements, (3) nonverbal communication behaviors, and (4) speech behaviors (see pp. 58-62).

Taxonomy Continuum	Levels	Definitions	Behavioral Activity
1.10 Segmental 1.20 Inter-segmental 1.30 Supra-segmental	1.00 Reflex Movements	Actions elicited without conscious volition in response to some stimuli	Flexion, extension, stretch, postural adjustments
2.10 Locomotor 2.20 Non-Locomotor 2.30 Manipulative	2.00 Basic-Fundamental Movements	Required: 1.00 Inherent movement patterns which are formed from a combining of reflex movements, and are the basis for complex skilled movement	2.10 Walking, running, jumping, sliding, hopping, rolling, climbing 2.20 pushing, pulling, swaying, swinging, stooping, stretching, bending, twisting 2.30 handling, manipulating, gripping, grasping, finger movements
3.10 Kinesthetic Discrimination 3.20 Visual Discrimination 3.30 Auditory Discrimination 3.40 Tactile Discrimination 3.50 Coordinated Abilities	3.00 Perceptual Abilities	Required: 1.00–2.00 Interpretation of stimuli from various modalities providing data for the learner to make adjustments to his environment	The *outcomes* of perceptual abilities are observable in *all purposeful* movement. Examples: Auditory—following verbal instructions. Visual—dodging a moving ball. Kinesthetic—making bodily adjustments in a hand-stand to maintain balance. Tactile—determining texture through touch. Coordinated—jump rope, punting, catching.

Classification	Definition	Description
4.00 Physical Abilities	Functional characteristics of organic vigor which are essential to the development of highly skilled movement	
4.10 Endurance		All activities which require strenuous effort for long periods of time—Examples: distance running, distance swimming.
4.20 Strength		All activities which require muscular exertion—Examples: weight lifting, wrestling.
4.30 Flexibility		All activities which require wide range of motion at hip joints—Examples: touching toes, back bend, ballet exercises.
4.40 Agility		All activities which require quick precise movements—Examples: shuttle run, typing, dodgeball.
5.00 Skilled Movements	A degree of efficiency when performing complex movement tasks which are based upon inherent movement patterns	
5.10 Simple Adaptive Skill		All skilled activities which build upon the inherent locomotor and manipulative movement patterns of classification level two.
5.20 Compound Adaptive Skill		
5.30 Complex Adaptive Skill		These activities are obvious in sports, recreation, dance, and fine arts areas.
6.00 Non-discursive Communication	Communication through bodily movements ranging from facial expressions through sophisticated choreographies	
6.10 Expressive Movement		Body postures, gestures, facial expressions, all efficiently executed skilled dance movements and choreographies.
6.20 Interpretive Movement		

Figure 3.2 Taxonomy for the Psychomotor Domain: Classification Levels and Subcategories. From Anita J. Harrow, *A Taxonomy of the Psychomotor Domain* (New York: David McKay Company, Inc., 1972), pp. 104-106. Reprinted with permission of the publishers.

CLASSIFICATION OF PSYCHOMOTOR BEHAVIOR[4]

1.00 GROSS BODILY MOVEMENTS

Behaviors in this category are characterized by movements of entire limbs in isolation or in conjunction with other parts of the body. The movements may be performed by a person alone, by a person in conjunction with another object, or between two or more persons. Although some coordination of movements with the eye or ear is obviously necessary, primary emphases usually are on strength, speed, or precision in objectives involving gross movements. Objectives which primarily are dependent upon coordination with eye or ear are placed in the second category (2.00) of psychomotor skills.

1.10 Movements Involving the Upper Limbs

Objectives in this category are related primarily to behaviors focusing on the use of arms and shoulders, such as throwing, catching, and pulling oneself up.

To be able to throw a baseball 35 feet.
To be able to do 10 chin-ups.

1.20 Lower Limbs

Objectives in this classification focus primarily on the use of feet and legs. Behaviors which would fall in this class include such activities as running, jumping, marching, and kicking.

To be able to run the 100 yard dash in 15 seconds.
To be able to march around the room three times in step to a military march.
To be able to raise and lower the right leg 10 times in succession from a prone position to a 45-degree angle.

1.30 Movements Involving Two or More Bodily Units

The behaviors represented by objectives in this class involve a combination of arm and leg movements or of movements using the entire body. Examples of activities in this behavioral class are swimming, diving, gymnastics, and dancing.

To be able to swim 100 yards using the Australian crawl.
To be able to execute a 1½ gainer with an average rating of 5.5 (on a 10-point scale) by a panel of three expert judges.
To be able to execute the five basic ballet positions with a minimum rating of 5, by two or three judges (on a 7-point scale).

2.00 FINELY COORDINATED MOVEMENTS

Behaviors in this classification primarily involve coordinated movements of the extremities, usually in conjunction with the eye or ear. The emphasis is on a pattern or sequence of coordinated movements, usually in combination with some external object. Objectives in this area may be found in fine arts, handicraft, woodworking (industrial arts), applied music, recreation, commercial arts, and written communication, to name but a few.

---

4. Robert J. Kibler, Larry L. Barker, and David T. Miles, *Behavioral Objectives in Instruction* (Boston: Allyn and Bacon, Inc., 1970), pp. 68-75. Reprinted with the permission of the publisher.

The behaviors in this class are often produced through a conditioning process. Measurements of these behaviors often represent an attempt to assess the degree of conditioning which has occurred at a given point in time. It is the degree of learning necessary to perform coordinated skills which primarily serves to differentiate them from the more gross bodily movements placed in the first classification.

2.10   Hand-Finger Movements

Behaviors in this class are characterized by the sense of touch rather than the sense of sight. The use of Braille by the visually-handicapped is a primary example of this class of behavior.

To be able to translate a paragraph in Braille accurately.

To be able to differentiate between a quarter and a nickel solely by touch.

2.20   Hand-Eye Coordination

Objectives related to this classification emphasize hand-eye relationships. Activities involving hand-eye coordination are extremely numerous. Several of the most common are playing a musical instrument, typing, writing, sewing, painting, sculpting, and weaving. Note that in all of these behaviors the feedback provided from visual inspection is critical to the successful performance of the task.

To be able to type an average of 60 words per minute for five minutes with fewer than four errors.

To be able to paint a portrait of a woman in the cubistic mode.

To be able to print the letters of the alphabet, duplicating the model in the writing manual.

2.30   Hand-Ear Coordination

Behaviors in this area focus on the relationships between sound stimuli and hand or finger movements. The sound in this case may serve as a stimulus for the hand movement or as a source of feedback concerning the success of the movement pattern. Examples of activities involving hand-ear coordination are found primarily in applied music (not involving sight-reading music), the broadcast media, and some other performing arts.

To be able to move the microphone lever to the right within two seconds after the music stops.

Given a note played on the violin, to be able to find the same note on the piano.

2.40   Hand-Eye-Foot Coordination

Objectives in this classification relate to movements which involve coordinated movements by hands, feet, arms, and fingers in conjunction with the eye. Most objectives in this area relate to such activities as physical education and operation of technical equipment and machinery.

To be able to punt a football 20 yards.

To be able to operate a sheet metal lathe safely.

2.50   Other Combinations of Hand-Foot-Eye-Ear Movements

This classification of objectives includes more complex behaviors that involve coordinated movements other than those specified in classes 2.10 through 2.40. Activities which might be included in this classification include piano tuning (eye-ear-hand), playing such musical instruments as organ, harp, and trap drums (eye-ear-hand-foot), and driving a car (eye-ear-hand-foot).

To be able to tune a piano through the use of a tuning fork.

To be able to drive a car along a prescribed route for three blocks without violating any traffic laws.

To be able to sight-read and play a given piece of organ music with no more than three mistakes.

3.00   NONVERBAL COMMUNICATION BEHAVIORS

Objectives relating to nonverbal communication behaviors are frequently found in public speaking, theatre, dance, and related performing arts curricula. The nonverbal communication behaviors included in this section (1) are learned and (2) attempt to convey a message to a receiver without the use of words. Some nonverbal behaviors serve to complement verbal communication. For purposes of clarification, those objectives will be classified under Category 4.00 as an integral part of speech communication. Nonverbal communication behaviors in this section include facial expressions, gestures, bodily movements, or a combination of the three.

3.10   Facial Expression

This classification focuses primarily on the mouth and eyes as communicators of moods or messages. Objectives involving facial expressions are especially important in theatre.

To be able to portray the emotion "rage" via facial expressions.

To be able to exhibit a range of six facial expressions which communicate different emotions identifiable by a panel of observers.

3.20   Gestures

Objectives in this class of behaviors involve the use of hands and arms to communicate specific messages. Areas in which gestures are primary forms of communication range from the complex language of the deaf to some forms of dances (for example, the hula), to the gesture of the thumb used by the hitchhiker. Most objectives related to the use of gestures are found in public speaking, theatre, and dance curricula.

To be able to communicate accurately a given message in hand-sign language.

To be able to communicate a series of five messages solely by the use of gestures so they may be understood by a panel of observers.

3.30   Bodily Movement

Objectives in this classification relate to total bodily movements whose primary emphases are the communication of a message or series of messages. Frequently, facial expressions and gestures are incorporated into a total pattern of movement. The defining characteristic of this class of behaviors is the movement of the trunk in addition to the other limbs in an attempt to communicate a message. Pantomimes are the most common activity which incorporate entire patterns of bodily movement.

To be able to portray, without words, a lady golfer hitting a hole-in-one.

To be able to pantomime a message selected at random so that a panel of observers can verbalize the message accurately.

4.00   SPEECH BEHAVIORS

Objectives related to speech behaviors primarily are found in speech communication, public speaking, and speech correction curricula.

The communication cycle may be subdivided into component processes—message invention, organization, encoding, transmission, reception, decoding, evaluation, and response. Some of these processes are primarily cognitive and affective, while others may be classified more readily in the psychomotor domain. Objectives related to message invention, organization, encoding, decoding, and evaluation are classified under Levels five and six (Synthesis and Evaluation) of the cognitive domain. Most objectives related to these processes would be classified under Section 5.10 (Production of a Unique Communication).

Message reception and response would be classified under Levels one and two of the affective domain (Receiving and Responding). Consequently, the only phase of the speech communication process related to this classification is transmission. This involves the formation, production, and projection of sound.

Gestures and other physical movements which tend to complement or reinforce verbal messages also are classified in this section. Those gestures and physical movements which are designed to replace or substitute for verbal messages are classified in Section 3.00.

4.10   Sound Production

Objectives in this classification relate to the ability to produce *meaningful* sounds. This involves the processes of respiration and phonation or the forcing of air past the vocal folds in such a way as to produce an audible sound which is designed to communicate to a listener. Random babbling of infants is not considered to be meaningful sound production.

To be able to produce the vowel sounds.
Given a series of sounds on a tape recorder, to be able to imitate them vocally.

4.20   Sound-Word Formation

This involves the ability to coordinate sounds into meaningful words and messages. The processes involved in word formation include articulation and modification of the oral cavity to form a battery of different sounds.

To be able to say the words "red" and "read" so that their meaning may be distinguished by a group of non-expert listeners.
To be able to recite a given passage without mispronouncing any words.

4.30   Sound Projection

Objectives in this classification involve the ability to project sounds across the air waves at a level adequate for reception and decoding by the listener. The processes of respiration and modification of the resonators are involved primarily in sound projection.

To be able to say a given word in a soundproof chamber at a level of 15 decibels.
Given a room filled with people generating a noise level of 20 decibels, to be able to convey an oral message to another person across the room 25 feet away with 95 percent comprehension.

4.40   Sound-Gesture Coordination

This classification deals with the ability to coordinate facial expression, movement, and gestures with verbal messages. The goal of nonverbal and verbal coordination is the enhancement of the verbal message through the nonverbal channels. Objectives which involve total nonverbal communication are placed in Section 3.00.

> Given a message three minutes in length, to be able to transmit the same message with no significant reduction in comprehension in half the time through the addition of coordinated gestures and bodily movement to the verbal message.
>
> Given an ambiguous verbal message, to be able to transmit the intended meaning accurately to your classmates through the addition of meaningful facial expressions.

Summary

The author of the present text believes that the taxonomies can be valuable educational tools but that they are not appropriate to all objectives, especially those involving complex behaviors. The above discussion of the three behavioral domains is intended as a guide for the classification of behavioral objectives. It should not be regarded as an absolute answer to the problems associated with classifying educational objectives and human behavior.

The Taxonomy of Questions

Sanders states that the basic ideas underlying his *Taxonomy of Questions* come from the *Taxonomy of Educational Objectives,* edited by B. S. Bloom. Some explanation is necessary to show how a book on objectives has significance to the topic of questions.

The purpose was to develop a system that could be used to classify any educational objective and thereby would provide a useful pattern in a hopelessly confused area in educational thinking. Within the cognitive domain, a number of categories of thinking were defined that encompassed all intellectual objectives in education and were called memory, translation, interpretation, application, analysis, synthesis, and evaluation. One of the ways each category was defined was by using examples of questions that required students to engage in the specified kind of thinking. This is the point at which the *Taxonomy of Educational Objectives* is carried in a new direction by the "taxonomy of questions" which Sanders developed in his volume.

Sanders developed the following definitions of Bloom's categories of thinking.[5]

5. Norris M. Sanders, *Classroom Questions, What Kinds?* (New York: Harper & Row Publishers, Inc., 1966), pp. 2-3.

1. *Memory:* The student recalls or recognizes information.
2. *Translation:* The student changes information into a different symbolic form or language.
3. *Interpretation:* The student discovers relationships among facts, generalizations, definitions, values, and skills.
4. *Application:* The student solves a life-like problem that requires the identification of the issue and the selection and use of appropriate generalizations and skills.
5. *Analysis:* The student solves a problem in the light of conscious knowledge of the parts and forms of thinking.
6. *Synthesis:* The student solves a problem that requires original, creative thinking.
7. *Evaluation:* The student makes a judgment of good or bad, right or wrong, according to standards he designates.

It should be pointed out that, in Bloom's book, the category of "memory" is called "knowledge." Also, that "translation," "interpretation," and "extrapolation" are placed under the heading of "comprehension." Sanders also reminds his readers that these preliminary definitions are by no means adequate for distinguishing the categories. He has submitted them only as a necessary background to a discussion of the way in which ideas from the *Taxonomy of Educational Objectives* can be used by classroom teachers.

D. How Does One Develop a Clear Statement of Objectives?

The procedure to be described here emphasizes the stating of objectives as learning outcomes and the defining of these objectives in terms of student behavior; that is, in terms of the specific types of behavior that students are expected to demonstrate (e.g., lists names) at the end of the learning experience. This procedure assumes that effective teaching and measurement require a clear conception of the desired learning outcomes.

Some teachers have a tendency to state their objectives in such broad terms that the expected learning outcomes are vague and ambiguous. Some state them in such specific terms that they end up with long, unmanageable lists of tasks to be performed by the students, rather than goals for them to work toward. What is needed is an approach which would avoid both extremes, one which would include statements of objectives that are general enough to provide direction, without overly limiting the instructional process, and specific enough to be clearly defined by the behavior that students exhibit when they achieve the objectives. The objectives should be from all domains and from the simple to the complex to the degree that the lesson, unit, or course warrants this scope.

Gronlund believes that the above can be accomplished by:[6]

1. Stating the instructional objective as a general learning outcome.
2. Listing, under each instructional objective, a representative sample of the specific types of behavior that indicate attainment of the objective.

To illustrate, take a unit on working with fractions in about the fifth grade.

1. Knows basic concepts of fractions.
   1.1 Identifies proper fractions from improper fractions.
   1.2 Labels numbers of a fraction either as a numerator or denominator.
   1.3 Defines the terms numerator and demoninator.

Stating it in this way is more than literary form. It emphasizes that the instructional objective is *knows* and not *identifies, labels,* or *defines.* These latter types of behavior are simply *samples of the types of performance that represent the word knows.* The teaching efforts must be directed toward the *general objectives* of instruction and not toward the specific samples of behavior selected to represent each objective. When measuring the students, however, one will devise instruments to measure growth toward the *samples of behavior* and accept as evidence of growth the attainment of the general objective. It is impractical to measure everything that children have learned just as it is impractical to list all of the behaviors to show knowledge of the basic concepts of fractions. One must be satisfied with a sample, a sample of the fractions the students have studied during instruction and a sample of the many types of behavior that could be used as evidence of the students' knowledge of basic concepts of fractions. If the samples are representative enough, generalization can then move from measurement to the larger domain of behavior. That is, one can judge how well the students have achieved the instructional objective—"The student knows basic concepts of fractions."

Stating the General Objective

It would appear simple enough to state the general learning outcome, e.g., knows basic concepts of fractions or applies concepts and principles. However, sometimes teachers tend to focus on the *teaching process,* on the *learning process,* or on the *subject matter* rather than on the expected *outcomes* of instruction. Sometimes, there is also difficulty in stating the general outcome at a satisfactory level of generality; that is, a middle-of-the-road approach between broad, undefinable statements and long, unmanageable lists of specific types of behavior.

6. Reprinted with permission of Macmillan Publishing Co., Inc. from *Stating Objectives for Classroom Instruction,* 3rd ed. by Norman E. Gronlund. Copyright © 1978, Norman E. Gronlund.

Gronlund lists six criteria to follow in producing a good set of general instructional objectives.[7]

1. Begin each general instructional objective with a verb (knows, understands, appreciates). Omit such unnecessary refinements as "The student can. . . ." or "The student develops the ability to. . . ."
2. State each objective in terms of *student performance* (rather than teacher performance).
3. State each objective as a learning *product* (rather than in terms of the learning process).
4. State each objective so that it indicates *terminal behavior* (rather than the subject matter to be covered during instruction).
5. State each objective so that it includes only *one* general learning outcome (rather than a combination of several outcomes).
6. State each objective at the proper level of generality, that is, at a level of generality that clearly indicates the expected learning outcome and that is readily definable by specific types of student behavior. Stating from eight to twelve general instructional objectives will usually suffice.

As to form, objectives will contain a P (participant); B (behavior); and PR (a product). Take the following objectives.

1. The student (P) knows (B) basic concepts of fractions (PR).
2. The learner (P) applies (B) concepts and principles (PR).
3. The pupil (P) understands (B) changes in tempo (PR).

Some authors recommend that you add C (conditions) and MC (measurement criterion).

Seventh grade pupils (P) will label (B) congruent angles (PR) of a parallelogram having the vertices labeled A, B, C, D (C) with 100 percent accuracy (MC).

Whether the objective contains three or five elements is something a teacher must decide. Objectives should, however, contain the minimum of P (participant); B (behavior); and PR (product).

Stating the Specific Behavioral Outcomes

After a basic list of general instructional objectives has been identified, the next step is to define each objective in terms of *specific learning outcomes;* that is, identify and list under each objective a representative sample of specific types of behavior that are to be used as evidence that the objective has been achieved. While the verbs of knows, understands, applies, appreciates, and thinks critically were all right for the general outcomes, it

---

7. Gronlund, *Stating Objectives for Classroom Instruction*, 3rd ed., p. 11.

is necessary now to define, in terms of *specific* student behavior, what is meant by each of these general outcomes. The list of illustrative verbs found in Appendix C will be helpful. This is not an exhaustive list. The best behavior in a specific objective is the one which best conveys the terminal behavior a teacher desires the student to achieve. The criterion is that the behavior is in behavioral terms. Terms such as sees, gains, realizes, and acquires are examples of non-behavioral terms. They are internal, not observable.

There are certain criteria to check if you are stating these objectives properly. According to Gronlund, they are:[8]

1. State the general instructional objectives as *expected learning outcomes.*
2. Place under each instructional objective a list of specific learning outcomes that describes the *terminal behavior* students are to demonstrate when they have achieved the objective.
   a. Begin each specific learning outcome with a *verb* that specifies definite, *observable behavior.*
   b. List a sufficient number of specific learning outcomes under each objective to describe adequately the behavior of students who have achieved the objective.
   c. Be certain that the behavior in each specific learning outcome is *relevant* to the objective it describes. (If the general objective is in the cognitive domain, the specific objectives must also be. If the general behavior term is *understands,* then the specific behavioral terms must be *forms* of understands.)
3. When defining the general instructional objectives in terms of specific learning outcomes, revise and refine the original list of objectives as needed. You may find that your original objective was too general or broad and needs to be subdivided. An objective of *solves problems creatively,* for example, might better express instructional intent if it is broken down into *verbal* and *performance skills.* At other times, you might note that the specific types of behavior overlap to such a degree that it is desirable to combine two statements into a single objective. Thus, *demonstrates self-confidence* and *drives defensively* might be combined into *applies laws to behind-the-wheel driving.*
4. Be careful not to omit complex objectives (e.g., critical thinking, appreciations) simply because they are difficult to define in specific behavioral terms. Sometimes the more complex objectives, although difficult to define, are usually more important from an educational viewpoint. Objectives relating to thinking skills, attitudes, and appreciations should not be slighted because of the difficulty of clearly defining them.
5. Consult reference materials for help in identifying the specific types of behavior that are most appropriate for defining the complex objectives.

8. Gronlund, *Stating Objectives for Classroom Instruction,* 3rd ed., p. 17.

Adding a Fourth and Fifth Element to the Specific Objectives

Many schools are now moving toward criterion-referenced instruction and evaluation. The idea is to set a minimum criterion of growth toward the objective toward which the pupil, or all pupils, will grow. This is accomplished by adding a *condition* and a *measurement* criterion. A condition is a description of the conditions under which the participant will be able to demonstrate mastery of the objective (time limit, equipment, tools, and the like). The measurement criterion is a specific statement as to the minimum acceptable level of performance to indicate mastery of the objective (80% correct, four out of five, to the nearest tenth, for example).

Following are some examples of the general objective with three components and the specific objectives with five components.

Cognitive

1.0 The student (P) understands (B) the concepts and processes relating to whole numbers (PR)

   1.1 The student (P) explains (B) the four fundamental processes in arithmetic (PR) *without reference to material* (C) *correctly* (MC)

   1.2 The student (P) describes (B) how to estimate answers (PR) *from a sample in the book* (C) *without error* (MC)

   1.3 The student (P) recalls (B) how to round off numbers (PR) *from a given sample* (C) *using the correct principles* (MC)

Affective

1.0 The pupil (P) exhibits (B) eagerness to succeed (PR)

   1.1 The pupil (P) helps (B) self (PR) *during free time* (C) *without urging* (MC)

   1.2 The pupil (P) attempts (B) tasks (PR) *in assignments* (C) *by himself* (MC)

   1.3 The pupil (P) accepts (B) instructions (PR) *during exercises* (C) *willingly* (MC)

Psychomotor

1.0 The learner (P) enunciates (B) sounds correctly (PR)

   1.1 The learner (P) articulates (B) consonants (PR) *when called upon* (C) *with 80 percent accuracy* (MC)

   1.2 The learner (P) sustains (B) vowels (PR) *from a sampling* (C) *regularly* (MC)

   1.3 The learner (P) sings (B) vowel exercises (PR) *from laboratory manual* (C) *satisfying a five-point checklist* (MC)

E. How Does One Plan for Measurement of a Lesson or Unit?

In Chapter 1, the three main steps or tasks in the teaching process were introduced: Setting of Objectives, Determining the Methods or Procedures, Measuring and Evaluating Progress. This chapter indicates how to develop the first task. When both the methods and materials of instruction and the procedures for evaluating student progress are selected in light of the desired learning outcomes, they are expected to be more relevant and effective.

One way to do this is to prepare a planning chart which includes all three. The examples given in Table 3.3 illustrate the procedures for preparing such a chart.

F. What Are the Limitations in the Measurement and Evaluation Process?

As in any teaching task, there are obstacles or limitations which the teacher must recognize. In measurement and evaluation, there are basically three limitations which seem especially important.[9]

1. Teacher's Time for Planning Good Measurement

It takes considerable time to make an overall guide for a unit including measurement.

Solution: Take one unit at a time. The teacher will then find, with practice, that the units will come into focus, and the task becomes easier as new units are approached.

2. Teacher's Time for Actual Measurement

Teachers may find that time does not allow them to use all of the measurement devices which they believe would be appropriate.

Solution: It is wise to look at all of the possible ways to measure; from these, one can select those which will give, in the time available for measurement, the best picture of the child's growth. The task is not always done as thoroughly as desired. The teacher must be content to do what can be done in the time available.

3. Lack of Opportunities to Measure All Behavior

Mr. McGraw, a ninth grade teacher, might have the following general objective for a unit in Science: *The pupil uses the scientific method in solv-*

---

9. R. Murray Thomas, *Judging Student Progress* (New York: David McKay Co., 1960), pp. 31-33. © Longmans, Green & Co., Inc., 1960. Reprinted with permission of the publishers.

TABLE 3.3
Instructional Planning Chart

INSTRUCTIONAL OBJECTIVES	TEACHING METHODS	MEASUREMENT AND EVALUATION
THE LEARNER:	*Cognitive*	
1. *Understands* the concepts and processes relating to whole numbers.		
1.1 *Explains* the four fundamental processes in arithmetic correctly.	Reviews the four fundamental processes, and the pupils will discuss them in class. Show a film strip on how to estimate answers correctly, and the pupils will do a practical exercise from the book, explaining how they arrived at the correct answers. Use visual aids to explain the rounding off process, and the pupils will participate in oral problems that involve rounding off of numbers, explaining how they arrived at the correct answers.	1.1 Essay (Short Answer); Participation Chart of Discussion
1.2 *Describes* how to estimate answers correctly.		1.2 Simple Recall (Basic); Participation Chart
1.3 *Recalls* how to round off numbers correctly.		1.3 Completion (Basic); Graded Written Assignment; Alternative Response (Basic)
	Affective	
2. *Exhibits* eagerness to succeed		
2.1 *Helps* self voluntarily	Provide many opportunities in small group or individual activities for the learner to be able to take care of himself.	2.1 - 2.3 Rating Scale (Changing Alternatives)
2.2 *Attempts* tasks by himself		
2.3 *Accepts* instructions willingly		
	Psychomotor	
3. *Enunciates* sounds correctly		
3.1 *Articulates* consonants properly	Stress the importance of proper enunciation for proper execution of music and listener understanding. Provide practice exercises using the tape recorder. Use small groups to practice singing vowel exercises.	3.1 - 3.2 Checklist (Basic)
3.2 *Sustains* vowels correctly		
3.3 *Sings* vowel exercises well		3.3 Rating Scale (Constant Alternatives)

ing problems. He would separate this general objective into specific behaviors as follows:

The pupil:
1. Effectively *defines* the problem to be studied.
2. *Gathers* appropriate data related to the problem.
3. Properly *analyzes* the data.
4. *Suggests* solutions to the problem based on the facts presented.
5. *Uses* the scientific method in solving daily problems.

In describing his problem, Mr. McGraw therefore might state: "I realize that I can provide opportunities for pupils to grow toward some of these objectives, and their progress can be measured directly. However, with the objective, 'Uses the scientific method in solving daily problems,' I do not have much opportunity to observe the pupils outside of class, and I can't follow the pupils around to see if they are using the scientific method to solve their daily problems.

"Therefore, there are objectives like this one and others for which I do not have opportunities to measure pupil growth directly—thus, they are not measurable."

Mr. McGraw's conclusion is partially correct. It is obvious that there are not adequate opportunities, at times, to measure pupil growth *directly.* However, there are levels of evaluation other than direct measurement. These are compromises, but they can and must be used. The following section outlines a solution that has been used successfully by many teachers.

G. What Are the Different Levels of Measurement and Evaluation?

R. Murray Thomas,[10] in his book, *Judging Student Progress,* presents three levels of measurement and evaluation.

1. Behavioral Level

Measures *directly* the pupil's performance by the observation of his oral, physical, or written performance.

Whenever possible, the teacher should measure the pupil's behavior directly. For example, if the goal is *speaks clearly,* the teacher observes the pupil speaking. If the goal is *writes a paragraph correctly,* the teacher has the pupil write a paragraph. This is the highest level, direct measurement, since it measures the pupil's actual behavioral change as he grows toward an objective.

10. Thomas, *Judging Student Progress,* pp. 33-37. Reprinted with permission of the publishers.

However, some goals are not appropriately measured directly. When this happens, one must compromise and use an indirect level of measurement. Two levels of indirect measurement are explained in the following paragraphs.

2. Planning Level

Measures *indirectly* the pupil's performance by requiring him to tell or show what he would plan to do if a real situation were to arise.

Measuring the pupil's plan rather than his actual behavior is obviously a compromise position, inasmuch as people do not always behave as they plan. For example, a teacher may deviate from lesson plans; a pupil may not do the homework as planned.

Therefore, when the teacher measures what the pupil plans to do rather than what he or she actually does do, the teacher knows that his measurement of the goal may not be as accurate as one would like. However, when measuring on the planning level, one must assume that the pupil will act as planned.

There are many examples of occasions when one uses the planning level. For example, if the goal is *Eats properly balanced meals,* the teacher would probably have the pupils tell what they would plan to eat. If the goal is *Leaves the room properly during a fire,* the teacher could simulate a fire situation and then require that the pupils show what they would do. Any time that a mock simulated situation is used, the measurement is on the planning level.

The preceding examples indicate that when a teacher cannot judge behavior directly, he can compromise by judging what the pupil would plan to do. The teacher must assume, in many cases, that the pupil will act as planned.

3. Understanding Level

Measures *indirectly* the pupil's preformance by having him or her tell or explain what knowledges and understandings he or she has about a subject.

There are some objectives which apparently are not appropriately measured on either the behavioral or planning level. These are normally considered basic knowledges and understandings. For example, in social studies, one might list the following:

1. *Understands* how the geography of Mexico affects the lives of its people
2. *Knows* the important industries of Mexico

3. *Knows* the contributions that Mexico has made in art, music, and architecture.
4. *Understands* how people live in a culture much more simple than his own

Understands and *knows* are general action words and cannot be measured concretely. However, if one thinks of how pupils can show that they understand or know something, such specific action words as *explains, tells, describes,* and *recognizes* come to mind. Therefore, one can substitute the appropriate specific action word in objectives which call for understanding.

Taken in this light, understanding objectives are relatively easy to measure through the use of traditional teacher-made tests, oral or written. They also can be measured through the more routine measurements of written assignments, oral reports, and reading reports.

The understanding level is listed as the lowest level of measurement; however, for given objectives, it may be the highest, most appropriate level of measurement possible. The difficulty arises when a teacher uses the understanding level for measurement when one of the higher levels would be possible. For example, if an objective is *The pupil plays in safe areas,* the best measurement would be the behavioral level, if feasible, or the planning level. To leave the measuremnt at the understanding level would be assuming too much. The children may know where they are to play, but the "proof of the pudding" is whether they carry their knowledge into actual behavior.

In summary, teachers must choose an evaluation device on which they can directly judge the behavioral goal whenever possible. When this is not possible, they must judge on the planning level, and when neither is feasible, they must measure the degree to which the pupil's knowledge and understanding may be expected to guide him to proper action when required. Sometimes the nature of the objectives causes overlapping among the three levels. This need not be a concern, since the teacher should strive to select the level which is as near as possible to actual behavior.

H.   What Is Minimum Competency Testing?

Introduction

There appear to be four major aspects of minimum competency testing:

1. Historically, its development.
2. Some key questions about minimum competency testing.
3. Three major implications of minimum competency testing.
4. Some characteristics of a good minimum competency testing program.

Historically, our schools have been charged with two functions: Instruction and the certification of competence in a number of areas, depending on the local school philosophy. Traditionally, the major focus has been on the instructional function of the school, with certification of competence implicit in the successful completion of twelve years of schooling.

More recently, the focus has been shifting to the certification function of the school. This shift in focus is due largely to litigation involving high school graduates who do not possess certain valued competencies. Public concern and legal charges have forced legislators and school district officials into a position where competency testing programs are mandated as a solution to the problem, without proper consideration of the issues involved. No more, goes the argument, can we afford to have incompetent high school graduates and incompetent schools.

Aside from isolated lawsuits regarding high school graduates who do not possess skills that have been defined by society as essential, another factor that has stirred a great deal of public concern is the highly publicized decline in college entrance examination scores. These two factors, in particular, have led to a widespread belief that schools are becoming less effective in performing one of their primary functions: the preparation of youth for survival in society.

The evidence seems to point to the fact that high school students, in particular, are not performing as well as students did twenty and thirty years ago on present indicators of educational attainment. Although a standard solution to the problem has been to institute minimum competency testing programs, therefore holding the schools more accountable, perhaps one should not accept the school as the cause of the problem so readily.

Perhaps the problem has something to do with youth alienation during the 1963-1978 period. Everyone is aware of reports that suicide, drug usage, delinquency rates, teenage pregnancies, and other social indicators of alienation have been on the increase during this period. Perhaps television has had something to do with it. Dramatic figures indicate that a 17-year-old is likely to have viewed some 15,000 or more hours of television, more time than the youth has spent in schools. Perhaps, it has had something to do with curriculum changes. The breadth of course offerings has increased, generally resulting in a decrease in the frequency of the number of "basic" courses that each student takes during high school. Perhaps, it has had something to do with the tests themselves. It may be that the perceived decline in literacy is little more than an effect created by an increasing content gap between the test and the curriculum.

Although several singular explanations have been offered, it is likely that there is no one cause for the perceived decline in literacy. The most sensible explanation is that the decline is a result of multiple causes, not all within the control domain of the school. Regardless of the causes, and whether some or all of these can be influenced by the process of schooling, competency programs are seen as a step in the solution for the problem through the fact that society holds schools accountable for certain valued outcomes. Because of this, mandated programs must be a major concern of school officials.

Who Will Do It?

The current posture of the Congress of the United States appears to be one of cautious interest in the areas of competency-based education. While no mandates have come out of the Congress for a national system of CBE/T (competency-based education/testing), the congressional interest is exemplified by provisions to include some kind of voluntary assistance to states. Since the federal government already underwrites a good deal of the costs of the National Assessment of Educational Progress, it may be unlikely, in this period of fiscal concern, to substantially extend this effort to include CBE.

Many departments of public instruction in the states have competency-based education as a local responsibility with the state's interest being expressed by some technical assistance to local school districts as they pursue independent goals and objectives in this matter. We do know that most states have established some form of competency requirement for high school graduation.

It would appear, then, that competency-based education is a local school district responsibility in most instances and that decisions in respect to requirements for promotion and graduation are left to the individual school district.

Five Keynotes on Minimum Competency Testing

Adopting a policy on minimum competency testing requires answering at least five major questions. Those questions and some possible answers are presented here.

1. What are the competencies to be measured?
   First, one should distinguish between school skills and life skills. Competencies having to do with school skills will indicate whether the student is ready for the next course in school; the life skills will indicate whether the student is ready for the shopping center. But this division seems much too simplistic. Actually, there are five choices: (1) basic skills, (2) school subjects, (3) life area, (4) basic skills applied in each school subject, and (5) basic skills applied in each life area. The obvious choice is (1) basic skills. But, wait! Look at the others! Unless one selects (2), teachers of art and music and science and social studies and foreign languages and driver education and vocational subjects will

have no minimum standards. Unless one chooses (3), the teacher may teach about school and not teach about life. Unless one chooses (4), the students may be able to spell a list of words correctly in an English class but will misspell them in their science laboratory notebooks. Unless one selects (5), students may learn to add and subtract but may be unable to balance their checkbooks. But one can't select them all because schools do not have the time and money for that much testing. So one must choose very thoughtfully! Regardless of choice, one will have to live with the consequences.

2. How does one measure the competencies?

The possibilities range from testing through experience in actual performance situations to testing with paper and pencil. Between these two extremes lie two other alternatives: simulated performance situations and school products and performances. Actual performance situations in later school or on the job is ideal testing, but the problem is that it takes too long for the results to come back to help either the school or the student. Simulated performance situations set up in school to resemble those in later life or on the job is good testing. It is cheaper, takes less time, and gives quicker results; but it isn't perfect: the situations are not real, there are very few good tests available, and it takes more time and money than using paper and pencil. School products and performances include essays, painting, clarinet solos, brake jobs, speeches, touchdowns, things which the students make or do. This is not as good as simulated since the student usually has had help, the test pressures are missing, and it is difficult to score the results. But it takes less time and money than arranging special simulations.

Most of the paper-and-pencil tests in the classroom measure a narrow band of knowledge or skill and are far removed from actual performance situations. But those tests are quick, easy, and available.

To summarize, as you move away from actual performance situations in real life and move toward paper and pencil, testing becomes easier and cheaper, but the test results become less likely to predict later success. A possible solution is to test life skills by simulated performance situations and use paper and pencil to test school skills.

Another decision is whether you should develop your own tests or use what is available. There are many paper-and-pencil tests available on the market but not many simulated performance tests of ethical behavior or other life skills. Many test publishers are making contracts with schools to help them develop their programs. Some experts believe that tests should be purchased if the school can afford it; a lot of time will be saved. Others maintain that tests should be built locally to reflect local objectives.

To the author, the answer has to be a practical one and also has to meet minimum testing conditions that will be mentioned later. If a test publisher has a test which reflects adequately the objectives you have built, fine; if not, it would be much more valid to get help from a test expert or a test company and build your own. It is assumed that most districts are interested in what is called "criterion-referenced testing" rather than "norm-referenced testing." Criterion-referenced means how well the student meets the minimum standards established for the competency; norm-referenced says where one stands in relation to other students.

3. When does one measure the competencies?

Will competencies be measured during school or at the end of school?

a. Measure them during school if you believe:

—you want to measure students' competence to advance from grade to grade.

—students and their parents deserve a distant early warning if there is trouble ahead.

—administrators need to make changes any time students do not progress—changes in curriculum, course selection, faculty inservice training. Only formal competency tests will alert administrators to unsatisfactory learning early enough to do something about it.

b. Measure them at the end of school if you believe:

—you want to measure students' competence to move out of school and into the next school or into life.

—students learn at different rates. All students deserve enough time to reach the minimum.

—teacher-made tests and daily classroom contact will identify students who are not making progress during school. Formal competency testing is not needed.

The author believes that a competency testing program, if implemented, should not focus only on the senior year, but should provide a monitoring system that will bring students, from their first day of school, to their maximum potential. The system should contain provisions so that students (or schools) are not held to minimum competency restrictions without several years prior notice. Both the student and the school need time to adjust.

4. Does one measure a single minimum competency or many?

A single standard, or minimum, can be too hard for a dull student but too easy for a bright student; impossible for the dull and thus not motivating, trivial for the bright and thus not motivating; objectionable to parents and teachers of the dull, laughable to parents and teachers of the bright; and thus acceptable to none of them.

Obviously, some sort of compromise is necessary. One can use a low minimum for every student regardless of ability, and a graduated minimum for a student of, say, above average ability. This does not expect the impossible for anyone, but it does expect more from students who clearly can do more. The old problem, such as how to measure ability and translate it into performance terms is still present, however. This is not an impossible situation.

5. What is done with the incompetent?

What will one do about incompetent students? Verify the findings independently before acting? Give them several more chances? Lower the standards so that they can pass? Remediate so that they can pass? Refuse to promote or graduate them until they can pass? Promote or graduate with a restricted diploma or certificate of attendance? These are important questions which each district must consider carefully in order to answer this fifth question.

Three Major Implications

Three major implications need to be fully considered before a school district moves into establishing CBE/T.

Accountability Funding Implications

Regardless of intent, any state or district that uses a common competency test across schools may be opening itself up to a test-based system of accountability or funding. Any time that common tests are used across schools within districts or across districts within a state, comparison of scores is involved. Generally, because of different curricular emphases, different teaching styles, and different student demographics, such comparisons are unfair and provisions should be made so that this common abuse does not occur. In some instances, state-wide testing programs have been used to allocate funds to districts. Generally, this means that those districts with more low scoring students receive a higher proportion of funds for remediation purposes.

At this point, the evidence clearly indicates that competency testing programs should not be used for personnel or funding decisions. The singular defensible use of such programs lies in their diagnostic and subsequent remediation functions.

Curricular Implications

If competency testing programs are to be instituted, then consideration must be given to curricular changes that may evolve as a result of their implementation. These changes may be intended or unintended. This has always been one of the uses of a regular testing program and is really nothing new.

Another implication that must be considered if competency-based testing is established is the mechanism that must be formulated for remediation. If one institutes a competency testing program, then presumably some students will be shown to be incompetent, in which case it is the school's responsibility to remediate. This factor has both its good and its bad points. On the one hand, remediation is desirable. On the other hand, educators and parents should be prepared to accept unequal resource allocations per pupil and to sacrifice some curricular diversifications for repetition if such formal programs are implemented.

Legal Implications

The full legal implications of competency-based testing programs are not yet known. To be sure, some legal consequences are likely to arise as a result of the movement. Particularly in systems such as in Florida, where individuals are given a "certificate of attendance" or "diploma" depending upon test performance, the potential for litigation is strong.

To avoid some of the more obvious legal problems, the following factors should, at a minimum, be considered in establishing such an assessment system: (a) A competency-based testing program should have curricular validity; that is, test content should match curriculum content. This assures that the test covers outcomes that are valued by the school and are included in the curriculum. A test that stresses outcomes other than those cannot be justified for use in making a decision regarding promotion or graduation. (b) A competency testing program should have instructional validity; that is, assurances must be made that the content in the curriculum, reflected in the test, was actually taught. If services were not delivered, the potential for litigation exists. (c) A competency testing program should insure content validity; that is, the test should adequately and equitably reflect the domains of skills stressed in the schooling process. (d) Consideration should be given to secondary screening techniques, using methods other than tests for those students failing to achieve minimum competencies. This avoids the use of a test as the sole indicator of competence. (e) Any test used in such a process should be thoroughly examined for discrimination potential, particularly on the basis of race or disabling conditions. If such potential exists, alternative procedures for special populations should be explored.

Some Characteristics of a Good Minimum Competency Testing Program

Most experts recommend that each school district which implements a competency-based education program should establish a developmental model which contains the following elements or characteristics.

1. Involves local community citizens.
2. Provides training to professional staff.

3. Establishes both minimum and optimum student competency levels.
4. Provides remedial training for students who fail to attain desired competencies.
5. Notifies the public of competency-based education goals and objectives prior to implementation of the program.
6. Provides for periodic evaluation of student competencies during the K-12 school years.
7. Provides for continuing evaluation of program competencies to allow for planned modification.

Thus, one sees, in planning a minimum-competency program, that there are several key questions to be answered, including: Who will do it? What are the competencies to be measured? How does one measure the competencies? and the like. There are some implications including funding, curricular, and legal aspects which must be noted. Finally, there are certain characteristics that a good competency program should meet. It is the author's viewpoint that it is not a question of whether a school district should have a minimum competency program—all districts will have some form of program—rather, it is the format and structure of the program to fit the individual needs of the district which will determine its pattern and scope.

Summary Statements

1. Basically, measurement is good if it measures appropriately toward the goal of instruction.
2. The core of the problem in planning for good measurement is a clear statement of specific objectives at the very beginning of the unit.
3. The *Taxonomy of Educational Objectives* classifies objectives into three domains; namely, the cognitive domain, the affective domain, and the psychomotor domain.
4. The cognitive domain includes those which are related to the recall of knowledge and the development of intellectual abilities and skills. The affective domain includes those objectives concerning changes in pupil attitudes, interests, values, and appreciations. The psychomotor domain includes objectives related to the motor skills which pupils are to develop.
5. Teachers can lead students into all kinds of thinking through careful use of questions, problems, and projects. Some teachers ask questions of high quality, but far too many overemphasize those that require students only to remember, and practically no teachers make full use of all worthwhile kinds of questions.

6. Specific objectives should be stated in behavioral terms and should meet the other criteria for stating specific objectives correctly.
7. One useful way of outlining an instructional unit in order to reduce the possibility of overlooking the important goals of the unit is to draw up a *matrix*, a table with specific objectives along one axis and the content categories along the other.
8. Correct sequence in planning for effective measurement is objectives, methods, measurement.
9. The behavioral level is the highest form of measurement and should be used whenever possible; when this is not possible, one should judge on the planning level; when neither is feasible, the understanding level may be utilized.
10. It appears that it is not a question of whether a school district should have a minimum competency program; rather, it is the format and structure of the program to fit the individual needs of the district which will determine its pattern and scope.

Discussion Questions

1. Summarize the criteria in determining whether a measurement instrument is good.
2. Explain why a clear statement of specific objectives is extremely important as the basis for planning good measurement and evaluation.
3. Study the "Taxonomy of Questions" definitions as presented by Sanders and be ready to classify the following questions into the proper definition of thinking.
   a. What did Abraham Lincoln mean when he said, "Fourscore and seven years ago our forefathers brought forth on this earth a new nation . . ."?
   b. Compare the relationship between an ape and a human in regard to physical and mental structure.
   c. True or False. The sun is the only significant source of heat for the earth's atmosphere.
   d. Describe the requirements of a well-balanced diet. Plan a menu for your family for one day in terms of this diet.
   e. John Jones has red hair.
      John Jones has a bad temper.
      All red-haired men have bad tempers.
   What kind of reasoning do these statements involve? Discuss their reliability.
4. Describe the process of developing behavioral objectives as to:
   a. Defining learning outcomes as a two-step process.
   b. The guidelines for producing the general objectives.

   c. The guidelines for producing the specific learning outcomes.

   d. The way to use the taxonomy in developing a comprehensive list of objectives.

   e. Relating objectives to classroom instruction.

5. Study the Guide for Planning a Unit (Table 3.3). Be ready to discuss what you have learned about measurement and valuation from the development of this guide.

6. Discuss the common theme permeating the first two limitations of measurement and evaluation.

7. Mr. Wutti teaches seventh-grade industrial arts. His objectives might be to have the pupil: (a) describe the basic woods used in construction, the geographical sources of each, and the finishes appropriate to each, and (b) work well with others in group projects. To measure pupil progress toward these objectives, he decides, "I'll give them 50 multiple-choice items." What would you recommend to Mr. Wutti as a better approach to evaluation?

8. Below is a list of specific objectives from many fields and levels of education. Study each one and be ready to indicate the highest level of measurement (B, P, or U) possible for each. The pupil:

   a. *respects* the opinions of others.

   b. *describes* the four basic foods.

   c. *carries* sharp objects properly.

   d. *recognizes* the parts of an equation.

   e. *writes* a friendly letter correctly.

   f. *explains* the procedure for mouth-to-mouth resuscitation.

   g. *leaves* the room properly during a fire.

   h. *introduces* people properly.

9. If you were asked to be on a committee of teachers to plan an in-service program for new teachers on the topic "The Measurement and Evaluation Program in Our School," what would be the topics you would suggest for discussion so that the new teachers would have a complete understanding of measurement and evaluation and its purposes in the classroom?

10. Assume that you have been assigned to a committee of teachers, administrators, and School Board members to develop a philosophy and general character for a minimum competency testing program. What would be the ideas that you would include under each of these two topics?

Student Activities

1. Select an objective for a unit and suggest two or three ways of measuring pupil progress toward the objective. Then apply the criteria for

determining if measurement is good. Do the instruments meet the criteria?

2. Find a few specific objectives in any teaching units or curriculum guides available to you and apply the seven criteria for stating specific objectives properly. Write out your analysis of the degree to which your examples meet these criteria.

3. You will be assigned to a group each of which will be responsible for working with one of Sanders' definitions of the levels of thinking. Each group should develop the following for the definition to which it is assigned:

   a. Definition

   b. Explanation of the nature and function of this category (no more than 75 words)

   c. Examples of specific objectives and test items for each

   You may be assigned to do this on a specific level of education. If so, be sure the objectives and test items are appropriate for this level.

4. Develop an instructional planning chart like that in Table 3.3. Produce *an objective* in each of the cognitive, affective, and psychomotor domains. In the middle column for each, briefly describe a teaching method; and in the third column, name one or more ways of measuring the learner's growth toward the objectives. You may combine objectives to be served by one measurement or isolate them for measurement as appropriate. The objectives need not all come from the same subject or grade level, but be ready to name the subject and grade level for each.

Selected Readings

Ahmann, J. Stanley, and Glock, Marvin D. *Evaluating Pupil Growth*, 5th ed. Boston: Allyn and Bacon, Inc., 1975. Chapter 2.

———. *Measuring and Evaluating Educational Achievement*, 2nd ed. Boston: Allyn and Bacon, Inc., 1975. (Paperback) Chapter 2.

Bennion, Donald H. *Assessing Student Learning*. Dubuque, Iowa: Kendall-Hunt Publishing Company, 1977. Chapters 1 and 2.

Bloom, Benjamin S., et al. *Handbook on Formative and Summative Evaluation of Student Learning*. New York: McGraw-Hill Book Co., 1971. Appendix.

Bloom, Benjamin S., et al. *Taxonomy of Educational Objectives, Handbook I: Cognitive Domain*. New York: David McKay Co., Inc., 1956. Part II.

Clark, D. Cecil. *Using Instructional Objectives in Teaching*. Glenview, IL: Scott, Foresman, & Company, 1972.

Cramer, Ward, and Trent, Roger. *Performance Objectives*. Cincinnati, Ohio: Educational Horizons Publishers, 1972.

Davies, Igor K. *Objectives in Curriculum Design*, New York: McGraw-Hill Book Co., 1976. Chapters 1-10.

Gronlund, Norman E. *Measurement and Evaluation in Teaching*, 3rd ed. New York: The Macmillan Company, 1976. Chapters 2 and 3.

———. *Readings in Measurement and Evaluation*. New York: The Macmillan Company, 1968. Chapters 2 and 3.

Harrow, Anita J. *A Taxonomy of the Psychomotor Domain.* New York: David McKay Co., Inc., 1972. Chapters 2 and 3.

Hopkins, Charles D., and Antes, Richard L. *Classroom Measurement and Evaluation.* Itasca, IL: G. E. Peacock Publishers, Inc., 1978. Chapter 2.

Kibler, Robert J., Barker, Larry L., and Miles, David T. *Behavioral Objectives and Instruction.* Boston: Allyn and Bacon, Inc., 1970.

Krathwohl, David R., et. al. *Taxonomy of Educational Objectives, Handbook II: Affective Domain.* New York: David McKay Co., Inc., 1964. Part II.

Mager, Robert F. *Preparing Instructional Objectives,* 2nd ed. Palo Alto, California: Fearon Publishers, Inc., 1975.

Mehrens, William A., and Lehmann, Irvin J. *Measurement and Evaluation in Education and Psychology.* New York: Holt, Rinehart, and Winston, Inc., 1973. Chapter 2.

Noll, Victor H., Scannell, Dale P., and Craig, Robert C. *Introduction to Educational Measurement,* 4th ed. Boston: Houghton Mifflin Co., 1979. Chapter 5.

Payne, David A., and McMorris, Robert F. *Educational and Psychological Measurement.* Morristown, NJ: General Learning Press, 1974. Chapters 14 and 15.

Popham, W. James, and Baker, Eva. *Establishing Instructional Goals.* Englewood Cliffs, NJ: Prentice-Hall, Inc., 1970.

———. *Planning an Instructional Sequence.* Englewood Cliffs, NJ: Prentice-Hall, Inc., 1970.

Sanders, Norris M. *Classroom Questions, What Kinds?* New York: Harper & Row Publishers, 1965. Chapter 1.

Tuckman, Bruce W. *Measuring Educational Outcomes: Fundamentals of Testing.* New York: Harcourt Brace Jovanovich, Inc., 1975. Chapters 2 and 3.

Vargas, Julie S. *Writing Worthwhile Behavioral Objectives.* New York: Harper & Row Publishers, Inc., 1972.

Wick, John W. *Educational Measurement. Where Are We Going and How Will We Know When We Get There?* Columbus, Ohio: Charles E. Merrill Publishing Company, 1973. Chapters 2 and 3.

4

Construction and Use of Classroom Tests (Teacher-Made)

What are the purposes and functions of teacher-made tests?

How does one ask questions to produce diversity of thinking?

What is the difference between criterion-referenced and norm-referenced testing?

What are the basic types of test items and the variations of each?

How do the objective test and the essay test differ on basic traits?

What are the general principles of test construction which a teacher should realize before attempting to plan or make any type of test?

What are the steps in the construction of a test?

How does one construct and use the specific types of items?

How does one evaluate an achievement test?

A. What are the Purposes and Functions of Teacher-Made Tests?

Schwartz and Tiedeman state that the unique purpose which may be served by using teacher-made tests in the classroom are that they permit the teacher to:[1]

1. Measure and appraise student progress in terms of specific classroom objectives.
2. Provide motivation for learning specifics as well as generalizations.
3. Secure evidence of individual and group strengths and weaknesses while the students are at work on a specific unit.
4. Measure frequently, since check tests as well as unit or final tests may be used.
5. Secure specific information for reporting purposes.
6. Locate evidence which will be useful in making immediate modifications of curriculum and instructional procedures.

1. Alfred Schwartz and S. C. Tiedeman, *Evaluating Student Progress in the Secondary School* (New York: David McKay Co., 1957), p. 110. Reprinted with permission of the publishers.

B. How Does One Ask Questions to Produce Diversity of Thinking?

Teachers should give particular attention to the teaching of and the measurement of critical thinking and reasoning. As used here, critical thinking and reasoning are defined as questions requiring thought processes beyond the memory level of learning.

Chapter 3 discussed Bloom's *Taxonomy of Educational Objectives,* in which he and his colleagues categorized all educational objectives of the cognitive domain into the six categories of Knowledge, Comprehension, Application, Analysis, Synthesis, and Evaluation. One way of helping the reader understand each category was to use examples of questions which required students to engage in the particular kind of thinking. Sanders carried on from this structure in a book which stressed the "taxonomy of questions." He predicated his writing on two hypotheses: First, teachers can lead students into all kinds of thinking through careful use of questions, problems, and projects; and second, some teachers intuitively ask questions of high quality, but far too many overemphasize those that require students only to remember, and practically no teachers make full use of all worthwhile kinds of questions. Thus, his emphasis was on requiring students to use ideas rather than simply to remember them. He modified Bloom's taxonomy to produce seven categories with the following definitions:

1. *Memory:* The student recalls or recognizes information.
2. *Translation:* The student changes information into a different symbolic form or language.
3. *Interpretation:* The student discovers relationships among facts, generalizations, definitions, values, and skills.
4. *Application:* The student solves a life-like problem that requires the identification of the issue and the selection and use of appropriate generalizations and skills.
5. *Analysis:* The student solves a problem in the light of conscious knowledge of the parts and forms of thinking.
6. *Synthesis:* The student solves a problem that requires original, creative thinking.
7. *Evaluation:* The student makes a judgment of good or bad, right or wrong, according to standards he designates.[2]

Sometimes definitions are difficult to translate into actual use. To assist the reader, following is an example of an educational objective followed by a question appropriate to it for each of the classifications above. (The word *question* here refers to any oral or written question or test item asked of a pupil on a given level.)

2. Norris M. Sanders, *Classroom Questions: What Kinds?* (New York: Harper & Row Publishers, Inc., 1966), pp. 1-3.

1. Memory

   Objective: The pupil identifies some of the early explorers who came to the New World.

   Question: Circle the early explorers—Columbus, Lincoln, Magellan, Washington.

2. Translation

   Objective: The pupil identifies the same idea expressed in another manner.

   Question: Choose the statement which is most like this one: "An adjective is any word which modifies a noun."

   A. A word which describes an action word is an adjective.

   B. Any person, place, or thing which is described by a single word has been modified by an adjective.

   C. A word which tells about another word is an adjective.

3. Interpretation

   Objective: The pupil recognizes the importance of South American countries.

   Question: Compare the two countries of Brazil and Argentina in regard to population, main products, geographic features, and climate.

4. Application

   Objective: The pupil explains why paper currency is a good medium of exchange.

   Question: The main product of country X is fish. Therefore fish is used as a basis for purchasing other items. In other words, if Mr. Jones wanted to buy a car from Mr. Smith, he would pay Mr. Smith 2,000 fish. Can you suggest a better method of payment? Explain why in a short essay.

5. Analysis

   Objective: The pupil identifies a well-balanced meal.

   Question: Tell why the reasoning in these statements is correct or incorrect:

   We need carbohydrates in our meals.

   This meal is made up of carbohydrates.

   Therefore, this meal is good.

6. Synthesis

   Objective: The pupil identifies the problems in marketing a product.

   Question: Discuss several ways in which you might improve upon the hula hoop to make it more marketable.

7. Evaluation

   Objective: The pupil discusses the accomplishments and terms of the presidents of the United States.

   Question: Who were the five most outstanding presidents of the United States and why?

A teacher might ask about the possible uses of the "taxonomy of questions." There are many uses, some of which are indicated as follows:

1. It will help the teacher to discover whether he is offering a variety of intellectual experiences. Teachers are usually amazed when they take time to classify their questions to discover that they are overemphasizing some areas of cognition and ignoring others.
2. It will assist in determining which instructional materials are going to provide experiences for a variety of intellectual thought. Since the methods, procedures, and materials of learning are the vehicles for accomplishing the objectives, a check must be made to determine their effectiveness.
3. It will help to evaluate the degree to which critical thinking is being stressed. If the teacher can be satisfied that he is asking questions ranging from translation to evaluation, he can be assured that he is providing instruction in critical thinking.
4. It provides some interesting ideas for action research. More and more teachers are becoming producers of research as well as consumers. One teacher evaluated the questions teachers ask in the fourth, sixth, and eighth grades of social studies in a school to determine range of intellectual thought required, and it was not consistent from one grade to the other. This research can be immediately translated into curriculum reform.
5. It can help the pupil become more active in the learning process. It is a standing axiom that "one gets out of something what he puts into it." Too often pupils have been inactive participants in learning. By stressing the "taxonomy of questions" the pupil is forced into intellectual activity of a meaningful nature.

A few final thoughts relative to the principles undergirding the use of the taxonomy of questions are presented here. Sometimes teachers are concerned when they have difficulty agreeing upon the category into which a given question fits. This should not cause great concern since it should be classified at the highest category within which it would fall. If this is done consistently, then each question will be found at its highest level. At times, teachers believe that a certain type of question will elicit the same kind of thinking among all the pupils. For example, if a teacher wanted students to determine which era in literature was best portrayed by quotations, for some students it would require interpretation. However, for those who may remember the quotation by a certain author and era, it would be exhibiting only memory. Teachers should also realize that the entire realm of questions can be used on any level and with almost all types of students. The difference in questions between the first and the twelfth grades should be in complexity rather than by type. Likewise, slow learners can find questions above the memory level as challenging and stimulating as the brighter children. Again it is a matter of content and complexity rather than kinds of questions.

C.   What Is the Difference Between Criterion-Referenced and Norm-Referenced Testing?

It is important that anyone reading any assessment reports be able to differentiate between an objective-referenced test and a norm-referenced test. An objective-referenced test is designed to determine whether a student has mastered a specific learning objective. The objective that is measured is one that has been determined to be important for an individual student or group of students. Test items are designed to determine mastery of the objective. Ususally a criterion for mastery is established, such as: the students should be able to answer two or three test items to demonstrate the mastery of an objective. The use of objective-referenced testing procedures has become increasingly popular since subject material actually taught in the classroom is measured.

Norm-referenced tests, or grade-level achievement tests, are developed to show the level at which, on the average, students are able to answer a number of questions on a test. To construct achievement tests, an initial pool of test items is created on the basis of content or face validity and is administered to a sampling of individuals representative of the population for which the test is being developed. Each test item is then evaluated in terms of its ability to discriminate good from poor students; that is, items are identified which only good students (defined by high total scores or high grades in the content area) usually answer correctly and poor students (defined by low total test scores or low grades in the content area) usually answer incorrectly. The remaining test items are ineffectual for discriminating between good and poor students, but better reflect average student ability. Test items with a high proportion of items in the middle level of difficulty and a low proportion at the extremes are then selected for the final version of the test. The final test is administered to a relatively large number of students who are representative of the population whose achievement the instrument is designed to measure. The results are then analyzed and transposed to insure that individual scores on the total test are distributed in a statistically predictable manner. Usually, test developers strive to convert raw data to a normal distribution with equal numbers falling above and below the mean (M). This distribution then becomes the "norm," and thereafter students receiving scores equal to the mean of this distribution are assigned grade level.

THIRD GRADE OBJECTIVE/ITEM EXAMPLE	State Sample	CESA 12 Students
1. *Can use ordinal numbers beyond tenth.*	62%	70.27%
2. *Can identify 2/3 and 3/4 of a whole.* Which circle is 3/4 shaded?	32%	80.33%

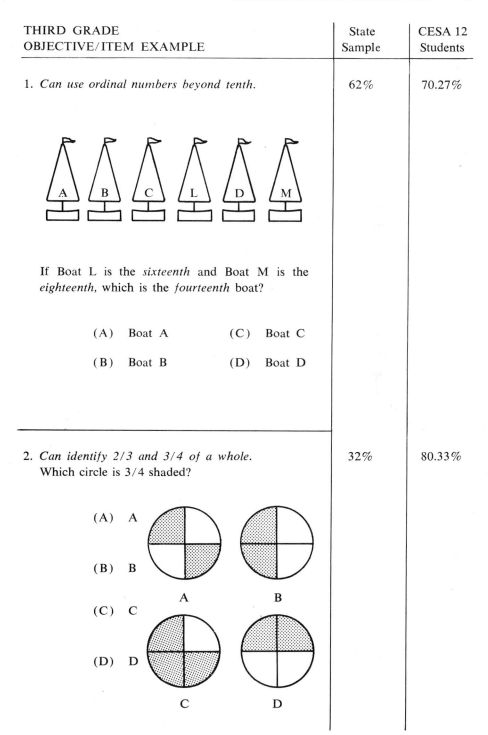

If Boat L is the *sixteenth* and Boat M is the *eighteenth*, which is the *fourteenth* boat?

(A) Boat A   (C) Boat C

(B) Boat B   (D) Boat D

2. *Can identify 2/3 and 3/4 of a whole.*
Which circle is 3/4 shaded?

(A) A

(B) B

(C) C

(D) D

OBJECTIVE/ITEM EXAMPLE	State Sample	CESA 12 Students
1. Can represent rational numbers by decimals and fractions. $\frac{4}{5} =$ ☐ A) .4 B) .8 C) .04 D) .08	24%	35.18%
2. Can use exponential notations in representing numbers. $3648 =$ ☐ A) $(3 \times 10^1) + (6 \times 10^0) + (4 \times 10) + 8$ B) $(3 \times 10^0) + (6 \times 10^1) + (4 \times 10) + 8$ C) $(3 \times 10^2) + (6 \times 10^1) + (4 \times 10 \div 8$ D) $(3 \times 10^3) + (6 \times 10^2) + (4 \times 10) \div 8$	60%	50.34%
3. Can recognize that $1/1$ or 1 is an identity element for multiplication in the set of rational numbers. ☐ $\times \frac{1}{1} = \frac{7}{8}$ A) $\frac{8}{7}$ C) $\frac{7}{8}$ B) $\frac{6}{8}$ D) $\frac{7}{7}$	40%	80.41%
4. Can recognize the multiplicative inverse (reciprocal) for every set of positive rational numbers except zero and use it in the division of rational numbers. $\frac{1}{2} \div \frac{2}{7} = \frac{1}{2} \times$ ☐ A) $\frac{2}{7}$ C) $\frac{1}{7}$ B) $\frac{7}{2}$ D) $\frac{3}{14}$	36%	41.18%

SEVENTH GRADE OBJECTIVE/ITEM EXAMPLE	State Sample	CESA 12 Students
1. Can add rational numbers whose fractions have unlike denominators. $$\frac{1}{8} + \frac{1}{5} =$$ (A) $\frac{2}{13}$ (C) $\frac{13}{40}$ (B) $\frac{1}{40}$ (D) $\frac{5}{8}$	40%	49.97%
2. Can add rational numbers expressed in terminating decimal form. $3.02 + 3.1 =$ (A) .612 (C) 3.33 (B) 6.12 (D) 6.42	81%	69.56%
3. Can subtract rational numbers expressed in terminating decimal form. $7.93 - 1.71 =$ (A) 622 (C) 62.2 (B) .0622 (D) 6.22	89%	68.12%

The mathematics assessment program in CESA 12 (Cooperative Educational Service Agency 12)[3] utilized objective-referenced testing procedures. Briefly stated, these procedures included:

1. Classroom teachers at each grade level selected, from DPI (Department of Public Instruction) sources, the objectives which they felt were most essential for students to have attained.
2. For each of the objectives deemed essential, three test items designed to measure attainment were developed.
3. Pilot test instruments were developed and administered to students from schools outside of CESA 12.
4. Results of pilot instruments were analyzed and test reliability coefficients determined.
5. The final form of the test instrument was developed and administered to all third, sixth, and seventh graders in CESA 12 during the first week of May.
6. Results were mailed back to school officials during the third week of May, and included:
   a. Overall CESA results
   b. District results
   c. Building results
   d. Classroom results
   e. Individual student results

Since the objectives used in developing this assessment program were from state sources, data do exist on how well students from throughout the state performed on each objective. On the previous pages, a comparison of CESA 12 students and a state sample of students is displayed. Under each objective is a test item that was used to determine student attainment of that objective. It should be noted that procedures and test items used by the state were different from the assessment in CESA 12.

D. What Are the Basic Types of Test Items and the Variations of Each?

The listing below is to indicate the varied nature and scope of teacher-made tests. *Illustrations of many of these are given later in the chapter under specific test types.*

1. Essay Tests
   a. Essay (Short Answer)
   b. Essay (Discussion)

---

3. Cooperative Educational Service Agency 12. *1974 Mathematics Assessment Program Report, Grades 3, 6, and 7.* CESA 12, Portage, WI, 1974.

2. Objective Tests (Recall Type)
   a. Simple Recall (Basic)
   b. Simple Recall (Problem Type)
   c. Simple Recall (Maps, Charts, etc.)
   d. Completion (Basic)
   e. Completion (Matching)
   f. Completion (Analogies)
   g. Completion (Maps, Charts, etc.)
3. Objective Tests (Alternative-Response)
   a. Alternative-Response (Basic)
   b. Alternative-Response (Two-Clause)
   c. Alternative-Response (Three Alternatives)
   d. Alternative-Response (Converse)
   e. Alternative-Response (With Correction)
   f. Alternative-Response (With Qualifications)
   g. Alternative-Response (With Diagrams)
   h. Alternative-Response (With Analogies)
4. Objective (Multiple-Choice)
   a. M-C (Basic)
   b. M-C (Recall)
   c. M-C (Common Principle)
   d. M-C (Results)
   e. M-C (Causes)
   f. M-C (Charts, Maps, etc.)
   g. M-C (Analogies)
5. Objective (Matching)
   a. Matching (Basic)
   b. Matching (Three Columns)
   c. Matching (Master List)
   d. Matching (Analogies)
6. Objective (Rearrangement)
   a. Chronological
   b. Order of Importance
   c. Order of Difficulty
   d. Length, Weight, Logic, etc.
7. Objective (Analogies)
   (See possibilities in 2-5 above)
8. Situational-Interpretive Items

E. How Do the Objective Test and the Essay Test Differ on Basic Traits?

In Table 4.1, a comparison of what the pupil is expected to do in the objective test and in the essay test on some basic traits is made.

TABLE 4.1

Comparison of the Objective and Essay Tests

Trait	Objective Test	Essay Test
1. Type of Structure	The pupil operates within an almost completely structured task	The pupil organizes his/her own response with a minimum of constraint
2. Type of Response	The pupil selects one of a limited number of alternatives or recalls a short answer	The pupil uses his/her own words and expression in his response
3. Sampling of Knowledge	The pupil responds to a relatively large number of items (extensive sampling)	The pupil responds to a relatively small number of questions (intensive sampling)
4. Credit in Scoring	The pupil receives a score for each answer according to a predetermined key (usually right or wrong with no partial credits)	The pupil receives a score for each question depending upon the degree of completeness and accuracy
5. Learning Outcomes Measured	Very good for measuring knowledge of facts. Some types can measure higher levels of thinking. Usually inappropriate for measuring ability to select and organize ideas, writing abilities, and some types of problem-solving skills	Inappropriate for measuring knowledge of facts. Can measure higher levels of thought. Appropriate for measurement of ability to select and organize ideas, writing abilities, and problem-solving skills
6. Effect on Learning	Encourages students to develop a comprehensive knowledge of specific facts and to discriminate among them. Can encourage development of higher level thinking skills if properly constructed	Encourages students to learn ability to organize, integrate, and express ideas effectively. Usually asks students to concentrate on larger units of materials

F. What Are the General Principles of Test Construction Which a Teacher Should Realize Before Attempting to Plan or Make Any Type of Test?[4]

1. In Planning the Test:

a. The nature of the test must take into consideration the purpose it is to serve, such as motivation, diagnosis, mastery, and achievement.

b. The nature of the test must take into consideration the conditions under which it is to be administered, such as age, level, ability, and time.

c. Make a plan for the construction and use of the measuring device. This includes:

>   Listing the specific objectives for which the device is to be used
>
>   Listing the main ideas of content or traits which will show growth toward the objectives.
>
>   Stating the value of the device in relation to other devices to be used (this is a percentage based on 100% for all of the devices to be used).

2. In Preparing the Test:

a. The preliminary draft of the test should be prepared as early as possible.

b. Generally, the test should include more than one type of item.

c. The kind of test item which a teacher selects to evaluate for a specific goal should be as appropriate as possible to that goal.

d. The content of the test should range from very easy to very difficult.

e. It is usually desirable to include more items in the preliminary draft of the test than will be needed in the final form.

f. The items should be phrased so that the content, rather than the form, will determine the answer (language of the text—*intelligence* answers).

g. The items should be worded so that the whole content functions in determining the answer rather than only part of it (specific determiners—word clues).

h. All items of a particular type should be placed together in the test.

i. Items should be arranged in order of difficulty.

j. A regular sequence in the pattern of responses should be avoided.

k. The answering system should be consistent for given types of items.

l. The directions should be clear, curt, and complete.

m. A sample item, correctly done, should follow the directions for any items or type of test which is unfamiliar to the pupils.

4. Parts of this section consist of headings from Julian Stanley, *Measurement in Today's Schools,* 4th ed. (Englewood Cliffs, N.J.: Prentice-Hall, Inc., 1964), pp. 171-201.

n. Be sure that the items are of the proper degree of difficulty for the grade level.

o. Be sure that the items are worded properly and that appropriate vocabulary and grammar are used.

p. Be sure that there are no items which will be answered by all or failed by all. There is one exception to this rule. Usually the first item or so, depending on the length of the test, is so easy that all can answer it correctly. This is known before the test is administered. This type of item is for motivational purposes only—that is, to get the student started on the test with some feeling of self-confidence.

q. Be sure that no trick or catch questions are used.

r. Be sure that the test is long enough to measure what it is supposed to measure.

s. Be sure that the individual items differentiate between the good and and the poor pupils in the class. To determine this, one makes an item analysis. This technique is discussed in section I of this chapter.

3. **In Administering the Test:**

a. Every reasonable precaution should be taken to insure normal conditions for the test (such as heat, light, ventilation, seating, and time).

b. The time allowance for the test should be generous (it is generally believed that, for an achievement test, 80%-90% of the pupils should have an opportunity to finish).

c. The scoring procedure should be as simple as possible.

d. Before the actual scoring begins, answer keys and scoring rules should be prepared.

4. **In Evaluating the Test:**

a. The difficulty of the test is a general indication of its validity.

b. An item analysis should be made to determine which items are discriminating between the good and the poor pupils.

c. Pupils should have an opportunity to indicate those items which were ambiguous or which were misinterpreted by them.

d. The test results should be checked against an outside criterion for validity.

e. On unit or final tests, the reliability coefficient should be determined.

G. What Are the Steps in the Construction of a Test?

1. **Preliminary Steps**

a. List the objectives for which the test is to measure.

b. Gather together the outline of content, notes, books, and materials used in the instruction.

c. Recall and jot down the methods used to teach toward objectives.

2. **Actual Steps**
   a. Prepare a plan for the test.
   b. Draft the items in preliminary form.
   c. Decide upon the length of the test.
   d. Edit and select the final items.
   e. Rate the items for difficulty.
   f. Rearrange the items in order of difficulty.
   g. Prepare the instructions for the test.
   h. Decide upon rules for scoring and prepare answer key.
   i. Produce the test, being sure of good mechanical make-up.

3. **Explanation of Actual Steps**
   a. Draw up a plan for the test

   Good tests do not just happen—they are carefully planned. Just as one would have a blueprint for a home being built, so one must have a "blueprint" for a test. Its purpose is to emphasize the need for a general guide or "skeleton" before the actual items are constructed. This plan is an assurance that all objectives are covered, that there is balance in the test, and that the test will reflect the emphasis in the specific unit or course.

   A sample plan for a unit test is shown in Table 4.2. Other two-way grid-tables of specifications are shown in Tables 4.3 and 4.4.

   b. Draft the items in preliminary form

   With the plan for the test at hand, the next step is that of writing down tentative test items. In doing this, little attention needs to be given to the percentages. One can review each topic and sub-topic in turn and then write out items which cover the high points of each. The teacher should not spend much time refining the wording. The important tasks in this step are:

   1. Covering the topic, unit, or course thoroughly, but at the same time, avoiding trivial points. It is advisable to try to construct from 25%-50% more items than your estimate indicates will be kept in the final test. This enables the teacher to "cull out" in a later step, thereby providing proper emphasis and balance in the test.
   2. Deciding which type of test item is best suited to the particular situation—Objective (True-False, Multiple-Choice, Matching, Simple Recall, Completion) or Essay (Short Answer, Discussion). The type of test item should be decided principally upon the adaptability of that item to a particular bit of subject matter. Certain bits of subject matter seem to fit into one of the types; others are not very readily adaptable to any of the types. REMEMBER, the nature of the objective and the content should determine the type of item; do not

TABLE 4.2

*Plan for a Test (on the Unit): Construction and
Use of Teacher-Made Tests*

Objectives	*Content*	*% of Items**
After studying this unit, the pupil:		
1. *Explains* the place of teacher-made tests in evaluation.	Functions and purposes of teacher-made tests.	10%
2. *Lists* the sequential steps in constructing a test.	The preliminary and actual steps in test construction.	10%
3. *Outlines* the types of teacher-made tests.	Objective and essay types.	20%
4. *Recognizes* the advantages and limitations of each type.	Advantages and limitations of each of objective and essay types.	25%
5. *Writes* good test items of the various types.	Principles of construction of each type.	25%
6. *Interprets* the three criteria of a good test.	Validity — Reliability — and Usability.	10%
	Total	100%

* These percentages are not assigned arbitrarily but represent the teacher's careful judgment as to the value of each objective and the emphasis given it in the unit. These percentages remain as such and no attempt is made at this time to convert these into actual numbers of items. This conversion can be made more intelligently under the step of deciding upon the length of the test.

force objectives or content into items of a specific type into which they do not fit. When each type of item is discussed later, the teacher will have a good idea as to what types of objectives and content can best be measured by each type. Most teachers, for a unit or final test, prefer to prepare their items on 3″ × 5″ cards rather than to write them consecutively on sheets of paper. Cards then may be arranged, shuffled, discarded, or inserted without necessitating any rewriting of items. Each card should contain: (a) the type of item; (b) a key to designate the objective; (c) the test item, double-spaced to allow for corrections; and (d) the indicated answer. An abbreviated sample follows which relates to the plan in Table 4.2:

Multiple-Choice

6. The nearest synonym for the term
Validity is (A) dependability
(B) usability (C) *worthwhileness*
(D) economy (E) objectivity

TABLE 4.3

Matrix: Objectives and Content—Reading, Grade Two

Content / Objectives	Consonants: 1. Beginning sounds 2. Ending sounds 3. Blends & diagraphs	Vowels: (A, E, I, O, U) 1. Long sounds 2. Short sounds	Word Meanings: 1. Opposites 2. Categories	Sentence Readings: 1. Understanding 2. Determine the missing word	Paragraph Reading: 1. Predicting the outcome 2. Sequence of material 3. Main idea	Drawing
The Student						
Memory (30%) 1. Recognizes alphabet letters and sounds intelligently. 2. Recalls 5 basic vowels and their sounds meaningfully.						
Translation (20%) 1. Transfers random words into a sentence meaningfully. 2. Recognizes missing words from sentence context intelligently.						
Interpretation (15%) 1. Formulates a best title successfully utilizing paragraph meaning. 2. Determining a group classification readily utilizing 2 or more words.						
Application (15%) 1. Draws conclusions meaningfully. 2. Determines opposites meaningfully from word clues.						
Analysis (10%) 1. Recognizes chronological relationship intelligently.						
Synthesis (10%) 1. Creates an original idea meaningfully.						

c. *Decide on the length of the test*

After drafting the items in preliminary form, the teacher will have an idea of the number of items needed to sample the lesson or unit rather thoroughly. It will be necessary to allow for shrinkage of 25% or more when the refining process begins.

Factors which must be considered are: (1) purpose of the test; (2) number of items needed to sample thoroughly; (3) age and grade level of the learners; (4) time available to devote to the test; and (5) types of items being used.

The teacher should remember that, for general achievement testing, approximately 80%-90% of the students should have an opportunity to complete all items.

TABLE.4.4

Matrix: Objectives and Content—The Chemical and Cellular Make-up of Life

Objectives \ Content	History of Biology / 1. Mechanism vs. Vitalism / 2. Importance Experiment	Laws of Conservation / 1. Mass / 2. Energy	Atomic Theory / 1. Structure of atoms / 2. Chemical notation / 3. Chemical reaction / 4. Molecular bonds	Principle Cell Compounds / 1. Water / 2. Proteins / 3. Carbohydrates / 4. Fats / 5. Nucleic acids	Role of Enzymes / 1. Function of enzymes / 2. Structure of enzymes	Cell Structure & Function	Cell Energy / 1. Source / 2. Process / 3. Control	Energy Relationships
The Student:	15%	10%	10%	15%	10%	20%	15%	5%
Memory (30%) 1. Recalls scientific definitions. 2. Assigns Distinct properties to chemical units. 3. Describes the function and location of cell structures. 4. Describes cellular respiration. 5. Identifies energy relationship. 6. Recognizes group characteristics of cell compounds.								
Translation (10%) 1. Associates compounds with chemical formula. 2. Identifies inter-relationships of life functions.								
Interpretation (20%) 1. Solves simple chemical equations correctly. 2. Draws inferences from data accurately.								
Application (15%) 1. Predicts outcome of experiments consistently. 2. Detects relationships between cell shape and function effectively.								
Analysis (15%) 1. Recognizes unstated assumptions consistently. 2. Discriminates between facts and hypothesis accurately. 3. Uses the Scientific Method logically.								
Evaluation (10%) 1. Appraises experimental results critically. 2. Judges the validity of conclusions reliably.								

d. Editing and selecting the final items

This is the "culling out" stage of the test. It is performed preferably a day or two after the preliminary draft of the items is made. This editorial stage is one of the most important steps and one which many teachers do not do. The result is usually a poor test if the step is eliminated.

The teacher must scrutinize each test item in a manner similar to the way an editor critically examines every line of an important manuscript. The teacher should place himself, so far as possible, in the attitude of the pupil. He must try to misread the meaning to determine whether there are possibilities of misinterpretations which would mislead the pupil or which would prove ambiguous. The teacher should keep in mind the fact that good sentence structure is a prime requisite for a valid test item. One can ask whether an easier synonym can be found for any difficult word or term. Punctuation must be such that it will assist in making the intent of the test item clear. In an objective type item for which only the right answer is given credit and all others are wrong, the teacher should be sure that the item is worded so that the right answer will be called forth and can be defended. In an essay type item where partial credit is given for partial answers, one must be sure that the item indicates to the pupil the nature of the desired response (many essay items are so broad or vague that a pupil does not know specifically what the teacher is asking).

A few examples are cited here which will indicate the nature of this step.

ITEM: The force of gravitation causes water to run _____.

ANALYSIS: This item does not require understanding of gravitation and can be answered by general intelligence. Rephrase to: The force which causes water to run downhill is called _____.

ITEM: Discuss what is needed for good health (Essay).

ANALYSIS: Pupil must guess both what material is wanted and length of answer. Rephrase this so that it is more specific and so that it indicates the length of response.

ITEM: George Washington was _____ of the _____ in the _____ and _____ of the _____.

ANALYSIS: Discard it. This violates the principle of a completion item which indicates that only the important ideas should be required, and enough key ideas must be left so that the pupil knows what is wanted. Shorten this to ask for one or two main things, with key words left in the question.

e. *Rate the items for difficulty*

Validity of a test is raised by having items presented in a proper degree of difficulty. Items passed by every child or failed by all contribute nothing to the test. In addition, the validity of a test is increased by having the simpler items first and the more difficult ones last. The mechanics of this rating is simple, but it takes the teacher's best judgment to give the most accurate rating.

The ratings may be done on either a 5- or 10-point scale. Regardless of the scale used, the procedure is as follows: (1) Rate 1 for those items which are so easy that all or nearly all of the pupils may be expected to answer them correctly; (2) rate 5 (or 10, depending upon the scale used) for those items which, in the teacher's estimation, will be the most difficult; (3) assign the intermediate ratings (2 to 4 or 2 to 9) to those intermediate in difficulty; (4) write the ratings on the item cards.

f. *Rearrange the items in order of difficulty*

When the items have been rated, the teacher rearranges them in proper order for placement on the test. One must remember that test items of the same type should be grouped together on the test so that, upon completion of this step, the easier type of item will be first, and, within each grouping, test items will be in order of difficulty. It has already been mentioned that this step will increase reliability because pupils will be better motivated and will distribute their time and effort over the test more adequately.

g. *Prepare the instructions for the test*

Best instructions or directions for a test are those which the teacher knows will make the test absolutely clear to the pupils. The three criteria of good directions are clearness, conciseness, and completeness. In written tests, there are both general directions at the beginning and specific directions before each part. General directions tell the pupil the type of tests which follow, how he is to proceed on the test, and the time available. Specific directions are geared to the specific type of items within each part. In the lower grades, teachers prefer to give directions orally; a little later, the teacher reads them while pupils follow the printed directions silently; in upper grades, high school, and college, the directions are read silently by the pupils unless an explanation is needed.

The amount of detail in directions will depend largely on: (1) how familiar pupils are with the types of item being used; (2) the age or mentality of the pupils.

Following are general rules which may help to emphasize the significant features of a good set of directions.

1. General directions at the beginning of the test should indicate to the pupil the type(s) of tests to follow, how to proceed, and how to budget the time for the test.
2. Phrase the directions to meet the level of the lowest mentalities in the group.
3. Use the simplest synonyms for all words or ideas.
4. Be generous in the use of samples, especially with younger children or with new types of items. Be sure that samples are filled out correctly.
5. Tell the pupil where and how to record his answers and provide space for them.
6. Tell the pupils how each type will be scored—such as total right or right minus wrong.
7. If each part is timed, the pupil should be told how much time is alloted for each section of the test.

Examples of Test Directions

1. *Essay*
   In the following essay question(s), be sure to read the question carefully to understand it, outline your response mentally or on scratch paper, write your response carefully and clearly, and then re-read your response, making any necessary corrections.
   (The question itself will usually give an indication of length.)

2. *Recall Type*
   a. In the following question(s), place your answer completely, but concisely, following the question. (A recall answer is usually limited to a word, phrase, or a sentence.)
   b. In the following completion question(s) write, in the space provided, the word or phrase which correctly answers the question.

3. *Alternative-Response*
   Determine whether each of the following statements is true or false. If the statement is true, place a + in the space before the item; if the statement is false, place a 0 in the space.

(Sometimes there is a correction formula for guessing. If it is applied, the students should be told what it is.)

4. *Multiple-Choice*

   For each of the following, choose the *best* answer from among the choices given. Write the letter of your choice in the blank to the left of the question. (On the primary level, the pupil will be told to draw a line under, circle, or X the correct answer.)

5. *Matching*

   Match the item in the left column with the choices in the right column by writing the letter of the correct choice in the blank to the left of the first column.

   (If there are the same number of choices, or a lesser number than items, you would normally indicate whether the choices can be used more than once. If there are more choices than questions, normally the choices are used only once. On the primary level, the pupil will be asked to connect the two columns with a line.)

6. *Rearrangement*

   (The directions here will vary, depending on the nature of the rearrangement. Following is an example of one of sequence.) Indicate the sequence of presidents by giving 1 to the earliest and then proceeding with 2-3-4 and on until all are ranked.

7. *Analogies*

   In this exercise, you are given two terms or ideas the relationship of which you must infer. These are followed by a third term or idea and you must select, identify, or match (depending on type) a fourth term or idea which bears the relationship to the third that exists between the first two. A more simple modification of this will need to be made for the primary level.

h. *Decide on the rules for scoring, and prepare answer key*

   Certain aspects of scoring have been mentioned previously, but a few general statements will help to clarify the issue.

For Objective-Type Tests:

   1. Avoid giving partial credits. Except in rare cases, mark the answer either right or wrong.

    2. Give each test item one point of credit in such tests as true-false, simple recall, and multiple-choice; in completion tests, give one point for each blank correctly completed; in matching exercises, one point for each match.

For Essay Tests:

    1. Read over the material in the text, lesson plans, course outline, and notes that are related to the question asked.

    2. Make a checklist (key) of the main points or ideas for which credit will be given in each question. Decide upon the scoring for each of the questions, as well as for the parts of each question.

    3. In scoring a given question, the teacher first reads through the entire response to try to understand the whole response and intent of the pupil before going back to score for the important points.

    4. Grade one question throughout all papers before going on to the next question.

    5. The pupil's total score on the test is the sum of the credit given for each of the questions. Make a special, separate provision for consideration of sentence structure and spelling if these are to be considered in grading in relation to the objective being measured.

H. How Does One Construct and Use the Specific Types of Items?

Construction and Use of the Essay Examination

Definition

    The essay examination is a free-response type of test in which the pupil organizes his response in reply to a specific question or issue.

When used

    In general, this type of test is used to measure the FUNCTIONING OF KNOWLEDGE rather than its mere *possession*. The following examples (not exhaustive) of key or directional words that might be used in essay type questions give an idea of the mental functions which can be measured by the essay test:

Explain	Make accurate inferences	Discriminate	Give conclusions
Relate	Interpret	Organize	Generalizations
Compare	Detect relationships	Select significant idea	Sequences
Contrast	Show differences	Summarize	Relationships Associations

Suggestions for constructing essay examinations[5]

1. Draft the essay question carefully, defining important directional or key words (see above) to eliminate semantic difficulties. For example, one might say: "By 'compare,' I mean to give a full answer in which you consider like and unlike factors in the situation." Each key word should be defined, for each calls for a different approach in the writing of the item.

2. Phrase the questions to give hints concerning the structure of the answer expected, unless this is inconsistent with the objectives to be measured. The question, "Discuss the Articles of Confederation," becomes more specific for both the pupil and the teacher grading it if phrased: "Discuss the Articles of Confederation with respect to their origin, their operation in actual practice, and their relationship to the present Constitution."

3. Write questions which can be readily answered within the time allowed for the examination. Allow enough time for pupils to outline, write, and read through their answers. Suggest a time allowance for each question if more than one essay question is included in the examination.

4. Construct the questions so that they are of such a range of difficulty as will allow ALL pupils to demonstrate their level of competence.

5. Require all students to write on the same questions; avoid choices among several questions.

6. To get better sampling, increase the number of questions and reduce the length of discussion expected in each.

Oral questioning

History of oral examinations or questioning is a long one. Until the current century, it was the prevalent form of examination in the common schools. In its more formal sense it is still used a great deal today on higher levels of education and in adult life. It is used as "orals" in the doctoral examination, as admission to graduate schools, for scholarships or awards, and for the employment interview, to mention a few.

In the informal sense, oral questioning or oral discussion is used on all levels of instruction. It is used from the first day a student enters school, as it should be. The author stresses the fact that principles of the essay test should be incorporated into oral questioning on the primary level. Assuming that the written essay test cannot be used until about the third grade in its simplest form, one can use the principles of the essay test in oral questioning in kindergarten and in grades one and two. Then, the pupils

5. Schwartz and Tiedeman, *Evaluating Student Progress in the Secondary Schools*, p. 147-149. Reprinted with permission of the publishers.

will have had experience and training in thinking through questions and organizing their response so that, when the written essay is required, the pupils can proceed much more effectively.

There are many advantages to the oral question.

1. It is personal; it can be geared to the level of the individual student.
2. One can observe immediate reaction, verbal approach, forthrightness, stress tolerance, speech quality, and the like.
3. The examinee can be asked to expand on an answer, to clarify, or to justify.
4. By asking leading questions, the examinee can be led along the road from where he or she is to a desirable response.
5. The student can ask for a clarification of a question.
6. The student can be reassured if an emotional situation develops; the teacher can calm the student.

There are obviously some limitations.

1. It covers only a very limited sampling of content per pupil.
2. It is time consuming.
3. It has low rater reliability.
4. It may produce pupil trauma and embarrassment.

Construction and Use of the Recall Type of Objective Item

Definition

Simple Recall—A supply type of item which requires a student to furnish a word, phrase, or sentence in response to a question or a statement.
Completion—A supply type of item which consists of a sentence or a series of sentences in which certain important words or phrases have been omitted, and blanks provided for pupils to fill in.

When used

Both types have the following functions or purposes:

When responses are of the who, what, when, or where type
For isolated facts
Descriptive information
Definitions

Acquisition and use of vocabulary
Basic concepts
Solution of problems or situation type material

Suggestions for constructing recall type items

1. As to form, the simple recall type can be written in either a question or a statement form, but the question form is preferable.

2. The item must be stated in specific terms so that pupils have no difficulty in knowing the kind of answer desired.
3. Use this type of item when more than two alternatives are possible for the response.
4. Ask for the most important information.
5. Be sure to retain key words which are necessary for the pupil to know what is required in his answer.
6. Begin by asking for only one word in lower grades to progressively asking for more words or a phrase or sentence on the higher grade levels.
7. Make minimum use of textbook language—refrain from lifting sentences from text.
8. Avoid *a* or *an* or similar words before the blank.
9. Avoid items which can be answered by general intelligence, without knowledge of the subject matter.
10. The question should be worded so that there is only one correct response.
11. A single blank should be provided for each idea, not for each word in the response.
12. Put blanks for answers in straight column at right for ease of scoring except in lower grades.
13. The important word or words to be entered by the pupil should be at or near the end of the question.
14. Blanks should be of uniform length, providing no clue to the correct response.

Construction and Use of Alternative-Response Items (Objective)

Definition

A type of recognition (select) item in which each question provides a choice between two alternatives of which only one is correct.

When used

Understanding of principles and generalizations

Knowledge of facts

Measure for persistence of misconceptions

Reasons underlying an idea

Discriminate for value judgments

For soundnes of conclusions

Suggestions for constructing alternative-response items

1. Construction is facilitated by first making all items true and then converting to false those that can be so converted (this is usually done by changing a single important word or short phrase, the truth or falsity should be without question).

2. As a general rule, the total number of items in all tests of this type employed during a term should be about equally divided as to true or false, but the proportion on any single test should be at random.

3. Questions should be stated directly, clearly, simply, and usually should be a rather short, single clause (avoid trick or catch questions). Example: "Roosevelt's first inauguration was in 1933 B.C." (Poor) Omit any B.C. or A.D.; change the date if you want to make it false.

4. When two clauses are used, there must be pupil understanding of the approach. In such cases, the main clause should be true and the subordinate clause (usually the reason, cause, effect, or explanation) should be true or false, as desired. This fact should be made known to the pupil. Examples: "Wisconsin has a milder climate than Virginia because of the Great Lakes." (Poor) "Virginia has a milder climate than Wisconsin because it is farther south." (Better)

5. Unnecessary and complicated content should be avoided. Examples: "Kennedy, who served in World War II, was the thirty-fifth president of the United States." (Poor) "Eisenhower, who was born in Texas, was once Army Chief of Staff." (Poor)

6. Alternative elements should be such that their truth or falsity depends upon a single point, not upon two or more. Examples: "Lincoln was born in 1809 and died in 1965." (Poor) "An adverb may correctly modify a verb, an adjective, or another adverb." (Poor) "A growing child should drink much milk and tea." (Poor) (The first and third of these examples should be two questions; the second should be three.) It is particularly undesirable to employ elements involving two or more points when all are not true or all are not false.

7. Generally, the crucial portion of a statement should come toward the end rather than at the beginning.

8. Avoid using the exact language of the text; rephrase to measure understanding.

9. Items should be free of careless or confusing wording. Examples: "Good health depends upon exercise." (Poor) Some would say true (thinking partial dependence); others say false (total dependence). "Pets *may* be given candy." (Poor) Some interpret *may* as *may well* or *should* and mark *false;* others say "Of course they may," and mark *true.*

10. Negatives should be avoided in alternative tests. Their presence tends to confuse some pupils who really know the points at issue. This applies not only to such words as *not, no, never,* and *none,* but also to negative prefixes and suffixes. Even worse than single negatives are double ones. "Iowa is *not unlike* Illinois in climate." (Poor)

11. Avoid specific determiners such as *because, generally, may, most, often should, some, usually* (usually *True*) *all, alone, always, only, no, not, never, none* (generally *False*).

Examples of alternative-response type of items

Constant-alternative or alternative-response items require the pupil to choose his answer from two or more alternatives, *which remain the same for a whole series of items.*

a. Basic Type: True-false, yes-no, right-wrong, synonym-antonym, agree-disagree.

   Directions: For each of the following statements encircle *T* if the statement is true and *F* if the statement is false.

   T F 1. The Parthenon of Greece was the chief temple of the goddess Athena.

b. Three Alternatives: True-false-doubtful; true-false-can't say; positively related, negatively related, or unrelated.

   Directions: Below is given a list of variables influencing test validity. Before each variable write:

   $+$ if validity is positively related to it

   $-$ if validity is negatively related to it

   0 if validity is not related to it

   _____ difficulty of items

   _____ ease of scoring

c. True-False-Converse

   Directions: Below are statements for which you are to encircle the *two* correct answers from among the following:

   T: The statement is true.

   F: The statement is false.

   CT: The converse is true.

   CF: The converse is false.

   T F CT CF 1. All "shooting stars" are meteors.

d. True or False with Corrections

   Directions: For each of the following statements if the statement is true, underline the letter *T*. If the statement is false, underline the letter *F*, and write the substitute for the underlined word necessary to make it true.

   T F 1. Orbit is the term for the path traveled by a body in space.

   _____

e. True or False with Qualifications

   True-false items with qualifications require the pupil to indicate whether the item is true or false or whether it can be made true by adding certain qualifications to be given or selected by him. Example:

   Statements

   *T F*_____ 1. The President may grant reprieves and pardons.

   *T F*_____ 2. The President may appoint ambassadors.

Qualifications
- A. With the consent of the Senate
- B. With the consent of the House of Representatives
- C. No qualification
- f. True or False with Diagrams, Charts, Maps, or Other Visual Aids
  True-false items with diagrams, charts, or maps present a series of visual media for which the pupil is to make one of a small number of possible judgments.
- g. Other Forms
  1. True or false for a series of statements based on a given topic
  2. True or false with inferences
  3. Checklist for a given characteristic
  4. Master list of characteristics, explanations, or evaluations

Construction and Use of Multiple-Choice Items (Objective)

Definition

A recognition (select) type of item which includes a stem and three or more (at least four in high school) possible choices from which a student selects the best one to answer a problem or complete a statement.

When used

Value judgments and discriminating ability

Logical reasoning and relationships

Insight and critical analysis

Solving problematic situations

Application and interpretation of data

Cause-and-effect relationships

Performance of mental processes
  (Arithmetic-Math; Language Arts-English; Science)

Suggestions for constructing multiple-choice items

- a. Suggestions for stating problem (The Stem)
  1. The lead or stem of the item must present a single, central problem. The test for this is to cover the choices and note whether the stem, standing alone, is intelligible. Every multiple-choice item should be usable as a free-response item.
  2. The stem should be stated simply and accurately and should contain all material relevant to its solution. Errors occur here primarily because of omission of a statement of assumption, because of its being stated ambiguously, or because it contains complex sentence structure.

3. In most cases the stem or problem should contain only material relevant to its solution.

"Johnny goes to the hardware store to buy some nails. If the price of nails is ten cents a pound, what does he pay for twelve pounds?" (Poor) "What is the price of twelve pounds of nails at ten cents a pound?" (Better)

4. The stem is better stated in direct question or in direct statement form rather than in an incomplete statement form since, in the latter, verbal clues may be given to lead to the best choice.

5. The problem should be stated in positive form for two reasons: (a) Students respond to negative statements many times as though they were positive. This can be prevented by underlining the key or negative words like <u>not</u> and <u>never.</u> (b) Leads containing negative statements are usually trivial.

6. If an item requires the pupil to express an opinion or value judgment, it should, in most cases, ask the student to express the opinion of an authority specified in the stem, and not the student's own opinion.

b. Suggestions for developing choices (The Responses)

1. Put choices in logical order of presentation (example: numbers lowest to highest).

2. Correct choice should be placed at random among choices (no fixed pattern).

3. In elementary school, a minimum of three choices should be given; in high school, a minimum of four.

4. The right solution should be unquestionably right; most of the time, errors are made here by not having the answer complete enough or by failure to indicate the units in which the answer is to be given.

5. The suggested wrong choices should represent errors commonly made by the students in class discussion rather than general misconceptions. The wrong choices must be wrong for a specific reason (too general, too restricted, or incomplete).

6. The suggested choices should be as brief as possible. Avoid the necessity of measuring reading skills.

7. Except in lower elementary grades, the choices should be lettered and capital letters should be used for ease of scoring.

8. Irrelevant clues should direct the examinee away from the right answer if the examinee is unable to answer the problem. They should never direct attention to the right answer. This principle is of great importance because so many clues are given in mul-

tiple-choice items. The clues usually fall in the following categories:

> There is similarity of wording in stem and the best choice.
> The key word in lead is associated with key word in choice.
> Choices are from different or varied domains.
> Grammatical inconsistencies between stem and choices eliminate some choices.
> Not all choices are plausible.
> Choices vary in length and complexity.

Examples of the multiple-choice item, basic and variations

The multiple-choice or changing-alternatives item differs from the alternative-response in that the multiple-choice requires a choice between changing alternatives whereas the alternative-response item has a constant alternative. Following are some examples of various types of multiple-choice items:

a. Correct or Best Answer

Directions: Select the best response and place its letter in the space provided.

    ———1. What is the leading industry in Wisconsin? (A) agriculture (B) mining (C) manufacturing (D) forestry

b. Incorrect or Worst Answer

Directions: Of the four alternatives presented as completions to each statement, choose the worst and write its letter in the space provided.

    ———1. Why do some people prefer to live in a brick house? (A) it is cooler in the summer (B) it does not have to be painted (C) it lasts a long time (D) it never needs repair

c. Common Principle or Most Inclusive

Directions: Following are sets of four words or terms, one of which includes the other three. You are to select the inclusive term from each set and write its letter in the space provided.

    ———1. (A) red (B) white (C) blue (D) color
    ———2. (A) measles (B) diseases (C) mumps (D) chicken pox

d. Most Dissimilar Answer

Directions: Following are sets of four words or terms, one of which does not belong with the other three. Select the word or term which does not belong and write its letter in the space provided.

    ———1. (A) Everett Dirksen (B) Margaret C. Smith (C) Mike Mansfield (D) Dean Rusk
    ———2. (A) camelia (B) poppy (C) oak (D) rose

   e. Result from Among Causes
       Directions: In each group of four alternatives given below, there
       are one result and three causes which contributed to bringing about
       this result. Select the result and write its letter in the space provided.
       _____1. (A) spoken word (B) conditioning (C) repetition
                  (D) reinforcement
   f. Causes from Among Results
       Directions: From the following groups of four alternatives, select
       the one which may best be considered to be a cause of the other
       three.
       _____1. (A) punishment (B) nervous (C) withdrawal
                  (D) depression

Construction and Use of Matching Tests (Objective)

Definition

   A recognition (select) type of item which consists normally of two
columns, one a stimulus (left) column and one a response (right) column
from which the pupil selects the correct response in reply to the element in
the stimulus column. (Usually two columns, but may be more; differs from
multiple-choice in that there is a single set of responses rather than a set of
responses for each question.)

When used

Measure for association of concepts and meanings
Measure for the who, what, when, and where types
Modified forms can measure for logical reasoning and judgment
Measure for degree of truth or falsity of a concept
Measure for application of knowledge

Suggestions for construction of matching tests

1. The content of any single exercise should be homogeneous—each column
    must have a heading common to all entries in the column.
2. The stimulus column should be on the left, the response column on the
    right. Sometimes which is stimulus and which is response is hard to de-
    termine and may not make a difference (common fractions—decimal
    fractions; states—capitals). At other times the difference is important
    (matching authors and works; using maps, charts, or diagrams).
3. Responses should be put in the most appropriate order (alphabetical,
    chronological, small to large). This saves time and enables a pupil to
    recognize an answer more quickly.
4. Longer statements usually should be on the left, as the stimuli; the
    responses are usually the shorter of the two.

5. If each stimulus has only one answer or if each response can be used only once, one should be sure to have more responses than stimuli. The general rule is to have three more responses (decoys) than stimuli. If responses can be used more than once, no need exists to have more responses than stimuli.
6. The stimulus column should be numbered, the response column lettered (capitals). The letter of the response chosen should be placed in a blank provided before each element in the stimulus column. In lower grades, two columns are presented and the pupil merely draws a line to connect the stimulus item with his response.
7. Directions should state what relationship exists between the columns and in what way they are to match. The directions should also indicate whether each response can be used once or more than once. The sample for the matching exercise can be the first element in the stimulus column properly completed.
8. The length of the matching exercise is usually limited by the principle that all material in each column must be homogeneous. However, it is believed that the range should be a minimum of five items or a maximum of ten in the stimulus column and a maximum of fifteen in the response column. The entire matching exercise must be on one side of the page.

Examples of matching items

  a. Basic Type

States	Capitals
_____1. Alabama	A. Baton Rouge
_____2. Arkansas	B. Bismarck
_____3. California	C. Denver
_____4. Colorado	D. Little Rock
_____5. Louisiana	E. Madison
	F. Montgomery
	G. Sacramento
	H. Saint Paul

  b. Three-Column Type

States	Capitals	State Flower
_____1. Alabama	A. Baton Rouge	I. Apple blossom
_____2. Arkansas	B. Bismarck	J. Blue columbine
_____3. California	C. Denver	K. Goldenrod
_____4. Colorado	D. Little Rock	L. Golden poppy
_____5. Louisiana	E. Madison	M. Magnolia
	F. Montgomery	N. Camelia
	G. Sacramento	O. Violet
	H. Saint Paul	P. Zinnia

c. Master List Type

Seven Functions of Measurement

A. To assist in guidance of pupils
B. To select pupils
C. To maintain standards
D. To motivate pupils
E. To guide teaching
F. To furnish instruction to pupils
G. To evaluate educational methods, facilities, and procedures

_____1. A pretest is given prior to the beginning of a unit.
_____2. A reading readiness test is given to first graders.
_____3. A checklist is used to determine strengths and weaknesses of pupils in work habits.
_____4. Arithmetic exercises are given, and pupils are asked to check answers with those in the back of the book.
_____5. A spelling test is given to two groups of ninth graders, one of which has had experience in typewriting.

The Analogies Type of Item

Analogies are a type of test item which has been used considerably in standardized tests but has not been utilized as freely in teacher-made tests. This is a good type of item to measure the student's ability to associate meanings and to infer relationships. It can be used on any grade level with proper instruction. The students are presented with two terms or ideas the relationship of which they must infer. A third term or idea is then presented, and they must supply or select a fourth term or idea which bears the relationship to the third that exists between the first two.

Examples

1. Madison: Wisconsin : : Little Rock:_____
                                                  A. Minnesota
  B 2. Madison: Wisconsin : : Little Rock: B. Arkansas
                                                  C. Rhode Island
  + 3. Madison: Wisconsin : : Little Rock: Arkansas

Thus it can be seen that the analogies type of item is not a distinctive type of test item, but it is a form of asking questions which can be adapted to almost any basic type of item. In the first example above, it is in the form of a completion item; in the second, it is a multiple-choice; and in the last, it is an alternative-response item. It can also be adapted to a matching form with a list of analogies presented in the stimulus column and a list of alternatives in the response column.

Teachers on the primary level must be sure that directions are very clear and are understood by young children. A practice exercise is suggested on this level before the actual test items are presented. After a pupil becomes more sophisticated in test-taking, a sample item is sufficient before the actual test.

Rearrangement Items

Rearrangement test items are sometimes called continuity, sequence, or logical arrangement exercises. This type of item puts more emphasis on relationship of ideas than on specific facts. Material in this type of item is presented in random order, and the pupil is required to rearrange the material in some specified order.

Almost any kind of specified order may be requested, such as chronology, sequence, difficulty, importance, preference, and the like. The item is very objective. The difficulty of the item is determined by the degree of discrimination required within the set and by the number of items within a set. Generally, the finer the discrimination required and the greater the number of items, the more difficult this type of test becomes. It is suggested on the elementary level that three to six items be used in a set; a maximum of approximately ten items can be used on the higher levels.

In constructing the test, a blank usually is placed before or below the item and in it a pupil indicates his response by a number or letter.

The scoring of this type of test is relatively simple if the set includes up to three or four items. In this case, usually one point of credit is given only if the set is entirely correct. When there are more than four items in a set, the scoring becomes a little more difficult. Consider the sample given below in which the pupil is asked to rank the correct order of presidents holding office.

Names of Presidents	Pupil's Rank	Correct Order
John Kennedy	4	3
Richard Nixon	3	5
Dwight Eisenhower	2	2
Lyndon Johnson	5	4
Harry Truman	1	1

The simplest method would be to count the set either right or wrong. In this case, the student would not receive any credit. Equally as easy, but just as crude, is the method of counting as correct those items in which the pupil's response agrees with the correct response. This way, the pupil's score for the above sample would be two. Both of these methods are a little unjust, since they do not distinguish between pupils who have varying degrees of knowledge.

The author suggests the *squares of differences method* for scoring this type of item when there are five or more items in a set. In calculating a score by this method, first determine the worst possible arrangement and its cor-responding score by this method. It would be:

Correct order	3	5	2	4	1
Worst possible order	3	1	4	2	5
Difference	0	4	2	2	4
Squares of differences	0	16	4	4	16
Total squares of differences = 40					

Then, in a similar table, replace the worst possible order listing with the pupil's response. For the above example, it would be:

Correct order	3	5	2	4	1
Pupil's order	4	3	2	5	1
Difference	1	2	0	1	0
Squares of difference	1	4	0	1	0
Total = 6					

By this method, one can see that the lower the score a student receives, the more correct his response. To coordinate the scoring of this type of exercise with the scoring of other types of tests on which the higher score is always better, one can subtract the pupil's score (6) from the worst possible score (40) and the pupil receives a score for this exercise of 34. The teacher may want to reduce this value to a smaller number if it seems that it will have too much weight in relation to other items. One can use any divisor desired, but you may want to divide it by the number of items in the set, disregarding any fractional remainder. In the sample just given, this would be dividing 34 by 5, or a score of 6. Obviously, there would be no negative scores and any dividend less than one-half of the divisor would receive no credit.

The author believes that there is yet a better mousetrap to be built in the scoring of rearrangement tests. However, until a new scoring method is devised, the above two methods are recommended: scoring as one item for sets of four or fewer items and use of squares of differences method for five or more items. Actually, the squares of differences method is not diffi-cult once the basic format is established.

Interpretive or Situational Items

Like the analogies type, the interpretive or situational item is not a dis-tinct or different type of item; rather, it is a different way of presenting material into already existing types of items. The most common types of items in which it is found are the multiple-choice and true-false. Basically, interpretive exercise consists of a series of objective items based on a common set of data. The data may be in the form of written materials, tables, charts, graphs, maps, or pictures. *A variety of learning outcomes can be measured by this type of item.*

Most of these outcomes are getting at a measurement of higher mental processes than just knowledge—that is, more complex achievement. Some examples of these outcomes are as follows:

Ability to interpret relationships
Ability to recognize the relevancy of information
Ability to recognize valid conclusions
Ability to apply principles
Ability to recognize inferences
Ability to recognize significant problems
Ability to recognize assumptions underlying conclusions

There are several advantages and limitations of the interpretive or situational item. Here are some advantages.

They are applicable to the measurement of understanding, interpretation, and evaluation.

Materials may be presented in different media: paragraphs, charts, diagrams, tables, pictures, and the like.

The questions can be asked in more than one mode, such as multiple-choice, true-false.

There is little room for ambiguity in the item; all material is relevant.

Some limitations or disadvantages are:

If in paragraph form, this type does place a heavy demand on reading skill.

It is difficult to prepare because it is time consuming to take; it is difficult to measure a very large sampling of material.

It measures only recognition, not whether the student could supply evidence to demonstrate his problem-solving skills and his ability to organize his thoughts.

There are many forms and uses of this type of exercise.

It is impossible to illustrate all of them. What is presented in the following illustrations are some examples from the primary level through the adult level and in different subject areas. It is hoped that those interested in other areas may be able to make application from these examples.

Interpreting Stories on the Primary Level (2.6-3.5)

The Koala looks like a toy teddy bear. It grows to a length of 2½ feet. It has a round head with large, round, furry ears and a stout body. It has no tail. Its legs are large, and each foot has five toes. The baby Koala is kept in the mother's pouch for about three months after birth.

Koalas are found only in southeastern Australia. Koalas sleep curled up on the limbs of trees hanging on with their special hands and feet. The Koala holds on tight even when sleeping. It is very gentle and will make a nice pet. It will not run away, even in areas which are not fenced.

1. The Koala looks most like a
   ○ dog
   ○ teddy bear
   ○ monkey

2. Why are the baby Koalas safe?
   ○ The are hidden in a cave.
   ○ They are kept in a nest.
   ○ They are carried in the mother's pouch.

3. What makes the Koala a good pet?
   ○ They are small.
   ○ They are gentle.
   ○ They don't bark.

Interpreting Pictures on the Primary Level (2.6-3.5)[6]

S1 The _____ is reading a book to the children.
   ○ school   ○ teacher   ○ student
   ○ theater

1. The story is about a
   ○ cow   ○ donkey   ○ squirrel
   ○ barn

2. In the picture, there are
   ○ boys   ○ girls   ○ teachers
   ○ boys, girls, and teacher

Interpreting in Reading Comprehension (Grades 5.5-6.9)[7]

The birds, like human beings, apparently enjoy variety; at least, every type builds a different kind of nest. Some build with mud, while certain woodpeckers make holes in trees for nests. Some birds simply lay

6. Picture and question S1 are used by permission of Houghton Mifflin Company and are from the *Iowa Tests of Basic Skills, Primary Battery, Level 8, Form 6*. Copyright 1972 by The University of Iowa.

7. Reproduced from the *Stanford Achievement Test, Intermediate Level II*, copyright © 1973, by Harcourt Brace Jovanovich, Inc. Reproduced by special permission of the publisher.

eggs on the ground, while nearby another expectant mother weaves a complex nest of grass, branches, and leaves. Some nests are at the tops of one-hundred-foot trees; others are solidly supported by the ground itself. Nests also vary in size from nine feet in diameter down to no more than one inch. All of these differences call attention to the great variety of birds in the world and to their ways of self-preservation.

1 The eggs of some birds may be found on the —
  1 floor   3 tree trunk
  2 water   4 ground   **1** ① ② ③ ④

2 Different kinds of birds build nests which are —
  5 mostly in trees
  6 of various types
  7 basically the same
  8 different only in size   **2** ⑤ ⑥ ⑦ ⑧

3 For their nests, some woodpeckers use —
  1 leaves   3 houses
  2 holes   4 mud   **3** ① ② ③ ④

Interpretation in Mathematics Applications (Grades 5.5-6.9)[8]

Use the following graph to answer questions 27–29.

This graph shows the number of students in five schools.

Number of students in 100's

Which school has about 1200 students?

Central   King
Edison   Park
               Lincoln

Lincoln has about how many more students than King?

1400	575
275	150
	400

A new school will soon take all the students from King and Edison. About how many students will go to the new school from King and Edison?

1250	1475
1025	1100
	1550

Interpretation in Social Science (Grades 7.0-9.5)[9]

Questions 32-36 are based on the poster below.

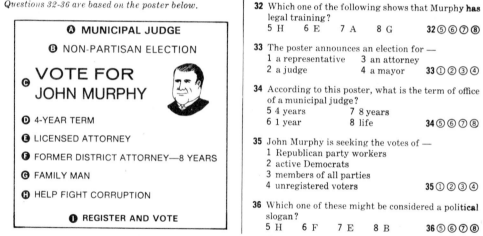

Ⓐ MUNICIPAL JUDGE

Ⓑ NON-PARTISAN ELECTION

Ⓒ VOTE FOR JOHN MURPHY

Ⓓ 4-YEAR TERM

Ⓔ LICENSED ATTORNEY

Ⓕ FORMER DISTRICT ATTORNEY—8 YEARS

Ⓖ FAMILY MAN

Ⓗ HELP FIGHT CORRUPTION

Ⓘ REGISTER AND VOTE

32 Which one of the following shows that Murphy **has** legal training?

5 H   6 E   7 A   8 G   **32** ⑤ ⑥ ⑦ ⑧

33 The poster announces an election for —
1 a representative   3 an attorney
2 a judge   4 a mayor   **33** ① ② ③ ④

34 According to this poster, what is the term of office of a municipal judge?
5 4 years   7 8 years
6 1 year   8 life   **34** ⑤ ⑥ ⑦ ⑧

35 John Murphy is seeking the votes of —
1 Republican party workers
2 active Democrats
3 members of all parties
4 unregistered voters   **35** ① ② ③ ④

36 Which one of these might be considered a political slogan?
5 H   6 F   7 E   8 B   **36** ⑤ ⑥ ⑦ ⑧

Interpretation in Mechanical Reasoning (Gr. 8-12, Adult)[10]

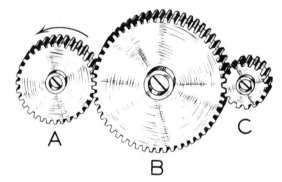

39

Which gear turns most times in a minute?

---

9. Reproduced from the *Stanford Achievement Test, Advanced Form A,* copyright © 1973 by Harcourt Brace Jovanovich, Inc. Reproduced by special permission of the publisher.

10. From the *Differential Aptitude Test, Form L.* Reproduced by permission. Copyright 1947, © 1961 by the Psychological Corporation, New York, New York. All rights reserved.

Interpretation in Science (Grades 7.0-9.5)[11]

For questions 6-8, use the chart below.

The chart shows the data recorded from observations of a stone falling under the action of its weight alone.

Time (sec.)	Distance (ft.)	Speed (ft./sec.)
0	0	0
1	16	32
2	64	64
3	144	96
4	256	128
5	400	?

6 At the end of 1 second, how many feet had the stone fallen?

5 64   6 0   7 16   8 32   **6** ⑤ ⑥ ⑦ ⑧

7 When the stone had fallen a distance of 144 feet, at how many feet per second was it falling?

1 144   2 96   3 128   4 160   **7** ① ② ③ ④

8 It takes 5 seconds for the stone to fall a distance of 400 feet. How many feet per second will the stone probably be traveling then?

5 160   6 128   7 400   8 144   **8** ⑤ ⑥ ⑦ ⑧

Some suggestions for writing the interpretive or situational item.

1. Select material which lends itself to the outcomes for which this test can be used.
2. Select material which is new to students so that application can be made.
3. Keep introductory material brief.
4. If the exercise can be kept shorter, more items can be made and a better sampling obtained.
5. The items must be relevant to the introductory material.
6. Media presentations other than the written word (charts, pictures, tables, and the like) must be relevant and of high quality.
7. Get as much as you can out of the interpretive exercise—have several items to go with each illustration.
8. The regular guidelines for making test items should be followed.
9. Items should be those which ask for analysis or interpretation.

11. Reproduced from the *Stanford Achievement Test, Advanced Form A,* copyright © 1973 by Harcourt Brace Jovanovich, Inc. Reproduced by special permission of the publisher.

I. How Does One Evaluate an Achievement Test?

1. Purpose and Scope of Item-Analysis Methods

A technique by which a teacher can evaluate the strengths and weaknesses of achievement tests is called *item analysis*. Its existence is based on the hypothesis that the total test is or is not good depending upon the worth of individual items. Thus by evaluating the aggregate of the items in a test one can infer the goodness of the total test. The technique serves as a self-instruction device for the teacher. One can determine whether the current test is a good one, which items were effective and which were not, and one generally can learn how to produce better items for future tests.

2. Structure of an Item Analysis Chart

Basically, the item analysis chart will determine two things: the level of difficulty of an item and its discriminating power; that is, does it show a difference between the upper and lower groups of students on this test? Usually a five-column chart is structured. In order, the headings are as follows:

Item Number	*Success of Upper Group*	*Success of Lower Group*	*Index of Discrimination (U—L)*	*Level of Difficulty (U+L)*

The item number is where one lists each item in the test from beginning to end.

3. Determining the Index of Discrimination

The index of discrimination is the difference between the number of correct responses between the upper and lower groups. Therefore, the success of each group on each item must be determined. To do this, each pupil's test is marked and a total raw score is found. The test papers are then ranked according to the total scores and the top and bottom thirds become the upper and lower group. *The middle third is ignored.* For each item, the number of pupils in the upper and lower groups who respond correctly are tabulated. The formula for finding the index of discrimination then becomes:

$$D = U - L$$

Where:

D = index of discrimination.

U = number of students in upper group who successfully answered the item.

L = number of students in lower group who successfully answered the item.

The arithmetic difference between the numbers in the second column and third column are determined for each item and placed under the column—*Index of Discrimination.* (See Item Analysis Chart in Section 5.)

4. Determining the Level of Difficulty

The level of difficulty is the sum of the number of pupils in both groups who got the item right. Thus,

$$LD = U+L$$

Where:

    LD = level of difficulty.
    U = number of pupils in upper group who got the item right.
    L = number of pupils in lower group who got the item right.

The arithmetic summation of the second and third column is calculated for each item and placed under the column—*Level of Difficulty.* (See example in Section 5.)

5. Interpreting the Item Analysis Table

Table 4.5 shows a sample Item Analysis Chart. It is only partially complete since each item number should be shown and, in this example, only a sampling of items is shown. In this example, there were 30 pupils in the class and 10 pupils in each of the upper and lower groups.

TABLE 4.5

Item Analysis Chart

Item Number	Success of Upper Group U	Success of Lower Group L	Index of Discrimination (U—L)	Level of Difficulty (U+L)
1	10	10	0	20
5	9	8	1	17
10	6	8	—2	14
15	8	2	6	10
20	6	2	4	8
30	3	1	2	4
	N = 10	N = 10		

The *Index of Discrimination* describes the discriminating power of each item. Obviously, the items at the beginning of the test are going to be easier and show less discrimination. This should then increase and then possibly decrease as the harder items toward the end are figured. The principle upon which the index of discrimination is based is that a good item will differentiate between the good and poor students on the test but always in favor of the upper group. To give you a guide to interpretation, the following might be used.

Any difference:

$$\begin{array}{ll}
\text{Above 50\% of N} & = \text{good discriminator} \\
\text{20-50\% of N} & = \text{fair} \\
\text{Below 20\% of N} & = \text{poor} \\
0 & = \text{none} \\
- & = \text{negative}
\end{array}$$

Some writers suggest that a good achievement test should have 50% of the items exceeding $+ 0.40$, less than 40% should have values between $+ 0.40$ and $+ 0.20$, less than 10% between $+ 0.20$ and 0, and none should have negative values. Negative values identify items which differentiate between pupils in the wrong direction, that is, favoring the lower group over the upper group.

Using the figures above, one would interpret the *Index of Discrimination* for Table 4.5 as follows:

No. 1 = no discriminating power   (0)
No. 5 = poor discriminating power   (1)
No. 10 = negative discriminating power (−2)
No. 15 = good discriminating power   (6)
No. 20 = fair discriminating power   (4)
No. 30 = fair discriminating power   (2)

In general, one would say that this test, as indicated by the sample, does not have sufficient items which are good discriminators since only one of six has good discriminating ability. The items should be studied to determine how they could be improved to provide better discrimination.

The *Level of Difficulty* tells basically two things: whether one is producing items with the proper range of difficulty and whether they are placed in the test from the easiest to the most difficult. Again, a general guide might be:

Above 70% successful = easy

30%-70% successful   = moderate

Below 30% successful = difficult

Most of the items should be in the 30-70% bracket so that the majority of the students can have a good opportunity to answer the question. A few should be easy, to get them into the test; a few should be difficult, to challenge the better students. We could interpret Table 4.5 as follows:

No.   1 = very easy
No.   5 = easy
No. 10 = moderate
No. 15 = moderate
No. 20 = moderate
No. 30 = difficult

Notice that 3 of the 6 items were moderate; 2 of 6 were easy; and 1 of 6 was difficult. Normally, items which are answered by all or failed by all are invalid and would not be kept. However, one or two, depending on the length of the test, of the items which everyone answered correctly might be used as motivational items, even though invalid.

Some teachers may wish to explore further uses of the Item Analysis Chart. One technique especially useful on a multiple-choice item is to find out the worth of each choice, the distractors as well as the correct response. Each choice should be so plausible that it is chosen by some students and therefore would be a good distractor for those who have limited knowledge. Another procedure of analysis is to produce a chart for analyzing pupil responses to each item in an achievement test. This is accomplished by putting the pupils' names vertically on the left and the test item numbers across the top. For each item, a pupil is given a + if he answers it correctly, a − if it is incorrect, and a 0 if omitted. The chart can then be studied for individual strengths and weaknesses and a class summary can be made of aggregate strengths and weaknesses. This contributes to excellent post-test discussion and learning.

6. A Note of Caution on Item Analysis

Although the technique of item analysis is extremely useful for the improvement of achievement tests, a few words of caution must be expressed.

In the first place, such analysis is usually based on a relatively small sampling of pupils. This forces the teacher to make some judgments on items with limited data. Second, although it is possible to use the technique with short-answer essay tests, the resultant information is not as useful as for objective items. Third, the technique works best on tests in which the items are highly intercorrelated—most achievement tests cover such a wide sampling of knowledge that they do not meet this criterion very well. Last, so many other factors can affect the data on item analysis. Some of these variables include the specific test make-up, the conditions under which the test was given, the teacher-pupil attitude, and the general quality of the class.

Nevertheless, with these limitations considered, the technique is still worth-while for the in-service education of the teacher and the improvement of achivement tests.

Summary Statements

1. Teacher-made tests have unique functions in the measurement of pupil progress and should be used for the objectives for which they can do the best job.
2. Sanders based his taxonomy of questions on two hypotheses: First, teachers can lead students into all kinds of thinking through careful use of questions; and second, some teachers intuitively ask questions of high quality but far too many overemphasize those which require students only to remember, and practically no teachers make full use of all worthwhile kinds of questions.
3. The several uses of the taxonomy of questions might assist the teacher: in discovering whether he is offering a variety of intellectual experiences; in determining which instructional materials are going to provide experiences for a wide variety of intellectual thought; in evaluating the degree to which critical thinking is being stressed; in providing some interesting ideas for action research; and in helping the pupil become more active in the learning process.
4. The entire realm of the taxonomy of questions can be used on any level and with all types of students; the difference is in the content and complexity of questions rather than in type.
5. Most teachers are familiar with the basic types of items; however, there are many variations of each and combinations of items which might be considered by the teacher because sometimes the variations can measure the objectives more adequately and can produce more interesting items.
6. One of the first decisions a teacher must make when tests are to be used is whether to use an objective type or an essay type test. Familiarity with the basic differences between these two types is important in making the correct decision.
7. Knowledge of general principles of test construction will enable a teacher to produce tests which have validity, reliability, and usability.
8. There are sequential steps to follow in the development of a test which, if followed, will facilitate test construction and which will produce a test that pupils can solve, knowing what they are to do and how they are to do it.
9. Teachers must be familiar with both the function of a specific type of item and its construction if it is to be used properly to measure growth toward a specific objective.

10. Item analysis is one of the best self-instruction devices for the teacher. It can determine whether the current test is a good one and which items were effective, and the teacher generally can learn how to produce better items for future tests.

Discussion Questions

1. Summarize the unique functions served by teacher-made tests.
2. Define critical thinking and reasoning as they relate to teaching and learning.
3. Discuss how the Essay (Short Answer) differs from the Essay (Discussion) as to length and function.
4. What is another name for the recall type of test and for the recognition type of test? Basically, what is the functional difference between these two types of tests?
5. What are the two ideas which should be inferred from the following statement: Those objectives of the unit or course for which tests are the most appropriate form of measurement should be identified.
6. Discuss the following statement relative to evaluating a test: The difficulty of the test is a general indication of its validity.
7. What is the implication in the following statement: Remember, the nature of the objective and the content to be measured should determine the type of item to be used.
8. Describe the main point which pupils should be taught so that they can approach the essay examination with confidence and respond to it more adequately.
9. For each of the main types of test items described in this chapter, discuss the ones which could be used appropriately on the grade level (elementary) or subject (secondary) of your choice.
10. Formulate some basic principles relative to the interpretation of the *level of difficulty* and *index of discrimination* in item analysis.

Student Activities

1. Select any three of the elements of critical thinking suggested in the text of this chapter, and for each devise a question which might be asked of the pupils on the grade level and subject of your choice.
2. The nature of the test must take into consideration the purpose it is to serve. Characterize each of the following purposes as to length, type of sampling, and use made of the results: motivation, diagnosis, mastery, and achievement.
3. Give examples of test items which would produce correct responses because: (a) word clues were given and (b) only an "intelligence" answer was called for.

4. For any short unit of your choice, formulate a plan for a test following the format presented in this chapter.
5. Rearrange the following types of tests in order of the length of time it would take a pupil to do each type. Use 1 for the type which the pupil could complete in the briefest time, 2 for the next shortest, and the like.

> Essay (Short Answer)
> Essay (Discussion)
> Simple Recall (Basic)
> Completion (Basic)
> Alternative-Response (Basic)
> Multiple-Choice (Basic)
> Matching (Basic)

6. Using the same listing as for the previous question, rate the types of tests for item difficulty using 1 for the least difficult type, 2 for the next most difficult type, and the like. How do your two rankings compare?
7. For each of the following types of tests, write a set of directions, including the simplest mode of pupil response for a grade level of your choice.

> Alternative-Response (Basic)
> Multiple-Choice (Basic)
> Matching (Basic)
> Completion (Basic)

8. Following is a list of factors comparing essay tests and objective tests. For each factor, indicate whether the essay or the objective test would be most appropriate to use. Use E to denote the essay type and O to denote the objective type.
   a. To measure depth, rather than breadth, of understanding
   b. To obtain the highest reliability of grading or scoring
   c. To measure critical reasoning through extensive sampling
   d. To reduce the possibility of the pupil's guessing or bluffing
   e. To enable the pupil to organize his response with a minimum of constraint
   f. To reduce the labor required in the construction of the tests
   g. To reduce the labor required in scoring of the tests.
   h. To enable the pupil to obtain a score based upon the completeness and accuracy of his response.
9. Complete an item-analysis chart, following the structure in Table 4.5, using the following data. Write a basic interpretation of the index of discrimination and index of difficulty.

Test Given to 30 Pupils of Which 10 Were in
Upper and Lower Groups

Item Number	Success of Upper Group	Success of Lower Group
1	10	10
10	9	7
20	8	5
30	6	2
40 (last question)	2	0

Selected Readings

Adkins, Dorothy C. *Test Construction: Development and Interpretation of Achievement Tests*, 2nd ed. Columbus, Ohio: Charles E. Merrill Publishing Company, 1974. Chapters 4-7.

Ahmann, J. Stanley, and Glock, Marvin D. *Evaluating Pupil Growth*, 5th ed. Boston: Allyn and Bacon, Inc., 1975. Chapters 3-6.

———. *Measuring and Evaluating Educational Achievement*, 2nd ed. Boston: Allyn and Bacon, Inc., 1975. Chapters 3-6.

Bennion, Donald H. *Assessing Student Learning*. Dubuque, Iowa: Kendall-Hunt Book Co., 1977. Chapters 3-6.

Brown, Frederick G. *Principles of Educational and Psychological Testing*, 2nd ed. New York: Holt, Rinehart and Winston, Inc., 1976. Chapter 13.

Cooperative Educational Service Agency 12. *1974 Mathematics Assessment Program Report. Grades 3, 6, and 7*. Portage, Wisconsin: CESA 12, 1974.

Ebel, Robert L. *Essentials of Educational Measurement*, 3rd ed. Englewood Cliffs, New Jersey: Prentice-Hall, Inc., 1979. Chapters 3, 10, and 13.

Green, John A. *Teacher-Made Tests*, 2nd ed. New York: Harper & Row Publishers, Inc., 1975. Chapters 1-7.

Gronlund, Norman E. *Measurement and Evaluation in Teaching*, 3rd ed. New York: The Macmillan Company, Inc., 1976. Part II.

———. *Readings in Measurement and Evaluation*. New York: The Macmillan Company, Inc., 1968. Part II.

Hopkins, Charles D., and Antes, Richard L. *Classroom Measurement and Evaluation*. Itasca, IL: F. E. Peacock Publishers, Inc., 1978. Chapters 4-7.

Hunkins, Francis P. *Questioning Strategies and Techniques*. Boston: Allyn and Bacon, Inc., 1972.

Linneman, Richard H., and Merenda, Peter F. *Educational Measurement*, 2nd ed. Glenview, IL: Scott, Foresman and Company, 1979. Chapter 4.

Mehrens, William A., and Lehmann, Irvin J. *Measurement and Evaluation in Education and Psychology*. New York: Holt, Rinehart and Winston, Inc., 1973. Chapters 7-11.

Noll, Victor H., Scannell, Dale P., and Craig, Robert C. *Introduction to Educational Measurement*, 4th ed. Boston: Houghton Mifflin Company, 1979. Chapters 6 and 7.

Noll, Victor H., Scannell, Dale P., and Noll, Rachel P. *Introductory Readings in Educational Measurement*. Boston: Houghton Mifflin Company. 1972. Section 3.

Payne, David A., and McMorris, Robert F. *Educational and Psychological Measurement*. Morristown, NJ: General Learning Press, 1974. Part IV.

Popham, W. James. *Criterion-Referenced Instruction*. Belmont, CA: Fearon Publishers, 1973.

———. *Criterion-Referenced Measurement*. Englewood Cliffs, NJ: Prentice-Hall, Inc., 1978.

Sanders, Norris M. *Classroom Questions, What Kinds?* New York: Harper & Row Publishers, 1965.

Sax, Gilbert. *Principles of Educational Measurement and Evaluation*. Belmont, California: Wadsworth Publishing Company, Inc., 1974. Chapters 3-5.

Stanley, Julian C., and Hopkins, Kenneth D. *Educational and Psychological Measurement and Evaluation*. Englewood Cliffs, New Jersey: Prentice-Hall, Inc., 1972. Chapters 8-11.

TenBrink, Terry D. *Evaluation. A Practical Guide for Teachers*. New York: McGraw-Hill Book Company, 1974. Chapter 13.

Thorndike, Robert, and Hagen, Elizabeth. *Measurement and Evaluation in Psychology and Education*, 4th ed. New York: John Wiley & Sons, Inc., 1977. Chapter 7.

Tuckman, Bruce W. *Measuring Educational Outcomes: Fundamentals of Testing*. New York: Harcourt Brace Jovanovich, Inc., 1975. Chapters 4 and 5.

Wick, John W. *Educational Measurement. Where Are We Going and How Will We Know When We Get There?* Columbus, Ohio: Charles E. Merrill Publishing Company, 1973. Chapter 4.

5

Construction and Use of Observational Tools

What is meant by observational tools?
What are the uses and advantages of observational tools?
What are the limitations of observational tools?
How does one construct and use the basic types of observational tools?
　　Participation Charts
　　Checklists
　　Rating Scales
　　Anecdotal Records
What are some methods of evaluating personal-social adjustment?
　　Additional Observational Tools
　　Sociometric and Related Techniques
　　Self-Report Inventories
　　Projective Measures of Personality

A.　What Is Meant by Observational Tools?

Observational tools are subjective instruments or instruments of judgment which may yield quantitative data or results but, more often, qualitative or descriptive results.

B.　What Are the Uses and Advantages of Observational Tools?

Because observational tools are subjective instruments, some teachers avoid using these methods. They may believe that, unless an instrument can be classified as objective, it has little value for measurement and evaluation. Sometimes, objective type instruments may be more appropriate than observations; at other times, however, observation is of more value. There are five uses and advantages of observation.

1. Observation of the student's daily work as he applies principles and procedures provides a continuous check on the student's daily achievement. Observation provides an incentive for the student to show growth toward goals, and it enables the teacher to note errors as they occur.
2. Observation provides a check on certain important outcomes of instruction without encroaching on instructional time or disrupting training in any way.
3. If observation can be made reliable and objective, the results, more than those of any other measure, should be a valid indication of the student's ability to use and apply what has been taught. In Chapter 3, the three levels of measurement and evaluation were described. In order of preference, these were behavioral, planning, and understanding. Observational tools are an example of the behavioral level of evaluation, since they are a direct measure of the student's performance.
4. The time, equipment, and personnel required to administer carefully controlled performance tests make extensive use of them impractical. Observational tools can be used as a very effective supplement to a few carefully prepared performance tests and written examinations.
5. Observational tools have wide applicability to nonacademic growth (cooperation, consideration, initiative, enthusiasm, and the like) as well as to subject matter growth.

C.   What Are the Limitations of Observational Tools?

Limitations of observational tools center around the mechanics of using them rather than the value of the tools themselves. The first limitation relates to the specific planning necessary to the use of observation, the second to factors affecting the reliability of observation, and the third to opportunities for systematic observation.

1. Failure to plan for the use of observational tools

Many teachers confuse casual observation with systematic observation. Casual observation does not relate to specific learnings but is merely the process of noting general student behavior. In contrast, systematic observation is planning observation with specific objectives in mind.

The teacher should consider the major objectives of the lesson, unit, or course and identify the objectives for which observational tools would be the most appropriate. For each objective, the teacher can decide which pupil traits would best characterize student growth toward the objective. These traits become the basis for the focal points of observation. When organized into an observational form, the teacher will observe all the students on the same set of traits or criteria.

2. Failure to eliminate factors which tend to reduce the reliability of the results of observation

The following factors will reduce the reliability of observational results unless the teacher can control them. These might be classified as "faults of human nature," since they are temptations to which all are susceptible as teachers evaluate student growth. If one realizes that these items affect the reliability of the results, one can avoid being influenced by them. These factors include:

    a. Tendency to give high ratings to students who appear to be busy without critically examining the quantity or quality of their work.

    b. Tendency to be influenced by the student's past record or previous performance.

    c. Tendency to rate all students the same on a trait—thus, to defeat the purpose of differentiating degrees of growth.

    d. Tendency to base final evaluation on the most recent observation or on the one or two most vivid impressions obtained throughout the unit or course.

    e. Tendency to contribute to the "halo effect" of some students. Some students have pleasant personalities and are attractive to other students and teachers alike. There is a tendency to rate these students high regardless of their specific performances.

3. Failure to coordinate observation with teaching

Systematic observation requires that a teacher plan opportunities for observation during the lesson, unit, or course just as he would plan for instructional procedures. A teacher who does not do this will set aside the use of observational tools until reports are due and then hurriedly will record some observations with little genuine effort to evaluate growth effectively. There are many opportunities each week when a teacher can plan ahead to observe for pupil growth. Such opportunities should be planned so that the cumulative results of observation will be based on adequate sampling of pupil behavior throughout the term or course.

D. How Does One Construct and Use the Basic Types Observational Tools?

Participation Charts

Definition

Thomas describes a participation chart as an observational device which is used for observing students in small groups or the observation of pupils in total class discussion; the chart indicates who contributes, how often each contributes, and how valuable the contributions are.[1]

General Purpose

It will show evidence, by charting of voluntary oral student participation, of the progress of pupils toward group goals. The oral nature of this participation should be emphasized. Other devices can be used for the measurement of written or physical performance, but participation charts are unique to oral participation. Also, the voluntary nature should be emphasized, since, again, other devices such as a checklist or rating scale may be used for forced responses.

Specific Purposes

The participation chart may be used in observing students in small groups or in general class discussion. Frequently, teachers will divide the class into small groups for planning of a project or presentation. Charting small-group discussion is simpler than charting large-group discussion, since the number of students involved is less. The leaders and followers can easily be identified. Following up the observation, the teacher can assist each child to understand his or her role in the group and can guide the child in becoming a better contributor. By comparing observations made early in the year with those made later in the year, the teacher can note the growth of pupil participation.

In observing general class discussion, the teacher can evaluate growth in group participation throughout the year, will have another source of evidence in determining pupil growth toward goals, and can produce evidence to aid in discussing oral participation with each student.

The participation chart does not indicate why some pupils will not participate in class discussion or why some pupils use this activity to gain attention from other pupils. Because oral participation is one of the principal methods each person can use to contribute as citizens of society, it seems worthwhile to promote this medium of communication for its own sake although this benefit is a by-product of the original purpose—that is, to measure growth toward group goals.

For What Objectives Can This Technique Be Used?

The major advantage of observational tools is that they have wide applicability. Thus, the participation chart can be used for any category of objectives as long as oral participation can be exhibited and observed.

---

1. R. Murray Thomas, *Judging Student Progress* (New York: Longmans, McKay Co., Inc., 1960), p. 271. Reprinted with permission of the publishers.

Plans for the Use of Participation Charts

ELEMENTARY: KINDERGARTEN OR FIRST GRADE, UNIT ON THE CIRCUS

Objectives	*Participation Rating*	*Weight of Device*
The pupil: 1. *Expresses* the ideas of how animals are trained 2. *Explains* how to buy a ticket 3. *Describes* how animals perform 4. *Discusses* the importance of circus people working together	Superior contribution Secondary contribution Uncertain or doubtful contribution Detracting contribution	25%*

SECONDARY: SOCIAL PROBLEMS (12th GRADE), UNIT ON THE UNITED NATIONS

Objectives	*Participation Rating*	*Weight of Device*
The pupil: 1. *Explains* the origin of the United Nations 2. *Discusses* the basic purposes of the United Nations 3. *Compares* the United Nations with previous world organizations 4. *Describes* the basic structure of the United Nations	Superior contribution Secondary contribution Uncertain or doubtful contribution Detracting contribution	15%*

*This percentage indicates the weight of this device in relation to the other instruments which would be used in this unit.

Charting Small Group Work

In Figure 5.1, Thomas suggests how a simple chart can be constructed to record oral participation within small groups.

The type of contribution is listed at the left, and the names of the students are across the top. A tally mark for each contribution is placed opposite the proper type of contribution. Note that the type of contribution is defined under the chart so that the same criteria may be used when rating each of the pupils.

| Type of Contribution* | Name of Committee | | | | |
	David	Susan	Richard	Toby	Pat
Superior	卅	///	////	/	
Secondary	卅 /	//	////	///	
Uncertain or Doubtful	/	////		/	//
Detracting		///	/		

*Type of Contribution Defined

Superior:	Introduction of significant idea
Secondary:	Introduction of important, but minor idea
Uncertain:	Contribution needs clarification
Detracting:	Contribution detracts from discussion

Figure 5.1   Charting Participation in Small Groups. (Adapted from R. Murray Thomas, *Judging Student Progress* (New York: Longmans, Green & Co., Inc., David McKay Co., 1960), p. 268. Reprinted with permission of the publishers.

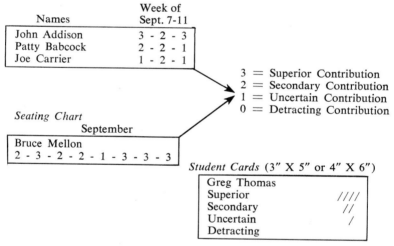

Figure 5.2   Charting General Class Discussion.

Charting General Class Discussion

Charting general discussion is a somewhat more difficult procedure since the teacher, in most cases, is leading the discussion. To chart participation while each student is contributing takes the teacher's attention away from the discussion momentarily and therefore might disrupt the discussion. The teacher might be able to chart participation "on the spot" if the pupils understand what the teacher is doing, but almost always some continuity is lost in the process.

A better procedure is to chart participation as soon as possible after the discussion has taken place. Some teachers who find it difficult to chart participation right after the discussion has been completed will rate each student once or twice a week on participation—a kind of analysis of each pupil's participation over the past few days.

Whether the rating is done during the discussion, after the discussion, or once or twice a week, similar procedures may be used. Figure 5.2 shows charting participation by roll-book tallies, by a seating chart, and by student cards. The teacher can modify these forms for individual usage. The main thing is that the charting of participation makes sense to the teacher and can be analyzed later with full realization of exact significance of the key to the chart.

Checklists

Definition

A checklist is usually a listing of steps, activities, skills, objectives, or topics in which the teacher checks the items as they are exhibited by the pupil.

Purposes

The basic purpose of a checklist is to keep a continual account of the student's progress as he performs tasks of various types. There are four specific purposes of this device.

1. A list of steps in performing a certain operation used by an observer in evaluating a student's proficiency in some skill.

    Work Habits (Typewriting)

    _____ Reports to class and desk promptly

    _____ Removes cover and places it away neatly

    _____ Readies machine for typing

    _____ Places paper in machine properly

2. A list of activities or characteristics which are checked if they exist and are left blank if they do not.

    Cooperation

    _____ Does his or her share

    _____ Contributes ideas

    _____ Listens to other viewpoints

    _____ Follows instructions promptly

3. A list of goals or objectives which are given check marks as they are achieved.

       Informal Speeches

_____Prepares outline correctly

_____Speaks slowly and clearly

_____Presents ideas effectively

_____Summarizes main points concisely

4. A list of topics or assignments which are checked as they are completed by a teacher or a student in a unit or segment of a course.

       Basic Printing

_____Draws type case

_____Sets a line of type in composing stick

_____Locks up type

_____Takes impression

_____Makes type corrections

The examples above show the basic format of a checklist; that is, the traits are listed and a check mark is given to show the presence of a trait. There are other uses of a checklist for which a different form is required.

In the case of marking a project, a combination checklist/rating scale may be constructed. It takes the basic format of the checklist, but instead of a check mark to reveal the presence of a trait, a number rating may be given.

Scrapbook	*Key*
_____Cover	5 — Excellent
_____Title page	4 — Very good
_____Follows theme	3 — Good
_____Printing	2 — Fair
_____Binding	1 — Poor

At times, a checklist may be used to check the sequence of a student's action or behavior. A listing is made of all possible steps in the sequence. The teacher observes the student at work and places a number 1, for example, opposite the first action or step the student does, number 2 opposite the next step, and so on. A glance at the completed checklist can determine which students have made the correct progression and those who have not. The errors for the latter group can readily be spotted and corrected.

       Steps in Constructing a Test

_____Makes a plan for the test

_____Drafts the items in preliminary form

_____Decides upon the length of the test

_____Edits the items for final form

_____Rates the items for difficulty

_____Rearranges the items for difficulty

Construction

The first step is to decide upon the objectives for which a checklist might be used. The teacher then analyzes and determines for each objective the specific skills, activities, or topics to be exhibited by the pupil. The individual items of the unit must be defined or stated in specific and functional terms as in the examples just given. When the individual items are determined and listed properly, the teacher can then place these into a format for observation. The checklist can be duplicated so that each child will be evaluated on a separate sheet, or a master checklist can be produced in which the names of all the children are listed at the left with the list of activities across the top. The latter has the advantage in that progress of the total class can be noted at a glance.

Uses

The checklist can be used by the teacher very readily in most subjects. Since it is highly adaptable to all types of objectives, it can be used to measure growth in knowledges, skills, and attitudes. Thus it can be used to observe for social studies concepts, mathematical skills, or traits of personality. Another important use is for pupil self-evaluation. Frequently, a teacher can devise a parallel checklist for pupil use. In a pupil-teacher conference, a comparison of the teacher evaluation and pupil self-evaluation can be discussed. The checklist can also be used as a diagnostic instrument by listing deficiencies or errors in a performance or skill. A check mark would indicate that the pupil needs to improve on particular items.

Rating Scales

Definition

Rating scales are observational tools to indicate the status of an individual on a series of traits by means of checking the degree to which the pupil has developed each characteristic.

Purposes

A rating scale is generally used when the teacher feels it necessary to obtain finer discrimination among the pupils than a checklist allows. The philosophy behind the checklist is that the trait is present or absent; on a rating scale, it is assumed that all pupils will show some growth toward a trait, but the growth will be in varying degrees. More specifically, rating scales assist the teacher in measuring the more intangible characteristics of pupils such as attitudes, appreciations, or skills that can be evaluated only in a limited way, if at all, by more objective measures. Rating scales also serve to motivate students. Students not only try to do better if they know that they are being rated, but if the students have knowledge of the traits being observed, they tend to develop growth toward specific goals. If the ratings are made known to the students in a tactful manner, the ratings then aid them in self-analysis. There is also a value to teachers in using rating scales in that the scales tend to direct their attention to the study of the individual student—to his or her individual development.

Construction

The general planning of rating scales follows the procedure outlined under the section on checklists except that, since there are degrees of a trait to be developed, a few additional criteria must be considered. One criterion is that the trait or characteristic must be clearly defined. Unless it is defined, each teacher might define the trait differently. The trait or characteristic must also be readily observable. This is particularly important because the teacher is asked to rate a pupil on a degree of growth. It also requires that the degrees of trait can be defined. The method of defining may vary depending on the format, but the criterion is that the exhibited behavior of the pupil can be easily identified with a degree of growth stated.

Types of Rating Scales

There are two basic types of rating scales which a teacher may devise. These include the numerical scale and graphic rating scale. The latter is usually classified into one of two types: the constant-alternative form or the changing-alternative form. Each of these scales is described below.

1. Numerical Scale

Numerical rating scales assign numbers for the various degrees of each trait from the least to the most.

Directions: Give the student a number from 1 to 5 to represent the degree to which he possesses each trait. 1 represents a minimum of the trait, 3 an average amount, and 5 a maximum amount of the trait.

Does the student
participate effec-
tively in group
planning? _____
         1   2   3   4   5

2. Graphic rating scales

The graphic rating scale is one in which a horizontal line represents a scale from low to high and under which a degree of the trait is described by a word or more complete description.

The *constant-alternative* form always uses the same descriptive words for each trait.

Does the student
participate effec-
tively in group
planning?

	Very little	Seldom	Occasionally	Frequently	Very often

Does the student
help to motivate
others?

	Very little	Seldom	Occasionally	Frequently	Very often

The *changing-alternative* form provides separate descriptions for each degree of each trait.

Does the student
participate effec-
tively in group
planning?

Ideas distract group from their goal	Is passive, usually agrees with others	Suggests an idea when called upon	Suggests ideas of secondary importance	Suggests ideas of major importance

Does the student
work efficiently
on his own?

Unable to work alone; needs constant help	Works alone only if constantly watched	Works alone but is inconsistent	Works alone well with some initial help	Works well alone and is a self-starter

The graphic rating scale has an advantage in that a profile can be produced by connecting the checked points from each trait. The continuous line allows the rater to check any part of the line—not necessarily right above a given description. In constructing the graphic rating scale, these suggestions would be followed.

1. Introduce each trait by a question that is phrased to describe the trait in objective and observable terms.
2. Make a continuous line above the traits so that rater can check any place on the line.

3. Adapt the words to describe each level to the understanding of the persons who will do the rating.
4. Avoid phrases at the ends which express levels of the trait so extreme that raters will never check them.
5. Make the meaning of the intermediate levels closer to the average or neutral phrase than to the extreme phrases. This might induce the raters to use a wider range of the line.
6. To reduce the halo effect, vary the desirable end of the rating line at random. This will prevent a profile from being drawn, but it may require the rater to read each degree of the trait carefully to choose the one desired.

Anecdotal Records

Definition

An anecdotal record is a written observation of a single, specific, significant incident in the behavior of the pupil. This is sometimes called an *observer-description* method of recording observation to distinguish it from rating scales, checklists, and participation charts which are considered *observer-evaluation* methods. The anecdotal record is a more time-consuming device to use, since there is an actual description of the incident observed. However, since they represent real behavior, anecdotal records serve an extremely useful purpose for the teacher who is attempting to synthesize other appraisal procedures into a meaningful picture of the student as a total functioning personality.

When Anecdotal Records Are Used

1. Observation of growth toward understandings, skills, and attitudes
2. Diagnosis of academic and social problems
3. Social development and skills
4. Health and physical growth
5. Provide feeder data for rating scales, checklists, and cumulative record

Characteristics of an Anecdote

1. It is factual: It records only the actual event, incident, uncolored by the feelings, interpretations, or biases of the observer.
2. It is an observation of only one incident.
3. It is an observation of an incident which is considered important and significant in the growth and/or development of the pupil.
4. It is short and informal yet gives pertinent information.
5. It contains information which may be either complimentary or uncomplimentary.

RECORDED ON PRINTED CARD FORM OR ON SLIPS OF PAPER

Name: John Warren   Grade: Seventh   Date: September 30, 1980

Incident:	John brought into class today an arithmetic problem which was assigned in science class, and he indicated that this was a good example of how we can apply arithmetic tools to other subjects.
Interpretation:	This was the first instance in which John has shown growth toward the objective of showing application of arithmetic to other subjects.
Suggestion:	This may be the spark that John needs to see relationships among subjects. A chart will be placed on the bulletin board with John's suggestion, and others will be encouraged to add other examples of arithmetic use in other subjects.

MULTIPLE ANECDOTAL RECORD FORM PRINTED ON 8½″ x 11″ PAPER

Name: John Warren   Grade: Seventh   Class: Arithmetic   Observer: Mr. Brown

Date	Incident	Interpretation and Suggestions
9/30/80	John brought into class today an arithmetic problem which was assigned in science class and indicated that this was a good example of how we can apply arithmetic tools to other subjects.	This may be the spark that John needs to see relationships among subjects. A chart will be placed on the bulletin board with John's suggestion, and others will be encouraged to add other examples of arithmetic use in other subjects.

RECORDED IN A RING NOTEBOOK. ONE OR MORE PAGES FOR EACH PUPIL WITH NAME TAB ON INITIAL SHEET.

1980-81

9-14	Showed lack of interest in American government	
10-18	Assignment late with no excuse	
11-2	Did not participate in "get out the vote" campaign	
12-7	In conference, he revealed home factors which affects attitude	
1-15	Took active part as discussion leader	
2-20	Gave some very good ideas for class skit on student government day	
3-17	Was elected to contact the mayor for visit to class	
4-10	Showed active interest in research paper on "Effect of State Government on Local Communities"	
5-20	Research paper showed excellent organization, good knowledge, and great improvement in basic attitude.	

(Tab: Government)

(Tab: Joe)

Figure 5.3   Examples of Anecdotal Records.

6. It shows growth or lack of growth toward certain objectives or purposes for which the teacher is teaching and for which the pupils are striving.
7. It serves its best purposes when a periodic summary is made of individual anecdotes over a period of time to reveal consistent patterns of growth or regression.

What It Contains

1. Identity of the pupil observed: name and class or activity
2. Date of observation
3. Name of observer
4. Incident
   Optional
   1. Interpretation of behavior
   2. Suggestions or recommendations concerning growth and behavior

To be most useful, the individual anecdotes of each pupil should be summarized periodically. In such a summary, the salient features of the pupil's growth and present status are recorded. These summaries can be placed in the pupil's cumulative folder to be used by future teachers and to be supplemented by them. In this manner, a complete and valuable "behavior inventory" of a pupil can be accumulated over a period of years. Recent legislation in some states allows students who have reached the age of majority and parents to view material in the cumulative folder.

E. What Are Some Methods of Evaluating Personal-Social Adjustment?

The process of adjustment is the individual's attempt to create a more harmonious relationship between himself and his environment. Learning can best take place when this relationship is harmonious and the student, teacher, and environment seem to fit together in a way which gives direction and significance to the learning process. The teacher plays a significant role in helping each child to develop good adjustment, in establishing a favorable environment for learning, and in adapting the learning process to each child's ability and interests.

A variety of instruments for evaluating personal-social adjustments are available. Some of these include additional teacher observational tools, others include reports by peers, some are self-reports, and others are projective types of techniques. Most of these can be developed and used by the teacher while others must be administered and interpreted by a clinician.

It is not the purpose of this introductory book to go into great detail on these techniques. Many books and articles have been written in this area and users are encouraged to study some of these sources for detailed information.[2]

The following outline is indicative of the variety of useful instruments and techniques in this area of evaluation. A short description of each will follow the outline.

> Additional Observational Methods
>> Interview
>> Time Sampling
> Sociometric and Related Techniques
>> Sociogram
>> Social Distance Scale
>> "Guess Who" Questionnaires
> Self-Report Techniques
>> Attitude Scales and Questionnaires
>> Autobiography
>> Biographical Data Blank
>> Diary
>> Interest Inventories
>> Personality Inventories
> Projective Techniques
>> Unfinished Sentences or Stories
>> Clinical Techniques

Additional Observational Methods

1. *Interview*

Counseling takes place largely through interviews. The basic purposes of interviews are to:

> Obtain Information
> Give Information
> Interpret Data
> Engage in Therapy

In the first one, Obtain Information, the objective is to bring together all information which may be relevant to the situation. Business, government, and clinical situations use this type of interview frequently through their entrance-and-exit interviews. The teacher can gather this information from records, from the child initially, or as the interview process continues.

---

2. Among there are Hatch and Costar, Horrocks and Schoonover, Ahmann and Glock, and Remmers, Gage, and Rummel, among others, whose references are included at the end of this chapter. The reader is also encouraged to check the topic of personal-social adjustment or personality measurement in the *Education Index* or *Review of Periodical Literature*.

In the second purpose, Giving Information, the matter may be as simple as giving factual information about school regulations, college requirements, and the like. On the other hand, the student may want to know more about himself for more realistic self-appraisal. The latter information may be found in the records or it may require additional testing or inquiry.

One of the main purposes of an interview, at times, is to Interpret Data or Information. This may be as simple as interpreting past progress from records or it may require interpreting a new test result or a profile of results. In most instances the interpretation is for a specific purpose, e.g., vocational goal, solving a personal problem, and the like.

The fourth activity in interviewing, on occasion, involves Therapy. This does not mean therapy as given by a clinician but does indicate counseling chosen to help the student eliminate or alleviate concern he may have about a problem. It could involve catharsis where an individual talks out his problem and thus is able to see more clearly the direction in which he must go. Or it could involve extended dialogue whereby both the student and the teacher-counselor together work out a satisfactory solution or reduce anxiety.

2. *Time Sampling*

Time sampling means that a predetermined period of time has been assigned in which an individual is to be observed. The objective is to make note of all significant behavior during this time. A time sampling of student behavior for an individual known to be singularly unproductive during study periods might appear as follows:

10:15-10:19   Hastily leafed through two books and a notebook as if trying to find assignments and to decide which to do. Finally opened algebra book to a set of problems.

10:19-10:22   Wrote name on paper and started first problem. Decided to sharpen pencil.

10:22-10:30   Returned to desk, stared at wall, doodled on paper, wadded it up, and walked up to throw it in waste basket.

10:30-10:33   Started on new sheet with first problem. Stopped work to watch another student walk to study hall proctor and continued to watch until student returned to seat.

It is obvious that the above time sampling not only showed the student's lack of productivity, but it is also valuable information which may help the student understand and change this behavior. Like other forms of observation, time sampling can be time-consuming and unproductive of significant behavior on occasion. It works best when it is used to observe for a problem already identified.

Sociometric and Related Techniques

1. *Sociogram*

Sociometry has to do with the study of how the student's classmates see him and with his degree of social acceptance by them. The basic step in making this study is to devise questions which will stimulate students to reveal their true feelings about other members of the class. Questions of the following types are appropriate.

a. Whom do you wish to sit next to in the classroom?
b. With whom would you like to work on a committee?
c. Whom would you like as a companion on a class project?
d. Who are your best friends?
e. With whom do you like to associate after school?

The first three are types of questions the results of which could be put to use by the teacher; the last two provide additional information but are not structured for a specific use. The second question might get at respect for a skill or work habits while the first and third get a friendship and pleasure in proximity.

The sociometric test should be administered in an informed manner. For lower grades, each question should be on a separate piece of paper. The student usually writes his name and lists his numbered choices. Generally it is desirable to request five choices rather than a smaller number. Children in the primary grades may have to limit their choices to three.

In drawing a sociogram, the general procedure is to locate individuals on a chart so that the "stars" (the most popular) are near the center; the "isolates," or unchosen, are on the outside; and other students are located so as to minimize the number of intersecting lines.

In interpreting sociometric data for individual students, the teacher is obviously most concerned about the isolates (not chosen) and the neglectees (very infrequently chosen). The teacher needs to dwell on these cases and to ask himself several questions as to why these students are isolates or neglectees. Possibly there are adjustment problems that might have been overlooked. However, it should not be assumed that all of the "stars" are perfectly adjusted. Sometimes these students may overstrive for popularity to conceal some lack of other adjustment. These data indicate that information from other sources must be brought in to adequately interpret sociometric data.

2. *Social Distance Scale*

The social distance scale is used to determine the degree to which the individual accepts or rejects the group as well as the degree to which the group accepts or rejects this person. Thus, it gives a little more complete information than the sociogram. In the sociogram the individual is limited to three to five choices; there is no information on why he or she failed to choose other classmates.

Examples of the degree of statements on a particular item are as follows:

_____a. Would like to have this person as one of my friends.

_____b. Would like to have this person in my group but not as a close friend.

_____c. Would like to be with this person once in a while but not too often or for a long time.

_____d. Do not mind this person being in the room but do not want to have anything to do with him/her.

_____e. Wish this person were not in our room.

As can be noted, the questions will point out those who are rejected. For this reason some teachers prefer not to use this scale since it does require reporting negative feelings toward others which may be in opposition to their goals.

3. "Guess Who" Questionnaires

The "Guess Who" technique is a device in which the pupils are asked to match their peers with a list of behavioral characteristics. The teacher produces a list of characteristics including both complimentary and uncomplimentary traits. The student can list himself/herself, another student, or as many as he or she believes fit the description. When the results are tabulated, the teacher is able to see which pupils are placed with each characteristic and those which are mentioned the most or not at all.

Examples of some characteristics are as follows:
Here is someone who likes to talk a lot, always has something to say.

_____

Here is someone who waits for somebody else to think of something to do and always likes to follow the suggestions which others make.

_____

Here is someone who is very friendly, who has lots of friends, who is nice to everybody. _____

Self-Report Techniques

1. Attitude Scales and Questionnaires

Remmers has defined an attitude as an emotionalized tendency, organized through experience, to react positively or negatively toward a psychological object.[3] There are certain terms that are used many times when one considers attitudes in the broad sense. Such terms or concepts are *interests, motives, values, appreciation, morale, ideals,* and *character.*

It is helpful to think of attitudes as having various dimensions. If a teacher keeps these in mind it will help in thinking about the attitudes of the students. Some of these dimensions are favorableness, intensity, salience, generality, public versus private attitudes, and common versus individual attitudes.

Measurement of attitudes and interests can take many forms. Attitudes usually have been measured by the single-question technique or by scales. Interests usually have been measured by informal teacher-assigned methods or by standardized inventories.

The simplest method of measuring attitudes is the ballot or single-response counting, as popularized by various public opinion polls. These devices are in effect two-point "scales." For example, in measuring attitude toward a democracy, the item in question might be "Majority rule is necessary." An analysis of the percentage of agreement would be taken as an index of the attitude of a group of persons. The wording of the question properly is a problem in this type of measurement since the error arising from wording cannot be eliminated completely.

Some of the basic attitude scales can be illustrated by reference to those by Thurstone, Remmers, and Likert. The Thurstone Type Scales illustrates the *equal-appearing-intervals* technique. This means that judges have taken all opinion-type statements about an attitude object and have placed these on a continuum from the least favorable to the most favorable. The student is asked to place a check mark after all the statements endorsed as expressing his or her own opinion or attitude. The score on the scale is the mean or median scale value of the opinions expressed. It is very difficult to build this type of scale for every type of attitude object.

Remmers' Master-Type Scales is an attempt to measure attitudes toward any one of a class of attitude objects such as occupational fields or professions. The statements are not specifically relative to any single attitude object but each can be focused on an object if it is named. It also uses the Thurstone's equal-appearing-intervals technique. However, whereas in Thurstone's scales the statements are arranged in random order, in Remmers' scales they appear in order of decreasing favorableness. This greatly decreases the time necessary for scoring.

The Likert-Type Scales are fairly easy to construct when one compares them with the two previous scales. Each scale contains statements which reflect favorable or unfavorable attitudes about an attitude object. The

3. Remmers, Gage, and Rummel, *A Practical Introduction to Measurement and Evaluation,* (New York: Harper & Row Publishers, Inc., 1965), pp. 308-316.

students are then asked to respond on a five-point scale: "strongly agree," "agree," "undecided," "disagree," and "strongly disagree." These alternatives are usually given a score value from 1 to 5, the 5 being at the most favorable end of the scale. The subject's score is the total of the values indicated. The scale can be scored rapidly and compares quite favorably in validity and reliability to the scales of Thurstone and Remmers.

2. Evaluation of Interests

Interests may be classified and measured in *four* categories: expressed, manifested, inferred, and inventoried. *Expressed* interests can be measured by asking a student to tell or write about the activities that he or she most and least enjoys. Teachers have found expressed interests useful in helping pupils find topics for English compositions, in selecting instructional materials, and in stimulating group discussion. The results of this form of measurement are most valid around the time they are expressed since maturity and environment can change these expressed interests.

When the teacher directly observes the student engaged in hobbies or other activities, he is measuring *manifest* interests. A student who builds model rockets, assembles model cars, and reads about modern rocketry and cars is manifesting interest in such activities. These interests are usually transitory and change with age and development.

Inferred interests are those which are assumed to be true by inference from high scores on certain aspects of achievement. The assumption is that if a student does well in a school subject or if he or she receives a high score on certain aspects on an achievement test, the student has high interest in these areas. There is not, of course, a perfect correlation between the two, ability and interest, but there is a tendency for the two to go together.

Inventoried interests are those which are measured by standardized instruments. These assume that persons successful in the same occupation or field have similar patterns of interests and that these differ from successful persons in another field of endeavor. Four types will be illustrated below. The first is designed for the elementary level, the second and third for junior or senior high, and the last for the senior high school level.

    a. What I Like To Do—An Inventory of Children's Interests[4]

        This inventory is designed for use in grades 4 through 7 and measures interests in eight areas: Art, Music, Social Studies, Active Play, Quiet Play, Manual Arts, Home Arts, and Science. It has two purposes: to identify pupil interests so that they may be used in guidance and instruction and as a research instrument for the psy-

4. Louis P. Thorpe et al., *What I Like To Do: An Inventory of Children's Interests* (Chicago: Science Research Associates, Inc., 1954).

chological study of children's interests. The inventory consists of 294 questions and asks a student to respond by indicating a Yes, No, or ?. Such questions are included as:

	No	**?**	**Yes**
Learn to play piano	_____	_____	_____
Swim under water	_____	_____	_____
Make jewelry out of shells	_____	_____	_____

Grade 4 would need two periods of about 30 minutes each; 5-7 could complete it in a 50-minute period.

b. Occupational Interest Inventory[5]

The Intermediate form of this test is useful in grades 7-12, the Advanced form for grades 9 to adult. It yields three groups of scores:

Fields of Interests:	personal-social, natural, mechanical, business, the arts, the sciences
Types of Interests:	verbal, manipulative, computational
Level of Interests:	in routine tasks, with tasks requiring considerable skill, with tasks requiring expert knowledge, skill, and judgment

Approximately 30-40 minutes are needed to complete the inventory. Answers may be marked in the test booklet or on separate machine-scorable or Scoreze answer sheets. A profile sheet enables scores to be plotted on a percentile scale. Major fields of interest are identified by those of the 70th percentile or higher, rejected fields by scores below the 30th percentile.

c. Kuder General Interest Survey[6]

This inventory is most useful in grades 6-12 since it is not directed solely at the professional level. This form has eleven scores: outdoor, mechanical, computational, scientific, persuasive, artistic, literary, musical, social service, clerical, and a verification scale. There is no time limit, but students usually complete it in 45-60 minutes. The instructions are so simple that it can be self-administered, scored, and profiled. The manual contains suggestions for interpreting the scores.

5. Edwin A. Lee and Louis P. Thorpe, *Occupational Interest Inventory* (Monterey, California: California Test Bureau, 1956).

6. Frederic Kuder, *Kuder E: General Interest Survey,* Revised (Chicago: Science Research Associates, Inc., 1971).

An example of an item is as follows: A student is asked to indicate the one of the triad that he or she would like *Most* and the one that he or she would like *Least*.

> Repair a broken lock
> Look for mistakes in a typewritten report
> Add columns of figures

d. Strong-Campbell Interest Inventory[7]

This inventory is the current combined-sex edition of the Strong Vocational Interest Blank (SVIB), an interest inventory that has the longest history of any psychological test in widespread use today. In this 1974 edition, the person is given a list of 325 items and is asked to respond either 'Like," "Indifferent," or "Dislike" to each of them. The respondent's answers are analyzed, generally by computer, in three main ways: first, for general overall trends; second, for consistency of response to 23 interest areas; and third, for the degree of similarity between the person's responses and the characteristic responses of men and women employed in a wide range of occupations. It is designed for persons 16 years of age and older.

For each item of the basic scales, the person is asked to mark "L" if he/she likes the item, mark "I" if he/she is indifferent, or mark "D" if he/she dislikes the item. Example:

Carpenter	L	I	D
Sports Reporter	L	I	D
Art Teacher	L	I	D
Make a Speech	L	I	D
Play Golf	L	I	D
Read Poetry	L	I	D

There is a modification of the above when it comes to "Preference between two activities" and describing "Your characteristics."

e. Minnesota Vocational Interest Inventory (MVII)[8]

The Minnesota Vocational Interest Inventory (MVII) has been prepared to provide systematic information on the interest patterns of men in *non-professional occupations*. It is intended to aid counselors working with students and others who are contemplating occupations at the *semi-skilled and skilled levels*. For each individual who completes the MVII, scores are derived to provide an index of similarity between his interests and the interests of persons

7. Edward K. Strong, Jr., and David P. Campbell, *Strong-Campbell Interest Blank,* Second Edition (Stanford, California: Stanford University Press, 1974).

8. Kenneth E. Clark and David P. Campbell, *Minnesota Vocational Interest Inventory* (New York: The Psychological Corporation, 1965).

in a variety of non-professional occupations. The MVII is designed primarily for use with those persons who contemplate entering occupations which do not require a college degree. The MVII has been administered at the ninth grade level with good results. Thus, the authors feel that it can be used with ninth grade or higher.

It includes 474 items grouped in threes, making a total of 158 triads. The person who completes the inventory is asked to select within each triad the one activity he would most like to do (L) and the one that he would like the least (D). This is a forced-choice method. An example is as follows:

L a. Varnish a floor
   b. Learn to use a slide rule
D c. Repair a broken electric iron

Scoring keys have been developed for twenty-one *Occupational Scales* including baker, food-service manager, retail sales clerk, stock clerk, printer, tabulating machine operator, warehouseman, hospital attendant, pressman, carpenter, painter, plasterer, truck driver, truck mechanic, industrial education teacher, sheet metal worker, plumber, machinist, electrician, and radio-TV repairman. Scoring keys are also available for the following *Homogeneous or Area Scales*. These scales differ from the occupational scales in that these were derived by identifying clusters of items that are related to each other. These scales include mechanical, health services, office work, electronics, food service, carpentry, sales-office, clean hands, and outdoors.

f. Ohio Vocational Interest Survey (OVIS)[9]

OVIS is an interest inventory designed to assist students in grades eight through twelve with their educational and vocational plans. In order to enhance interpretations of a student's measured interests, OVIS combines an information questionnaire with the interest inventory. The results of the questionnaire provide the student and the counselor with valuable background data for interpreting the interest scores. In addition, a school-wide summary of the questionnaire furnishes useful information for planning guidance services and curriculum changes.

The interest inventory profiles a student's interests along 24 scales. These scales represent the entire spectrum of occupations as defined in the 1965 edition of the *Dictionary of Occupational Titles*. These scales include manual work, machine work, personal services, caring for people or animals, clerical work, inspecting and testing,

9. Ayres G. D'Costa et al., *Ohio Vocational Interest Survey* (New York: Harcourt Brace Jovanovich, Inc., 1970).

crafts and precise operations, customer services, nursing and related technical services, skilled personal services, training, literary, numerical, appraisal, agriculture, applied technology, promotion and communication, management and supervision, artistic, sales representative, music, entertainment and performing arts, teaching-counseling-social work, and medical.

OVIS combines the 7-item *Student Information Questionnaire* and the 280-item *Interest Inventory* in a machine-scorable form. There is no time limit for administration, but high school students usually complete it in sixty to ninety minutes. The first six questions of the *Student Information Questionnaire* gather background information about the student's occupational plans, subject area preferences, curriculum plans, post-high school plans, and vocational course interests. Question 7, the *Local Survey Section* of the *Questionnaire,* enables the school to ask up to eight additional questions pertinent to the local situation.

The *Interest Inventory* asks the student to respond to job activities in terms of "Like very much," "Like," "Neutral," "Dislike," and "Dislike very much." An example:

1. Hire employees for a store D d n l L

OVIS may be used to help students choose a high school program and make post-high school plans; to help potential dropouts make vocational plans consistent with their interests and abilities; to assist guidance counselors in planning occupational units for group guidance classes; to serve as a basis for building an occupational information file; to help administrators plan for curriculum expansion; and to identify groups of students interested in specific educational and vocational plans.

g. Picture Interest Inventory (PII)[10]

The Picture Interest Inventory, for grades 7 to Adult, is designed to help an individual determine his or her pattern of occupational interests and, at the same time, indicate those specific occupational fields which have career possibilities based on interest. Since no words are used, the PII can be given to practically all youth from grades seven upward, regardless of their reading or writing ability or language comprehension.

---

10. Kurt P. Weingarten, *Picture Interest Inventory,* 7-adult (Monterey, California: CTB/McGraw-Hill, Inc., 1958).

Two groups of scores are obtained:

1. Fields of Occupational Interest
   a. Interpersonal Service
   b. Natural
   c. Mechanical
   d. Business
   e. Esthetic
   f. Scientific
2. Supplemental Scales
   a. Verbal
   b. Computational
   c. Time Perspective

The fields are self-explanatory as being broader categories of interest. The supplemental scales are not as clear. An interest in the *verbal scale* would mean a person is interested in activities involving the use of verbal symbols—the spoken or written word. An interest in *computational* indicates interest in the use of computational symbols and concepts—working with numbers. The *time perspective scale* gets at the amount of preparation and training required before competency in the occupation is reached. The willingness to forego the immediate wants and desires and the attainment of short-range goals in order to focus on those goals which can only be reached after relatively longer periods of time is the quality assessed by this scale.

3. *Personal-Social Adjustment Inventories*

Note that both interest and personal-social adjustment measurement refers to the use of inventories rather than tests. This is so since they do not call upon a pupil to perform at a maximum level of accomplishment. Rather, they ask the student to describe what is typical of himself or herself.

The inventories described in this section are called structured inventories. This term is used since it is designed so that all examinees interpret the items in the same way. There is some ambiguity as to meaning from time to time but the authors of these inventories try to keep this to a minimum. Most of the inventories have been developed, standardized, and researched by psychologists with a psychometric orientation. All students are presented with a uniform set of questions; their responses are scored objectively according to a key; and the results are interpreted in comparison with norming samples.

There are certain limitations and advantages in the transparent personality inventory.

a. If a student seeks guidance, the direct, transparent questions may be best. The student has come for help and believes that truthful answers will result in some assistance with his problem.

b. It is possible to create a good impression on a transparent inventory. It has been found, however, that if a student has volunteered for testing, has been assured that the results will be confidential and will be used as a basis for guidance, the "good impression" is reduced.

c. For selection and classification purposes, a more indirect type of question may be more profitable. Such an example is the *forced-choice technique.* In this technique, the student must choose one of two alternatives presented. It may reveal more than the student had intended to reveal.

d. It is not always possible for a student to really have insight into his or her own behavior—that is, the ability to describe his or her own reactions. It is difficult at times to be objective with oneself.

e. Interpreting a personality inventory correctly is difficult. Personality inventories can aid in the first level of diagnosis—identifying those who need help. They can also assist in the second level of diagnosis—locating areas of difficulty. For the third level, however, identifying causative factors, it is important that the results be regarded only as *leads* to be used for further study through other measures such as observation, interviews, and the like.

There have been several attempts to increase the validity of inventory results. One technique is the forced-choice question which tends to make the inventory fake-resistant since the student must make a choice from two alternatives. The use of verification or validation scores is another attempt at improving the validity of the results. An example of this is the Minnesota Multiphasic Personality Inventory (MMPI) which uses five validation scores: A lie score; a K-score of test-taking defensiveness; an F-score on deviant responses; a question score (total number of items on which a student chose "cannot say"); and an inconsistency score. Many types of validation scores enable the examiner to throw out an inventory result as being questionable, but the K-score on the MMPI is a *correction score.* The result is used to correct for the tendency to "fake good" or respond defensively. Thus a correct inventory is saved rather than discarded.

The Strong Vocational Interest Blank and the MMPI use another technique to improve the validity of results. This is called *selecting and keying items on the basis of empirical data.* In the Strong, the student's responses to items are assigned weights in different occupational keys in terms of the differential responses of occupational groups. That is, if a student is interested in engineering and answers items in a way in which successful engineers answer these, he will be given a high rating on the engineering scale. Th MMPI uses a similar technique in personality traits by keying items to certain personality classifications.

Some tests attempt to *obscure the scoring pattern* to increase the validity by arranging the items pertaining to each component (such as social skills) in random order throughout the test. When items unique to a component are all grouped together, the inventory becomes more transparent and students can respond to these items in such a way as to create a desired pattern. One of the most common ways to attempt to increase validity is by *disguising inventory items*. The idea is to try to get the student to rationalize his behavior. The following are a few examples from the *California Test of Personality*.

Have people often been so unfair that you gave up?
Do people often try to cheat you or do mean things to you?
Is your work often so hard that you stop trying?

These types of items seem to work best on normal subjects who might more normally attempt to respond in a socially desirable way. Abnormal subjects seem to react best to direct questions so that the results will more nearly indicate the nature of the help they need.

This book will not attempt to describe all of the published inventories in this area. A few of the more widely used ones will be described briefly as illustrations of the major types of inventories.

a. *Transparent Inventory*

The California Test of Personality is an example of a Transparent Inventory. It produces 16 scores with a scale divided into personal adjustment and social adjustment. Although care has been given to disguise items, it is quite obvious to the test-wise student as to what is really being asked. All items measuring one topic are grouped together so the student can recognize the group of questions which reveal withdrawing tendencies, for example.

This type of inventory should be used in situations where there is reason to believe that honest and frank answers will be given. Sometimes the better adjusted students and adults obtain lower scores on this type of inventory since they are more prone to admit weaknesses. The more insecure, trying to be accepted better, may try to answer items which place them in a more acceptable light.

b. *Empirically Keyed Inventories*

The California Psychological Inventory (CPI) is an empirically keyed inventory. The inventory yields 18 scores: Eleven of these are based on empirically derived scoring weights assigned to responses found to differentiate between criteria groups; four of the scores are based on weights originally judged by the author as indicating the presence of a designated variable and refined by internal consistency analysis. The remaining three scores were also derived empirically to detect tendencies of subjects to fake (good or bad) or to respond in a manner which makes the other scores of doubtful validity.

The author, Harrison C. Gough, suggests that, in interpretation, considerable weight be given to "interactions among scales," to patterns of profiles, and to "internal variability of the profile." The author suggests that when a high score on Ai (achievement through independence) is accompanied by a high score on Ac (achievement through conformity), the person is likely to be efficient, well organized, and stable; whereas a high score in Ai accompanied by a low score in Ac tends to be found in people who are demanding and dominant.[11]

c. *Forced-Choice Inventories*

An example of the forced-choice type of inventory is the *Edwards Personal Preference Schedule* (EPPS). Since its appearance about fifteen years ago it has been very widely used and has generated a tremendous amount of research. The test is designed to assess the relative strength of 15 manifest needs selected from Murray's need system.[12] Each need is represented by nine statements. A statement from each need is paired twice with one from every other need (210 items). Additionally, to allow an indication of the consistency of a subject's responses, for each need one of these pairs is repeated. The forced-choice technique indicates that the inventory is designed to be fake-resistant; that is, the examinee is unable to consistently choose socially desirable responses.

Although the test has proved to be especially popular on the college and adult level (high school norms are available), there are some limitations. The subtests tend to have low reliability since the student is uncertain of many of his choices and would probably change them on retesting. Many students resist this type of inventory since they are forced to make choices which they do not feel paint a desirable self-picture. Third, this design shows only intra-individual differences, not the relative strength of a trait with respect to other examinees.

11. Harrison C. Gough, *Manual, California Psychological Inventory* (Palo Alto, California: Consulting Psychologists Press, Inc. 1957).

12. Henry A. Murray and others, *Explorations in Personality* (New York: Oxford University Press, Inc., 1938).

d. *Problem Checklists*

A type of inventory or questionnaire which has been used a great deal is the problem checklist. The items included in such an inventory are intended to be representative of problems in different areas. Although really not intended to be a measuring device, it does accelerate the process of understanding the student and his or her problems. It is most effective in a counseling situation.

One of the most common is the Mooney Problem Checklists.[13] It has four forms—junior high, senior high, college, and adult forms. The junior high school form (7-9) produces seven scores including health and physical development, school, home and family, among others. The high school form (9-12) produces eleven scores and includes such additional scores as courtship-sex-marriage, morals and religion, vocational, and educational, among others. The forms are simply lists of common problems and the student is asked to mark those problems he or she has, to indicate those which are of most concern, and to write a statement about these problems in his/her own words. There is no mystery here, only a straightforward list of problems and an obvious approach which leaves the counselor free to communicate to the extent of his readiness to do so.

The SRA Youth Inventory is another example of the checklist type of evaluation. The instrument's value lies in helping school people identify quickly the self-acknowledged problems of students in grades 7-12. This is achieved by having the student respond to 298 problem statements. The subject checks each item that applies to him or her and makes no response to the remaining problem statements. The results are scored in nine categories: school, future, myself, people, home, dates and sex, health, general, and basic difficulty. The last scale, basic difficulty, attempts to determine whether the subject has any personality disturbance and in what area. This is the least valid of the results and should be used with caution.

It must be remembered that in checklists students check only those items on which they *consciously* feel problems. The results should be interpreted as suggesting areas worthy of exploration.

4. *The Autobiography*

The autobiography is a systematic account of his or her life as written by the student. It is usually starting at the high school level since the student has matured in writing and in ability to reflect back on past life

13. Ross L. Mooney, *Problem Checklists* (New York: Psychological Corporation, 1950).

more than previously. The format may be *structured* or *unstructured.* In the structured form, the student is given an outline of topics on which to write and to bring together as much information as possible. Such topics could include:

Early history and family background
Health and physical record
School history
Interests, leisure-time activities, hobbies, travel experiences, frendships
Occupational experiences
Educational-vocational plans
Desires and plans regarding marriage and a home

To be effective there must be a high degree of rapport established between the student and the one requesting the autobiography. If written for an English class as a regular assignment, it can only be as effective as the student feels that the writing will be held in confidence. It is usually quite effective when written for a counseling situation when the student feels that the thoughts revealed will contribute to a better understanding of the student on the part of the counselor. In any case, it must be considered a subjective technique for the collection of information.

5. *Pupil Questionnaire*

One of the most popular self-report techniques is the pupil questionnaire. It consists of a series of questions which elicits general information from the student or information for specific purposes. It is easy to administer and provides a great deal of information to the teacher or counselor. It can be used for:

a. Collection of basic information for individual cumulative record folders.
b. Collection of supplementary information for specific purposes.
c. Securing responses for use in validating information collected through other techniques.
d. Sampling pupil opinions and attitudes.
e. Making evaluation.

There are some limitations of the questionnaire. Weaknesses in wording, length, and kinds of questions result in inaccurate or incomplete responses. Parents are sometimes aroused by questions which try to reveal home environment and pupil-parent relationships. Questions about the economic status of the parents bring inaccurate results since many children do not know the income level of the parents. The questions must be worded so that the student feels he can give an honest answer. Threatening questions can arouse anxieties that may bias the responses. Complexly designed questionnaires usually do not receive as good attention and response as those which are simply designed and easily answered.

Figure 5.4 is an example of a questionnaire which can be used for collecting a variety of general information from the student.

Projective Measures of Personality

A projective test is a relatively unstructured, yet standard, situation to which a student is asked to react. Since the individual has no clues from the examiner, he will tend to react to the situation in terms of his own personality. Unlike the yes-no type of personality inventories which tend to measure surface or willing-to-share reactions, the projective techniques tend to measure inner or depth reactions because, unknown by the examinee, he is revealing his true or total feelings to a neutral situation.

There are several ways to classify projective measures. The simplest is to place them in two general categories: those which are content-centered and those which are form-centered. The content-centered type is one in which the student is reacting primarily to the theme or feeling expressed in the object. An example of this is the *Thematic Apperception Test* (TAT) in which the student is asked to tell or write a story about some relatively ambiguous pictures. The form-centered is one in which the examinee reacts primarily to the formal characteristics of the object or picture. Thus, in the *Rorschach Inkblot Test* the student responds to such formal factors as presence of movement, tendency to use parts or wholes, organization of form, and sensitivity to color and shading.

Lindzey has proposed a classification of projective measures in terms of five general types of responses: (1) association, (2) construction, (3) completion, (4) choice of ordering, and (5) expression.[14]

The *association technique* is one in which the examinee responds to the stimulus presented by the examiner with whatever word or concept occurs to him. Examples of this include the *Rorschach Inkblot Test* and the *Word Association Test*.

In the *construction technique,* the student constructs a story or draws a picture without any restrictions placed upon him. Examples here include the *Thematic Apperception Test* (TAT), the *Make-a-Picture-Story Test* (MAPS), and the *Blacky Pictures.*

In the *completion techniques,* the examinee is asked to complete an incomplete product in any manner which he feels most suitable. Examples here include sentence-and-story completion tests.

The *choice or ordering techniques* require the examinee to arrange the alternatives in some way to meet a given criterion or to select alternatives based on relevance, correctness, appropriateness, and the like. Examples here include the *Picture Arrangement Test* and the *Szondi Test.*

---

14. G. Lindzey, "On the Classification of Projective Techniques," *Psychological Bulletin* 56:158-168, 1959.

Name _____ Date _____

Home Address _____ Telephone _____

Date of Birth _____ Place of Birth _____

Instructions: Please write or print your answers as clearly and neatly as possible. Complete all of the blanks. Where no answer can be given, use the word "none." If you are in doubt as to the meaning of any question, consult your homeroom teacher or guidance counselor.

SECTION I. FAMILY BACKGROUND

1. With whom do you live? (check one)

   father and mother _____ father only_____ mother only _____ guardian _____

2. Status of parents (check those applying)

   married __ divorced __ separated __ father dead __ mother dead __

3. Name of parents (or guardian) _____

4. Address _____ Telephone _____

5. Nationality of father _____ mother _____

6. Occupation of father _____

7. Employer _____

8. Occupation of mother _____

9. Employer _____

10. Education of father: grade school ___ high school ___ college ___

    Education of mother: grade school ___ high school ___ college ___

11. Brothers and sisters (names and ages):

    _____ _____   _____ _____

    _____ _____   _____ _____

12. Language spoken in the home _____

13. Religious preference _____

SECTION II. PERSONAL BACKGROUND

1. Special interests or hobbies: _____

   _____

2. What do you do with most of your leisure time? _____

   _____

   _____

3. What kinds of books do you enjoy? _____

   _____

4. What magazines do you read regularly? _____

   _____

5. Do you read a daily paper? _____ How many? _____

   What parts do you read? (check)

   front page _____ sports section _____

   other general news _____ women's section _____

Figure 5.4 Pupil Personnel Questionnaire. (Robert L. Gibson and Robert E. Higgins, *Techniques of Guidance* [Chicago: Science Research Associates, Inc., 1966], p. 150 © 1966, Science Research Associates, Inc. Reprinted by permission of the publisher.)

Figure 5.4   Continued

editorials _____   comics _____

entertainment news _____   advertisements _____

other

6. What kinds of motion pictures do you like best? _____

_____

7. Health condition (good, fair, poor) _____

Any physical defects? _____

_____

Have you ever had a serious illness? _____   If so, what _____

_____

Have you ever been in a serious accident? _____

If so, what? _____

_____

SECTION III. EDUCATIONAL BACKGROUND AND PLANS

1. Do you enjoy school? (check one)

always ___ usually___ sometimes ___ seldom ___ never ___

2. What subjects do you enjoy the most? (a) _____

(b) _____   (c) _____

3. What subjects do you enjoy the least? (a) _____

(b) _____   (c) _____

4. What are your favorite school activities? (a) _____

(b) _____   (c) _____

5. What courses of study are you planning to take in this school? _____

_____

6. Do you plan to continue your education after high school? _____

At what kind of institution? _____

SECTION IV. OCCUPATIONAL BACKGROUND AND PLANS

1. What occupations are you interested in?   (a) _____

(b) _____   (c) _____

2. Past occupational experience:

Type of work	Employer	Dates
(a) _____	_____	_____
(b) _____	_____	_____
(c) _____	_____	_____

3. Are you working part-time now? _____

If so, what kind of work? _____

Employer _____

If not, are you interested in part-time employment? _____

What kind of work? _____

When one uses psychodrama, sociodrama, play, drawing, and painting techniques, the *expressive techniques* of projection are being used. This is where the examinee combines a number of different stimuli into some form of production. The clinician would look for the manner and style of presentation as well as the production itself.

Unfortunately, the classroom teacher generally is not trained to use projective techniques. However, by having à knowledge of what they are and can do, the teacher can refer a child to a clinician for testing and interpretation. Most schools will have developed some working relationships with a psychologist for such referral testing either as part of their staffs or with other units in the community or area.

Profiles of Interest and Personality Inventories

Following are descriptions and profiles of some common interest and personality inventories illustrative of those commonly used.

1. *Figure 5.5. Hall Occupational Orientation Inventory*[15]

The Hall has various forms dealing with Grades 7-16 and adults. It produces 22 scores. Some Needs Met by Jobs: creativity—independence, risk, information—knowledge, belongingness, security, aspiration, esteem, self-actualization, personal satisfaction, and routine-dependence. Job Traits: data orientation, things orientation, and people orientation. Worker Traits: location concern, aptitude concern, monetary concern, physical abilities concern, environment concern, co-worker concern, qualifications concern, time concern, and defensiveness. The profile is expressed in stanine form indicating 7-9 as strong, 4-6 as mixed, and 1-3 as weak.

2. *Figure 5.6. Kuder General Interest Survey*[16]

This KGIS, also called Kuder E, is a revision and downward extension of Kuder Preference Record—Vocational, Form C. It produces eleven scores: outdoor, mechanical, computational, scientific, persuasive, artistic, literary, musical, social service, clerical, and verification. It takes approximately 45-60 minutes although it is untimed. This test is designed for grades 6-12. The most recent revision is 1970. The scores are expressed in percentiles for male and female norms.

15. From Self-Interpreting Profile Sheet, *Hall Occupational Orientation Inventory* devised by L. G. Hall. Profile is reproduced with permission of Scholastic Testing Service, Inc., Bensenville, IL. © 1975.

16. From the *Kuder General Interest Survey*, Form E, by G. Frederic Kuder. © 1976, 1963, G. Frederic Kuder. Profile is reprinted by permission of the publisher, Science Research Associates, Inc.

Self-Interpreting Profile Sheet for the
Hall Occupational Orientation Inventory

Page 4 of your *Interpretive Folder* is a profile sheet to be used if you score the Inventory yourself. If the Inventory has been machine-scored, use this profile sheet instead of the one in your folder. To complete your profile, follow the directions at the bottom of this page; then insert this sheet as page 4 in your *Interpretive Folder*.

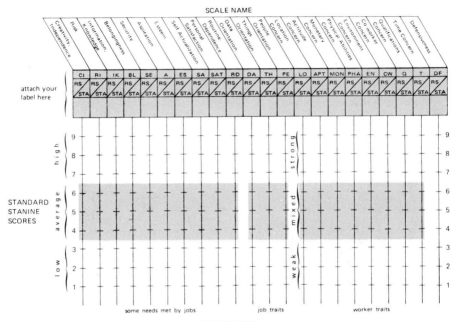

DIRECTIONS

1. Peel your label off its backing, and place it on the box above the profile chart. You do not need any glue or paste; the label will stick as you press it into place. Be sure you line up the abbreviations on the label with those printed on the profile sheet.

2. There are two numbers for each scale on your label. The top number is your raw score, and the bottom number is your stanine for that scale. Find your stanine for each scale and mark an X where the stanine line crosses the scale line. For example, if you have a stanine of 5 for "Creativity, Independence," you should mark an X where the line for stanine 5 crosses the vertical line under "CI." Mark the stanine for each of your 22 scales.

3. Now use a ruler to join the first X with the second X, the second X with the third X, and so on. This line is your career inventory profile.

Copyright © 1975 by L. G. Hall
Published by Scholastic Testing Service, Inc.
Bensenville, Illinois 60106

Figure 5.5 Sample Profile: Hall Occupational Orientation Inventory. (Reproduced with permission of Scholastic Testing Service, Inc., Bensenville, IL. © 1975.)

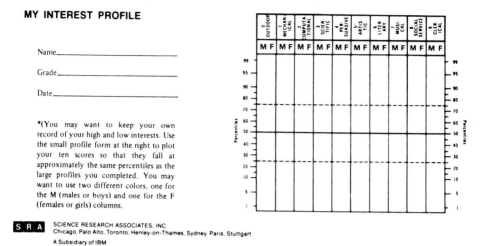

MY INTEREST PROFILE

Name

Grade

Date

*(You may want to keep your own record of your high and low interests. Use the small profile form at the right to plot your ten scores so that they fall at approximately the same percentiles as the large profiles you completed. You may want to use two different colors, one for the M (males or boys) and one for the F (females or girls) columns.

S R A SCIENCE RESEARCH ASSOCIATES, INC.
Chicago, Palo Alto, Toronto, Henley-on-Thames, Sydney, Paris, Stuttgart
A Subsidiary of IBM

Figure 5.6 Sample Profile: Kuder General Interest Survey. (From the *Kuder General Interest Survey,* Form E, by G. Frederic Kuder. © 1976, 1963, G. Frederic Kuder. Reprinted by permission of the publisher, Science Research Associates, Inc.)

3. *Figure 5.7. Strong-Campbell Interest Inventory*[17]

This new, unisex form of the SCII was designed to rectify the possible sexist editions previously published in which there were separate forms for men and women It is designed for ages 16 and over. There are 155 scoring scales (6 general occupational themes, 23 basic interest scales, 124 occupational scales, and 2 special scales) and 23 administrative indexes. The general theme scales yield scores on each of Holland's "personality-interest" types: realistic, investigative, artistic, social, enterprising, and conventional. These are expressed in standard scores units with a mean of 50 and an SD of 10. The Occupational Scales are expressed in descriptive phrases from very dissimilar to very similar.

4. *Figure 5.8. California Test of Personality*[18]

This test is produced on four levels: K-3, 4-8, 7-10, 9-14 adults. It provides for 15 scores divided into Personal Adjustment, Social Adjustment, and Total Adjustment. Under Personal Adjustment are included: self-reliance, sense of personal worth, sense of personal freedom, freedom from withdrawal tendencies, and freedom from nervous symptoms. Included

17. From the SCII Profile Sheet of the *Strong-Campbell Interest Inventory* by Edward K. Strong and David P. Campbell. Obtainable from and used with permission of NCS/Interpretive Scoring Systems, 4401 W. 76th Street, Minneapolis, MN 55435.

18. Profile from *California Test of Personality*. Reprinted by permission of the publisher, CTB/McGraw-Hill, Del Monte Research Park, Monterey, CA 93940. Copyright © 1953 by McGraw-Hill, Inc. All Rights Reserved. Printed in the U.S.A.

under Social Adjustment are: social standards, social skills, anti-social tendencies, family relations, school relations, and community relations. Each of the scores is expressed in percentile form. Although an old test (1953), it is still considered a good, simple inventory of adjustment.

5. *Figure 5.9. California Psychological Inventory*[19]

This highly researched instrument is designed for ages 13 and above. It has proven useful in counseling of high school and college students. Research indicates that it can help select talented youth and can predict delinquent behavior. It has been used in basic research on interactionism and moral development. It produces 18 scores: dominance, capacity for status, sociability, social presence, self-acceptance, sense of well-being, responsibility, socialization, self-control, tolerance, good impression, communality, achievement via conformance, achievement via independence, intellectual efficiency, psychological mindedness, flexibility, and femininity. The scores are expressed as standard scores with a mean of 50 and an SD of 10.

6. *Figure 5.10. Vineland Social Maturity Scale*[20]

This is one of the oldest personality measures. It is designed for use from birth to maturity. It is an age scale with items scaled for age under the headings of self-help general, self-help dressing, self-help eating, communication, self-direction, socialization, locomotion, and occupation. A total age equivalent and a total social quotient are obtained. It is an observational tool in which the subject may or may not be present. The informant should be someone closely related to the subject, like the parent or guardian.

7. *Figure 5.11. Jesness Behavior Checklist*[21]

This checklist was developed as a research instrument to be used to record data on delinquent boys in a training school setting. It offers two methods for the measurement of social behavior: self-ratings and observer ratings. It is designed for ages 10 and over. It produces scores in 14 areas: Unobtrusiveness, friendliness, responsibility, considerateness, independence, rapport, enthusiasm, sociability, conformity, calmness, effective communication, insight, social control, and anger control. The scores are expressed in T-score form and in percentiles.

19. Profile Sheet for the *California Psychological Inventory: Male,* devised by Harrison G. Gough. Obtainable from and used by permission of the NCS/Interpretive Scoring Systems, 4401 W. 76th Street, Minneapolis, MN 55435. © 1975.

20. Profile sheet from Test Booklet of the *Vineland Social Maturity Scale,* devised by Edgar A. Doll. Reproduced by special permission of American Guidance Service. © 1965.

21. Profile Sheet (Male Delinquent Norms) of the *Jesness Behavior Checklist.* Devised by Carl F. Jesness. Used by permission of the publisher, Consulting Psychologists Press, Palo Alto, CA. © 1971.

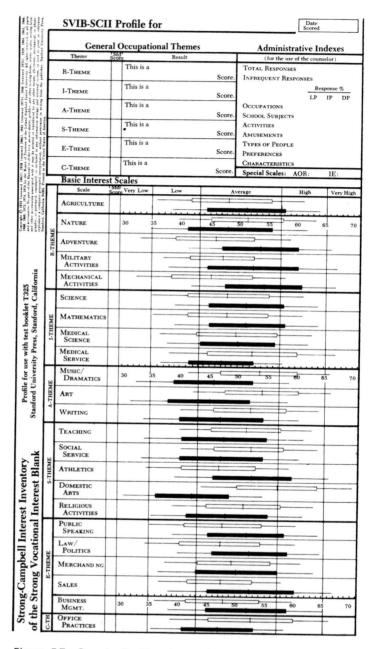

Figure 5.7 Sample Profile: Strong-Campbell Interest Inventory. Obtainable from and used with permission of NCS/Interpretive Scoring Systems, 4401 W. 76th Street, Minneapolis, MN 55435.

Occupational Scales

Code	Scale	Sex Norm	Std Score / Profile (Very Dissimilar · Dissimilar · Ave · Similar · Very Similar)
RC	Farmer	m	
RC	Instrum. Assembl.	f	
RCE	Voc. Agric. Tchr.	m	
REC	Dietitian	m	
RES	Police Officer	m	
RSE	Hwy. Patrol Off.	m	
RE	Army Officer	f	
RS	Phys. Ed. Teacher	f	
R	Skilled Crafts	m	
RI	Forester	m	
RI	Rad. Tech. (X-ray)	f	
RI	Merch. Mar. Off.	m	
RI	Navy Officer	m	
RI	Nurse, Registered	m	
RI	Veterinarian	m	15 25 45 55
RIC	Cartographer	m	
RIC	Army Officer	m	
RIE	Air Force Officer	m	
RIA	Occup. Therapist	f	
IR	Engineer	f	
IR	Engineer	m	
IR	Chemist	f	
IR	Physical Scientist	m	
IR	Medical Tech.	f	
IR	Pharmacist	f	
IR	Dentist	f	
IR	Dentist	m	15 25 45 55
IR	Dental Hygienist	f	
IRS	Phys. Therapist	f	
IRS	Physician	m	
IRS	Math-Sci. Teacher	m	
ICR	Math-Sci. Teacher	f	
IC	Dietitian	f	
IRC	Medical Tech.	m	
IRC	Optometrist	m	
IRC	Computer Progr.	f	
IRC	Computer Progr.	m	
I	Mathematician	f	
I	Mathematician	m	15 25 45 55
I	Physicist	m	
I	Biologist	m	
I	Veterinarian	f	
I	Optometrist	f	
I	Physician	f	
I	Social Scientist	m	
IA	College Professor	f	
IA	College Professor	m	
IS	Speech Pathol.	f	
IS	Speech Pathol.	m	
IAS	Psychologist	f	
IAS	Psychologist	m	15 25 45 55
IA	Language Interpr.	f	
ARI	Architect	m	
A	Advertising Exec.	f	
A	Artist	f	
A	Artist	m	
A	Art Teacher	f	
A	Photographer	m	
A	Musician	f	
A	Musician	m	
A	Entertainer	f	
AE	Int. Decorator	f	

Occupational Scales

Code	Scale	Sex Norm	Std Score / Profile (Very Dissimilar · Dissimilar · Ave · Similar · Very Similar)
AE	Int. Decorator	m	
AE	Advertising Exec.	m	
A	Language Teacher	f	
A	Librarian	f	
A	Librarian	m	
A	Reporter	f	
A	Reporter	m	
AS	English Teacher	f	
AS	English Teacher	m	
SI	Nurse, Registered	f	
SIR	Phys. Therapist	m	
SRC	Nurse, Lic. Pract.	m	
S	Social Worker	f	
S	Social Worker	m	15 25 45 55
S	Priest	m	
S	Dir., Christian Ed.	f	
SE	YWCA Staff	f	
SIE	Minister	m	
SEA	Elem. Teacher	m	
SC	Elem. Teacher	f	
SCE	Sch. Superintend.	m	
SCE	Public Administr.	m	
SCE	Guidance Couns.	m	
SER	Recreation Leader	f	
SEC	Recreation Leader	m	
SEC	Guidance Couns.	f	
SEC	Soc. Sci. Teacher	m	15 25 45 55
SEC	Soc. Sci. Teacher	m	
SEC	Personnel Dir.	m	
ESC	Dept. Store Mgr.	m	
ESC	Home Econ. Tchr.	f	
ESA	Flight Attendant	f	
ES	Ch. of Comm. Exec.	m	
ES	Sales Manager	m	
ES	Life Ins. Agent	m	
E	Life Ins. Agent	f	
E	Lawyer	f	
E	Lawyer	m	15 25 45 55
EI	Computer Sales	m	
EI	Investm. Fund Mgr.	m	
EIC	Pharmacist	m	
EC	Buyer	f	
ECS	Buyer	m	
ECS	Credit Manager	m	
ECS	Funeral Director	m	
ECR	Realtor	m	
ERC	Agribusiness Mgr.	m	
ERC	Purchasing Agent	m	
ESR	Chiropractor	m	
CE	Accountant	m	
CE	Banker	f	15 25 45 55
CE	Banker	m	
CE	Credit Manager	f	
CE	Dept. Store Sales	f	
CE	Business Ed. Tchr.	f	
CES	Business Ed. Tchr.	m	
CSE	Exec. Housekeeper	f	
C	Accountant	f	
C	Secretary	f	
CR	Dental Assistant	f	
CRI	Nurse, Lic. Pract.	f	
CRE	Beautician	f	

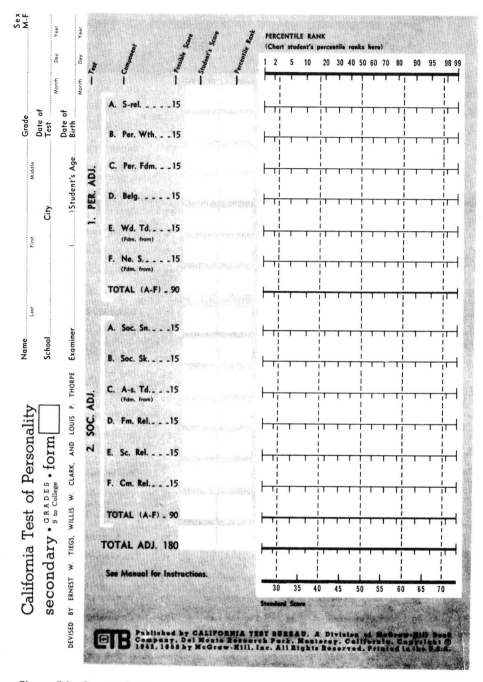

Figure 5.8   Sample Profile: California Test of Personality. (Ffrom *California Test of Personality*. Reprinted by permission of the publisher, CTB/McGraw-Hill, Del Monte Research Park, Monterey, CA 93940. Copyright © 1953 by McGraw-Hill, Inc. All Rights Reserved. Printed in the U.S.A.)

PROFILE SHEET FOR THE *California Psychological Inventory*: **MALE**

Name _____ Age _____ Date Tested _____

Other Information _____

Notes:

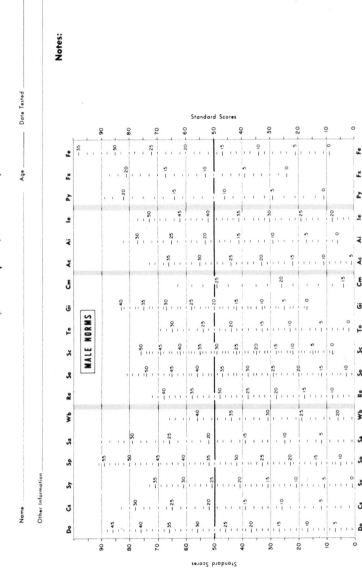

MALE NORMS

Standard Scores

Male Norms

Figure 5.9 Sample Profile: California Psychological Inventory. (Obtainable from and used with permission of NCS/Interpretive Scoring Systems, 4401 W. 76th Street, Minneapolis, MN 55435.)

AGS

Vineland Social Maturity Scale

BY EDGAR A. DOLL, Ph.D.

NAME .... Sex .... Grade .... Date .... Year .... Month .... Day
Last   First

Residence .... School .... Born .... Year .... Month .... Day

M.A. .... I.Q. .... Test Used .... When .... Age .... Years .... Months .... Days

Occupation .... Class .... Years Exp. .... Schooling ....

Father's Occupation .... Class .... Years Exp. .... Schooling ....

Mother's Occupation .... Class .... Years Exp. .... Schooling ....

Informant .... Relationship .... Recorder ....

Informant's est. .... Basal Score* .... Additional pts. .... Total score ....

Age equivalent ....

Social quotient ....

R E M A R K S :

Age Periods

O - I

Category†	Score*	Items	LA Mean
C		1. "Crows"; laughs	.25
SHG		2. Balances head	.25
SHG		3. Grasps objects within reach	.30
S		4. Reaches for familiar persons	.30
SHG		5. Rolls over	.30
SHG		6. Reaches for nearby objects	.35
O		7. Occupies self unattended	.43
SHG		8. Sits unsupported	.45
SHG		9. Pulls self upright	.55
C		10. "Talks"; imitates sounds	.55
SHE		11. Drinks from cup or glass assisted	.55
L		12. Moves about on floor	.63
SHG		13. Grasps with thumb and finger	.65
S		14. Demands personal attention	.70
SHG		15. Stands alone	.85
SHE		16. Does not drool	.90
C		17. Follows simple instructions	.93

† Key to categorical arrangement of items:

S H G — Self-help general C — Communication L — Locomotion
S H D — Self-help dressing S D — Self-direction O — Occupation
S H E — Self-help eating S — Socialization

* For method of scoring see "The Measurement of Social Competence."

AMERICAN GUIDANCE SERVICE, INC.
PUBLISHERS' BUILDING, CIRCLE PINES, MINNESOTA 55014

Figure 5.10 Sample Profile: Vineland Social Maturity Scale (Reproduced by special permission of American Guidance Service.)

175

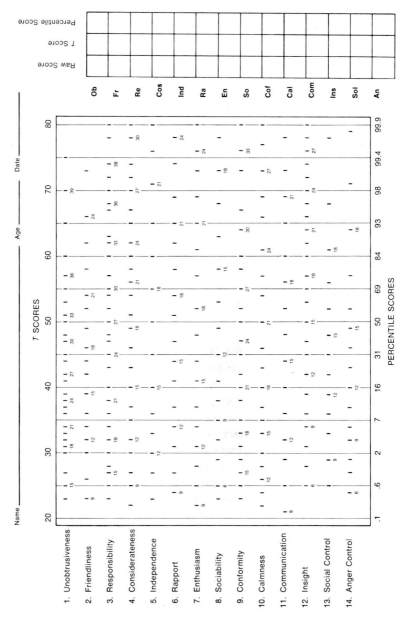

Figure 5.11 Sample Profile: Jesness Behavior Checklist. (Devised by Carl F. Jesness. Used by permission of the publisher, Consulting Psychologists Press, Palo Alto, CA.)

Summary Statements

1. Observation is the use of the more subjective instruments or instruments of judgment that may yield quantitative data or results but more often qualitative or descriptive results.
2. If observation can be done objectively and reliably, it can be a very valid measurement because it is a direct measure of pupil performance.
3. The limitations of observations can be classified under three categories: failure to keep in mind specific behaviors to be observed; failure to use good principles of observation; and failure to plan opportunities for observation.
4. There are four basic types of observational tools: Participation Charts; Checklists; Rating Scales; and Anecdotal Records.
5. The process of adjustment is the individual's attempt to create a more harmonious relationship between himself and his environment.
6. The basic methods of evaluating personal-social adjustment can be grouped under four main headings: observational tools, sociometric and related techniques, self-report inventories, and projective techniques.
7. *Self-Report Inventories* are those in which an individual tells about himself through varied degrees of structured instruments.
8. *Projective Measures of Personality* are relatively unstructured, depth type of measures which consciously or unconsciously reveal the subject's inner reactions or feelings.
9. Many standardized Interest and Personality inventories are available, the results of which can aid the teacher and/or counselor in working with individuals of all ages.

Discussion Questions

1. How do you justify observational tools, admittedly subjective, as measurement devices?
2. Explain the reference to the idea that the results of observation should be a more valid indication of the student's ability to use and apply what has been taught than any other measurement.
3. Discuss the difference betwen casual observation and systematic observation.
4. Describe the process by which a teacher develops an observational tool from the beginning to the actual format of the device.
5. Explain how you would defend the use of a participation chart to someone who said: "But Mary is timid and shy; she will never voluntarily discuss issues in class."
6. Explain how you would determine whether you would use a checklist or a rating scale for a given objective.

7. Discuss the difference between an *observer-description* type of observation and the *observer-evaluation* type. Give an example of each type.
8. Describe the basic objective in each of the four types of interviews included in this chapter: Obtain information, give information, interpret data, and engage in therapy.
9. Explain the common theme underlying each of the techniques listed under *Sociometric and Related Techniques* in this chapter. Then tell how each differs from the others.
10. Based on the description of each in this chapter, discuss which grade levels, K-12, each of the *Self-Report Inventories* might be realistically used.
11. Explain what the student does in each of the five types of projective measures as classified by Lindzey in this chapter.

Student Activities

1. Study Figure 5.1 in this chapter, Charting Participation in Small Groups, and write a page summary of your analysis of each student's participation. Be prepared to read your analysis in class. Will other summaries be similar to yours?
2. Select an objective for which a basic checklist might be used. Develop the specific traits or characteristics which will serve as check points and place them into a format for actual use.
3. Select a specific trait for which a rating scale may be used. Develop each type of rating scale format for this trait—numerical, graphic (constant alternatives and changing-alternatives). Summarize your views on the difficulties of preparing each type and which type you believe most functional.
4. Write a review of the following anecdote using the principles on pages 144-146 as your criteria.

> Name: Sue Kelly
> Date: 2/9
> Observer: Harriet Stevens
>   Sue has won our first art contest. When she was offered a prize for her second success, she gave it to Darlene, who was runner-up. Darlene accepted it without any expression of appreciation. Sue seems to be a well-adjusted child and quite sensitive to the needs of other children. It was a particularly noble gesture for her to give Darlene the prize since Darlene is very selfish and uncooperative with her peers.

5. Select your own subject and topic and conduct an interview which has as its basic purpose that of *Obtaining Information*. Write a report of the interview in 200-300 words.

6. Observe a child or a fellow student in an academic situation for a 30-minute period of time using the *Time Sampling Technique*. Write a report in the manner shown in this chapter.
7. From direct observation or from your knowledge of child or adolescent development, list six characteristics which would be appropriate for a *"Guess Who" Questionnaire*.
8. Select a personal-social adjustment inventory reviewed in Buros' *Mental Measurements Yearbook* and write a 200-300 word critical review of its value and use on the grade levels for which it is designed.
9. Using the format of the *Pupil-Personnel Questionnaire* illustrated in Figure 5.4, fill it out on a child or youth of your own choosing. Leave out questions which would not be appropriate for a specific age or grade level. Add a paragraph at the end indicating the degree to which you learned additional knowledge which helped you better understand the child or youth.

Selected Readings

Ahmann, J. Stanley, and Glock, Marvin D. *Evaluating Pupil Growth*, 5th ed. Boston: Allyn and Bacon, Inc., 1975. Chapters 7 and 13.

Anastasi, Anne. *Psychological Testing*, 4th ed. New York: The Macmillan Company, 1976. Chapters 17-20.

Bennion, Donald H. *Assessing Student Learning*. Dubuque, Iowa: Kendall-Hunt Book Co., 1977. Chapters 7 and 8.

Brown, Frederick G. *Principles of Educational and Psychological Testing*, 2nd ed. New York: Holt, Rinehart and Winston, Inc., 1976. Chapters 17 and 18.

Cartwright, Carol A., and Cartwright, G. Phillip. *Developing Observation Skills*. New York: McGraw-Hill Book Co., 1974.

Cronbach, Lee J. *Essentials of Psychological Testing*, 3rd ed. New York: Harper & Row Publishers, Inc., 1970. Chapter 17.

Ebel, Robert L. *Essentials of Educational Measurement*, 3rd ed. Englewood Cliffs, NJ: Prentice-Hall, Inc., 1979. Chapter 19.

Gronlund, Norman E. *Measurement and Evaluation in Teaching*, 3rd ed. New York: The Macmillan Company, 1976. Chapter 16.

Hopkins, Charles D., and Antes, Richard L. *Classroom Measurement and Evaluation*. Itasca, IL: F. E. Peacock Publishers, Inc., 1978. Chapter 3.

Mehrens, William A., and Lehmann, Irvin J. *Measurement and Evaluation in Education and Psychology*. New York: Holt, Rinehart and Winston, Inc., 1973. Chapter 12.

Noll, Victor H., Scannell, Dale P., and Craig, Robert C. *Introduction to Educational Measurement*, 4th ed. Boston: Houghton Mifflin Company, 1979. Chapter 12.

Thorndike, Robert L., and Hagen, Elizabeth. *Measurement and Evaluation in Psychology and Education*, 4th ed. New York: John Wiley & Sons, Inc., 1977. Chapter 11-13.

Tuckman, Bruce W. *Measuring Educational Outcomes: Fundamentals of Testing*. New York: Harcourt Brace Jovanovich, Inc., 1975. Chapter 14.

6

Judging Procedures, Products, and Performances

What is the need for judging procedures, products, and performances?
What are the assessment methods and instruments available?
What are examples of standardized instruments?
What are examples of teacher-made instruments?
    Work-Sample Tests
    Identification Tests
    Simulated Conditions Tests
    Assignments and Projects

A. What Is the Need for Judging Procedures, Products, and Performances?

There are many clichés which serve to introduce the need for judging procedures, products, and performances. For example, "He knows what he is talking about, but he can't do it" or "Those who can, do; but those who can't, teach" or "He knows his economic theory, but he can't balance a budget." These all emphasize the idea that knowledge and understanding are important, but if you can't *apply* it, your education is partly lacking.

Although everyone should learn to apply the information one is learning, the application is especially important in such fields as speech, music, art, drama, foreign languages, physical education, science, journalism, and vocational education, among others.

Performance-type assessment has many values.

1. It is suitable for many learning objectives.
2. It is application-oriented.
3. It is less dependent on reading or writing skills.
4. It eliminates much paper-and-pencil testing.
5. It serves as an alternative assessment for those with reading or writing problems.

6. It promotes creativity.
7. It makes learning relevant.
8. It gets the student involved.
9. It helps the student assess his own learning.
10. It is fun.

Judging procedures, products, and performances poses some problems. Some users have said that these types of assessment are difficult to make; it is difficult, at times, to break a task down into its parts for evaluation; these techniques are limited to certain fields; these assessments are difficult to administer and are very time consuming; and it is difficult to check for the validity of these assessments. Although each of these statements may have some truth in it, the same problems might be stated for many other forms of assessment. The key point is that in a good program of evaluation there must be a diversity of assessment instruments to reach the various objectives. Also, it provides another avenue by which the student can show his growth toward the goals of instruction.

B. What Are the Assessment Methods and Instruments Available?

The instruments available in this area fall into three basic categories: (1) Standardized Tests; (2) Teacher-Made Instruments; and (3) Observational Tools. *The first two will be discussed in this chapter and the third one, Observational Tools, were covered in the previous chapter.*

C. What Are Examples of Standardized Instruments?

In Chapter 10, a section is devoted to aptitude tests. Some of these can be classified as performance assessment. Following are some titles with a statement of the performance which is covered in each case.

1. *Bennett Hand-Tool Dexterity Test.* This tests proficiency in the use of wrenches and screwdrivers.
2. *Detroit Clerical Aptitude Examination.* This measures eight clerical skills, including a handwriting scale.
3. *General Aptitude Test Battery.* The GATB measures aptitude in ten areas including spatial, clerical perception, eye-hand coordination, finger dexterity among others.
4. *Modern Language Aptitude Test.* Through the use of a tape recording, this test measures the individual's probable degree of success in learning a foreign language.
5. *Seashore Measures of Musical Talent.* Includes tests of pitch, loudness, rhythm, timbre among others.
6. *Torrance Tests of Creative Thinking.* These tests appear in verbal and figural versions.

In addition to measuring performance in specific areas such as the above, there are performance tests, or parts of tests, in the area of mental measurement. These are very helpful in trying to obtain a more accurate measure of ability where understanding of the language or working with verbal symbols would be difficult. Following are a few examples.

1. *Wechsler Intelligence Scales—Nonverbal or performance parts.* The Wechsler Scales include both a verbal and nonverbal or performance scale. The latter is helpful in measuring the non-language or performance ability of an individual. This includes such tests as picture arrangement, block design, object assembly, and coding, among others. This part produces a performance or nonverbal IQ.

2. *Goodenough Draw-a-Man Test.* In this test, the individual is simply instructed to make a picture of a man, to make the very best picture that he can. Emphasis is placed on the child's accuracy of observation and on the development of conceptual thinking rather than on artistic skill.

3. *The Leiter International Performance Scale.* This is an individual performance scale. It is almost devoid of verbal instructions. All tests are administered by attaching the appropriate card, containing printed pictures, to a frame. The examinee chooses the block with the proper response pictures and inserts them into the frame.

4. *The Bender Visual Motor Gestalt Test.* This test consists of nine designs, presented one at a time on cards. The subject is instructed to copy each design. The test has promise as a rapid screening device, especially for detecting the more serious forms of disturbance.

D.   What Are Examples of Teacher-Made Instruments?

The teacher-made instruments of performance include (1) work-sample tests; (2) identification tests; (3) simulated conditions; and (4) assignments and projects.

Work--Sample Tests

In this type of exercise, a job analysis is made of the task for which the student is trained. From this job analysis, a sampling of the basic elements is included on the test. Where possible, the actual tools and tasks should be used. It may be as simple as putting together a woodworking plane and getting it ready for use or as complex as completing a federal income tax return. It is applicable to any course where a task or process can be broken down into component parts and the student is asked to perform the tasks in either a timed or untimed fashion. Following is an example of a problem situation presented in a Consumer Education course in high school. Discussion has been held on how to figure the costs of cars and the student is asked to figure the total cost for a car with standard transmission or one with automatic transmission.

You want to buy a new car and have decided on the Honda Civic, 2-door sedan. You aren't sure whether you want the car with standard transmission, 5 radial tires, and AM radio; *or* with automatic transmission and AM radio. Listed below are the dealer's prices and other costs of purchasing a car. Items marked with an asterisk (*) are necessary costs. Figure the cost of each of the 2 choices.

DEALER'S PRICES

*Base price (standard transmission)	$3989.00
*Dealer preparation	80.00
Automatic transmission	400.00
AM radio	85.00
*Shipping (from Baton Rouge)	185.00
Radial tires (per tire)	35.00

OTHER COSTS

*License (this is your first car)	18.15
*Registration	1.00

*4% sales tax—to be figured on total
      cost of car excluding license and
      registration

To figure the cost of each of the two choices, do this:

1. Add (a) costs related to the choice.
        (b) necessary dealer's prices.
2. Multiply the total by 4%.
3. Add costs for license and registration to total.

The final answers are _____ and _____.
           (choice 1)   (choice 2)

Identification Tests

As the title implies, the student is asked to identify parts of an object, drawing, picture, chart, and the like. It might be used as a recall-supply type in which the student is asked to identify a specific part of the object or drawing and write down the answer on an answer sheet. It might be a recognition-select type where the pupil is given a list of possible answers and then selects the letter of the correct part and writes it down (as in a matching type). When possible, the real object should be used. When this is not possible, a drawing or a picture of the object is duplicated and students work from a dittoed or mimeographed sheet on which to make their identification.

Sometimes in addition to identifying the part, the student is asked to explain its function. For example, in art a student might be asked to identify the various wood finishes and explain when each would be used. In music

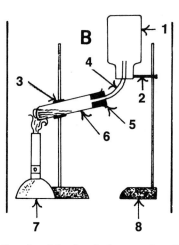

Directions: In the blanks below write in the correct name of each of the numbered parts of the apparatus pictured above.

1. _____
2. _____
3. _____
4. _____
5. _____
6. _____
7. _____
8. _____

Figure 6.1   Example of an Identification Test in Science.

appreciation, a student might be asked to identify the instruments of a symphony orchestra and the function they normally perform. In English, a paragraph might be presented and a student asked to identify the topic sentence, main idea, as well as the subject, verb, and object of each sentence. A sample division problem might be presented and the student asked to identify the dividend, divisor, remainder.

Figure 6.1 is an example of an identification test in a general science unit.

Simulated Conditions Tests

In this type of test, the teacher tries to simulate in the classroom the actual conditions which the real situation includes. In a business education office practice class, a simulated business office is developed and students are asked to perform specific tasks. In driver education, the use of trainers and visual media is coordinated to have the student perform in an almost life-like situation. In science class, the students have been studying how to test for the goodness of water and to purify it for drinking. Although it would be possible to take the class out to a stream and run the experiment, it might be difficult for the entire class to participate. In this case, you might want to simulate a situation on paper and have the students tell how they would purify the water to make it consumable. Such as: The English class of Whitewater High School went on a picnic to Wakonda Park. They brought everything along for the picnic except something to drink. Dick said, "There is a stream over there; let's get some water to drink." Tell how you would purify the water to make it safe to drink.

Assignments and Projects

Most teachers give assignments and projects, the frequency depending upon the subject and level. These are considered learning activities to help the students grow toward the goals of instruction. However, if they are carefully constructed, administered, and analyzed, they can provide much evaluative information.

TenBrink summarizes the design of projects and assignments in the following manner.[1] Even though the principles appear to be more closely designed for assignments, many of the same principles apply toward projects.

1. Assignments or projects designed to provide the teacher with useful evaluative information should: (a) engage the student at some stage in the attainment of specific instruction goals; (b) include complete instructions clearly presented; (c) be reasonable; and (d) result in a performance or product which could be readily analyzed.
2. The following suggestions should help you to select or design projects and assignments which will be useful for obtaining evaluative information. These will just be listed here and then each will be developed in the following points starting with No. 3.
   a. Decide what the student is supposed to learn from the experience.
   b. Decide what information you wish to obtain about the student.
   c. Determine what the students are to do.
   d. Determine how the students are to communicate the results of what they have done.
   e. Formulate instructions to the students.
   f. Establish the rules and the rationale for the analyses to be made.
3. *Decide what the student is supposed to learn from the experience.* Every assignment you give should be designed specifically to help the student reach (or move toward) some instructional goal. It may take several assignments to help a student reach a particular goal. In that case, you should state precisely how each assignment is to help the student attain the goal and you should decide exactly what the student should learn if he completes the assignment correctly.

1. Terry TenBrink, *Evaluation: A Practical Guide for Teachers* (New York: McGraw-Hill Book Company, 1974), p. 335.

The kind of learning, the level of learning, and the stage of the learning process all make a difference in what you should have the student do. It is valuable for you to know what kinds of learning a student is having trouble with and at what stage in the learning process the trouble is occurring. *The kind of learning* refers to whether it is in the cognitive domain, the affective domain, or the psychomotor domain. The *level of learning* refers to the levels within a domain (e.g., cognitive: knowledge, comprehension, application, and the like). The *stage of learning* refers to the stage at which the learning occurs:

Acquisition Stage—The student is learning new information.

Retention Stage—The learned information or skill is practiced so it will be retained.

Transfer Stage—Retrieve information and use it in a new situation.

4. *Decide what information you wish to obtain about the student.* We have said above that every assignment or project should provide information about the student's progress toward *expected learning outcomes.* By analyzing the assignments or projects of the students, one can discover both good and bad *unexpected outcomes.* This might include additional information learned; misinformation or bad habits learned; attitudes, opinions, and interests resulting from the learning activities; and additional communication skills developed.

5. *Determine what the students are to do.* The question that must be answered here is, "What kind of assignment will help the students reach the instructional goals which have been established and will, at the same time, make it possible for me (the teacher) to obtain needed evaluative information?" There are basically three kinds of assignments which were alluded to in No. 3: The acquisition assignments, the review (or retention) assignments, and the transfer assignments. Remember that the *acquisition assignments* are designed primarily to help students acquire new information or skills. There are three major questions that acquisition assignments can help to answer.

   a. Did the students learn the knowledge or skill, that is, grow toward the objective?

   b. How fast did the students acquire the knowledge or skill?

   c. What kinds of errors did the student make during acquisition or what misinformation did he acquire?

Assignments designed to help the student *review* and practice can make the difference between students who take the newly gained knowledge and skills with them and those who forget the knowledge and skill. Occasional review assignments allow you to find out, at various times after acquisition, how much is being retained. They can also help you spot unexpected learning outcomes early, such as misinformation or bad habits. These can then be corrected before the student is asked to transfer the information. In review assignments, you usually ask the student to show his work or attach his work so you can spot where errors occur.

Transfer assignments should provide an opportunity for the student to apply or relate his new knowledge and skills to new situations. By varying the conditions under which transfer is required, you can learn under what conditions transfer of particular knowledge or skills does occur and under which conditions it does not occur.

6. *Determine how the students are to communicate the results of what they have done.* There are three important characteristics of the student's response to an assignment: the mode of the response, the length of response, and the relative freedom to respond. The mode of the response must provide the opportunity for the student to grow toward the objective for which it is designed (e.g., if the *action* in the objective is "writes," than an oral response would not be appropriate). Also, the mode should allow you to make the kind of analysis you want to make. A performance (speech) gives you limited analysis whereas a product (written work, object, drawing) allows you to make an extended analysis. Observational tools can be used to analyze nonverbal performances (tennis) and nonverbal products (table). Content analysis procedures can be used to evaluate verbal performances and products.

   Also to be considered here is the length of the response and the sampling. The length will give you greater opportunity to check learning and therefore will be more reliable. A greater length will allow for greater sampling. Here, one must be sure that the sample is uniform over the outcomes being measured.

7. *Formulate instructions to the students.* Instructions should be very clear so the student knows the purpose for which the assignment is given; second, so he knows how to go about doing it; and third, how the results will be used.

   In the first place, share with the student the objective or outcome for which the assignment or project is given. For example:

Outcome:	Give examples of valid types of measurement for a specific purpose.
Assignment:	This assignment will help you grow toward understanding the concept of validity.

   In helping him with the learning activity, describe for him the parameters within which he can work. What is the length? Should it be typed? Do you want footnotes? Can students work together on it? The more they know about the boundaries of the assignment or project, the faster and better they can approach and complete it.

   Third, tell the students how you plan to use the results. Will you mark it up and return it to them to correct? What are the criteria you will use to evaluate it? Will it be graded? If so, how much will it count? Then, when you have included these main facets or characteristics of a good assignment or project, you can have more assurance that students know what is expected of them.

8. *Establish the rules and the rationale for the analyses to be made.* Before you give an assignment or project, decide what kind of an analysis you plan to make: content analysis or observation. Content analysis is useful for analyzing oral or written verbal communications. Observation is best for analyzing performance and nonverbal products. This is then followed by asking what things you will look for. For example, in the evaluation of students developing test items, the author might indicate:

   The items will be checked for the following:
   —Does the item measure growth toward the objective?
   —Does it follow the principles of making that item?
   —Is it produced properly, including space where the answer is to be given?

Measurement and Evaluation
March 14

ASSIGNMENT ON RUNNING A CORRELATION AND INTERPRETING THE COEFFICIENT

Instructions: Two unit objectives have been to run a correlation and to interpret the coefficient obtained from it. This will help you sharpen your skill in running a correlation and check your understanding of interpreting correlation coefficients.

Be sure to work slowly and carefully; double check every entry. In showing your progression under the formula, be sure to include each step as in the model. Show division on the back of the paper. Think through your interpretation very carefully and write it so that it is clear to anyone reading it.

The paper will be checked for:

—accuracy within the correlation table.
—correct progression to the answer under the formula.
—reporting the answer correctly to two places.
—making the correct interpretation including both the sign and the size of the coefficient.

Use of Results

This is a review assignment and will not be graded. I will mark it so you profit from your mistakes. We will go over common errors in class. I will check with each of you to see if you understand any difficulties you had. This assignment will be followed by one asking you to apply your skill in running a correlation and interpreting it in a new situation. That one will be graded for evaluation.

Figure 6.2   Giving an Assignment.

Application of results

The items will not be graded but will be marked up for you to profit from any errors. Some of you will be asked to place yours on the board for class discussion as an example of a good item.

Figure 6.2 is a sample of a measurement course assignment.

Summary Statements

1. It is important to have knowledge and understanding of things, but it is equally, if not more, important to be able to apply the knowledge one has learned through performance and procedures or in products.
2. There are three basic assessment tools in this area: standardized tests; teacher-made instruments; and observational tools.
3. Standardized instruments usually take the form of aptitude tests; e.g., measuring ability in a specific field. However, some performance or nonverbal scales are built to measure general ability or to diagnose for specific visual or motor skills.
4. Teacher-made instruments may take four forms: work-sample tests; identification tests; simulated conditions tests; and assignments and projects.

5. A work-sample test is given when a job analysis is made of a performance and a student is to perform the tasks in either a timed or untimed situation.
6. An identification test is one in which the student is asked to identify parts of an object, drawing, picture, chart, and the like. When possible, the real object should be used but, if impossible, the object can be duplicated on paper and the student can identify from the reproduction.
7. A simulated conditions test is one in which the teacher tries to simulate in the classroom the actual conditions which the real situation includes. By having the student perform in this mock situation, the instructor can determine the quality of performance.
8. Although assignments and projects are considered learning activities, if they are carefully constructed, administered, and analyzed, they can provide much evaluative information.

Discussion Questions

1. The use of procedures, products, and performances has many values and some drawbacks. Summarize briefly the values and limitations of this area of evaluation.
2. Discuss the validity of standardized tests as a means of judging the performance of an individual. What is the assumption on which aptitude tests are built which enables us to use them in a counseling situation?
3. Develop a general objective with 2-3 specific, sample behavior objectives under it for each of the types of teacher-made instruments—work-sample tests; identification tests; simulated conditions tests; and assignments and projects.

Student Activities

Using the same or a new objective from the ones in number 3 above, develop a measuring instrument for each of the teacher-made instruments—work-sample tests; identification tests; simulated conditions tests; and assignments and projects.

Selected Readings

Ahmann, J. Stanley, and Glock, Marvin D. *Evaluating Pupil Growth*, 5th ed. Boston: Allyn and Bacon, Inc., 1975. Chapter 7.
———. *Measuring and Evaluating Educational Achievement*, 2nd ed. Boston: Allyn and Bacon, Inc., 1975. Chapter 7.
Cronbach, Lee J. *Essentials of Psychological Testing*, 3rd ed. New York: Harper & Row Publishers, Inc., 1970. Chapters 12 and 13.

Green, John A. *Teacher-Made Tests*, 2nd ed. New York: Harper & Row Publishers, Inc., 1975. Chapter 5.

Hopkins, Charles D., and Antes, Richard L. *Classroom Measurement and Evaluation*. Itasca, IL: F. E. Peacock Publishers, Inc., 1978. Chapter 11.

TenBrink, Terry D. *Evaluation. A Practical Guide for Teachers*. New York: McGraw-Hill Book Company, 1974. Chapter 12.

Tuckman, Bruce W. *Measuring Educational Outcomes: Fundamentals of Testing*. New York: Harcourt Brace Jovanovich, Inc., 1975. Chapter 6.

Describing Educational Data and Standardized Testing

7

Describing
Educational Data

What is meant by statistical methods?
What is a simple frequency distribution and how is it constructed?
What is the first step of analysis?
What are the measures of central tendency and how are the basic ones
    computed?
When are the various averages used?
What are measures of variability, and how are the basic ones computed?

A.   What Is Meant by Statistical Methods?

Statistical methods may be defined as the presentation and analysis of
numerical data collected through measurement.

In Chapter 1, it was noted that the ability to analyze data is one of the
basic requirements in effective measurement and evaluation. Teachers may
do their measurement with considerable insight and skill, but if they do not
know how to organize and analyze this data, they will have a mass of meaningless impressions which will not aid them in determining where they have
succeeded, where they have failed, and what to do next.

When data is collected, it is usually listed in random order in a column
called the Raw Score Column. (See sample problem, Table 7.1) *Raw scores*
are nothing more than a series of scores presented in random order. The
scores are counted, and the total *number of cases (N)* is recorded at the
bottom of the column.

What is the highest score? In this grouping, it is 99. What is the lowest
score? Here, it is 49. The range of scores is 50 points from 99 to 49. Then,
what is the average score? Which score starts the upper quarter? Which
score starts the lower quarter? Which scores are in the middle 50%? These
questions cannot be answered accurately because the data is not organized
properly.

Raw scores are of little value in understanding what the scores mean. However, one must have a starting point, and the Raw Score Column is the starting point for the presentation and analysis of data. The next step in organizing the data for analysis is that of preparing a frequency distribution.

B.   What Is a Simple Frequency Distribution and How Is It Constructed?

A simple frequency distribution is a graphic representation of a distribution of raw scores. Steps in the construction of a simple frequency distribution (Table 7.1) are these:

1. Make a Score Column *(X)*. Place the scores in order of size from high to low, listing each score value only once.
2. Make a Tally Column. Tabulate, by a vertical mark, the number of pupils receiving each score. Total tally column to be sure that this total coincides with the total number of raw scores.
3. Make a Frequncy Column *(f)*. Count the number of tallies for each score and enter this total as a number in *f* column. Total *f* column.

One can see that the raw scores now have been reorganized (presented) into a new framework for more efficient analysis. The teacher then can note at a glance the top score and the lowest score, can even approximate the average score, and can estimate the location of the top-quarter and of the lowest-quarter scores. However, the purpose of a simple frequency distribution chart is to *present* the scores—the first part of statistical analysis. The further columns in the simple frequency distribution charts are columns used for analysis of data.

C.   What Is the First Step of Analysis?

Usually, the first step in analysis is to rank the scores. On page 24 there is a discussion of ranking scores in introducing the technique of correlation. Refer to table 2.1 and subsequent discussion in Chapter 2 to review the material on ranking scores.

It may be well to note here that, by ranking, one determines the relative position of a score in a series of scores. This is accomplished by assigning the rank of 1 to the highest score (see Table 7.2) and then proceeding down the list of scores (remember the modification when there are duplicate scores). Ranking serves two purposes in analysis: first, it indicates the position of each score, and thus of each pupil, within the group; and second, it can be used as a means of grouping pupils into whatever number of sections desired.

TABLE 7.1

Simple Frequency Distribution

		Simple Frequency Distribution		
Raw Scores		X	Tally	f
77	62	99	/	1
84	57	93	/	1
67	87	87	/	1
77	67	84	////	4
73	73	77	/////	5
93	62	73	///	3
84	77	67	///	3
62	67	62	///	3
77	84	57	/	1
49	N-24	52	/	1
73		49	/	1
99			N-24	N-24
84				
52				
77				

TABLE 7.2

Measures of Central Tendency

X	f	Rank	fX
99	1	1	99
93	1	2	93
87	1	3	87
84	4	5.5	336
77	5	10	385
73	3	14	219
67	3	17	201
62	3	20	186
57	1	22	57
52	1	23	52
49	1	24	49
	N-24		1764

Mean	Median	Mode
$M = \dfrac{\Sigma fX}{N}$	$Mdn = \dfrac{N+1}{2}$	Score that occurs most frequently
$= \dfrac{1764}{24}$	$= \dfrac{25}{2}$	$= 77$
$= 73.5$	$= 12.5$ Count Up	
$= 74$	$= 75$	

D. What Are the Measures of Central Tendency and How Are the Basic Ones Computed?

Measures of central tendency are points which represent all of the scores made by the group, and they give a concise description of the performance of the group as a whole. These measures are more commonly called *averages*. There are three basic averages: The mean, the median, and the mode.

1. What Is the Mean and How Is It Determined?

a. Definition

The mean is the sum of the individual scores *(ΣfX)*[1] divided by the number of cases *(N)*. The mean is known as the *arithmetic average*.

b. Formula

$$M = \frac{\Sigma fX}{N}$$

Here, M means the mean, Σ stands for "sum of," ΣfX means the sum of the individual scores times the frequency of scores, and N equals the number of cases.

In the sample problem, the mean equals 74.

2. What Is the Median and How Is It Determined?

a. Definition

The median is a point on either side of which there is an equal number of cases. This is known as the *counting average*.

b. Formula

$$Mdn = \frac{N + 1}{2} \quad \text{Result Count Up}$$

Here, Mdn stands for the median, $N + 1$ for the number of cases plus one.

The figure which one obtains from the formula is not the median, but must be used to count upward into the distribution to find the median or middle point. In the illustrated problem, one counts upward from the bottom either in the frequency column or in the tally column. The twelfth frequency is on the score of 73 but there is still a .5 frequency remaining. It is important for the teacher at this point to count downward from the top to be sure of the exact and correct

---

1. See Appendix E for Statistical Symbols and Formulas Commonly Used in Measurement.

point of the median. When counting downward from the top, the twelfth frequency is on 77 with a .5 frequency remaining. This means that the median is midway between 73 and 77 which is 75.

Sometimes, the median is on an exact score; at other times, it will be the midpoint between two scores. When checking the first calculation by counting downward from the top, the median point can be determined accurately.

3. What Is the Mode and How Is It Determined?

a. *Definition*

The *mode* is the score that occurs most frequently (the inspectional or observational average).

b. *Formula*

The formula for the crude mode is its definition.

In Table 7.2, one can observe the fact that the score of 77 has the greatest number of frequencies; therefore, the mode is 77.

c. *Irregularities in determining the mode*

The mode is easily determined in a distribution in which one score has the greatest frequencies. It is not uncommon, however, for a distribution to have more than one score with the highest frequency. It is in this situation that the teacher must know how the mode is reported.

Following is the middle of the distribution with a new set of frequencies.

$$84 - ////$$
$$77 - \cancel{////}$$
$$73 - ///$$
$$67 - \cancel{////}$$
$$62 - ///$$

Here, the highest number of frequencies is found at 77 and at 67. Since the two scores are not adjacent, the distribution is reported as *bimodal* (two modes), and it is reported as being 77 and 67.

Sometimes there are more than two high points which have the same numbers of high frequencies, and they are not adjacent.

$$84 - ////$$
$$77 - \cancel{////}$$
$$73 - ///$$
$$67 - \cancel{////}$$
$$62 - ///$$
$$57 - \cancel{////}$$

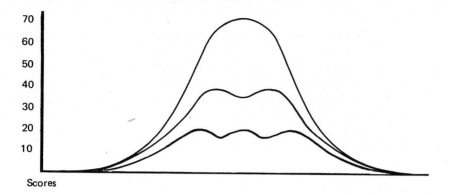

Figure 7.1   Modal, Bimodal, and Multimodal Distribution

The three high points are 77, 67, and 57. This is called a *multimodal* distribution, and the three modes are reported. Any distribution of more than two modes is called multimodal. Figure 7.1 illustrates the three types of modes.

The previous two paragraphs indicate how the modes are reported when the highest frequencies are not adjacent to each other. If the high frequencies *are all adjacent* to each other in either the bimodal or the multimodal distribution, it is normal to average these values and report the average as the modal point. If *all* high frequencies are not adjacent, however, the mode is reported as bimodal or multimodal as explained in the previous paragraphs.

Whenever there is more than one mode, it indicates that there is more than one point of concentration. This gives a clue to the teacher that there probably are various groups within the class. This can assist the teacher in working with these groups for more individualized instruction.

E.   When Are the Various Averages Used?

1.   The Mean Is Used When:

a.   The measure of central tendency having the greatest reliability is desired. This means that the mean is the average which is most stable from sample to sample—it is the most consistent. The mean, therefore, is the average which is used most commonly.

b.   Further statistical techniques are to be computed. Many times, the mean is a "prerequisite" to figuring a statistical result as in standard deviation or correlation coefficients.

c.   Grades are to be determined using the mean as a reference point.

2. **The Median Is Used When:**

   a. There are extreme scores which would make the mean unreliable. For example, there are five teachers with salaries of $10,600; $10,700; $10,800; $10,900; $13,000. The mean would be $11,200, but it would hardly be a representative average of the majority of the teachers. Here, the middle salary of $10,800 (the median) would be a more representative average.

   b. A quicker average is required for reporting purposes. Many times in reporting scores to pupils or parents, a teacher wants to report an average as a reference point. In most cases, the median can be obtained much more quickly than the mean and probably is accurate enough for a rough average. The author uses the median in reporting the average on check tests and other measurements which carry minimal weight.

   c. Certain scores could influence the average, but all that is known about them is that they lie outside of the distribution. Sometimes pupils do not complete a test in the allotted time and are marked DNC (did not complete), or they may receive such a high score that it "runs off the scale" at the upper end of the distribution. The median can easily be figured since each "score" counts only as one in finding the median point. The mean could not be figured since the exact value of each score must be known.

3. **The Mode Is Used When:**

   a. A quick, approximate measure of concentration is all that is needed.

   b. The most frequently obtained score is desired.

   The mode is not a very reliable average as can be observed in its computation. There may be one mode, two modes, or many modes. Thus, it is not a decision as to whether to use the mode when a mean or median can be computed; rather, the decision is whether to use the mode as an additional index when using the mean or the median. Sometimes, it is of value in this situation. For example, the mean IQ of a class may be 110 and the mode is 100. This means that the arithmetic average (mean) indicates that the class, as a whole, has an average IQ at the upper end of the average range, but the greatest concentration of IQ's seem to be around the "normal" IQ of 100.

F. What Are Measures of Variability and How Are the Basic Ones Computed?

Measures of variability are indices which describe the spread or scatter of scores in a distribution. These measures are distances, not points. Sometimes, they are called ranges.

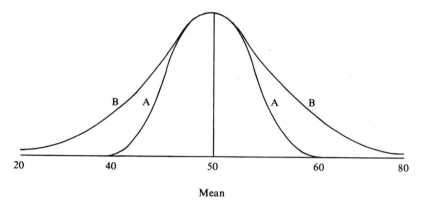

	40	50	60	

Mean

Figure 7.2   Mean Score of Two Distributions

In comparing two sets of scores, one may find that the means are equal, but this does not mean that the distributions of the scores are identical. In Figure 7.2, the mean scores of both distributions are the same, 50. However, distribution A has scores ranging from 40 to 60, whereas distribution B has scores from 20 to 80. It is obvious, then, that the two groups are not identical and that they would require different approaches to teaching. To understand the differences within a distribution or between two distributions, it is necessary to know more than the average score.

There are three basic measures of variability which a teacher may have occasion to use or at least to understand in reading professional literature. These are the external range, the range by quartiles, and standard deviation.

1. The External Range

a. Definition

The external range is the difference between the highest and the lowest score in the distribution.

b. Formula

Range = H − L

In a previous sample problem, the highest score was 99; the lowest was 49; therefore, the range is 50. (See Table 7.4.)

The range is useful because it indicates the variability of the group from one extreme to the other. A large range would mean a heterogeneous group on the measurement; a small range would mean a rather homogeneous group.

The external range is somewhat unreliable. It is influenced by the extreme scores only, and one extreme score can increase the external range by such an amount that it would not produce a reliable index of the variability of the majority of the group.

What should the size of the range be? There is no perfect size of the range since, usually, one will compare one range with another to compare variability. However, in a normal curve of distribution, it is often considered the range to extend from three standard deviations below to three standard deviations above the mean. But the distribution of scores from a class of 30 students will not typically show a range from high to low of six standard deviations. Table 7.3 indicates that the following ratio of range to standard deviation can be expected for the samples of sizes shown.

TABLE 7.3

Ratio of Range to Standard Deviation

Sample Size	Typical Range in Standard Deviation Units
10	3.0
50	4.5
100	5.0
1000	6.5

The values shown are averages so some samples will be higher and some lower. However, it would be helpful for the teacher to know that in a class of 25-30 test scores the range will be between three and four standard deviations rather than six.

2. The Range by Quartiles

Because the external range gives the distance from one extreme to the other, sometimes one may obtain an erroneous picture of the variability within the distribution. To obtain further insight into the variability within the distribution, it might be desirable to determine the range by quartiles.

The range by quartiles is finding the range of the upper quarter, of the lowest quarter, and of the middle 50%. This must not be confused with quartile deviation, which is also an index of variability. The range by quartiles is useful in finding the variability of the groups within the distribution. It also can be used for dividing students into three sections for small-group instruction, for interpreting placement of pupils in the group, and for grading purposes. The last point will be explained further in Chapter 13, Grading, Marking, and Reporting Practices.

a. Range of the upper fourth

In order to find the range of the upper fourth, it is necessary to locate the *point* which starts the upper fourth. This point is known as the 75th percentile, or the point of Q_3.

Q_3 is determined by the same procedure as was used for the median or Q_2 except that, this time, one must count upward 75% of the way into the distribution. The formula is:

$Q_3 = 3/4N$ or $3N/4$. Result Count Up.

In the sample problem in Table 7.4, the N was 24. Therefore:

$Q_3 = 3/4$ of 24 or 18. Result Count Up.

By counting upward into the distribution 18 frequencies, the point of Q_3 is on 84. The point which begins the top quarter, then, is 84. The range of the top quarter in the distribution is 84-99; thus, a range of 15 points.

b. Range of the lowest fourth

Q_1 is the point below which lies the lower 25% of the cases, or the lowest fourth.

The formula is:

$Q_1 = N/4$. Result Count Up.

In the sample problem, the substitution would be:

$Q_1 = 24/4$ or 6. Result Count Up.

By counting upward six frequencies (and down 18 frequencies), one locates 64.5. The point of Q_1 is 64.5, but the lowest quarter range of actual scores is from 49-62, or a range of 13 points.

c. Range of the middle 50%

The range of the middle 50%, or the typical group, is then easily determined. It is between the starting points of the upper and lower quarters. In the sample problem in Table 7.4, the middle range would be between 67 and 77, or a range of 10 points.

The middle 50% of this sample group appears to be a very closely knit group with the difference being 10 points; the top quarter is only slightly greater in range than the lowest quarter (15 points as compared to 13).

Grade or class groups can be compared with one another through the use of the range by quartiles, and one can determine the quartile distributions within a single class or group. If one group had a range within the top quarter of 15 points and another group on the same measurement had a range of 30 points, the second group

TABLE 7.4

Measures of Variability

X	f	Rank	fX	d	fd	fd²
99	1	1	99	25	25	625
93	1	2	93	19	19	361
87	1	3	87	13	13	169
84	4	5.5	336	10	40	400
77	5	10	385	3	15	45
73	3	14	219	-1	-3	3
67	3	17	201	-7	-21	147
62	3	20	186	-12	-36	432
57	1	22	57	-17	-17	289
52	1	23	52	-22	-22	484
49	1	24	49	-25	-25	625
	N=24		1764			3580

Range	Top Fourth	Lower Fourth	Standard Deviation
$R = H - L$	$Q_3 = \dfrac{3N/4 \text{ Result}}{\text{Count Up}}$	$Q_1 = \dfrac{N/4 \text{ Result}}{\text{Count Up}}$	$SD = \sqrt{\dfrac{\Sigma fd^2}{N}}$
$= 99 - 49$	$= 72/4$	$= 24/4$	$= \sqrt{\dfrac{3580}{24}}$
$= 50$	$= 18$ Count Up	$= 6$ Count Up	
	$= 84$	$= 64.5$	$= \sqrt{149.17}$
	$= 84 - 99$	$= 49 - 62$ (actual)	$= 12.21$

has a variability twice as great as the first group within the top quarter. The teaching procedures and the materials of instruction, therefore, would vary from one group to the other.

3. Standard Deviation

The standard deviation, or *SD*, is a measure of varability calculated around the mean. The *SD* is the most stable measure of variability and is customarily used in research problems and in studies involving correlation. The symbol for the *SD* is the Greek letter σ (sigma).

Teachers will find *SD* used as a measure of variability when they read the manuals accompanying standardized tests and when they read research studies using statistical analysis. Teachers generally have not used *SD* in their own analysis of data primarily because it appeared to be a complex measure to compute and to interpret.

The formula is: $SD = \sqrt{\dfrac{\Sigma fd^2}{N}}$

If one will realize, however, that *SD* is a unit of distance, it can be more readily understood. A foot is a unit of distance and, in measuring a room, the results are expressed in feet. Similarly, in a distribution of scores, the variability or distance can be stated in SD units (here d stands for "deviation from the mean," f for frequency of scores, N for number of cases, and Σ for sum of). In the sample problem in Table 7.4, the mean has been computed so that the deviation of each score from the mean is stated in the d column. Since some scores are duplicated, one multiplies the deviation by the frequency (fd) to obtain this column. Then fd^2 is obtained by multiplying the d column by the fd column. The resulting computation shows the SD value to be 12.21. Refer to Appendixes F and G for assistance with square root.

What does the SD value indicate about the nature of the distribution? Bartz states the value as follows:

> Obviously, it tells *how much* the scores in a distribution deviate from the mean. If the value of the SD is small, there is little variability, and the majority of the scores are tightly clustered around the mean. If the SD is large, the scores are more widely scattered above and below the mean. The SD can be used for comparing two groups to see how they differ in variability.[2]

It is very difficult to say in simple words what the standard deviation is or what it corresponds to. What is a large standard deviation? What is a small standard deviation? "Large" and "small" have primarily relative meaning, that is, larger or smaller than that found for some other group or some other test. There is one reference point with which it is sometimes useful to compare the standard deviation. This is the mean. The ratio 100 (Standard Deviation) / Mean is called the *coefficient of variation,* and is sometimes used to compare variability of different groups and measures.

The standard deviation obtains its clearest meaning from the normal curve of distribution. The "normal curve" is a symmetrical curve having a bell-like shape. A normal curve is pictured in Chapter 2. For the normal curve, there is an exact mathematical relationship between the standard deviation and the proportion of cases. The relationship is shown in Table 7.5.

The same proportion of cases will always be found within the same standard deviation limits. Thus, in any normal curve about two-thirds (68.2 percent) of the cases will fall between $+1$ and -1 standard deviations from the mean. Approximately 95 percent will fall between $+2$ and -2 standard deviations from the mean, and practically all of the cases will fall between $+3$ and -3 standard deviations from the mean. This unvarying relationship of the standard deviation unit to the arrangement of scores in the normal distribution gives the standard deviation a type of standard

2. Albert E. Bartz, *Elementary Statistical Methods for Educational Measurement* (Minneapolis: Burgess Publishing Company, 1963), p. 31.

TABLE 7.5

*Proportion of Cases Falling Within Certain Specified Standard
Deviation Limits for a Normal Distribution*

Limits Within Which Cases Lie	Percent of Cases
Between the mean and either $+1.0$ SD or -1.0 SD	34.1
Between the mean and either $+2.0$ SD or -2.0 SD	47.7
Between the mean and either $+3.0$ SD or -3.0 SD	49.9
Between $+1.0$ and -1.0 SD	68.2
Between $+2.0$ and -2.0 SD	95.4
Between $+3.0$ and -3.0 SD	99.8

meaning. It becomes a yardstick in terms of which different groups may be compared or the status of a given individual may be evaluated.

The meaning of being a given number of standard deviations above or below the mean may be expressed in terms of the percent of cases in the group whom the individual surpasses. A short table showing the percent of cases falling below different standard deviation values on the normal curve is given in Appendix K. This table enables one to translate any score, expressed in standard deviation units, into the equivalent percentile on a normal curve. Supposing there is a distribution with a mean of 25 and a standard deviation of 10. An individual received a score of 35. Since the mean is 25 he falls 35–25 or 10 points above the mean. The 10 points above is equal to 10/SD (10) or 1 standard deviation above the mean. From the table in Appendix K, 1 standard deviation above the mean places the student above 84.1 percent of the cases within the group.

A score expressed in SD units has much the same meaning from one set of scores to another. If a student is one-half standard deviation above the mean of his group in arithmetic and one standard deviation above in spelling, we can describe him as better in spelling than in arithmetic. The standard deviation provides a unit in terms of which scores can be directly compared from one test to another from one time to another. In Chapter 8, you will realize that it is basic to converting scores into standard scores such as the z-score, T-score, stanines, deviation IQ, and the like.

The *SD* statistic alone can be used for placing grades in a distribution. More detailed information concerning grade distribution will be presented in Chapter 13.

The importance of the *SD* cannot be overemphasized. Because the concept is basic to the construction and interpretation of tests, teachers should familiarize themselves thoroughly with the preceding discussion and calculations. Then, they should use these techniques to improve their analysis and thereby will improve their teaching procedures.

Summary Statements

1. Statistical procedures include the presentation and analysis of numerical data collected through measurement (the analysis phase of measurement and evaluation).
2. Analysis of data is one of the basic skills which a teacher needs to develop because it is an indication where he has succeeded, where he has failed, and what he must do next.
3. A simple frequency distribution is the means by which one assembles a set of raw scores into a meaningful organization.
4. The first step of analysis is to determine the relative position of a score in a series of scores (ranking).
5. The second step of analysis is to determine a measure of central tendency. This measure is a point which represents all of the scores made by the group and, as such, gives a concise description of the performance of the group as a whole. The basic ones are the mean, median, and mode.
6. The third step of analysis is to determine a measure of variability. This measure is a distance that describes the spread or scatter of scores in a distribution. The basic ones are the range, the variability by quartile, and standard deviation.

Discussion Questions

1. Discuss the significance of a teacher having the ability to analyze data for effective evaluation.
2. Explain the method of ranking scores when there are duplicate or multiple frequencies for given scores.
3. Describe what the rank of a score indicates. What is its limitation in analysis of data?
4. In your own words, what do measures of central tendency tell us about a distribution of scores?
5. Summarize the irregularities in determining the mode.
6. Describe what you consider to be the main criteria in determining when you would decide to use the mean, the median, or the mode.
7. Why is it important to determine a measure of variability as well as a measure of central tendency for a set of scores?
8. What is the limitation of the "external range"?
9. Describe how the "range by quartiles" relates to a marking and grading system?
10. In your own words, describe what standard deviation means.
11. What are other names for the points of Q_1, Q_2, and Q_3?

Student Activities

1. Define the following terms:

Raw Score	Measures of Variability
Frequency Distribution	External Range
Measures of Central Tendency	Quartile Range
Mean	Standard Deviation
Median	
Mode	

2. Construct a simple frequency distribution using the following scores:

57	89	39	57	42
83	67	63	63	57
47	57	67	74	52
67	74	52	67	74
63	52	77	47	77

3. Rank the following scores:

30	24	22
28	24	22
28	24	21
26	23	20

4. Determine the mode in the following examples:

A	B	C
89 — ///	89 — //	89 — //
86 — ////	86 — ////	86 — ////
84 — ##//	84 — ///	84 — ////
82 — ////	82 — ////	82 — //
80 — ///	80 — //	80 — /

5. For each of the following, indicate whether the mean, the median, or the mode would be most appropriate:
   a. When the measure having the highest reliability is desired
   b. When the point of concentration is wanted
   c. When a quick average for reporting purposes is desired
   d. When there are extreme scores, but all that is known about them is that they are above or below a certain point
   e. When a supporting measure is desired to a main average
   f. When there are extreme scores which could affect an average disproportionately

6. Using the simple frequency distribution constructed in Activity 2 above, construct further columns and determine the following:

Rank of each score	Range
Mean	Upper Fourth
Median	Lower Fourth
Mode	Standard Deviation

Selected Readings

Bartz, Albert E. *Basic Statistical Concepts in Education and the Behavioral Sciences.* Minneapolis: Burgess Publishing Company, 1976.

————. *Descriptive Statistics for Education and the Behavioral Sciences,* 5th ed. Minneapolis: Burgess Publishing Company, 1979. Chapters 1-6.

Brown, Frederick G. *Principles of Educational and Psychological Testing,* 2nd ed. New York: Holt, Rinehart and Winston, Inc., 1976. Chapter 3.

Ebel, Robert L. *Essentials of Educational Measurement,* 3rd ed. Englewood Cliffs, NJ: Prentice-Hall, Inc., 1979. Chapter 11.

Garrett, Henry E. *Elementary Statistics,* 2nd ed. New York: Longmans, McKay Co., 1962.

Green, John A. *Teacher-Made Tests,* 2nd ed. New York: Harper & Row Publishers, Inc., 1975. Chapter 10.

Gronlund, Norman E. *Measurement and Evaluation in Teaching,* 3rd ed. New York: The Macmillan Company, 1976. Appendix A.

Guilford, J. P., and Fruchter, Benjamin. *Fundamental Statistics in Psychology and Education,* 6th ed. New York: McGraw-Hill, Inc., 1978. Chapters 1-6.

Hopkins, Charles D. *Describing Data Statistically.* Columbus, Ohio: Charles E. Merrill Co., 1974.

Hopkins, Charles D., and Antes, Richard L. *Classroom Measurement and Evaluation.* Itasca IL: F. E. Peacock Publishers, Inc., 1978. Chapter 8.

Linneman, Richard H., and Merenda, Peter F. *Educational Measurement,* 2nd ed. Glenview, IL: Scott, Foresman and Company, 1979. Chapter 2.

Mehrens, William A., and Lehman, Irvin J. *Measurement and Evaluation in Education and Psychology.* New York: Holt, Rinehart and Winston, Inc., 1973. Chapter 4.

Noll, Victor H., Scannell, Dale P., and Craig, Robert C. *Introduction to Educational Measurement,* 4th ed. Boston: Houghton Mifflin Company, 1979. Chapter 2 and Appendix A.

Nunnally, Jum C. *Introduction to Statistics for Psychology and Education.* New York: McGraw-Hill Book Co., 1975.

Sax, Gilbert. *Principles of Educational Measurement and Evaluation.* Belmont, CA: Wadsworth Publishing Company, Inc., 1974. Chapter 6.

Smith, G. Milton. *A Simplified Guide to Statistics for Psychology and Education,* 4th ed. New York: Holt, Rinehart and Winston, Inc., 1970.

Stanley, Julian C., and Hopkins, Kenneth D. *Educational and Psychological Measurement and Evaluation.* Englewood Cliffs, NJ: Prentice-Hall, Inc., 1972. Chapter 2.

Thorndike, Robert L., and Hagen, Elizabeth. *Measurement and Evaluation in Psychology and Education,* 4th ed. New York: John Wiley and Sons, Inc., 1977. Chapter 2.

8

The Interpretation of Test Scores: Norms and Derived Scores

What is meant by norms?
What are the different types of norms?
What are grade and age norms?
How do you calculate and interpret percentile norms?
How do you calculate and interpret the various standard scores: z-scores;
   T-scores; stanines; deviation IQ's?
How are norms usually presented?
How do you judge the adequacy of norms?
How can you develop and use local norms?

A.   What Is Meant by Norms?

In the absence of additional interpretive data, a raw score on a psychological test is meaningless. To say that a learner has correctly computed 10 problems in an arithmetic computation test, or has translated 20 words on a Spanish test, or has written a computer program in 20 minutes conveys little information about his standing in any of these tasks. Likewise, the familiar percentage scores do not provide a satisfactory solution to interpreting test scores. A score of 60 percent on one arithmetic test, for example, might be equal to 40 percent on another, and to 80 percent on a third. The difficulty level of the items making up each test will determine the meaning of the score. All raw scores, then, can be interpreted only by reference to *norms*.

Norms are aids or guides in the interpretation and application of results. They are *not* standards for each learner to meet; rather, they are guideposts which tell where a student stands. They will aid the teacher in planning the work with the individual student.

When a raw score is converted into some relative measure, it is called a derived score. These derived scores serve two purposes. First, they indicate the individual's relative standing in the normative sample and thus permit an evaluation of his performance in reference to other learners. Second, they provide comparable measures that permit a direct comparison of the individual's performance on different tests. In the first case, if a student receives a percentile score of 80 on a spelling test for fourth graders, we can say that he is above 80 percent of fourth graders in spelling for this test. In the second case, if the student receives a stanine of 8 in typing, 3 in accounting, and 5 in business law, we can say that he appears best in typing, second in business law, and lowest in accounting.

There are various ways in which raw scores may be converted to fulfill the above objectives. The various types and how they are calculated and used will be discussed in succeeding sections.

B.   What Are the Different Types of Norms?

Norms can be classified as to the different types of *derived scores* into which raw scores can be converted and they can be differentiated as to whether they are *norm-referenced* or *criterion-referenced*.

A summary of the most common types of norms and their derived scores is presented in Table 8.1.

There is another way of adding additional information to test interpretation, that is, whether the test is criterion-referenced or norm-referenced. A test is said to be *criterion-referenced* when provision is made for translating the test score into a statement about the behavior to be expected of a person with that score. A test is *norm-referenced* when the translated score

TABLE 8.1

Most Common Types of Test Norms

Type of Norm and Derived Score	Meaning in Terms of Test Performance	Type of Group
Age Norms (Age Equivalent)	The developmental age to which pupil's raw score entitles him/her.	Successive age groups
Grade Norms (Grade Equivalent)	The grade in school to which the pupil's raw score entitles him/her.	Successive grade groups
Percentile Norms (Percentile ranks or percentile scores)	Percentage of pupils in the reference group surpassed by the individual.	Single age or grade group to which the individual belongs
Standard Score Norms (Standard Scores)	Distance of pupil's raw score above or below the mean of the reference group in terms of standard deviation units.	Same as above

tells where the person stands in some population of persons who have taken the test. The same test can be used in both ways. An example of a criterion-referenced statement is that "Fred's score indicates we can expect him to solve multiplication problems with 80 percent accuracy." An example of norm-referenced is "Fred performed better in multiplication problems than 60 percent of ninth graders."

Up to relatively recent times, test specialists have emphasized norm-referenced but criterion-referenced and norm-referenced are both helpful. The former tells what the person is able to do, the latter tells how he compares with others. Criterion-referenced is useful in judging him as a particular individual, while norm-referenced aids in judging his ability to compete. With much emphasis in today's schools on individualized instruction, criterion-referenced tests are expected to increase. Criterion-referenced scores are most appropriate for programmed instruction, formative evaluation, and mastery levels. Several standardized criterion-referenced tests have been developed. The ones produced by the Instructional Objectives Exchange[1] can serve as a sample of the types of test collections produced.

Reading
    Word Attack Skills, K-6
    Comprehension Skills, K-6
Mathematics
    Sets and Numbers, K-6
    Elements, Symbolism, and Measurement, 7-9
    Algebra I, 10-12
Science
    Life Science, K-6
Social Studies
    American Government, 10-12
Language Arts: Several collections from K-9

In summary, both kinds of information, how well a pupil performs relative to others and how well he or she performs relative to a behavioral criterion, are desirable in order to assess more completely pupil performance in an educational program. Where standardized criterion-based instruments are not available or when mastery testing is desired more frequently than the standardized instruments would normally be used, teachers are building their own criterion-referenced tests. Some reading, language arts, and mathematics publishers are producing mastery tests to go with their particular series.

---

1. Instructional Objectives Exchange, Box 24095, Los Angeles, California 90024.

C.   What Are Grade and Age Norms?

1.   Grade Norms Refer to the Grade in School to Which the Student's Raw Score Entitles Him.

These are used widely with standardized achievement tests, especially at the elementary school level. They are based on the average scores earned by pupils in each of a series of grades and are interpreted in terms of grade equivalents. For example, if students in the standardization sample who are beginning the sixth grade earn an average raw score of 30, this score is assigned a grade equivalent of 6.0. Tables are made up of such pairs of raw scores and their corresponding grade equivalents. Grade equivalents range from .0 to .9 for any grade—thus, for sixth grade from 6.0 to 6.9, the zero denoting the beginning or first month and .9 indicating the last month.

Grade equivalents have been very popular over the years because it is so easy for pupils and parents to relate them to school grades. For example, assume that the following grade equivalents were obtained by Tom, who is in the middle of the sixth grade.

Reading 10.0
Language 7.5
Arithmetic 6.5

In interpreting these scores, one would recognize that Tom is exactly average in arithmetic, one year advanced in language, and three and one-half years advanced in reading. However, the ease of interpreting grade equivalents leads to interpretations which are misleading or inaccurate to those who are unaware of their limitations. Some of these limitations are as follows:

a. The units are not equal on different parts of the scale, or from one test to another. A year of growth in reading achievement from 2.0 to 3.0 might represent a much greater improvement than an increase from grade 4.0 to 5.0 or 8.0 to 9.0. The reason is that growth in school subjects is uneven. At grade levels where educational growth is rapid, grade units indicate large differences in achievement; where growth slows down, grade units correspond to very small differences. Also, patterns of growth vary from one subject to another. For example, it would be difficult to compare growth in height with growth in reading since each has a different pattern of growth rate. At the elementary level, those subjects like arithmetic, reading, or language skills probably are easiest to compare since they receive consistent emphasis through the grades.

b. Extremely high or low grade equivalents have dubious meaning. If two students in the fifth grade received grade equivalents of 10.5

and 2.5 respectively in arithmetic, the unknowing might interpret the first as saying the child is five years ahead of his or her grade level in arithmetic, while in the second the child is 2-3 years below. Neither would probably be right. Most fifth grade achievement tests are designed and standardized on fifth grade students or on fourth through sixth grades. Thus, the grade equivalents of 10.5 and 2.5 are just "paper projections"—that is, extrapolated, not based on actual cases. On repeated testings, both would probably obtain scores inward toward the fifth grade. The only interpretation for such scores is that they did very well or very poorly, but the exact grade equivalent would have little value.

c. Assuming that a person earns a certain grade equivalent score in a subject, he is ready to do work at that level. For example, we might conclude that a fifth grade pupil should be doing seventh grade work in reading comprehension if he earns a grade equivalent of 7.0 on a reading comprehension test. The fact may be that he answered the less difficult test items more rapidly and accurately than the average fifth grader. Thus, the grade equivalent of 7.0 may really represent a thorough mastery of reading comprehension through the fifth grade. Pupils at different grade levels who earn the same grade equivalents may be ready for quite different types of instruction.

2. Age Norms Refer to the Developmental Age to Which the Pupil's Raw Score Entitles Him

They are based on the average scores earned by pupils at different ages and are interpreted in terms of age equivalents. They have essentially the same characteristics and limitations as grade norms. Age norms differ in that the test performance is expressed in age level rather than by grade. The age equivalents divide the calendar into twelve parts instead of ten. Age equivalents for nine-year-olds, for example, range from 9-0 to 9-11. They have the same limitations as grade equivalents in unevenness of growth units, extrapolated scores, and questions of readiness to do work at whatever age equivalent is obtained.

In summary, grade and age norms are based on the *average* performance of pupils at various grade and age levels. They are characteristically unequal and especially subject to misinterpretation above the elementary school level. Age norms are most useful for expressing growth in mental ability, arithmetic ability, and similar characteristics which have fairly consistent growth paterns. If interpreted with caution, they can be a useful means of grouping pupils with similar ability and for making general comparisons of academic ability and achievement.

D.   How Do You Calculate and Interpret Percentile Norms?

A percentile scale is one from 0 to 100 into which a student's raw score is converted. A percentile rank, or percentile score, indicates the pupil's relative position in a group in terms of the percentage of pupils scoring below him. Thus, if a student's raw score of 23 is equal to the 70th percentile, we say that 70 percent of the pupils in the norm group obtained raw scores lower than 23. Or, stating it in a more common way this student is above 70 percent of the norm group.

Although every percentile can be determined, there are some key percentiles. These are the 50th percentile (the median), the 75th percentile which starts the upper quarter, and the 25th percentile which delineates the lower quarter. Thus, students can be reported into different quarters of the distribution.

In standardized tests which use percentile scales, there will be a table with the raw scores listed and the percentile equivalents. At times, you will want to determine percentile ranks for local norms. In the *first example* that follows here a percentile rank is figured for *ungrouped data;* in the *second,* for *grouped data.*

UNGROUPED DATA

Formula $PR_X = 100 - 100 \dfrac{R-50}{N}$

Where 100 = Constant
R = Rank of score
50 = Constant number
N = Number of cases

X	f	Rank	Example: Find PR of score of 80
99	1	1	$PR_{80} = 100 - \left(\dfrac{100(6)-50}{22}\right)$
95	1	2	
87	2	3.5	
80	3	6	$= 100 - \left(\dfrac{600-50}{22}\right)$
77	4	9.5	
72	4	13.5	
65	3	17	$= 100 - \dfrac{550}{22}$
60	2	19.5	
57	1	21	$= 100 - 25$
50	1	22	
	N=22		$= 75$

The score of 80 is equal to the 75th percentile or the student who obtained a score of 80 is above 75 percent of the students in this distribution.

GROUPED DATA

Formula

$$PR_X = 100 \left[\frac{i\ (cfb)\ +\ f\ (X\text{-}LL)}{iN} \right]$$

Where cfb = Number of frequencies *below* interval which contains PR_X

f = Frequency of scores within the interval which contains PR_X

X = Score

LL = Lower real limit of interval

N = Number of cases

i = Length of interval

Intervals	f	Cum. f
90-99	2	22
80-89	5	20
70-79	8	15
60-69	5	7
50-59	2	2
	N=22	

$$PR_{70} = 100\left[\frac{10(7)\ +\ 8(70-69.5)}{10(22)}\right]$$

$$= 100\left[\frac{70\ +\ 8\ (.5)}{220}\right]$$

$$= 100\left[\frac{70\ +\ .4}{220}\right]$$

$$= 100\ \frac{74}{220}$$

$$= 100\ (.34)$$

$$= 34$$

The score of 70 is equal to the 34th percentile or the student who obtained a score of 70 is above 34 percent of the cases in this distribution.

Percentile norms are among the most popular and widely used norms in standardized testing. A distinctive feature is that one can interpret a pupil's performance in terms of any group in which he/she is a member or wishes to become a member. The interpretations given to a particular score are limited only by the types of decisions one wishes to make and the availability of the appropriate set of norms. Most commonly, of course, performance is reported in terms of the student's relative standing in his or her own grade or age group.

Even though one of the more popular of norms, the percentile scale is not without some limitations or drawbacks.

1. Percentile Units Are Not Equal on All Parts of the Scale

That is, because most students' scores cluster around the middle of the scale, the difference between percentile points is much smaller in the middle of the distribution than near the ends. The difference between the 40th and 50th percentile might be only a few raw score points while the difference between the 85th and 95th percentile would require a considerable difference in raw score values. This has two implications: First, a difference of several percentile points should be given greater weight at the extremes of the distribution than near the middle; and second, percentile ranks should not be averaged arithmetically.

2. When Interpreting a Percentile, One Must Always Refer to the Norm Group on Which It Was Based

A student in the freshman year in college might be at the 80th percentile compared with state college norms, 75 with university norms, and 70 with liberal arts college norms. A person, then, always has a percentile rank *in some particular group.*

3. Sometimes, Numerous Sets of Norms Are Required

On the elementary level, this is usually not bothersome since most comparisons are made with the pupil's age and grade. However, in high school and college, you may want to compare a person with several groups for selection or guidance purposes. Since standardized test publishers cannot provide innumerable sets of tables, it may require building local norms for local use.

Percentile Bands

A principle of measurement is that all measurement is subject to error. This matter was discussed with the topic of reliability in Chapter 2. Bearing in mind the *standard error of measurement* characterizing a test score, some publishers have prepared norm tables in the form of percentile bands. For each raw score the manual reports, a range of percentile values will be given within which the true ability of the examinee is presumed to lie. For example, in the *STEP Reading Test,* a sixth grade pupil with a raw score of 55 would have a percentile band of 66-83 reported.

The objective of percentile bands is to keep the test user from putting too much emphasis on an exact score and to encourage awarenes and understanding of the variability of pupil performance from day to day and from one form of the test to another form. The band that is usually reported extends from one standard error (1 SE) below the percentile to one standard error (1 SE) above the percentile. To interpret this band, we would say something like: "There are about two chances in three that the examinee's true ability falls within these percentile limits." Thinking in terms of a band rather than a point helps us to understand whether differences in scores are significant. If the bands overlap each other, the difference is not significant; if the bands *do not overlap,* there would appear to be a differ-ence large enough *to be significant.* This can be used to compare scores of groups as well as for an individual.

In general, percentile norms are one of the most popular of ways of interpreting a test. If used with its limitations and/or drawbacks, they can be one of the easiest for students and parents to understand.

E. How Do You Calculate and Interpret the Various Standard Scores?[2]

Sooner or later, every textbook discussion of test scores introduces the bell-shaped normal curve. The student of testing soon learns that many of the methods of deriving meaningful scores are anchored to the dimensions and characteristics of this curve. And he learns by observation of actual test score distributions that the ideal mathematical curve is a reasonably good approximation of many practical cases. He learns to use the standard prop-erties of the ideal curve as a model.

Let us look first at the curve itself. Notice that there are no raw scores printed along the baseline. The graph is generalized; it describes an ideal-ized distribution of scores of any group on any test. We are free to use any numerical scale we like. For any particular set of scores, we can be arbitrary and call the average score zero. In technical terms we "equate" the mean raw score to zero. Similarly we can choose any convenient number, say 1.00, to represent the scale distance of one standard deviation.[3] Thus, if a distri-bution of scores on a particular test has a mean of 36 and a standard devia-tion of 4, the zero point on the baseline of our curve would be equivalent to an original score of 36; one unit to the right, $+1\sigma$, would be equivalent to 40 $(36 + 4)$; and one unit to the left, -1σ, would be equivalent to 32 $(36 - 4)$.

The total area under the curve represents the total number of scores in the distribution. Vertical lines have been drawn through the score scale (the baseline) at zero and at 1, 2, 3, and 4 sigma units to the right and left. These lines mark off subareas of tht total area under the curve. The numbers printed in these subareas are percents—*percentages of the total number of people.* Thus, 34.13 percent of all cases in a normal distribution have scores falling between 0 and -1σ. For practical purposes we rarely need to deal with standard deviation units below -3 or above $+3$; the percentage of cases with scores beyond $\pm3\sigma$ is negligible.

The fact that 68.26 percent fall between $\pm1\sigma$ gives rise to the common statement that in a normal distribution roughly two-thirds of all cases lie between plus and minus one sigma. This is a rule of thumb every test user should keep in mind. It is very near to the theoretical value and is a useful approximation.

Below the row of deviations expressed in sigma units is a row of per-cents; these show *cumulatively* the percentage of people which is included *to the left* of each of the sigma points. Thus, starting from the left, when we

2. James H. Ricks, Jr. "Local Norms—When and Why." *Test Service Bulletin No. 58* (New York: The Psychological Corporation, 1971).

3. The mathematical symbol for the standard deviation is the lowercase Greek letter sigma or σ. These terms are used interchangeably in this article.

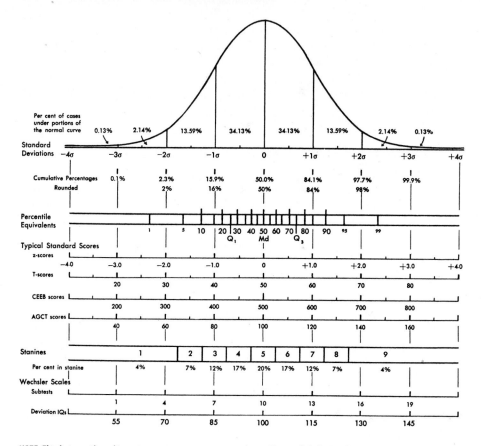

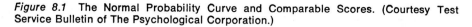

NOTE: *This chart cannot be used to equate scores on one test to scores on another test. For example, both 600 on the CEEB and 120 on the AGCT are one standard deviation above their respective means, but they do not represent "equal" standings because the scores were obtained from different groups.*

Figure 8.1 The Normal Probability Curve and Comparable Scores. (Courtesy Test Service Bulletin of The Psychological Corporation.)

reach the line erected above -2σ, we have included the lowest 2.3 percent of cases. These percentages hav been rounded in the next row.

Note some other relationships: the area between the $+1\sigma$ points includes the scores which lie above the 16th percentile (-1σ) and below the 84th percentile $(\pm1\sigma)$—two major reference points all test users should know. When we find that an individual has a score 1σ above the mean, we conclude that his score ranks at the 84th percentile in the group of persons on whom the test was normed. (This conclusion is good provided we also add this clause, at least sub-vocally; *if this particular group reasonably approximates the ideal normal model.*)

The simplest facts to memorize about the normal distribution and the relation of the *percentile* system to deviations from the average in sigma units are seen in the chart. They are

Deviation from the mean	-2σ	-1σ	0	$+1\sigma$	$+2\sigma$
Percentile equivalent	2	16	50	84	98

To avoid cluttering the graph, reference lines have not been drawn, but we could mark off ten percent sections of area under the normal curve by drawing lines vertically from the indicated decile points (10, 20, . . . 80, 90) up through the graph. The reader might do this lightly with a colored pencil.

We can readily see that ten percent of the area (people) at the middle of the distribution embraces a smaller *distance* on the baseline of the curve than ten percent of the area (people) at the ends of the range of scores, for the simple reason that the curve is much higher at the middle. A person who is at the 95th percentile is farther away from a person at the 85th percentile in units of *test score* than a person at the 55th percentile is from one at the 45th percentile.

The remainder of the chart, that is, the several scoring scales drawn parallel to the baseline, illustrates variations of the *deviation score* principle. As a class these are called *standard scores*.

1. z-Scores

First, there are the *z-scores*. These are the same *numbers* as shown on the baseline of the graph; the only difference is that the expression, σ, has been omitted. These scores run, in practical terms, from −3.0 to +3.0. One can compute them to more decimal places if one wishes, although computing to a single decimal place is usually sufficient. One can compute z-scores by equating the mean to 0.00 and the standard deviation to 1.00 for a distribution of any shape, but the relationships shown in this figure between the z-score equivalents of raw scores and percentile equivalents of raw scores are correct only for normal distributions. The interpretations of standard score systems derives from the idea of using the normal curve as a model.

A z-score is possible provided the mean and the standard deviation for the distribution are known. The formula is:

$$z = \frac{X - M}{SD}$$

Where X equals the raw score
M equals the mean
SD equals the standard deviation

To illustrate the use of the formula, suppose these were three raw scores: an 80 for a personality test; a 60 for an intelligence test; and a 40 for an achievement test. For the personality test, assume that the mean standard deviation are 60 and 10 repectively.

$$z = \frac{80 - 60}{10} = \frac{20}{10} = 2.0$$

Using the same mean and standard deviation as for the personality test, one would determine that the z-score for the intelligence test was 0.00 and for achievement, −2.0. For example, one might note that the student is as much below his class average in achievement (−2 z) as he is above the class average in personality (+2 z); or that his score in personality is two z-units above the intelligence score. Or, if one wishes to combine the three scores, one can do this by simply averaging them. Thus, the mean z-score equal $+2.0 + 0.0 + (-2.0)$ divided by 3. The mean z-score is 0.0. In this case, equal weight was given to each result; differential weighting can be applied by multiplying each z-score by the desired weight before combining them. It must be noted that this procedure for comparing and combining scores is not valid unless the scores came from the same group of subjects.

2. T-Scores

As can be seen, T-scores are directly related to z-scores. The mean of the raw scores is equated to 50, and the standard deviation of the raw scores is equated to 10. Thus a z-score of $+1.5$ means the same as a T-score of 65. T-scores are usually expressed in whole numbers from about 20 to 80. The T-score plan eliminates negative numbers and thus facilitates many computations.

The formula used for calculating z-scores can be easily modified into a formula for T-scores:

$$T = 10z + 50$$

The z-score of the personality test previously analyzed can now be converted to a T-score.

$$T = 10(2) + 50 = 20 + 50 = 70$$

During World War II, the Navy used the T-score plan of reporting test status. It is used today by many standardized tests and many teachers are using them for regular marking.

3. Stanine Scores

The stanine scale refers to a "standard nine-point scale." Raw scores are converted to score levels from 1 (low) to 9 (high) with 5 being exactly average.

The plan divides the norm population into nine groups, hence, "standard nines." Except for stanine 9, the top, and stanine 1, the bottom, these groups are spaced in half-sigma units. Thus, stanine 5 is defined as including the people who are within $+0.2.5\sigma$ of the mean. Stanine 6 is the group defined by the half-sigma distance on the baseline between $+0.25\sigma$ and $+0.75\sigma$. Stanines 1 and 9 include all persons who are below -1.75σ, and above $+1.75\sigma$, respectively. The result is a distribution in which the mean is 5.0 and the standard deviation is 2.0.

Just below the line showing the demarcation of the nine groups in the stanine system there is a row of percentages which indicates the percent of the total population in each of the stanines.·Thus 7 percent of the population will be in stanine 2, and 20 percent in the middle group, stanine 5.

The stanine method of interpretation is used quite widely because it has several advantages. It has broader units which parents can more readily understand. Stanines can be compared from test to test or among tests if the group on which they are based remains the same and if they represent more nearly equal steps or ranges of ability or achievement than other methods. It can be explained to parents that stanines 1, 2, and 3 together represent the same range of ability as 4, 5, and 6 or 7, 8, and 9, since this breakdown is usually used in sectioning. The big advantage of stanines over percentiles is that the stanine scale has equal units from 2 through 8 (stanines 1 and 9 are open-ended to pick up all extreme scores) whereas the percentiles are uneven throughout the scale. It can normally be explained to parents that stanines 1, 2, and 3 represent the low group; 4, 5, and 6 the average group; and 7, 8, and 9 the high group. Table 12.1, Chapter 12, shows the percentages of cases at each stanine level along with a description.

You can convert raw scores to stanine scores in two ways: First is by transforming the z-score to a stanine score. As you look at Figure 8.1, you can see that, whereas the z-score has a mean of 0 and an SD of 1, the stanine scale has a mean of 5 and an SD of 2. So, to transform from a z-score to a stanine score, the following formula is used.

$$\text{Stanine} = 2z + 5 \text{ (rounded to the nearest whole number)}$$

The z-score of the personality test previously analyzed can now be converted to a stanine score. The z-score for the personality test score was 2.

$$\text{Stanine} = 2(2) + 5 = 4 + 5 = 9$$

The second method of deriving stanines is more of a manual method and is explained in Appendix H. This method proposes to take a distribution of scores and convert the raw scores to stanines without first figuring the z-scores. It is a very direct method and fits in nicely when you are building a simple frequency distribution. Some teachers add columns to the simple frequency distribution including the percentile rank and the stanine and manually compute them as a normal part of the analysis process.

4. Deviation IQ's

Interpretation of the Wechsler scales, the 1960 revision of the Stanford-Binet, and many of the current group standardized ability tests depends on a knowledge of the standard score called the *Deviation IQ*. The *Wechsler Scales* (WPPSI, WISC, and WAIS) will be used as an example of how the deviation scores are produced and interpreted.

A subject's raw score *on each of the subtests* in these scales is converted, by appropriate norms tables, to a standard score, based on a mean of 10 and a standard deviation of 3. The sums of standard scores on the Verbal Scale, the Performance Scale, and the Full Scale are then converted into IQ's. These IQ's are based on a standard score mean of 100, the conventional number for representing the IQ of the average person in a given age group. The standard deviation of the IQ's is set at 15 points. In practical terms, then, roughly two-thirds of the IQ's are between 85 and 115, that is, $\pm 1\sigma$. IQ's of the type used in the Wechsler scales have come to be known as *deviation IQ's* as contrasted with the IQ's developed from scales in which a derived mental age is divided by chronological age.

Users of the Wechsler scales should establish clearly in their minds the relationship of subtest scaled scores and the deviation IQ's to the other standard score systems, to the ordinary percentile rank interpretation, and to the deviation units on the baseline of the normal curve. For example, every Wechsler examiner should recognize that an IQ of 130 is a score equivalent to a deviation of $+2\sigma$, and that this IQ score delimits approximately the upper two percent of the population. If a clinician wants to evaluate a Wechsler IQ of 85 along with percentile ranks on several other tests given in school, he can mentally convert the IQ of 85 to a percentile rank of about 16, this being the percentile equal to a deviation from the mean of -1σ. Of course he should also consider the appropriateness and comparability of norms.

Table 8.2 summarizes the characteristics of standard scores that have been discussed.

Efficiency in interpreting test scores in teaching, counseling, screening, clinical diagnosis, and in personnel selection depends, in part, on facility in thinking in terms of the major interrelated plans by which meaningful scores are derived from raw scores. It is hoped that this graphic presentation and discussion will be helpful to all who, in their daily work, must help others understand the information conveyed by numerical test scores.

TABLE 8.2

Summary of Characteristics of Standard Scores

Characteristic	z	T	Stanine	(Wechsler)	CEEB*
Mean	0.0	50	5	100	500
Standard Deviation	1.0	10	2	15	100
Maximum	+3.0	80	9	145	800
Minimum	−3.0	20	1	55	200
Negative values	Yes	No	No	No	No
Decimals	Yes	No	No	No	No

* College Entrance Examination Board Test

F.   How Are Norms Usually Presented?

This section will focus on two methods of presenting normative data: conversion tables and profiles. Some books will include expectancy tables in a discussion like this, but the author prefers to include them in Chapter 12 with the discussion on interpreting data to pupils and parents. However, it may be brought into discussion here if the instructor wishes.

1. Conversion Tables

The most basic and easiest technique is the conversion table or norm table. It is simply a table showing the raw score and its equivalent derived score whether it be in percentiles, stanines, age or grade equivalents, or standard scores, for a particular norm group. The table normally includes a list of raw scores, corresponding list(s) of derived scores, and a description of the norm group.

An illustration of a conversion table might be as follows:

Raw Score	Percentile Rank	Standard Score (T-score)
42	99	68
41	96	65
40	89	62
39	78	58
38	67	55
37	54	52
36	42	49
35	31	46
etc.	etc.	etc.

$N = 100$ freshmen in ninth grade in a midwestern public school.

Thus, if a student's raw score was 36, the percentile rank would be 42 and the standard score 49. One would interpret this by saying that, compared to other ninth graders in this midwestern public school, she was above 42 percent of ninth graders (percentile) or below 58 percent. The standard score of 49 would place her just below the mean (Standard Score which has a Mean of 50 and an SD of 10). Notice some things about this interpretation. First, it compared the person with a particular norm group; second, the interpretation was made only for the derived scores presented, e.g., percentiles and standard scores; third, it described the relative position of the student within the norm group. Since the trait for which the chart was developed is not specified, one cannot describe performance in relation to a specific trait. If the chart had been built for a test of academic aptitude, one could make some inferences as to success in school, for example.

2. Profiles

Sometimes, rather than a conversion table, profiles are constructed whereby a student's raw score can be plotted right on a profile and then the derived score read from the sides of the profile. On the top in vertical order, it would show the possible score, the raw score obtained, the grade equivalent, and the percentile rank. The grade equivalent would be found from a conversion table, but the percentile rank could be read right from the sides of the profile after plotting the raw score for each part of the test and the total.

For example, one could interpret a student's performance on a profile by saying that, in comparison with others in the same grade on whom this test was standardized, this student was above 57 percent in composite reading ability; above 60 percent in aptitude for reading; above 41 percent in auditory association; above 74 percent in word recognition; above 61 percent in word attack; and above 44 percent in reading comprehension. Or, stating it in another way, the student was slightly above average in total reading ability and, except for auditory association and reading comprehension in which she was slightly below average, she was above average in all other facets of reading skills.

G. How Do You Judge the Adequacy of Norms?

Adequacy of test norms is a very important consideration in the selection of a test. The test could be highly valid and reliable but if the norms are not adequate for the group you want to measure, the test is not very usable.

Gronlund lists five criteria[4] which are indicative of the qualities desired in test norms.

1. Test Norms Should Be Relevant.

Test norms are based on a variety of groups. In some cases, they may be a random sample nationally of a given age or grade while sometimes they may be limited to a specific region of the country or even a specific state. Sometimes they are normed for special types of schools—parochial, private, or public. The great variation requires study and analysis of the norms before purchase of the test or use for local purposes. The basic question which must be answered is: *Are the norms appropriate for the students being tested and for the decisions to be made with the results?*

If you merely want to compare your students with a general group to describe how your students compare, national norms may be more appro-

---

4. Norman E. Gronlund. *Measurement and Evaluation in Teaching*, 3rd ed. (New York: The Macmillan Company, 1976), pp. 411-413. © Norman E. Gronlund.

priate. If you want to consider how a high school senior might do in the various types of colleges within a university, you need norms on each of the specific groups involved. For example, on the ACT (American College Test), the student record form provides an expectancy table in which a percentile is obtained for each student as he/she is compared with students enrolled in the various colleges within a university. For example, Dave may have a percentile of 80 in the liberal arts college, 70 in the college of business, and 40 in the college of education. If all other factors were equal, you obviously would guide him to consider enrolling in the college of liberal arts or business rather than in the college of education.

Sometimes, if you want to use results for selection and placement in the local system for instructional purposes, you may want to develop local norms for this purpose. This procedure will be discussed in Section H.

2. Test Norms Should Be Representative.

Being sure that the norms are relevant is important but is not sufficient to meet all norm criteria. *A second important factor is to be sure that the norms are truly representative of the group it purports to represent.* It would be best if they could be a random sample of the population they represent. This is difficult and is hardly ever achieved. One should insist, however, that they be truly representative of the various sub-groups of the population. National norms should include a proper proportion of such sub-groups as boys and girls, various sizes of schools, geographic regions, racial groups, rural-urban areas, and socio-economic levels. This proportion is best represented if it follows the distribution from the last national census data.

One should be cautious in selecting a test where sheer numbers within the sample are stressed. There may be a very large sample, but it may be the wrong sample. It is better to select the carefully chosen, representative sample rather than a large, possibly biased sample, obtained wherever it was possible to get cases.

3. Test Norms Should Be Up-to-date.

There may have been a time in the history of education when things were stable over a period of time and the necessity to update norms was not too important. Today, however, with the constant changes in curriculum and methods, concomitant with the changes in children and youth, it is important that relatively current norms be available.

There are a few suggestions to note as you check for the recency of norms. The copyright date could mislead you. Sometimes, a slight change is made in the package of test materials and a new copyright date is put on; however, the norms may be from the original. Second, look at the norm tables themselves and the description accompanying them to check the information for which the data was gathered. Third, be sure if a revision is made that the norms are based on data collected by the new revision. Sometimes norms are updated without a revision. The original is used but a new sampling is established on which more current data is used.

4. Test Norms Are Comparable

In comparing results for different tests, it is important that the norms for the different tests are comparable. This is usually true on a survey battery of achievement tests so that you can compare directly a student's score in reading, arithmetic, and language skills, for example. Some test publishers will use the same sample for both an academic aptitude test and an achievement test so an expectancy chart can be built to compare potential with performance. If two or more tests are not normed on the same group, sometimes test experts have made them comparable through research means.

5. Test Norms Should Be Adequately Described.

It may be fair to say that many publishers are stingy with the amount and type of information they give about norms. They should realize that their tests would sell more readily if such information were available. The following information should be available in the test manual: (a) method of sampling, (b) date of the testing, (c) number and distribution of cases, (d) extent to which standard conditions of administration and motivation were maintained during the testing, and (e) characteristics of the norm group with respect to age, sex, race, aptitude, educational level, socio-economic status, types of schools represented, and geographic location. This information is needed to judge the adequacy of norms.

H. How Can You Develop and Use Local Norms?

Sometimes, local norms are more useful for instructional or administrative uses than are national norms. In sectioning students into mathematics classes with students of similar achievement, local norms would be useful. If the students do not seem to fit with the descriptions of students on which the test was standardized, local norms again would be useful. So there are many instances where local norms would be helpful. James H. Ricks, Jr., in a test bulletin entitled "Local Norms—When and Why," presents two propositions,[5] both debatable, he admits, for which local norms may be useful.

1. Local norms often make sense when we are looking back at what a group or individual has done but are less likely to make sense when we are looking ahead to what may be expected in the future.

5. James H. Ricks, Jr. "Local Norms—When and Why." *Test Service Bulletin No. 58*, August, 1971. The Psychological Corporation.

2. Local norms are frequently useful for administrative purposes but are less often valuable for counseling purposes.

By the first, he means that it is fairly easy to compare a student with a group with which he has been affiliated currently or in the past, but it would be unreasonably limiting to give him advice about his future that requires the assumption that he will always remain a member of this group. In the second instance, administrative purposes are usually for current decisions; counseling is many times forward-looking.

Determining local norms is not difficult. Some test manuals provide directions for preparing local norms. Percentile ranks or stanines are the norms most commonly computed. If a computer is available, the process is, of course, much faster. A typical procedure is illustrated in Figure 8.2 using percentile ranks and stanines. The procedure is as follows.

Set Up Your Distribution

1. The scores are grouped in intervals (Column 1).
2. The tallies and frequency column are determined (Column 2 and 3).
3. The cumulative frequency column is found by adding the frequencies cumulatively from the bottom (Column 4).

To Find the Percentile Rank (Use Interval 60-64 For Example).

1. Find one-half the *frequency* of the score interval (½ of 14 = 7).
2. Add the result of (1) to the *cumulative frequency* for the score interval *just below it* (7 + 26 = 33).
3. Divide the result of (2) by the *total number of students in the norm group,* and multiply by 100 (300 ÷ 100 = .33 × 100 = 33). The percentile rank for scores in the interval 60-64 is 33.

Score Group	Tally			Frequency	Cumulative Frequency	Percentile Rank	Stanine
95-99	/			1	100	99	9
90-94	////			4	99	97	9
85-89	7HH /			6	95	92	8
80-84	7HH ///			8	89	85	7
75-79	7HH 7HH			10	81	76	6
70-74	7HH 7HH ////			14	71	64	6
65-69	7HH 7HH 7HH //			17	57	49	5
60-64	7HH 7HH ////			14	40	33	4
55-59	7HH 7HH			10	26	21	4
50-54	7HH ///			8	16	12	3
45-49	7HH			5	8	6	2
40-44	//			2	3	2	1
35-39	/			1	1	1	1
	100			100			

Figure 8.2 Figuring Percentile Ranks and Stanines for Local Norms.

For Stanines

1. Refer to Table H.1 in Appendix H to find the number of stanine values to give for the appropriate N. In this case the numbers are 4 - 7 - 12 - 17 - 20 - 17 - 12 - 7 - 4 respectively from 1 to 9.
2. Distribute the stanine values either starting from the top or bottom or from the middle outward.

Summary Statements

1. Norms are *aids or guides* in the interpretation and application of results; they are *not standards*.
2. Measurements which are criterion-referenced indicate what a person can do; those which are norm-referenced tell how the person compares with others.
3. Age and grade norms are based on the *average* performance of pupils at the various age and grade levels. When used with their limitations in mind, they are a very useful type of interpretation.
4. Percentile norms are among the most popular and widely used in standardized testing. A distinctive feature is that one can interpret a pupil's performance in terms of any group in which he is a member or wishes to become a member.
5. A standard score is based on the number of standard deviations a person is from the mean. Standard scores include *z-scores, T-scores, stanines,* and *deviation IQ's*.
6. The adequacy of test norms is a very important consideration in the selection of a test. Are the norms relevant, representative, current, comparable, and do they contain an adequate description of the sample?
7. Local norms are sometimes more useful than national norms. For example, to section ninth graders on mathematics achievement or when the local students don't seem to fit the description of the students on which the test was standardized.

Discussion Questions

1. Explain why norms cannot be considered as standards for all groups or individuals to meet.
2. Explain the following two statements as they relate to criterion-referenced or norm-referenced interpretation. "Joe's score indicates that he can write a paragraph with 90 percent accuracy." "Joe performed better in writing paragraphs correctly than did 80 percent of fourth graders."

3. Discuss the limitations of grade or age norms as to:
   a. Inequality of units on different parts of the scale.
   b. Extremely high or low grade or age equivalents.
   c. Readiness of the student to work at any equivalent level he receives on the test.
4. Explain the following statements about percentile norms.
   a. Percentile units are unequal over the scale.
   b. A difference of *ten* percentile points at the extremes of one distribution should be given greater significance than near the middle.
   c. Percentile ranks should not be averaged arithmetically.
5. Describe how you find a T-score, stanine, and deviation IQ once you know the z-score and why.
6. Discuss the implications of the following statements as they relate to the adequacy of norms.
   a. A test is being considered for use in a public school and the norms are based on a parochial school population.
   b. If a random sample cannot be achieved, national norms should include a proper proportion of the appropriate sub-groups of our population according to the last federal census.
   c. A test is being considered whose norms were established fifteen years ago.
   d. Can I compare directly the results of the Stanford Reading Test with the Metropolitan Arithmetic Test and the California Language Test?
   e. In reading about the norms, I found material on the method of sampling and date of testing, but I could find nothing on the number and distribution of cases, the extent to which standard conditions of administration were met, and characteristics of the norm group.
7. Discuss what Rick means when he says that local norms often make sense when looking back at what a group or individual has done but are less likely to make sense when looking ahead to what may be expected in the future.

Student Activities

1. Assume that a student received a 10.2 grade placement in reading, an 8.2 in language, and a 7.2 in arithmetic. Build your arguments as to why you might *not* be able to say that he or she is far more superior in reading than in language or arithmetic. What other data would you want to have to make a correct interpretation?
2. Using the distribution of scores in the section on percentile norms for *ungrouped data*, figure the percentile rank of the X scores of 95, 72, and

57 using the formula given in the example. Do the same for these scores using the *grouped data* distribution and formula given in that example.

3. Given the following percentile points and standard error for each of the traits, first indicate the *percentile band* within which the true score would land two out of three times, and second, indicate if there is any significant difference between the performance on any of the traits.

    Reading   70 percentile and 5 SE
    Language   65 percentile and 5 SE
    Arithmetic   50 percentile and 5 SE

4. Given a distribution with a mean of 60 and a standard deviation of 5, find the z-score, T-score, and stanine of a score of 70.

5. Given a deviation IQ of 115 on the Wechsler scale, what is the student's percentile equivalent, z-score, T-score, and stanine?

6. Using the chart illustration on page 223 showing how one can read a conversion table of norms, read and interpret the percentile rank and standard score (T-score) for the raw scores of 37, 40, and 42.

7. Following the procedure outlined in the section on determining local norms on pages 227-228, figure out the percentile norms for students who have scores in the 45-49, 70-74, and 85-89 score group respectively. Check your answers with the chart.

Selected Readings

Ahmann, J. Stanley, and Glock, Marvin D. *Evaluating Pupil Growth,* 5th ed. Boston: Allyn and Bacon, Inc., 1975. Chapter 8.

————. *Measuring and Evaluating Educational Achievement,* 2nd ed. Boston: Allyn and Bacon, Inc., 1975. Chapter 8.

Anastasi, Anne. *Psychological Testing,* 4th ed. New York: The Macmillan Company, 1976. Chapter 4.

Brown, Frederick G. *Principles of Educational and Psychological Testing,* 2nd ed. New York: Holt, Rinehart and Winston, Inc., 1976. Chapters 10 and 11.

Cronbach, Lee J. *Essentials of Psychological Testing,* 3rd ed. New York: Harper & Row Publishers, Inc., 1970. Chapter 4.

Ebel, Robert L. *Essentials of Educational Measurement,* 3rd ed. Englewood Cliffs, NJ: Prentice-Hall, Inc., 1979. Chapters 14, 15, and 17.

Gronlund, Norman E. *Measurement and Evaluation in Teaching,* 3rd ed. New York: The Macmillan Company, 1976. Chapter 15.

————. *Readings in Measurement and Evaluation.* New York: The Macmillan Company, 1968. Part III.

Guilford, J. P., and Fruchter, Benjamin. *Fundamental Statistics in Psychology and Education,* 6th ed. New York: McGraw-Hill Book Co., 1978. Chapter 19.

Instructional Objectives Exchange, Box 24095, Los Angeles, CA 90024.

Mehrens, William A., and Lehmann, Irvin J. *Measurement and Evaluation in Education and Psychology.* New York: Holt, Rinehart and Winston, Inc., 1973. Chapter 6.

Noll, Victor H., Scannell, Dale P., and Craig, Robert C. *Introduction to Educational Measurement,* 4th ed. Boston: Houghton Mifflin Company, 1979. Chapter 3.

Ricks, James H., Jr. "Local Norms—When and Why." *Test Service Bulletin, No. 58.* New York: The Psychological Corporation, 1971.

TenBrink, Terry D. *Evaluation. A Practical Guide for Teachers.* New York: McGraw-Hill Book Company, 1974. Chapter 3.

Thorndike, Robert L., and Hagen, Elizabeth. *Measurement and Evaluation in Psychology and Education,* 4th ed. New York: John Wiley & Sons, Inc., 1977. Chapter 4.

Tuckman, Bruce W. *Measuring Educational Outcomes: Fundamentals of Testing.* New York: Harcourt Brace Jovanovich, Inc., 1975. Chapter 11.

9

Introduction to
Standardized Tests

What are standardized instruments?

What are the purposes of a standardized testing program?

How do you design a testing program?

What is a recommended program of standardized testing?

How does one select a standardized test?

What are some sources of information about educational and psychological tests?

What are some principles for administering standardized tests?

What are some principles for the scoring of standardized tests?

A. What Are Standardized Instruments?

A *standardized test is an instrument designed to measure objectively one or more aspects of a total personality by means of samples of verbal or nonverbal responses or by means of other behaviors.* Some might describe it as a measurement of behavior in which one is able to compare the performance of one with others. Still others, who would stress criterion-referenced instruments, would say that it is determining whether one is meeting the criterion established toward an objective.

Standardized instruments are characterized by having high technical quality since they are developed by test experts, have directions and scoring procedures which are extremely precise and uniform for all users, have norms which are usually carefully controlled so that the test is usable by most schools, have equivalent or parallel forms which add to the usefulness of an instrument, and include a test manual and other auxiliary materials which assist the user in administering, scoring, interpreting, and using the results.

Normally, a discussion of standardized tests will include chapters on introduction to standardized tests, intelligence or ability testing, achievement testing, and interest and personality testing. This book will include chapters on each of the first three, but the discussion on interest and personality inventories was included within the chapter on observational tools, more specifically on methods of evaluating personal-social adjustment.

B.   What Are the Purposes of a Standardized Testing Program?

One of the main weaknesses of many standardized testing programs today is that they do not have a philosophy and a purpose to guide them. A good testing program should be supplementary not duplicative, usable not confusing, economical not burdensome, comprehensive not sporadic, suggestive not dogmatic, progressive not static. Such a program, at least in tentative form, may cover an extended period rather than be adopted piecemeal year by year. Long-range planning makes it possible to have a varied program without leaving gaps or involving needless duplication.

In discussing the general considerations involved in organizing a plan of testing, Traxler states:

> The first item in the list of essentials is related closely to the need for stating educational objectives in the local situation. In defining the educational philosophy for a particular school, in setting up the broad general goals toward which changes in pupil behavior are to be directed, and in defining specific instructional objectives for various subject matter areas, there are needs for measurement and evaluation. To meet these needs, the testing program should provide information to assist in attainment of goals as well as checks to find if goals have been reached. Those goals, which can be served by test results, should be identified and stated clearly in planning the testing program.[1]

Stanley indicates that the first step in planning a program is to determine its purpose. "In doing so, three things should be considered: It should be cooperative; it should be practical; it should be definite."[2]

One may be asked: "Why have a testing program?" This is especially significant today when schools are developing so many of their own assessment instruments There appear to be four basic reasons why a standardized testing program is important.

1. *Tests may improve the instructional program.* Most teachers are conscientious about planning the best instruction for each individual student. To do this, the teacher needs as much data as possible to vary the materials, techniques, and goals in keeping with the nature of the learner.
2. *Tests may facilitate curriculum revision.* Teachers and curriculum leaders are constantly concerned with the relevancy of the curriculum for

1. Arthur Traxler et al., *Introduction to Testing and the Use of Test Results in Public Schools* (New York: Harper & Row Publishers, 1953), p. 14.

2. Julian Stanley, *Measurement in Today's Schools*, 4th ed. Englewood Cliffs, NJ: Prentice-Hall, Inc., 1964), p. 300.

the students. Having data on the ability and achievement levels of the students will assist them to plan the scope and sequence of subjects which will be offered to various levels of the learners.

3. *Tests may assist in educational and vocational counseling.* With the advent of career education, tests can assist the teacher and counselor in the career education program of the school at all levels. In the primary program, it may be assisting the child in self-awareness; in high school, it may help the learner match abilities and achievement with job specifications.

4. *Tests may help the administrative staff appraise the educational program.* Each school has its philosophy and objectives of education in that district. Tests, along with other data, can help the administrator evaluate how closely the school is reaching its objectives. It goes without saying that tests should not be used to evaluate the effectiveness of a certain staff member.

C. How Do You Design a Testing Program?

There are many guidelines for the planning of a new testing program or the revision of an established program. Many schools have a standing committee which might recommend a new program if one does not exist or might evaluate, at regular intervals, an established program.

Green suggests the following eight guidelines in planning a testing program.[3]

1. *The purposes of the program should be clearly formulated and written.* This may include the elaboration of classroom, guidance, and administration purposes.

2. *Provisions should be made to provide articulation and continuity throughout the grades in the district.* This is where the testing committee can come into the picture, especially if there is adequate representation from all levels of the district.

3. *The program should be comprehensive.* The basic program should include readiness, achievement, and ability tests. Some may want to add further tests, but it must include at least these areas.

4. *The testing program should be jointly planned by those who will use the results.* This not only means the types of tests but also the details of the schedule, scoring, recording of the results, and the like. Most testing committees will be careful to include representation from every user of the test results.

---

3. Reprinted and adapted by permission of Dodd, Mead & Company, Inc., from *Introduction to Measurement and Evaluation* by John A. Green. Copyright © 1970 by Dodd, Mead & Company, Inc.

5. *Trained personnel should administer and interpret the results.* This means that there should be an in-service program for teachers and others who will administer and interpret the results. Some states now have legislation which says the parents, and students who have reached the age of majority, have a right to see all the material in the students' records. It usually includes the statement that a school official must be available for proper interpretation.

6. *Testing should be a part of the educational program.* If all school personnel understand that measurement is an integral part of the teaching process, then the program will be viewed as being very important, and all personnel will be concerned that it is handled in a professional manner.

7. *Readily available aids, such as the test manuals and Buros'* Mental Measurements Yearbooks, *should be used in selecting the tests.* In the section in this chapter on selecting a test, many of the aids are listed which will help the committee to gather the necessary data on the test it wishes to consider.

8. *The results should be treated as confidential information, but they should be easily accessible to professional school personnel.* This is a very important principle. Students should know that the results will be seen only by professional school personnel or interpreted by them to properly authorized persons.

Another checklist which might be helpful to school administrators or to the school committee, as it is concerned with factors affecting the success of a testing program, is the following.

1. Purposes of the Program
   Clearly defined; Understood by parties involved
2. Choice of Tests
   Valid; Reliable; Appropriate difficulty level; Adequate norms; Easy to administer and score; Economical; Best available for purpose.
3. Administration and Scoring
   Administrators well trained; All necessary information provided; Scorers adequately instructed if hand-scored; Arrange for machine-scoring, if possible.
4. Physical Conditions
   Sufficient space; Sufficient time; Conveniently scheduled
5. Utilization of Test Results
   Definite plans for use of results; Provision for giving teachers all necessary help in using scores; Provision for systematic follow-up on use of results
6. System of Records
   Necessary for purpose; Sufficient for purpose; Convenient form for use; Computer printouts, if possible, with labels for cumulative folders

7. Personnel
   Adequately trained for the purpose
8. Affiliated Research
   Full advantage taken of results; Provision for special studies, analyses, and the like

Although there is some duplication, Traxler lists fifteen criteria of a testing program which school personnel should apply to their own testing program.[4]

1. Is the testing program comprehensive?
2. Does the testing program include all pupils in the school?
3. Are the tests given at regular intervals?
4. Are the tests well-timed?
5. Are the tests in the school's testing program comparable?
6. Do the tests used agree with the objectives and the curriculum of the school?
7. Are the specific tests carefully chosen?
8. Are the tests scored accurately?
9. Are the tests carefully administered to each group?
10. Are the test results interpreted in terms of appropriate norms?
11. Are the test results quickly reported to teachers and counselors in understandable terms?
12. Are the test results recorded on individual cumulative record forms?
13. Is a definite attempt made to relate the test scores to other kinds of information?
14. In addition to the regular testing program, is there provision for special testing, as needed?
15. Does the school have an in-service program for educating teachers in the use of test results?

D. What Is a Recommended Program of Standardized Testing?

It is rather difficult to refer to a testing program apart from the situation in which it is to operate. Differences in local philosophy and objectives in individual and community needs and in number and quality of staff members all operate to make ineffective in one situation that which may prove adequate in another. However, assuming that the basic purpose of testing is to help the teacher achieve a better understanding of the pupil and assum-

4. Arthur E. Traxler, "Fifteen Criteria of a Testing Program" in David A. Payne and Robert F. McMorris, *Educational and Psychological Measurement* (Morristown, NJ: General Learning Press, 1974), pp. 29-34.

ing that there are certain basic needs common to most educational situations, it is possible to deal generally with the relative importance of various parts of the testing program.

In relation to this topic, the author surveyed the members of his classes in measurement and evaluation over the years as to the testing programs conducted in their local schools. Although there were many variations of responses, several common points of agreement were noted. Tables 9.1 and 9.2 suggest programs for the elementary and secondary school.

In addition to the normal program shown, many schools will want to administer additional diagnostic tests in reading and arithmetic in grades 2-8. There is no definite pattern or time when these tests may be given. Each school should decide the type of special diagnostic testing most appropriate to its needs and the times that the tests should be administered.

The teacher will note that no mention is made of group personality and interest testing. Although the validity of such tests might be questioned on this level, an objective appraisal of this type may help the teacher understand the child better and reinforce observational findings. Some teachers will administer one of these group instruments to an individual child to

TABLE 9.1

*A Suggested Standardized Testing Program for
the Elementary School, K-8*

Type	*Purpose*	*When Given*
Screening	To determine through a pre-school screening program and an ongoing program for transfer students, any learning disabilities the child may have so that an adequate program can be planned, either of a remedial or development nature.	Pre-Kindergarten and to all new students entering a school.
Reading Readiness	To determine readiness and maturity for beginning reading and to assist in establishing reading groups.	End of kindergarten or beginning of first grade.
Reading Achievement	To determine growth in beginning reading and diagnosis of reading difficulties.	End of first and second grade.
Battery of Achievement	To determine growth in basic skills, including reading, mathematics, and language. Also, for diagnosis of learning difficulties and planning remedial programs.	Grades 3-8
Mental Maturity	To provide information on the nature and structure of abilities for guiding learning activities.	Grades 1-4-7 or 2-5-8 depending on organization of school.

TABLE 9.2

*A Suggested Standardized Testing Program for
the Secondary School, Grades 9-12*

Type	*Purpose*	*When Given*
Placement Tests English Mathematics	To assist in placement of students in basic freshman subjects	At the end of eighth grade or beginning of ninth grade
Battery of Achievement	To determine growth in basic subjects	Grades 9 and 11, or 10 and 12
Mental Maturity or Scholastic Aptitude Tests	To provide information on the nature and structure of abilities and aptitude for academic subjects	Grades 9 and 11, or 10 and 12
Battery of Aptitude Tests	To determine abilities in specific fields for educational and vocational guidance	Grades 11 or 12
Interest Inventory	To determine the likes and dislikes of a student for educational and vocational guidance	General inventory in ninth grade and more specific interest inventory at junior level
Personality Inventory	To provide information on personal-social development for educational and vocational guidance	Grades 9 and 11

obtain further information for guidance purposes. At times, an interest inventory is administered in the eighth grade to assist in programming for the secondary school. The elementary teacher must also be cognizant of the referral testing program, which is discussed in one of the following paragraphs.

Individual teachers may want to administer achievements tests in a specific subject field to determine student growth throughout the year. The teacher should also be aware of the *external testing program* of the secondary school which is usually planned by the guidance director. Some of these include the CEEB Tests (College Entrance Examination Board tests, commonly called College Boards), usually required by private colleges and universities; ACT Examination (American College Tests) commonly required by public colleges and universities; and State Employment Tests, administered in many states by the State Employment Service to non-college bound high school seniors. Many times, teachers can assist the guidance director in disseminating knowledge about these programs to students and in encouraging selected students to participate in them.

All teachers should become acquainted with the *referral testing program* of the school. This may include individual mental testing, psychological testing, tests in reading, speech correctional testing, and the like. These may be oral, performance, written, or a combination of all three. The teacher may be the initial source in spotting pupils who need special testing and therapy in order to profit from appropriate learning experiences. All of these tests require administration by specialized personnel. Usually, the teacher will confer with the principal or immediate supervisor to discuss the case. Larger schools may have these specialized personnel within the school staff; smaller systems usually will have referral arrangements with a city, county, or area agency.

Many states have passed legislation requiring the screening of all students to identify those who have learning disabilities and, subsequently, to plan a program of remediation for those so identified. The *Wisconsin* legislation will be used as an example. In 1973, Chapter 89, Laws of 1973, stipulated that the school district was responsible for insuring that appropriate special education programs are available to children with exceptional education needs between the ages of three and twenty-one. Special education is defined as "any educational assistance required to provide an appropriate education program for a child with exceptional education needs and any supportive or related services." The child with exceptional educational needs is defined as "any child who has a mental, physical, emotional, or learning disability which if the full potential of the child is to be attained requires educational services to the child to supplement or replace regular education."

As a result, school systems were asked to screen each child when the child first enrolls in school to determine if the child has exceptional education needs. Figure 9.1 is a flow chart of the screening process and implementation of the law produced by the Whitewater Unified School District No. 1.[5]

Briefly explained, the flow chart proceeds in this way. There are two mass screening sessions each year, one each in the spring and fall. There is also individual screening continuously throughout the year as needed. The areas in which screening takes place include speech, language, vision, hearing, perceptual motor, physical growth, and educational assessment. The special school personnel involved in this screening includes the speech therapist, school nurse, learning disability teacher, testing specialist, and school psychologist. There is an evaluation committee which supervises the screening program. After the results are in, the students for which there are needs for special help will be identified. If the Multi-Disciplinary Evaluation Team feels that the student's needs can be handled by staying with the regular teacher, the student will be "mainstreamed" in the regular program and

5. Unpublished report of the Whitewater Unified School District No. 1, March, 1974. From Whitewater Public School System, Whitewater, Wisconsin. Printed by permission of the school.

LOCAL SCREENING FLOW CHART

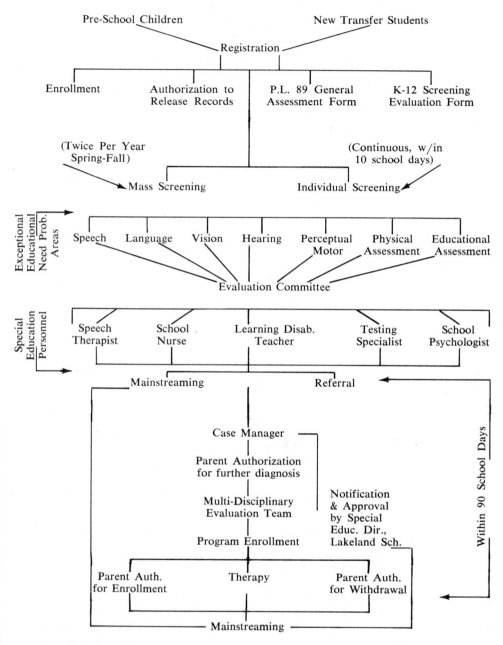

Figure 9.1   Local Screening Flow Chart.

observed. If a special program is warranted, a plan will be recommended and discussed with the parents. If the parents concur, the plan will be implemented. The final goal is to get the child back into the regular program (mainstreaming) whenever feasible.

The screening program for *group assessment* includes the following types of instruments.

1. Ability Testing
   K: Peabody Picture Vocabulary Test (individual)
   1-12:   Otis-Lennon Mental Ability Test

2. Achievement
   K-12:   The appropriate WRAT (Wide-Range Achievement Test)

3. Physical Assessment
   Perceptual Motor   Health History
   Visual   Speech and Language
   Hearing

The *individual assessment* is the same for the achievement and physical assessment as in the group program, but the ability part is changed as follows:

   Preschool: Peabody Picture Vocabulary Test (PPVT)
   K-1:   Wechsler Pre-Primary Scale of Intelligence (WPPSI)
   2-8:   Wechsler Intelligence Scale for Children (WISC)
   9-12:   Wechsler Adult Intelligence Scale (WAIS)

Examples of profiles of some tests used in early childhood education are found in Appendix J.

E. How Does One Select a Standardized Test?

In Chapter 2, three criteria of a good measuring instrument were discussed. A review of them here is important because they are basic to the selection of a standardized test: Validity—does the test measure what it is supposed to measure? Reliability—does the test produce a consistent, accurate result? Usability—can the test be used with a minimum expenditure of time, energy, and money?

With these three criteria in mind, what are some methods of selecting the best test for evaluation purposes?

1. Reputation—It is simple to ask others about a test which they have used and what their feelings are about its effectiveness. Although this method might be used along with some other methods, it should not be used as the only method. Other schools may have had different purposes or goals in mind in their instruction; the children may be

different as to background and current status; and the specific material in the test may not be valid, in terms of content, for the pupils for whom it is being considered.

2. *Mental Measurements Yearbook*—This reference book on standardized tests should be on each school's professional shelf (see bibliography at end of chapter). This book may be used in two ways: First, the book acquaints teachers with the good tests available in the various fields of instruction and guidance; second, reading the reviews of each test helps to reduce the number of tests to consider.

3. Manual of the Test—When one wishes to become acquainted more specifically with a test, it is desirable to obtain the manual for the test and to study it thoroughly. The manual will describe the test, how it was standardized, the validity and reliability of the test and how each was determined, the scorability, the administrability, and how the results may be interpreted and applied.

4. Obtain a Sample Set—The author believes that this is the culminating step in the selection of a test. When the number of tests to be considered is reduced to three or four, one can obtain a sample set of each, study them thoroughly, take each test himself/herself, and relate them to his/her purposes and pupils. A sample set usually includes a copy of the actual test, a manual, and a scoring key, and may be obtained at reasonable cost from the publisher. This method allows the teacher to place himself or herself in the position of the pupil and thereby check the vocabulary, content, and test processes. This aids in making the decision as to the suitability of the test for local purposes and pupils.

Payne and McMorris, in their chapter on "Designing and Implementing a Testing Program," give seven guidelines for selecting tests.[6]

1. The practice of measuring achievement in arithmetic and language in the primary grades is a questionable one, because (a) scores are heavily dependent on reading ability, (b) rote memory tends to play an unduly important role in the scores, and (c) too much pressure may be placed on the child at an age when his attitude toward school is of great importance in determining his success during the next several years.

2. The older the child the closer the agreement between his current measured intelligence and his adult intelligence; the results of intelligence tests in the early grades should be interpreted in the light of their relative unreliability.

3. Interests are usually not stable until middle or late adolescence, so interest inventories are of questionable value before then.

4. Regular intelligence and achievement tests often provide information which can be used to predict the probable degrees of academic success. A so-called "prognosis" test may only duplicate such information.

6. David A. Payne and Robert F. McMorris, *Educational and Psychological Measurement* (Waltham, Massachusetts: Blaisdell Publishing Co., 1967), p. 340.

5. Some achievement tests measure isolated aspects of formal education, and some emphasize the use of information in critical thinking and problem-solving. The appropriate test will reflect the philosophy of education of the school using it.

6. Since the reliability of a test is related to its length, a shortened version of a test gives convenience at the expense of consistency. A school must balance these two factors in deciding between a longer and a shorter test form.

7. Before making routine use of "personality" or "adjustment" tests, a school should (a) carefully examine the evidence of validity for the test to be used, (b) make certain that the community understands the purpose and function of such tests, and (c) be prepared to follow up identification with treatment or referral to available psychological or psychiatric resources.

The need for holding to rigorous critical standards of evaluation and for continual evaluation cannot be overstressed. If at any point in the procedure, the test fails to meet your standards, its use should be discontinued and other tests or procedures should be substituted.

In 1974, the American Psychological Association published a revision of its Standards for Educational and Psychological Tests and Manuals. As in the original documents, the essential principle underlying this revision is that a test manual should carry information sufficient to enable any qualified user to make sound judgments regarding the usefulness and interpretation of the test. These standards cover not only tests as narrowly defined, but they cover also most of the published devices for diagnosis, prognosis, and evaluation. The standards apply to interest inventories, personality inventories, projective instruments and related clinical techniques, tests of aptitude or ability, and achievement tests—especially those in an educational setting.

As such, this document has two sets of audiences: authors and publishers who are responsible for test development and test users who select tests for various school purposes. It is suggested that teachers study the following standards and translate them into a meaningful checklist with which to study and select tests.

In order to select the best possible test for the purpose desired, many schools use a test evaluation form similar to the one by Harrington in Figure 9.2. This enables a testing committee or an administrator to collect the same information on several tests which are being considered. The student will notice that this one includes six parts: Cost, Objectivity, Standardization, Test Manual, *Mental Measurements Yearbook*, and Personal Opinions of the test. When this information is available on several tests under consideration, it is much easier to make a decision than when varying information is available.

Directions: Complete each statement by circling or filling in the best response unless specific directions are given.

Evaluator _____

Name of Test _____

Author(s) _____

Publisher _____ Copyright _____

Level: Of the Test Grade _____ Age(s) _____

Type of Test (Mental, achievement, etc.) _____

I.   Cost: (Use prices as listed in Buros, Noll, or the test company catalog.)
    A. Financial
        1. Unit cost $ _____ per _____
        2. Answer sheets cost _____ (if separate)
        3. Is the test booklet reusable?   yes _____   no _____
    B. Time
        1. The time of administration is _____ hours _____ minutes
        2. Can the test be administered in parts? yes _____ no _____
    C. Equivalent Forms
        1. Number _____

II. Objectivity: The degree to which the examiner's judgment is eliminated. Comments to be completed only when any of the following items tend to be subjective.
    A. The directions for administration

    B. The scoring

    C. Interpretation of test results

III. Standardization
    A. Describe the standardization group. (Size, age, area, etc.)

    B. Validity: The degree to which the test measures what it is designed to measure.
        1. The coefficient of validity is: (Please use the lowest index given.)
            a. Insufficient   b. adequate   c. high   d. not given
               (below .40)   (.40 to .70)   (above .70)
        2. Indicate how validity was determined if the coefficient was not given.
        3. Comments by the evaluator on the validity (optional).

Figure 9.2   Test Evaluation Form (From William E. Harrington, *A Study Guide for Measurement.* (Dubuque: Wm. C. Brown Company Publishers, 1969), pp. 149-152. Reprinted by permission of William E. Harrington.

Figure 9.2 Continued

C. Reliability: The degree to which the test results are consistent.

1. The coefficient of reliability is: (Please use the lowest index given.)

   a. insufficient   b. adequate   c. high   d. not given

    (0-.70)   (.70-.90)   (above .90)

2. The coefficient of reliability was determined in what manner.

   a. Test   b. Equivalent   c. Odds   d. Split   e. Kuder   f. Other

    Re-test   Forms   Evens   Half   Richardson

3. Was the Spearman-Brown prophecy formula used? yes _____

                                         no _____

4. Comments by the evaluator on reliability (optional)

D. Norms

   Types of norms given (percentile, age, grade, etc.)

IV.   Test Manual: A complete manual contains all of the preceding information with the following additions.

A. List the advantages and purposes of the test.

B. List the suggestions for use of the test.

V.   Mental Measurements Yearbook: To gain other opinions of the test please review the mental measurements yearbook by Oscar Buros.

A. List advantages of the test.

B. List disadvantages of the test.

VI.   What are your opinions of the test?

THE STANDARDS[7]

I. Standards for Tests, Manuals, and Reports
    A. Dissemination of Information
        1. When a test is published or otherwise made available for operational use, it should be accompanied by a manual (or other published or readily available information) that makes every reasonable effort to follow the recommendations of these standards and, in particular, to provide the information required to substantiate any claims that have been made for its use.
        2. A test manual should describe fully the development of the test: the rationale, specifications followed in writing items or selecting observations, and procedures and results of item analysis or other research.
        3. The test and its manual should be revised at appropriate intervals. The time for revision has arrived whenever changing conditions of use or new research data make any statements in the manual incorrect or misleading.

    B. Aids to Interpretation
        1. The test, the manual, the record forms, and other accompanying material should help users make correct interpretations of the test results and should warn against common misuses.
        2. The test manual should describe clearly the psychological, educational, or other reasoning underlying the test and nature of the characteristic it is intended to measure.
        3. The test should state explicitly the purposes and applications required to administer the test and to interpret it properly.
        4. The test manual should identify any special qualifications required to administer the test and to interpret it properly.
        5. Evidence of validity and reliability, along with other relevant research data, should be presented in support of any claims being made.
        6. Test developers or others offering computer services for test interpretations should provide a manual reporting the rationale evidence in support of computer-based interpretation of scores.

    C. Directions for Administration and Scoring
        1. The directions for administration should be presented in the test manual with sufficient clarity and emphasis so that the test user can duplicate, and will be encouraged to duplicate, the administrative conditions under which the norms and the data on reliability and validity were obtained.
        2. Instructions should prepare the examinee for the examination: Sample material, practice use of answer sheets or punch cards, sample questions, and the like, should be provided.
        3. The procedures for scoring the test should be presented in the test manual with a maximum of detail and clarity to reduce the likelihood of scoring error.

7. Joint Committee of the APA, AERA, and NCME, *Standards for Educational and Psychological Tests* (Washington, DC: American Psychological Association, Inc., 1974). Pp. 9-73. Copyright 1974 by The American Psychological Association. Reprinted by permission.

D. Norms and Scales
   1. Norms should be published in the test manual at the time of release of the test for operational use.
   2. Norms presented in the test manual should refer to defined and clearly described populations. These populations should be the groups with whom the user of the test will ordinarily wish to compare the persons tested.
   3. In reporting norms, test manuals should use percentiles for one or more appropriate reference groups or standard scores for which the basis is clearly set forth; any exceptional type of score or unit should be explained and justified. Measures of central tendency and variability always should be reported.
   4. Local norms are more important for many uses of tests than are published norms. A test manual should suggest using local norms in such situations.
   5. Derived scales used for reporting scores should be carefully described in the test manual to increase the likelihood of accurate interpretation of scores by both the test interpreter and the examinee.
   6. If scales are revised, new forms added, or other changes made, the revised test manual should provide tables of equivalence between the new and the old forms. This provision is particularly important in cases where data are recorded on cumulative records.
   7. Where it is expected that a test will be used to assess groups rather than individuals (i.e., for schools or programs), normative data based on group summary statistics should be provided.

II. Standards for Reports of Research on Reliability and Validity

E. Validity
   1. A manual or research report should present the evidence of validity for each type of inference for which use of the test is recommended. If validity for some suggested interpretation has not been investigated, that fact should be made clear.
   2. A test user is responsible for marshalling the evidence in support of his claims of validity and reliability. The use of test scores in decision rules should be supported by evidence.
   3. All measures of criteria should be described completely and accurately. The manual or research report should comment on the adequacy of a criterion. Whenever feasible, it should draw attention to significant aspects of performance that the criterion measure does not reflect and to irrelevant factors likely to affect it.
   4. A criterion measure should itself be studied for evidence of validity and that evidence should be presented in the manual or report.
   5. The manual or research report should provide information on the appropriateness of or limits to the generalizability of validity information.
   6. The sample employed in a validity study and the conditions under which testing is done should be consistent with recommended test use and should be described sufficiently for the reader to judge its pertinence to his situation.
   7. The collection of data for a validity study should follow procedures consistent with the purposes of the study.

8. Any statistical analysis of criterion-related validity should be reported in the manual in a form that enables the reader to determine how much confidence is to be placed in judgments or predictions regarding the individual.
9. A test user should investigate the possibility of bias in tests or in test items. Whenever possible, there should be an investigation of possible differences in criterion-related validity for ethnic, sex, or other subsamples that can be identified when the test is given. The manual or research report should give the results for each subsample separately or report that no differences were found.
10. When a scoring key, the selection of items, or the weighting of tests is based on one sample, the manual should report validity coefficients based on data obtained from one or more independent cross-validation samples. Validity statements should not be based on the original sample.
11. To the extent feasible, a test user who intends to continue employing a test over a long period of time should develop procedures for gathering data for continued research.
12. If test performance is to be interpreted as a representative sample of performance in a universe of situations, the test manual should give a clear definition of the universe represented and describe the procedures followed in the sampling from it.
13. If the author proposes to interpret scores on a test as measuring a theoretical variable (ability, trait, or attitude), his proposed interpretation should be fully stated. His theoretical construct should be distinguished from interpretations arising on the basis of other theories.

F. Reliability and Measurement Error
1. The test manual or research report should present evidence of reliability, including estimates of the standard error of measurement, that permits the reader to judge whether scores are sufficiently dependable for the intended uses of the test. If any of the necessary evidence has not been collected, the absence of such information should be noted.
2. The procedures and samples used to determine reliability coefficients or standard errors of measurement should be described sufficiently to permit a user to judge the applicability of the data reported to the individuals or groups with which he is concerned.
3. Reports of reliability studies should ordinarily be expressed in the test manual in terms of variances of error components, standard errors of measurement, or product-moment reliability coefficients. Unfamiliar expressions of data should be clearly described, with reference to their development.
4. If two or more forms of a test are published for use with the same examinees, information on means, variances, and characteristics of items in the forms should be reported in the test manual along with the coefficients of correlation among their scores. If necessary evidence is not provided, the test manual should warn the reader against assuming equivalence of scores.
5. Evidence of internal consistency should be reported for any unspeeded test.

6. The test manual should indicate to what extent test scores are stable, that is, how nearly constant the scores are likely to be if a parallel form of a test is administered after time has elapsed. The manual should also describe the effect of any such variation on the usefulness of the test. The time interval to be considered depends on the nature of the test and on what interpretation of the test scores is recommended.

III. Standards for the Use of Tests

G. Qualifications and Concerns of Users
1. A test user should have a general knowledge of measurement principles and of the limitations of test interpretations.
2. A test user should know and understand the literature relevant to the tests he uses and the test problems with which he deals.
3. One who has the responsibility for decisions about individuals or policies that are based on test results should have an understanding of psychological or educational measurement and of validation and other test research.
4. Test users should seek to avoid bias in test selection, administration, and interpretation; they should try to avoid even the appearance of discriminatory practice.
5. Institutional test users should establish procedures for periodic internal review of test use.

H. Choice or Development of Test or Method
1. The choice or development of tests, test batteries, or other assessment procedures should be based on clearly formulated goals and hypotheses.
2. A test user should consider more than one variable for assessment and the assessment of any given variable by more than one method.
3. In choosing an existing test, a test user should relate its history research and development to his intended use of the instrument.
4. In general, a test user should try to choose or to develop an assessment technique in which "tester-effect" is minimized, or in which reliability assessment across testers can be assured.
5. Test scores used for selection or other administrative decisions about an individual may not be useful for individual or program evaluation and vice versa.

I. Administration and Scoring
1. A test user is expected to follow carefully the standardized procedures described in the manual for administering a test.
2. The test administrator is responsible for establishing conditions, consistent with the principle of standardization, that enable each examinee to do his best.
3. A test user is responsible for accuracy in scoring, checking, ending, or recording test results.
4. If specific cutting scores are to be used as a basis for decisions, a test user should have a rationale, justification, or explanation of the cutting scores adopted.
5. The test user shares with the test developer or distributor a responsibility for maintaining test security.

J. Interpretation of Scores

1. A test score should be interpreted as an estimate of performance under a given set of circumstances. It should not be interpreted as some absolute characteristic of the examinee or as something permanent and generalizable to all other circumstances.

2. Test scores should ordinarily be reported only to people who are qualified to interpret them. If scores are reported, they should be accompanied by explanations sufficient for the recipient to interpret them correctly.

3. The test user should recognize that estimates of reliability do not indicate criterion-related validity.

4. A test user should examine carefully the rationale and validity of computer-based interpretations of test scores.

5. In norm-referenced interpretations, a test user should interpret an obtained score with reference to sets of norms appropriate for the individual tested and for the intended use.

6. Any content-referenced interpretation should clearly indicate the domain to which one can generalize.

7. The test user should consider alternative interpretations of a given score.

8. The test user should be able to interpret test performance relative to other measures.

9. A test user should develop procedures for systematically eliminating from data files test-score information that has, because of the lapse of time, become obsolete.

F. What Are Some Sources of Information on Educational and Psychological Tests?

There are many sources of information about educational and psychological tests.

1. *Publishers' Catalogs.* Publishers of standardized tests usually provide free catalogs to qualified persons. These catalogs include such information as a brief description of the tests, their costs, purposes, appropriate age or grade levels, number of alternate forms, norms, time limits, scoring methods, and cost of a specimen set. (A partial listing of test publishers and their addresses is found in Appendix I).

2. *Specimen Set.* Most publishers put together a sample specimen set of each test they sell of a paper-and-pencil variety. This usually includes a manual, test booklet, answer sheet, and a scoring key. They will range in price from $1.00 to $10.00. This is a good way to check the things that you have read or heard about the test—the content, vocabulary, difficulty, format, and the like.

3. *Bulletins.* Many publishers issue bulletins including a variety of topics related to testing. The name of the company and an example of one or two of their bulletins follows. Some of these are free and others charge a minimum amount for each. An inquiry to the company will bring you this information.

a. California Test Bureau.
    Educational Bulletin No. 5. *Teacher Use of Test Results.*
    Educational Bulletin No. 21. *Guidance Testing and the Identification of Pupil Characteristics.*
b. Educational Testing Service
    Since 1967, ETS has published its *Test Collection Bulletin,* which contains up-to-date listings of new tests published in the United States and foreign countries. It also publishes a Test and Measurement Kit at a nominal cost. It includes such titles as:

    > Making the Classroom Test: A Guide for Teachers
    > Multiple-Choice Questions: A Close Look
    > Selecting an Achievement Test: Principles and Procedures
    > Short-Cut Statistics for Teacher-Made Tests

    In association with Rutgers University Graduate School of Education, ETS publishes *TM News* which includes up-to-date reports on measurement topics. TM Reports occasionally publishes summaries of conference papers dealing with measurement.
c. Harcourt Brace Jovanovich, Inc.
    A Glossary of Measurement Terms
    How Is a Test Built?
    Testing: A Tool for Curriculum Development
    Using Stanines To Obtain Composite Scores Based on Test Data and Teacher Ranks
d. Houghton Mifflin Company
    How To Construct a Good Multiple-Choice Test
    Changes in the Intelligence Quotient with Age
e. National Council on Measurement (NCME). This professional organization publishes quarterly reports concerned with the "practical implications of measurement and related research and their application to educational problems of individuals, institutions, and systems."
f. The Psychological Corporation
    No. 37 How Effective Are Your Tests?
    No. 38 Expectancy Tables—A Way of Interpreting Test Validity
    No. 48 Methods of Expressing Test Scores
    No. 54 On Telling Parents About Test Results

4. Yearbooks. Annual Review of Psychology
    National Society for the Study of Education (NSSE) has published yearbooks relating to measurement and evaluation every few years since 1915. The most recent ones include:

    > Sixty-Second Yearbook, 1963, Part II: *The Impact and Improvement of School Testing Programs*
    > Sixty-Eighth Yearbook, 1969, Part II: *Evaluation; New Roles, New Means.*
    > Buros, Oscar K. *Mental Measurements Yearbook,* Eighth Edition, 1978
    > Buros, Oscar K. *Reading Tests and Reviews,* 1968
    > Buros, Oscar K. *Personality Tests and Reviews,* 1968
    > (All from The Gryphon Press, Highland Park, N. J.)

5. Indices
    Education Index
    Psychological Abstracts

6. Journals
    American Educational Research Bulletin (Quarterly)
    American Psychologist (Monthly)
    Educational and Psychological Measurement (Quarterly)
    Journal of Counseling Psychology (Bimonthly)
    Journal of Educational Measurement (Quarterly)
    Measurement and Evaluation in Guidance (Quarterly)
    Psychological Bulletin (Monthly)
    Review of Educational Research (Five times a year)

7. University Research and Service Bureaus
    Many colleges and universities will have an office or bureau to which school personnel may turn for assistance in test information and selection. Most of these will have test catalogs, specimen sets of tests, and several reference books on standardized tests. The personnel at such a bureau will not try to sell any test but will provide information upon which a local school can make its own selection.

G.   What Are Some Principles for Administering Standardized Tests?

That correct administration of the tests is basic to obtaining good results cannot be emphasized too strongly. The purpose of the following principles is to enable the average teacher to approach the examination with confidence.

These principles may be divided into two categories: those which will assist the teacher in calling for the pupil's best efforts and those which will duplicate, as nearly as possible, the prescribed conditions under which the test was standardized.

1. Principles to call forth the pupil's best efforts.
    a. Provide for favorable testing environment.
        1. Give the test in a room away from direct noise.
        2. Give the test in familiar surroundings.
        3. Provide for proper light, heat, and ventilation.
        4. Arrange the desks and/or tables and chairs properly.
        5. Plan to have all distractions eliminated. Put a sign on the door: *Testing; Do Not Disturb.*
    b. Provide for the proper motivation of the pupil.
        1. Explain the purpose of the test.
        2. Emphasize the guidance use of the results.
        3. Indicate how his or her status will be affected.
        4. Emphasize that it will be an enjoyable task.
        5. Solicit his or her attention and cooperation.

2. Duplicate as nearly as possible the prescribed conditions under which the test was standardized.
   a. Be completely familiar with the manual.
   b. Read over the complete test booklet.
   c. Rehearse reading directions aloud several times.
   d. When giving the test, *read* the directions verbatim; do not try to memorize directions.
   e. Follow the timing precisely.
   f. Use the most accurate timepiece available (a stop watch or an ordinary watch with a sweep second hand).
   g. Keep a time chart:
      Parts of the Test / Time Allowed / Starting Time / Stopping Time
   h. Remember, the only help that can be given a pupil is that which is indicated in the manual. In general, questions of a mechanical nature can be answered (Where do I put the answer? May I use another pencil?). ANY QUESTIONS REGARDING CONTENT (What does this word mean? I don't understand the meaning of this question.) CANNOT BE ANSWERED. The response should be, on the latter type, "I'm sorry, I cannot help you; if you do not know it, go on to the next question." Your job is to keep them moving on the test.
   i. Go over the sample items with the pupils carefully.
   j. Ask if they have any questions BEFORE the actual test starts.
   k. Supervise during the test, but do not distract.
   l. Test only the number you can adequately supervise at one time. (The general rule is that there should be one supervisor for every 25 pupils on the high school level; on the elementary level, there should be only three or four tested at one time in the first grade, and one can gradually test more as the grade level increases, up to about 25 at the seventh-grade level.)

H.   What Are Some Principles for the Scoring of Standardized Tests?

In the scoring of standardized tests, the main objective is to score the tests as quickly as possible and with complete accuracy. The system which best accomplishes these objectives should be used. Sometimes, tests are machine-scored by the school itself, by a private agency, or by the test publisher. Such possibilities should be investigated by the school whenever the number of tests to be scored is extremely large and when it is believed that the tests will take an undue amount of the teacher's time.

When it may be necessary for the teacher to score the tests, certain principles should be followed. The principles might be classified under two headings: General Administration and Actual Scoring.

1. General Administration
    a. There should be a meeting of all teachers concerned, at which the supervisor would actually teach the proper procedure for scoring the test.
    b. The manual and scoring key should be studied and discussed.
    c. An actual demonstration should be presented.
    d. The specifics of scoring should be discussed—kinds of symbols to use in marking, how double checks should be made, the type of pencil to use, and where and how to record the score.

2. Actual Scoring
    a. Reread the scoring directions so that they are clearly in mind.
    b. Score the same page on all of the tests before proceeding to the next page. This makes the procedure more rapid and reduces the chance of error.
    c. Use the symbols agreed upon for marking or follow the suggestions in the manual. Most test parts ask for total right. Therefore, you may mark the correct ones with a C or mark the wrong ones with a ✔ counting omissions as wrong. Sometimes teachers use a + for a correct one, — for an incorrect one, and 0 for omitted items.
    d. Draw a horizontal line under the last item attempted.
    e. When the tests are scored, repeat the process using a different colored pencil to check your scoring.
    f. Count the number right if this is the procedure, or apply the correction formula, and place the final score in the space provided. Recheck your result.
    g. Transfer the score to the profile page.

If it is possible for two teachers to work together, the process is completed more quickly, and it probably is done so with less chance for error, since the second person checks the first's scoring as the process continues.

Some research has been done relative to scoring errors made by teachers. Such research has listed the type of error from most to least as follows: Counting, instructions, use of key, use of tables, and computation.

Summary Statements

1. A standardized test is an instrument designed to measure objectively one or more aspects of a total personality by means of samples of verbal or nonverbal responses, or by means of other behaviors.
2. Each testing program must have a philosophy and a purpose to guide it. The goals of the school which can be served by test results should be identified and stated clearly in planning the test program.

3. In designing a testing program, the committee should consider several established criteria which include concern for the purpose, proper articulation and continuity, comprehensiveness, input from all users, the use of trained personnel, a recognized part of the educational program, and confidentiality of results.

4. Ability and achievement tests form the backbone of a testing program. Additional tests of aptitude and personality may be added as the goals of individual schools warrant.

5. The essential principle underlying the APA *Standards for Educational and Psychological Tests and Manuals* is that the test manual should contain sufficient information to enable any qualified user to make sound judgments regarding the usefulness and interpretation of the test.

6. There are many sources of information from which a school can learn about tests. The final selection however, should be based on firsthand study of the complete test to determine its relationship to the purposes of the program and the pupils on which it is to be used.

7. A test evaluation form enables a testing committee or an administrator to collect the same information on several tests which are to be considered for the testing program.

8. A carefully conducted study of principles of test administration will enable the examiner to call forth the pupil's best efforts and to duplicate, as nearly as possible, the prescribed conditions under which the test was standardized.

9. A test may be scored efficiently if there are good scoring directions, an adequate key, and objective responses.

Discussion Questions

1. Compare the definition of a standardized test with the teacher-made classroom tests with which you are familiar. In what ways does a standardized instrument differ?

2. Summarize in your own words a response to the question: "Why have a testing program?"

3. Discuss how a testing committee would proceed to design a testing program for a school, K-12.

4. Describe the types of tests which are normally a part of a testing program and what each contributes to the program.

5. Discuss how, as a member of a testing committee, you would recommend the committee proceed to *select* a general survey achievement test.

6. In your own words, why should an examiner be thoroughly acquainted with the principles of administering standardized tests?

7. Compare the advantages and disadvantages of machine scoring and manual scoring of tests.

Student Activities

1. Either through an interview with testing personnel in a school or through your research, devise a set of objectives or purposes for a testing program for a specific school on a level of your interest.
2. Design a testing program for the purpose of objectives stated in No. 1. Suggest the types of tests and the purpose of each.
3. With the assistance of your instructor, select a standardized test and manual to evaluate using Harrington's *Test Evaluation Form.* You should have Buros' *Mental Measurements Yearbook* at your disposal to assist in filling out the form.
4. Write a summary of a review of a standardized test found in an educational or psychological journal. Compare this with the type of review in Buros. Is there a difference?
5. For a standardized test suggested by your instructor, study and be ready to simulate the administration of the test to another member of the class or a small group.
6. With the aid of your instructor, score a standardized test using the proper materials. Does everyone get the same score?

Selected Readings

Anastasi, Anne. *Psychological Testing,* 4th ed. New York: The Macmillan Company, 1976. Chapters 2 and 3.

Cronbach, Lee J. *Essentials of Psychological Testing,* 3rd ed. New York: Harper & Row Publishers, Inc., 1970. Chapters 2 and 3.

Greenbaum, William, Garet, Michael S., and Solomon, Ellen R. *Educational Progress.* New York: McGraw-Hill Book Co., 1977.

Gronlund, Norman E. *Measurement and Evaluation in Teaching,* 3rd ed. New York: The Macmillan Company, 1976. Chapter 14.

———. *Readings in Measurement and Evaluation.* New York: The Macmillan Company, 1968. Part V.

Hopkins, Charles D., and Antes, Richard L. *Classroom Measurement and Evaluation.* Itasca, IL: F. E. Peacock Publishers, Inc., 1978. Chapters 12 and 13.

Joint Committee of the American Psychological Association, American Educational Research Association, and National Council on Measurement in Education. *Standards for Educational and Psychological Tests and Manuals.* Washington, D. C.: American Psychological Association, Inc., 1974. Pamphlet.

Lennon, Roger T. "Planning a Testing Program," *Test Service Bulletin, No. 55.* New York: Harcourt Brace Jovanovich, Inc. Page 3.

Linneman, Richard H., and Merenda, Peter F. *Educational Measurement,* 2nd ed. Glenview, IL: Scott, Foresman and Company, 1979. Chapter 5 and Appendix C.

Mehrens, William A., and Lehmann, Irvin J. *Measurement and Evaluation in Education and Psychology.* New York: Holt, Rinehart and Winston, Inc., 1973. Chapter 13.

Noll, Victor H., Scannell, Dale P. and Craig, Robert C. *Introduction to Educational Measurement,* 4th ed. Boston: Houghton Mifflin Company, 1979. Chapter 13.

Popham, W. James. *Criterion-Referenced Instruction.* Belmont, CA: Fearon Publishers, 1973.

Samuda, Ronald J. *Psychological Testing of American Minorities.* New York: Dodd, Mead & Company, 1975. Chapters 1-6.

Sax, Gilbert. *Principles of Educational Measurement and Evaluation.* Belmont, CA: Wadsworth Publishing Company, Inc., 1974. Chapter 10.

Stanley, Julian C., and Hopkins, Kenneth D. *Educational and Psychological Measurement and Evaluation.* Englewood Cliffs, NJ: Prentice-Hall, Inc., 1972. Chapter 17.

TenBrink, Terry D. *Evaluation. A Practical Guide for Teachers.* New York: McGraw-Hill Book Company, 1974. Chapter 14.

Thorndike, Robert L., and Hagen, Elizabeth. *Measurement and Evaluation in Psychology and Education,* 4th ed. New York: John Wiley & Sons, Inc., 1977. Chapters 5 and 14.

Tuckman, Bruce W. *Measuring Educational Outcomes: Fundamentals of Testing.* New York: Harcourt Brace Jovanovich, Inc., 1975. Chapter 15.

10

Standardized Ability and Aptitude Tests

What are ability tests and how are they structured?
What are some typical tests of ability?
How does one interpret an ability test?
What are some uses of an ability test?
What are some examples of ability and aptitude test profiles?

A. What Are Ability Tests and How Are They Structured?

There are many definitions of intelligence. Generally, the definitions will fall into one or more of three categories: The capacity to: (1) think abstractly; (2) learn; or (3) integrate new experiences and adapt to new situations. Some of the common definitions are as follows:

Binet and Simon (1916)
    . . . the capacity to judge well, to reason well, and to comprehend well.
Terman (1916)
    . . . the ability to think in terms of abstract ideas.
Wechsler (1944)
    . . . the aggregate or global capacity of the individual to act purpose-
    fully, to think rationally, and to deal effectively with his environment.
Goddard (1946)
    . . . the degree of availability of one's experiences for the solution of
    immediate problems and the anticipation of future ones.

An aptitude test differs from a general ability test in that it measures a combination of abilities believed to be indicative of an individual's *ability to learn in some particular area.*

An ability test will reflect a theory or structure of intelligence. Some of the more common theories along with their proponents follow.

Binet's Position . . .

Binet believed that the mind is unitary and possesses one overriding function which is effective adjustment to environment. Of course, the Stanford-Binet test is an example here. Group tests would include the Henmon-Nelson Test of Mental Ability and the Otis-Lennon Mental Ability Test.

Spearman's Position . . .

In 1927, Spearman developed the two-factor theory suggesting that intelligence is composed of a general factor (g) and many specific factors (S_1, $S_2 \ldots S_n$). Individuals differ in the amount of g they possess. Specific factors are unique to each test and are therefore of lesser value than g. Examples here would include the Short Form Test of Academic Aptitude and the Lorge-Thorndike Intelligence Tests.

Thorndike's Position . . .

Thorndike believed that intelligence consists of a very large number of specific factors ($S_1 + S_2 + S_3 + \ldots S_n$). It is called the *multi-factor theory*. It casts doubt on the existence of any g, general factor. According to this theory, any mental act involves a number of minute elements operating together. Any other mental act also involves a number of the elements in combination. An example would be Thorndike's test called the CAVD. It was composed of four parts: sentence completion (C), arithmetic reasoning (A), vocabulary (V), and following directions (D). Thorndike tried to measure the number and variety of tasks (graded according to difficulty level) a person could complete.

Thurstone's Position . . .

Another *multi-factor* theory was developed by L. L. Thurstone of the University of Chicago. In 1938, Thurstone identified a relatively small number of "primary mental abilities" which are independent of each other. The ones with which he most often is associated are as follows:

M—*Memory:* The ability to memorize rote material.
N—*Number:* The ability to do calculations accurately and rapidly.
P—*Perceptual speed:* The ability to note visual details rapidly.
R—*Reasoning:* Primarily inductive reasoning.
S—*Space:* The ability to visualize patterns and objects when they are rotated or when they are part of a configuration change.
V—*Verbal:* Primarily measured by vocabulary and other verbal tests.
W—*Word fluency:* Measured by the number of words related in some way that can be produced in a specific period of time (such as ending in -*ing*).

TABLE 10.1

*Classification of Intelligence Quotients on the
Stanford-Binet and WAIS*

IQ Range	Percent	Classification

Stanford-Binet Intelligence Scale*

IQ Range	Percent	Classification
140 and above	1.6	Very Superior
120-139	11.3	Superior
110-119	18.1	High Average
90-109	46.5	Normal or Average
80-89	14.5	Low Average
70-79	5.6	Borderline Defective
69 and below	2.9	Mentally Defective

Wechsler Adult Intelligence Scale†

IQ Range	Percent	Classification
130 and above	2.2	Very Superior
120-129	6.7	Superior
110-119	16.1	Bright Normal
90-109	50.0	Average
80-89	16.1	Dull Normal
70-79	6.7	Borderline
69 and below	2.2	Mental Defective

*After Terman, L. M., & Merrill, M. A. *Measuring Intelligence*. Copyright © 1973 by Houghton Mifflin Company. Reprinted by permission of Houghton Mifflin Company. All rights reserved.
†From *Wechsler's Measurement and Appraisal of Adult Intelligence* by Joseph D. Matarazzo. Copyright © 1972 by Oxford University Press, Inc. Reprinted by permission.

According to Thurstone, intelligence is represented neither by *g* nor by a multitude of highly specific connections, as claimed by Thorndike, but by a more intermediate position between the two. The latest standardization of his *Primary Mental Abilities* (PMA), in 1962, contained five factors: Number, perceptual speed (K-6 only), reasoning (grades 4-12 only), spatial, and verbal.

B. What Are Some Typical Tests of Ability?

Primary or K-12

Cognitive Abilities Test (CAT). Houghton Mifflin Company, 1968. K-1, Grades 2-3. Primary level of Lorge-Thorndike Intelligence Test. Testing time: 40-50 minutes.

California Test of Mental Maturity. CTB/McGraw-Hill, 1963, K to Adult. Yields Language, Non-Language, and Total scores.

Davis-Eells Test of General Intelligence or Problem Solving Ability. Harcourt Brace Jovanovich, 1953. Purports to be a culture-fair test, free of reading demands, based on common experiences shared by all urban American children. Primary-6. Time: 30-90 minutes depending on level.

Kuhlmann-Anderson Intelligence Tests. Seventh Edition. Personnel Press, 1967. Eight levels from K-12. Yields verbal, quantitative, and total. Total can be converted to deviation IQ.

Otis-Lennon Mental Ability Test. Harcourt Brace Jovanovich, 1970. Six levels from K-12. Revision of familiar Otis Quick-Scoring Mental Ability Tests. Many derived scores including percentiles, stanines, mental ages, and deviation IQ's.

Cooperative Pre-School Inventory. Educational Testing Service, 1970. Ages three to six. Five scores: personal-social responsiveness; associative vocabulary; knowledge and application of numerical concepts, knowledge and application of sensory concepts, and total.

Ravens Progressive Matrices. The Psychological Corporation. Ages five and over. Illustrates Spearman's g. Claimed by some to be "culture-fair," but there is little evidence to support the claim. No time limits.

SRA Tests of General Ability (TOGA). Science Research Associates, 1962. Grades K-12 in five forms. All items in pictorial form, thus reducing reading ability. The reasoning test is supposed to be culture-fair, but there is no evidence to support this.

Elementary and/or Through High School

Cooperative School and College Ability Test. Cooperative Test Division of ETS. Grades 4-14 in five different levels. Testing time is 60-75 minutes. Yields three scores: verbal, quantitative, and total.

Henmon-Nelson Tests of Mental Ability, Revised Edition. Houghton Mifflin Company. Grades 3-14 in four levels. Testing time is 30-45 minutes. Yields a verbal, quantitative, and total score. One of the old names in ability testing.

IPAT Culture-Fair Intelligence Test. Institute for Personality and Ability Testing. Ages 8-superior adult in two scales. Testing time is 20-30 minutes. Although some claim it to be free from environmental influences, there is no evidence that it is culture-fair.

Lorge-Thorndike Intelligence Tests. Houghton Mifflin Company. Grades 3-College Freshmen. Testing time is 35-45 minutes. Yields a verbal and nonverbal score.

Quick-Word Test. Harcourt Brace Jovanovich, 1964. Grades 4-college in three levels. Untimed, but takes about 15 minutes. Yields a quick measure of verbal intelligence. Fifty words on elementary level, 100 words on higher levels.

SRA Tests of Educational Ability (TEA). Science Research Associates, 1962 Edition. Testing time is 30-70 minutes. Grades 4-12 in three levels. Yields four scores: language, reasoning, quantitative, and total.

Terman-McNemar Test of Mental Ability. Harcourt Brace Jovanovich, 1941. Grades 7-13. Seven subtests. Yields deviation IQ's and percentile ranks. Testing time, 40 minutes.

High School and College

American College Test (ACT). Revised annually. For high school seniors and college freshmen. Four tests: English usage, mathematics usage, social studies reading, natural science reading, and a composite score. Gives predictive data as well as current status with various norm groups.

College Entrance Examination Board Scholastic Aptitude Test (SAT). Revised continually. Educational Testing Service. Candidates for college entrance. Two scores: verbal and mathematical. Much normative data.

College Qualification Test. The Psychological Corporation, 1961. Candidates for college entrance. Six scores: verbal, numerical, science information, social studies information, total information, and total. Many norms in various majors.

Ohio State University Psychological Test. Science Research Associates, 1968. Grades 9-13. Yields three scores: vocabulary, word relationships, and reading comprehension.

Aptitude Tests

Bennett Hand-Tool Dexterity Test. Adolescents and adults. The Psychological Corporation. Time is 4-12 minutes. Tests proficiency in use of wrenches and screwdrivers.

Detroit Clerical Aptitudes Examination. Bobbs-Merrill Company, 1944. Eight parts including a handwriting scale.

Differential Aptitude Tests. The Psychological Corporation, 1973. Tests verbal reasoning, numerical ability, abstract reasoning, space relations, mechanical reasoning, clerical speed and accuracy, and language usage. Junior and Senior High School and young adults.

Flanagan Aptitude Classification Tests (FACT). Science Research Associates, 1960. High school and adults. Time: 2 hours and 46 minutes. Includes tests of inspection, coding, memory, precision, assembly, scales, coordination, judgment and comprehension, arithmetic, patterns, components, tables, mechanics, expression.

General Aptitude Test Battery. United States Employment Service, 1973. For ages 16 and up. Time: 2 hours and 15 minutes. Measures intelligence, verbal, numerical, spatial, form perception, clerical perception, eye-hand coordination, motor speed, finger dexterity, and manual dexterity.

Horn Art Aptitude Inventory. Stoelting Company, 1953. For Grades 12-16 and adults. Time: 50 minutes. Outline drawings of simple objects and creative composition.

Meier Art Judgment Test. Bureau of Educational Research and Service, Iowa City, 1928-1942. Grades 7-12 and adults. Student selects the better of 100 pairs of pictures.

Minnesota Paper Form Board, Revised. The Psychological Corporation, 1970. Grades 9-adult. Paper-and-pencil test measuring spatial perception.

Modern Language Aptitude Test. The Psychological Corporation, 1955-58. Grades 9 to adult. Designed primarily as a measure of an individual's probable degree of success in learning a modern foreign language. All directions on a tape recording.

Multiple Aptitude Tests. CTB/McGraw-Hill, 1959. Grades 9-13. Measures word meaning, paragraph meaning, language usage, routine clerical facility, arithmetic reasoning, arithmetic computations, applied science and mechanics, spatial relations—two dimensions, and spatial relations—three dimensions.

Pimsleur Language Aptitude Battery. Harcourt Brace Jovanovich, 1966. Grades 6-10. On tape. Includes grade-point average, interest in studying a foreign language, verbal ability, and auditory ability.

Seashore Measures of Musical Talent. The Psychological Corporation, 1919-1960. Probably best known of musical aptitude tests. Includes tests of pitch, loudness, rhythm, time, timbre, and tonal memory. All tests are on a record or tape.

Short Employment Tests. The Psychological Corporation, 1972. For adults. Vocabulary, arithmetic computation, clerical skill. Time: 15 minutes.

Torrance Tests of Creative Thinking. Personnel Press, 1966. These tests appear in verbal and figural versions. The verbal form tests are entitled "Thinking Creatively with Words," the figural, "Thinking Creatively with Pictures." Verbal test takes 45 minutes, figural test about 30 minutes. Grades 1-12.

Individual Ability Tests

Columbia Mental Maturity Scale. Third Edition (Burgemeister, Blum, and Lorge, 1972), Harcourt Brace Jovanovich. Useful in evaluating children who have sensory or motor defects or who have difficulty in speaking and, to some extent, in reading. The entire test, appropriate for children in the mental age range of 3-10 years, takes 15-20 minutes to administer.

Illinois Test of Psycholinguistic Abilities. Western Psychological Services. Widely used diagnostic instrument to delineate specific abilities and disabilities for remediation in children 2 to 10 years old. The 12 subtests provide a comprehensive evaluation of abilities in channels of communication, psycholinguistic processes, and levels of organization. Individually administered in about 60 minutes. Important for work in learning disabilities.

Leiter International Performance Scale. Stoelting Company, 1972. Administered without language to individuals from 2 years of age to adulthood, the task is to select the blocks bearing the proper symbols or pictures and insert them into the appropriate recesses on the frame. The scale is also useful in testing children who may be penalized by picture vocabulary tests, e.g., the illiterate child and perhaps some children from ethnic minority groups or from "culturally deprived groups."

Peabody Picture Vocabulary Test (PPVT). American Guidance Service, 1970. Nonverbal, multiple-choice test designed to evaluate children between the ages of 2½ and 18 years who have no hearing disabilities and who can indicate "yes" or "no" in some manner. The PPVT materials are 150 plates, arranged in ascending order of difficulty by age level and containing four pictures each. The examinee points to the picture on a given plate which best illustrates the meaning of a stimulus word provided by the examiner. Testing takes about 15 minutes. Used a great deal for screening purposes.

Pictorial Test of Intelligence. Houghton Mifflin, 1964. This test has a smaller age range than the PPVT, being suitable for children from 3-8 years. It takes about 45 minutes to administer and is designed to measure six facets of mental functioning: picture vocabulary, information and comprehension, form discrimination, similarities, size and number, and immediate recall. Norms are expressed in deviation IQ's, mental ages, and percentile ranks.

Quick Test. Psychological Test Specialists, 1962. This is a brief intelligence test based on vocabulary definitions. There are three forms of the test each containing 50 words. A single form of the test can be given in three minutes or less. It is a recognition test for word meaning, using pictures of objects and activities. The Quick Test appears to be useful as a screening device, that is, when precise estimates of intelligence are not of crucial importance; it should not be used as a substitute for the S-B or Wechsler tests.

Slosson Intelligence Test. (Slosson, 1963) An age-scale test that provides mental ages from 5 months to 27 years. No time limits. It takes between 10 and 30 minutes to administer. Scoring is fairly objective. The test can be used by relatively untrained examiners. It has merit as a quick screening device or as a device for retesting purposes. The test, however, should not be used uncritically as a substitute for the S-B or Wechsler scales.

Stanford-Binet Scale. The latest revision of the Stanford-Binet scale, published by Houghton Mifflin in 1973, is used to measure general intelligence of individuals from age 2 years to Superior-Adult III level.

Wechsler Preschool and Primary Scale of Intelligence. The Psychological Corporation, 1967. Age range from 4-6½. Produces a total, verbal, and performance IQ's. Similar to the Wechsler tests in format and administration. Has ten tests and takes over an hour to give; thus it usually must be given in two sessions.

Wechsler Intelligence Scale for Children (WISC). The Psychological Corporation, 1949, 1972. The WISC was developed as a downward extension of the Weschler-Bellevue Intelligence Scale. The original scale in 1949 had six verbal and six performance tests. It yielded a verbal, performance, and total IQ. Normally, one administers five of each type of the verbal and performance. It is a deviation IQ. The 1972 revision is similar in format. The revision does represent a synthesis of two somewhat opposing aims: (1) the retention of as much of the 1949 WISC as possible because of its widespread use and acceptance and (2) the modification or elimination of items felt by some test users to be ambiguous, obsolete, or differentially unfair to particular groups of children. In addition, a number of new items were added in order to strengthen the reliability of each test, although at the same time an effort was made not to make the tests unduly long.

Wechsler Adult Intelligence Scale (WAIS). The Psychological Corporation, 1955. One of the reasons Wechsler built this scale was that the Stanford-Binet did not satisfactorily measure the intelligence of adults. The WAIS can be used on adults from 16 to 64 years. Again, normally five tests each are given in the verbal and performance area. It produces deviation IQ's in these areas plus the total. It has a mean IQ of 100 and a standard deviation of 15.

C. How Does One Interpret an Ability Test?

Interpretation and use of standardized test results is one of the most crucial topics facing educators in today's schools. It is also one of the most difficult topics to discuss, primarily because of the many variables to be considered. If such discussions are to be meaningful, one would have to specify, at the outset, the kind of test under discussion—ability test, achievement test, interest measure, or personality measure. In addition to the kind of test, one must consider single-score tests versus multiscore tests or test batteries.

The key point to remember in interpreting any test score is that, while one can administer today's tests to large groups of pupils, the meaningful interpretation of test scores can only be done for individuals one at a time. The fact that ability tests are quick to administer and simple to score does not mean that they are either quickly or easily interpreted. Those who want to use ability tests as quick and easy ways of obtaining information about students are ignoring the fact that *understanding*, not the gaining of information, is the prime goal of pupil appraisal procedures.

Below are four questions which the person doing the interpreting should consider:

1. How High Is the Student?

This means that there must be a comparison of the pupil's score with some standard. There are three standards which are most meaningful in interpreting ability tests. These are: (1) a comparison of the pupil's score with scores made by other pupils against whom he is currently competing; (2) a comparison of the pupil's score with scores made by those pupils on whom the test was standardized; and (3) a comparison of the pupil's score on this test with his scores on tests of other kinds of ability. Each of these comparisons is important and each must be made for maximal use of ability test results. The first step in interpreting an ability test is determining how high the student is.

2. Do I Believe It?

One of the major errors made in the interpretation of any test is that of accepting too many of the results at face value. It is almost as though one is saying that nothing is known about the pupil and his potentialities before the administration of the test, and the teacher is looking to the standardized test to supply an answer to a question about which nothing was known previously. The teacher knows some facts about the pupil prior to administering any test, and there are many opportunities for the teacher to obtain estimates of the pupil's ability to learn and to profit from instruction. Whenever a test score differs much from that which the teacher has predicted on the basis of prior contacts with the pupil, he should ask himself why and, if still not satisfied, ask that the pupil be retested. Teachers cannot afford to use test results blindly or exclusively from the other means of estimating the pupil's potentialities for learning.

3. How Does This Knowledge Help the Teacher Understand This Pupil As a Person?

By this is meant: How does it help the teacher to understand the student better as a total functioning personality, not only as an IQ? It becomes immediately apparent that the results of ability tests must be considered in relationship to all other things known about the student. There is no meaningful way of using the results of ability tests unless other information about the student is also considered in decisions which the teacher makes.

4. **What Is the Significance of This Score in Terms of How the Teacher Should Treat This Pupil in the Classroom Or in the Counseling Situation?**

In attempting to answer this question, it is necessary to keep in mind the primary objective of being helpful to the pupil—of doing whatever one can to help the pupil grow and achieve the maximum potential of which he or she is capable. The interpretation of an ability test result which does not include an answer to the question of the significance of the test score in terms of *actions* the teacher should take with pupils is an incomplete interpretation indeed.

D. What Are Some Uses of an Ability Test?

Standardized tests, like any other measuring device, must be justified in the way the results are used. Everything done in measurement to this point is preliminary; the real crux of a good measurement program is in the utilization of results obtained.

Standardized test publishers are as concerned about this point as are educators in schools. Most standardized test manuals devote considerable time to suggestions for the most effective use of the results. A study of this section in the test manual will prove very beneficial to the teacher.

Following is a listing of the principal teacher uses of ability test results:

1. To determine the *level* at which the pupil is capable of learning. The mental age of the child reported in years and months or in grade-place-ment-form is a good index of the level in the curriculum at which the child will be most capable of working.
2. To determine the *rate* at which the pupil learns. The intelligence quotient is an index of the rate of learning, an index of brightness. It will suggest to the teacher the rapidity with which a child can proceed in the learning process. It might vary from one kind of learning to another; thus the breaking down of the total IQ into its subparts will assist the teacher in assessing the child's rate of learning in different abilities.
3. To determine the position of a pupil *in relation* to others. This can be best assessed if the test results may be reported in percentile or stanine form. Tables in the manual will then show where the pupil stands in relation to the children on whom the test was standardized. Local norms may be established after a period of time to indicate where the child stands in relation to his peers in his own learning situation.
4. To assist in general ability grouping.
5. To determine the structure and pattern of ability for educational and vocational guidance.

6. To determine whether ability is a factor in a learning or a behavior problem.
7. To aid the teacher in setting reasonable standards of attainment.
8. To provide information for better instruction in the areas of methods and materials.

E. What Are Examples of Aptitude Test Profiles?

Following are examples of standardized test profiles illustrative of the types of report forms available from aptitude tests.

1. Figure 10. 1. Short Form Test of Academic Aptitude[1]

This test has five levels: 1.5-3.4, 3.5-4, 5-6, 7-9, and 9-12. It is a revision of the still-in-print *California Test of Mental Maturity*. It produces three scores: Language, non-language, and total. Derived scores include mental age, intelligence quotient, and a percentile.

Figure 10.2. Differential Aptitude Test[2]

Forms L and M produced in 1969 gives scores in nine areas: Verbal reasoning, numerical ability, abstract reasoning, clerical speed and accuracy, mechanical reasoning, space relations, spelling, and grammar. Verbal reasoning and numerical ability are combined to give a total in these two areas. It can be used for grades 8-12 and adults. The derived score is in percentile form and, to assist in accuracy of interpretation, a percentile band is formed around each percentile score.

Summary Statements

1. Definitions of intelligence usually fall into one of three categories: The capacity to: (1) think abstractly; (2) learn; or (3) integrate new experiences and adapt to new situations.
2. An aptitude test differs from a general ability test in that it measures a combination of abilities believed to be indicative of an individual's *ability to learn in some particular area.*

1. From Individual Record Sheet, *Short Form Test of Academic Aptitude,* devised by Elizabeth T. Sullivan, Willis W. Clark, and Ernest Tiegs. Reprinted by permission of the publisher, CTB/McGraw-Hill, Del Monte Research Park, Monterey, CA 93940. Copyright © 1970 by McGraw-Hill Inc., All Rights Reserved. Printed in the U.S.A.

2. From Individual Report Form, Differential Aptitude Test, Form L. Reproduced by permission. Copyright 1947, © 1961, 1963, 1969 by the Psychological Corporation, New York, New York. All rights reserved.

Figure 10.1 Sample Profile: Short Form Test of Academic Aptitude. (From *Short Form Test of Academic Aptitude*. Reprinted by permission of the publisher, CTB/McGraw-Hill, Del Monte Research Park, Monterey, CA 93940. Copyright © 1970 by McGraw-Hill, Inc. All Rights Reserved. Printed in the U.S.A.)

INDIVIDUAL REPORT FORM

Computer-Produced Profile

DIFFERENTIAL APTITUDE TESTS [1963 EDITION]

G. K. Bennett, H. G. Seashore, and A. G. Wesman

Forms L and M

(Ψ)

Your Profile of DAT Scores

The numbers that tell how you did on each test are in the column marked "Percentile." Think of "percentile" as meaning "per cent of people." Your percentile tells where you rank on a test in comparison with boys or girls in your grade. These percentiles are based on test scores earned by thousands of students in numerous schools across the country. If your percentile rank is 50, you are just in the middle — that is, one-half of the students in the national group did better than you and one-half did less well. (If your school uses local norms, your counselor will explain the difference.)

The percentile shows what per cent of your national (or local) group scored no higher than you did. If your percentile rank on one test is 80, you are at the top of 80 per cent of the group—only 20 per cent made higher scores than yours. If you scored in the 25th percentile, this means about 75 per cent of the group did better than you on the test. Thus, a percentile rank always indicates your relative standing among a theoretical 100 persons representing a large "norm" group — in this case, students of your sex and grade. It does NOT tell you how many questions (or what per cent of them) you answered correctly.

On your profile, a bar of X's has been printed in the row for each test you took. The reason for the bar instead of a single X is that tests are not perfectly accurate; you cannot be sure that your score is a precise measurement of your ability, but you can be sure that you stand somewhere within the area covered by the bar. The percentile you earned is at the middle of the bar, except when the bar has been shortened in the case of an extremely high or low percentile so as not to run off the chart.

How Big a Difference Is Important?

Since tests of this kind cannot be perfectly accurate, your score might not be exactly the same if you could take the same test twice. Therefore, you should not overestimate the importance of small differences between two scores in comparing your stronger and weaker aptitudes. The bars on the profile help by indicating the more important differences.

Look at the bars for any two tests and notice whether or not the ends of the bars overlap. If they do not, chances are that you really are better in the kind of ability represented by the bar farther to the right than in that reflected by the left-hand bar. If they overlap but not by more than half their length, consider whether other things you know about yourself agree with this indication: the difference may or may not be important. If they overlap by more than half their length, the difference may be disregarded: so small a difference is probably not meaningful. This method of looking at the overlap of bars works for any two abilities you want to compare, whether they are listed next to each other or several rows apart on the chart.

Name: BLANCHE RIDGE
School: WASHINGTON Year* 1969 F Form L Grade 8 Sex F

Test	Raw Score	Percentile
Verbal Reasoning	15	40
Numerical Ability	17	45
VR + NA	32	40
Abstract Reasoning	39	90
Clerical Sp. & Acc.	30	15
Mechanical Reasoning	40	75
Space Relations	35	90
Language Usage Spelling	43	10
Language Usage Grammar	26	55

PERCENTILES: 1 5 10 20 25 30 40 50 60 70 75 80 90 95 99

Norms Used _____ (If no entry, percentiles are based on national norms)

*F—first (fall) semester testing and percentiles; S—second (spring) semester testing and percentiles.

69-171S

Figure 10.2 Sample Profile: The Differential Aptitude Test, Form L. (Reproduced by permission. Copyright 1947, © 1961, 1963, 1969 by the Psychological Corporation, New York. All rights reserved.)

3. Each ability test contains a structure which reflects a given theory of the make-up of intelligence. The theories usually fall into the categories of a general factor theory, a two-factor theory, or multiple-factor theories.

4. Whenever an IQ score is reported, it is important to specify the test on which it is obtained. For example, although the mean IQ for both the Stanford-Binet and the Wechsler Scales is approximately 100, a greater percentage of the Stanford-Binet norm group made very high or very low IQ's.

5. Although there has been much research on culture-fair or culture-free tests, it is fair to say that a test has not yet been developed which can truly be called culture-fair or culture-free.

6. The fact that ability tests are quick to administer and simple to score does not mean that they are quickly or easily interpreted; understanding, not the gaining of information, is the prime goal of pupil appraisal procedures.

7. There are many uses for ability test results. The key is to use the results for the purposes for which the test was selected in the first place.

Discussion Questions

1. It has been said by some that ability tests and achievement tests measure the same thing. Can you take the opposite viewpoint and defend what ability tests measure in contrast to achievement tests?

2. Discuss the differences between the three main theories of the structure of intelligence—the general factor theory, the two-factor theory, and the multi-factor theories.

3. How can you explain the statement: "Although the mean IQ for both tests is approximately 100, a greater percentage of the Stanford-Binet norm group made very high or very low IQ's"? You may refer to Table 10.1 for the percentage difference.

4. From the section on typical tests of ability, select any level or type of tests of your interest and describe what appear to be common elements among the various descriptions and what appear to be differences.

5. Discuss the difference between what the mental age tells you and what the IQ tells you. What uses can be made of each in implementation of results?

Student Activities

1. The first paragraph in this chapter states that most definitions of intelligence fall into one or more of three categories. Take each of the definitions given by the authorities quoted and categorize them into one or more of these categories.

2. With the help of your instructor obtain sample sets of three different ability tests and classify them as to the three different theories of the structure of intelligence. Be able to explain why you classified them as you did. Can you further classify them by the theory of an individual expert quoted in the text?

3. Take the following IQ's and interpret each according to Binet's classification and then Wechsler's found in Table 10.1. What problems do you foresee in interpretation between the two systems?

140	115
132	85

4. Select one of the typical tests of ability of your interest and obtain a sample set of it. Using Harrington's "Test Evaluation Form" and Buros' *Mental Measurements Yearbook,* make your own critical review of the test. You can follow the format of the reviews in Buros.

5. For the following listing of educational problems, indicate whether the IQ or the MA would be most helpful:
   a. rate of learning
   b. readiness for reading in the first grade
   c. criterion for ability grouping
   d. placement in a special class
   e. length of assignments
   f. difficulty of the curriculum
   g. amount of study time needed

Selected Readings

Ahmann, J. Stanley, and Glock, Marvin D. *Evaluating Pupil Growth,* 5th ed. Boston: Allyn and Bacon, Inc., 1975. Chapter 12.

Anastasi, Anne. *Psychological Testing,* 4th ed New York: The Macmillan Company, 1976. Chapters 3, 13, and 16.

Brown, Frederick G. *Principles of Educational and Psychological Testing,* 2nd ed. New York: Holt, Rinehart and Winston, Inc., 1976. Chapters 12 and 15-16.

Cronbach, Lee J. *Essentials of Psychological Testing,* 3rd ed. New York: Harper & Row Publishers, Inc., 1970. Chapters 7-9 and 12.

Ebel, Robert L. *Essentials of Educational Measurement,* 3rd ed. Englewood Cliffs, NJ: Prentice-Hall, Inc., 1979. Chapter 18.

Gronlund, Norman E. *Measurement and Evaluation in Teaching,* 3rd ed. New York: The Macmillan Company, 1976. Chapter 13.

———. *Readings in Measurement and Evaluation.* New York: The Macmillan Company, 1968. Chapters 29-33.

Hopkins, Charles D., and Antes, Richard L. *Classroom Measurement and Evaluation.* Itasca, IL: F. E. Peacock Publishers, Inc., 1978. Chapter 12.

Matarazzo, Joseph D. *Wechsler's Measurement and Appraisal of Adult Intelligence.* New York: Oxford University Press, 1972.

Mehrens, William A., and Lehmann, Irvin J. *Measurement and Evaluation in Education and Psychology.* New York: Holt, Rinehart and Winston, Inc., 1973. Chapter 14.

Noll, Victor H., Scannell, Dale P., and Craig, Robert C. *Introduction to Educational Measurement,* 4th ed. Boston: Houghton Mifflin Company, 1979. Chapters 9 and 10.

Noll, Victor H., Scannell, Dale P., and Noll, Rachel P. *Introductory Readings in Educational Measurement.* Boston: Houghton Mifflin Company, 1972. Section 5.

Sax, Gilbert. *Principles of Educational Measurement and Evaluation.* Belmont, CA: Wadsworth Publishing Company, Inc., 1974. Chapters 11 and 12.

Stanley, Julian C., and Hopkins, Kenneth D. *Educational and Psychological Measurement and Evaluation.* Englewod Cliffs, NJ: Prentice-Hall, Inc., 1972. Chapter 14.

Terman, Lewis M. *The Measurement of Intelligence.* New York: Arno Press, 1975.

Thorndike, Robert L., and Hagen, Elizabeth. *Measurement and Evaluation in Psychology and Education,* 4th ed. New York: John Wiley & Sons, Inc., 1977. Chapters 9 and 10.

Tuckman, Bruce W. *Measuring Educational Outcomes: Fundamentals of Testing.* New York: Harcourt Brace Jovanovich, Inc., 1975. Chapter 12.

11

Standardized Achievement Tests

What are achievement tests?
How is a standardized achievement test built?
How are achievement tests classified?
What are examples of diagnostic tests?
What are examples of achievement tests in single-subject areas?
What are examples of achievement test batteries?
What are some examples of individual and/or referral tests of achievement?
How do you interpret an achievement test?
What are some uses of achievement tests?
What are some examples of achievement test profiles?

A. What Are Achievement Tests?

Achievement tests are defined in several ways. Here are some of the common definitions.

California Test Bureau—A test which measures the amount a pupil has achieved in one or more subject fields or in the general aspects of schooling.

Ahmann and Glock—Tests which compare achievement of one with those students in other schools.

Gronlund—Measures outcomes and content common to majority of United States schools.

Stanley—A test which measures the extent to which a person has achieved something, that is, acquired certain information or mastered certain skills, usually as a result of specific instruction.

Noll and Scannell—A procedure or measuring instrument, usually a paper-and-pencil test, used to measure student progress toward curricular goals—knowledge or skills usually acquired through classroom instruction.

B.   How Is a Standardized Achievement Test Built?

It may be interesting to note how a standardized achievement test is built. Normally these steps are followed:

1. The publisher arranges a meeting of curriculum and subject matter specialists for the areas to be measured.
2. After thorough analysis of the syllabi, textbooks, and programs, a list of objectives for the subjects is prepared.
3. A two-way grid is built with objectives on the left and subject matter content across the top.
4. The number of items for each cell in the grid is agreed upon based on importance of the objective and topic.
5. A professional team of test writers prepares the items.
6. The items are reviewed carefully by the team and experimental items are put in a test booklet .
7. General instructions are built and a test is given to a sample of students.
8. After the tests are scored, an item analysis is made to remove the poor items.
9. The remaining items are refined and polished.
10. A representative sample of students are administered the final test and data on reliability, validity, and norms are obtained.

C.   How Are Achievement Tests Classified?

Achievement tests may be classified as *diagnostic, single subject-matter tests,* and *survey batteries.*

> *Diagnostic Tests*—These are designed to isolate specific strengths and weaknesses of an individual in some particular field of knowledge.
> *Single Subject-Matter Tests*—Measure the pupil's educational achievement in a single content area.
> *Survey Batteries*—Consist of a group of tests in *different content areas* standardized on the same population so that the results of the various components may be meaningfully compared.

D.   What Are Examples of Diagnostic Tests?

Diagnostic tests are basically concerned with the abilities or skills in such areas as reading, arithmetic, or spelling. These are the areas the subject-matter experts believe are essential in learning a particular subject. Because reading is an integral component of the learning process, most of the diagnostic tests are in reading. A diagnostic test will not only tell the teacher that a pupil is weak or deficient in a basic skill area but will also point out what parts are weak, such as addition of fractions or reference skills. In diagnostic testing, there is no single score. Rather, there is a detailed analysis of the parts of the test (auditory association, word recognition, etc.). Then, results are brought together, along with other information, to plan a remedial or developmental teaching program.

Following is an annotated listing of a few of the most frequently used tests of diagnosis.

In Reading

1. *Stanford Diagnostic Reading Test (SDRT)*. Harcourt Brace Jovanovich, 1977. Two levels: Level I (grades 2.5 to 4.5) and Level II (grades 4.5-8.5). Seven scores for Level I and eight for Level II. It is group administered. There are three timed tests and four untimed ones. The specific subtests in Level I are reading comprehension, vocabulary, auditory discrimination, syllabication, beginning and ending sounds, blending, and sound discrimination. The subtests of Level II are reading comprehension, vocabulary, syllabication, sound discrimination, blending, and rate of reading. Total testing time for Level I is 2½ hours and it is suggested that at least four separate testing sessions be used; Level II requires about 90 minutes and can be spread over a minimum of three sessions.

2. *Gates-McKillop Reading Diagnostic Tests*. Teachers College Press, Columbia University, 1962. Grades 2-6. Two alternate forms (1 and 2). Is individually administered. It provides 28 scores. It was designed to identify specific strengths and weaknesses in the child's reading skills by providing a variety of exercises in eight different subtests. The test is accompanied by a well-organized manual with many good suggestions for profile analysis. It takes several hours to give and would be distributed over several sessions. The test requires a well-trained examiner for valid interpretation.

3. *Durrell Analysis of Learning Difficulties*. Harcourt Brace Jovanovich, 1955. Grades 1-6. One form. Individually administered, it makes use of a series of paragraphs graded in difficulty, a simple tachistoscope, and a set of cards. The subtests are silent and oral reading, listening comprehension, word analysis, phonetics, faulty pronunciation, writing, and spelling. A good feature is the detailed checklist of difficulties which is provided. The manual contains suggestions for remedial teaching. Again, an experienced examiner is needed for valid interpretation.

In Arithmetic

Diagnostic tests in arithmetic are relatively few in number and, unfortunately, the old standbys such as the Diagnostic Tests and Self-Helps in Arithmetic (Grades 3-12), the Los Angeles Diagnostic Tests, Lee-Clark Arithmetic Fundamentals Survey Test, and the Stanford Diagnostic Arithmetic Test (Grades 2.5-8.5) may not be too valid today. The rapidly changing curriculum in arithmetic has posed a problem for test makers. On the one hand, there is the continuing need to measure the basic fundamentals; on the other, the tests must reflect the modern curriculum.

Because of the dearth of diagnostic tests in this area, only one will be described in order that the reader can become acquainted with the diagnostic procedure in arithmetic.

> *Diagnostic Tests and Self-Helps in Arithmetic.* CTB/Mcgraw-Hill, 1955. Grades 3-12. One form. Untimed. Four screening tests and 23 diagnostic tests. No norms.
>
> Six major areas are surveyed by the series: *basic facts* (five tests); *fundamental operations with whole numbers* (five tests); *operations with percentages* (one test); *fundamental operations with decimal fractions* (four tests); *operations with measures* (one test); and *fundamental operations with common fractions* (seven tests). Each of the 23 diagnostic tests is accompanied by a self-help that is on the back of the diagnostic test. The four screening tests are designed to measure pupil achievement in whole numbers, fractions, decimals, and general arithmetic skills and knowledge.
>
> The way it works is that a student takes the screening tests and, based on his performance on one or more of the screening tests, the appropriate diagnostic test(s) is/are administered. The diagnostic tests are given because they contain many items to locate the difficulties the student may have. The separate diagnostic tests are cross-referenced to assist the teacher in locating the nature of the difficulty. Thus, the teacher can see where the error is manifesting itself and can have the student take the appropriate test to help him.
>
> The diagnostic self-helps are keyed to the diagnostic test items. These are essentially remedial exercises that have been worked out in detail. Each one tells the student exactly what to do. After working through the self-help exercises, the pupil is encouraged to rework the items that he answered incorrectly.

E. What Are Examples of Achievement Tests in Single-Subject Areas?

Readiness Tests

Readiness today is concerned with physical maturation, educational readiness, and general mental ability. Readiness involves a variety of factors that are continually interacting. In assessing a child for first grade readiness, one would include such factors as mental maturity, perceptual maturity, experiential background, linguistic maturity, sensory acuity, social adjustment, and emotional adjustment. Many states, which have definite legislation for special education, have a screening program which includes many types of readiness tests. These will be discussed in a special section relating to screening later in this chapter.

Reading readiness is the most common of readiness tests. The major purposes of reading readiness tests are (1) to identify the children who are not ready to begin reading and (2) to identify, for grouping purposes, the children who are basically at the same level of readiness. Most of the reading readiness tests will include all or some combinations of the following: Motor skills, auditory discrimination, visual discrimination, vocabulary, and memory.

Some of the more common reading readiness tests are the following.

1. *American School Reading Readiness Test.* The Bobbs-Merrill Company, 1964. For K-1. Includes test of Discrimination of Geometric Forms, Discrimination of Letter Forms and Letter Combinations, Following Directions, Memory of Geometric Forms, Recognition of Words, and Vocabulary.

2. *Gates-MacGinitie Readiness Skills.* Teachers College Press, Columbia University, 1966. For K-1. Seven subtests: Listening Comprehension, Auditory Discrimination, Visual Discrimination, Following Directions, Letter Recognition, Visual-Motor Coordination, and Auditory Blending. Usually given in four sittings over a two-day period with 30 minutes for each part.

3. *Harrison-Stroud Reading Readiness Profiles.* Houghton Mifflin Company, 1956. For K-1. Six subtests: Using Symbols, Making Visual Discrimination, Using Content, Making Auditory Discrimination, Using Context and Auditory Clues, and Giving Names of Letters. Approximately 80 minutes of testing time needed. Usually administered in three sessions.

4. *Lee-Clark Reading Readiness Test.* CTB/McGraw-Hill, 1962. For K-1. Yields four scores: Letter Symbols, Concepts, Word Symbols, and a Total Score. Takes 20 minutes to administer. Serves as a good screening device and provides a fairly gross measure for initial grouping purposes.

5. *Metropolitan Readiness Tests.* Harcourt Brace Jovanovich, 1965. Grades K-1. Six subtests: Word Meaning, Listening, Matching, Alphabet, Numbers, and Copying. Requires three testing sessions. The total score and subtests are expressed in terms of five-level readiness status ratings.

6. *Murphy-Durrell Reading Readiness Analysis.* Harcourt Brace Jovanovich, 1965. Grade 1. Three subtests: Phonemes, Letter Names, Learning Rate. Also a total score. No time limits, but authors suggest two testing periods.

Although readiness tests in other areas are rare, one in arithmetic might be pointed out.

> *American School Achievement-Arithmetic Readiness Test.* The Bobbs-Merrill Company, 1941-55. Grade 1. Numbers.

Specific Subjects

Standardized achievement tests are available for nearly every subject and for every grade level. These specific tests have certain advantages over comparable tests from a battery. For example, the fact that they contain more items and a wider subject content makes it more likely that they will represent the instructional objectives of a particular teacher or school. Only a sampling of the many hundreds of specific subject-matter tests in reading, arithmetic, spelling, language arts, foreign language, social studies, and science will be described here. Other fields in which specific subject fields are common include: handwriting, health, home economics, industrial arts, library usage, literature, the Bible, music, speech, and driver education.

Reading

1. *Durrell Analysis of Reading Difficulty.* Harcourt Brace Jovanovich, 1956. Grades 1-6. Silent and Oral Reading, Listening Comprehension, Word Analysis, Phonetics, Faulty Pronunciation, Writing, and Spelling. 30-45 minutes.
2. *Gates-MacGinitie Reading Tests.* Teachers College Press, 1972. Six separate tests for grades 1-9. Measures vocabulary, comprehension, and speed and accuracy. New and attractively printed, easy to administer and score, and have norms which are representative of American school children.
3. *Lee-Clark Reading Test.* CTB/McGraw-Hill, 1965. Two levels: primer (grade 1), and first reader (grades 1-2). Testing time about 15 and 25 minutes for primer and first reader respectively. Scores obtained for auditory stimuli, visual stimuli, following directions, and total score. The first reader also has inference and completion scores.
4. *Nelson-Denny Reading Test.* Houghton Mifflin Company, 1973. For grades 9-16. Covers vocabulary, comprehension, and reading rate. Takes about 30 minutes. Some diagnostic features as well as survey.
5. *Nelson Reading Test.* Houghton Mifflin Company, 1962. For grades 3-9. Measures vocabulary, reading comprehension, ability to note details, ability to predict outcomes. 30 minutes administration time.
6. *Primary Reading Profiles.* Houghton Mifflin Company. For grades 1.5-2.5 and 2.5-3.5. Consists of five tests: aptitude for reading, auditory association, word recognition, word attack, and reading comprehension. Testing time is 70-85 minutes.

Other reading tests include:

Davis Reading Test. The Psychological Corporation, 1962. Grades 8-11 and 11-13.

Gray Oral Reading Tests. The Bobbs-Merrill Company, 1967. Grades 1-12.

Durrell-Sullivan Reading Capacity and Achievement Tests. Harcourt Brace Jovanovich, 1955. Grades range in two tests from 2.5-4.5 and 3-6.

Iowa Silent Reading Tests. Harcourt Brace Jovanovich, 1970. For elementary, grades 4-8; advanced, high school, and college.

Kelley-Greene Reading Comprehension Test. Harcourt Brace Jovanovich, 1952. For grades 9-13.

Gates-MacGinitie Primary CS-Speed and Accuracy. Teachers College Press, 1965. For grades 2-3.

Stanford Diagnostic Reading Test. Harcourt Brace Jovanovich. Grade range in two levels 2.5-4.5 and 4.5-8.5. Testing time 160-180 minutes for the lower level and 110-130 for the higher level.

Traxler High School Reading Test. The Bobbs-Merrill Company, 1967. For Grades 10-12. 45 minutes.

Traxler Silent Reading Test. The Bobbs-Merrill Company, 1969. Grades 7-10. 46 minutes.

Arithmetic

1. *Blyth Second-Year Algebra Test.* Harcourt Brace and Jovanovich, 1966. End of second-year albebra course in high school. Includes symbolic expression, factoring, radicals, exponents, logarithmic, simple progressions, linear and quadratic equations, and graphic methods. 45 minutes.

2. *Brief Survey of Arithmetic Skills.* The Bobbs-Merrill Company, 1947-53. For grades 5-12.

3. *Cooperative Mathematics Tests.* Educational Testing Service, 1965. A series of tests for grades 7-college. Includes tests in arithmetic, structure of the number system. Algebra I, Algebra II, Geometry, Trigonometry, Algebra III, Analytic Geometry, and Calculus. About 40 minutes for each test.

4. *Howell Geometry Test.* Harcourt Brace Jovanovich, 1969. For grades 9-12. About 40 minutes.

5. *Illinois Algebra Test.* The Bobbs-Merrill Company, 1956-58. Measures manipulative and mechanical skills. About 37 minutes.

6. *Illinois Plane Geometry Test.* The Bobbs-Merrill Company, 1957. About 37 minutes.

7. *Number Fact Check Test.* CTB/McGraw-Hill, 1946. For grades 5-8. Includes addition, subtraction, multiplication, and division facts. About 25 minutes.

8. *Orleans-Hanna Algebra Prognosis Test.* Harcourt Brace Jovanovich, 1968. For grades 1-8. Time is 50 minutes.

9. *Orleans-Hanna Geometry Prognosis Test.* Harcourt Brace Jovanovich, 1968. Grades 9-11. Time is 50 minutes.

10. *Wisconsin Contemporary Test of Elementary Mathematics.* Personnel Press, 1967. For grades 3-7. Stresses facts and concepts introduced into mathematics since 1962. Testing time is 50 minutes per form.

Spelling

1. *Lincoln Diagnostic Spelling Tests.* The Bobbs-Merrill Company, 1962. Grades 8-12. Measures pronunciation, enunciation, and use of rules in spelling. 50 minutes.
2. *The New Iowa Spelling Scale.* Bureau of Research and Service. Grades 2-8. Contains over 5,000 words chosen from Thorndike-Lorge Teacher's Word Book.

Language Arts

1. *A Look at Literature.* Educational Testing Service, 1968. For grades 4-6. Includes perception of literary qualities and devices, comprehension of meaning, and extension and application of meaning. 60-70 minutes.
2. *Brown-Carlsen Listening Comprehension.* Harcourt Brace Jovanovich, 1955. For grades 9-13. Measures ability to understand the spoken language. Takes 40-50 minutes. Gives scores in immediate recall, following directions, recognizing transitions, recognizing word meanings, and lecture comprehension.
3. *Cooperative English Tests.* Educational Test Service, 1960. Measures achievement in two fundamental areas: reading comprehension and English expression. For grades 9-14. Testing time is 40 minutes.
4. *Cooperative Primary Tests.* Educational Test Division, 1967. For grades 1-3. Designed to measure verbal and quantitative understanding, skills, and concepts basic to future development in reading, writing, listening, and mathematics. Time required is about 35 minutes.
5. *Essentials of English Test, Revised.* American Guidance Service. For grades 7-12. Includes punctuation, capitalization, sentence structure, correct usage, and spelling. 45 minutes.
6. *Purdue High School English Test.* Houghton Mifflin Company, 1962. For grades 9-13. Measures proficiency in grammar, punctuation, effective expression, vocabulary, and spelling. Time is 36 minutes.

Other tests frequently mentioned include the following:

1. *Campbell-Guiler Test in English Fundamentals.* The Bobbs-Merrill Co., 1957. Grades 9-12.
2. *Hoyum-Schrammel English Essentials Tests.* Bureau of Educational Measurements, 1956. Three levels for grades 3-4, 5-6, and 7-8.
3. *Pressey Diagnostic Tests in English Composition.* The Bobbs-Merrill Company. For Junior and Senior High School.
4. *Rinsland-Beck Natural Tests of English Usage.* The Bobbs-Merrill Company, 1957. For grades 9-13.

Foreign Language

1. *Modern Language Association Cooperative Foreign Language Tests.* Educational Testing Service, 1963. This is a series of tests of competence in five languages—French, German, Italian, Russian, and Spanish. Tests are at two levels of difficulty. Level L is for those who have had 1-2 years of the language in high school or 1-2 semesters in college. Level M is for those with 3-4 years of a language in high school or 3-4 semesters in college. Separate measures of listening, speaking, reading, and writing are provided. About 105 minutes of testing time.

2. *Modern Language Aptitude Test.* The Psychological Corporation, 1967. For grade 9 and above. Supposed to predict how easily and rapidly English-speaking students can learn a foreign language. There are five parts: Number listening, phonetic script, spelling clues, words and sentences, and paired associates. Time is one hour for the complete test and 30 minutes for a short form. There is an elementary form for grades 3-6.

3. *Pimsleur Language Aptitude Battery.* Harcourt Brace Jovanovich, 1966. For grades 6-10. The purpose is to screen and group students according to their ability to learn a modern foreign language. Test time is 50-60 minutes.

4. *Pimsleur Modern Foreign Language Proficiency Tests.* Harcourt Brace Jovanovich, 1967. A series of tests in French, Spanish, and German for grades 7-12 and college at two levels of difficulty. Form A is for high school students who have completed a first-level course in the language or college students with a semester course. Form C is for secondary students who have completed a second-level course or college students who have completed a one-year course. The four tests measure listening comprehension, speaking proficiency, reading comprehension, and writing proficiency. Total time is about 100 minutes.

Social Studies

1. *California Tests in Social and Related Sciences.* CTB/McGraw-Hill, 1946-53. Advanced form is for grades 9-12. Includes *Creating a New Nation* (to 1789), Nationalism, Sectionalism, and Conflict (1790-1876), Emergence of Modern America (1877-1918), The United States in Transition (since 1918). Each of the four tests takes 45 minutes.

2. *Cooperative Social Studies Tests.* Educational Testing Service, 1964. These tests measure achievement in seven areas of the secondary social studies curricula. These are American History (grades 7-8), Civics (8-9), American History (10-12), Problems of Democracy (10-12), American Government (10-12), Modern European History (10-12), and World History (10-12). Working time for each test is 40 minutes.

3. *Crary American History Test, Revised.* Harcourt Brace Jovanovich, 1965. This is to assess achievement of the contemporary objectives of a high

school course in American history. It assesses knowledge of facts, interpretation of information, map reading skills, ability to draw inferences, and the like. For grades 10-13. Testing time is 40 minutes.

4. *Emporia Geography Test.* Bureau of Educational Measurement. For Grades 4-7. Measures Part I—knowledge of United States geography tested by reference to a map; Part II—60 True-False items on World Geography; and Part III—40 Multiple-Choice items on World Geography.

5. *Emporia United States History Tests.* Bureau of Educational Measurement, 1937. Test I is for grades 5-6; Test II is for 7-8. Test I measures United States History through True-False and Multiple-Choice items. Test II includes True-False, Multiple-Choice, Matching, and historical-sequence items.

Science

1. *California Tests in Social and Related Sciences: Related Sciences.* CTB/McGraw-Hill, 1946-1955. For grades 4-8. Test 5 of the series measures Health and Safety; test 6 is on Elementary Science. Time for test 5 is 21 minutes; for test 6 is 19 minutes.

2. *Metropolitan Science Tests.* Harcourt Brace Jovanovich, 1959. For grades 5-9. Measures science information, generalizations, and understandings. About 20 minutes.

3. *Cooperative Science Tests.* Educational Testing Service, 1963. These tests measure achievement in four areas of secondary-school science: General Science (grades 7-9), Advanced General Science (8-9), Biology (high school), Chemistry (high school), and Physics (high school).

4. *Dunning-Abeles Physics Test.* Harcourt Brace Jovanovich, 1967. An end-of-the-course test in high school physics (grades 10-13). Measures performance in knowledge, comprehension, and application of physics concepts. Time is about 40 minutes.

5. *Read General Science Test.* Harcourt Brace Jovanovich, 1965. For junior-high science. Measures acquisition of knowledge, development of understanding, and application in science. Testing time is 40 minutes.

F. What Are Examples of Achievement Test Batteries?

Achievement Test Batteries consist of a group of tests in different content areas standardized on the same population so that the results of the various components may be meaningfully compared. They lend themselves best to those grade levels on which there is a common core of subjects. Thus, they find their greater use on the primary and elementary levels although there are some which go through the secondary school level.

There are many similarities between the various batteries. They usually contain tests in reading vocabulary, reading comprehension, arithmetic fundamentals, arithmetic reasoning, grammar, spelling, among others. Often, there are norms for various types of comparisons; e.g., rural-urban, age, grade, and the like. Raw scores are converted to grade equivalents, percentiles, stanines, and other standard scores.

Following is an annotated listing of some common achievement batteries on the elementary and secondary level. There are others and each school should study several to make a choice most consonant with its curriculum and teaching methods.

1. *California Achievement Test.* CTB/McGraw-Hill, 1972. Appropriate grade range is 1.5-12. Has five different levels: Lower Primary (1.5-2); Upper Primary (2-4); Elementary (4-6); Junior High (6-9); Advanced (9-12). On the lowest level, it measures language [Auding (Comprehension-Evaluation-Usage) mechanics, usage and structure, spelling]. On all other levels, it measures reading (vocabulary and comprehension), mathematics (computation, concepts, and problems), language (mechanics, usage, structure, spelling). Working time varies from about 90 minutes for the lower primary to 180 minutes for junior high and advanced batteries.

2. *Comprehensive Test of Basic Skills.* CTB/McGraw-Hill, 1973. Appropriate grade range is K-12. The K level measures pre-reading, language skills, elementary concepts of mathematics. The Grade 1 measures reading, language, and mathematics. Grade 2 and up is similar to the 1968 edition with the addition of social studies and science subtests. The previous edition measured reading, language, arithmetic, and study skills. Time required for the total batteries ranges from 170-190 minutes.

3. *Iowa Test of Basic Skills, Primary Battery.* Houghton Mifflin Company, 1972. Level 7 is for the grade range of 1.7-2.5; Level 8 is for 2.6-3.5. There are two forms. The areas tested are: Listening, Vocabulary, Word Analysis, Reading Comprehension, Spelling, Capitalization, Punctuation, Usage, Maps, Graphs and Tables, References, Mathematical Concepts, and Mathematical Problems. A basic edition is available which uses the vocabulary, word analysis, reading comprehension, spelling, mathematical concepts, and mathematical problems from the above. It is for testing pupils with short attention spans or where limited time is available. Working time for the standard edition is 3 hours, 32 minutes; for the basic edition, 1 hour, 53 minutes.

4. *Iowa Test of Basic Skills, Levels Edition.* Houghton Mifflin Company, 1972. For Grades 3-8. Two forms, 5 and 6. The five major areas tested are: Vocabulary, Reading Comprehension, Language Skills, Work Study Skills, and Mathematics Skills. The test requires about 280 min-

utes (4 hours and 40 minutes) and should be administered in four sessions. There is a modern mathematics supplement for Forms 1-4 which reflects the emphasis of modern mathematics on Sets, Properties of Number Systems, Geometry, Systems of Numeration, and Number Sentences. It may be used in addition to the regular battery or it may be administered as a separate test.

5. *Iowa Tests of Educational Development (ITED).* Science Research Associates, 1972. Grades 9-12. Measures educational development in English, mathematics, natural sciences, and social studies. There are nine tests including understanding of basic social concepts, background in the natural sciences, correctness and appropriateness of expression, ability to do quantitative thinking, ability to interpret reading materials in the social studies, ability to interpret reading materials in the natural sciences, ability to interpret literary materials, general vocabulary, and use of sources of information. Time is 22-40 minutes per test for the class-period version and 22-65 minutes per test for the full length version.

6. *Metropolitan Achievement Tests.* Harcourt Brace Jovanovich, 1972. There are 3 or 4 forms of the test at each of five levels: Primer (K.7-1.4), Primary I (1.5-2.4), Primary II (2.5-3.4), Elementary (grades 3.5-4.9), Intermediate (grades 5.0-6.9), and Advanced (7.0-9.5). These tests measure skills in language, reading, and arithmetic and, where appropriate, the mastery of study skills and science and social studies content. Testing time varies from 1 hour and 45 minutes for the Primary I batery to 4 hours and 15 minutes for the Advanced battery.

   There is a High School Battery which is designed for grades 9-13. The eleven subtests measure achievement in language arts, social studies, mathematics, and science. Testing time is 5 hours and 15 minutes.

7. *SRA Achievement Series.* Science Research Associates, 1973. For Grades 1-9. There are five different levels including 1-2, 3-4, 3-5, 5-7, and 7-8. The areas covered are reading, arithmetic, language arts, social studies, science, and work-study skills (optional). Testing time ranges from 4 to 6½ hours, depending on the level.

8. *Stanford Achievement Tests.* Harcourt Brace Jovanovich, 1973. For grades 1.5-12. Has nine different level tests. The K.1-1.8 is called the Stanford Early School Achievement Test (SESAT). This measures environment, mathematics, letters and sounds, aural comprehension, word meaning, and sentence reading. The remaining levels and grade ranges are as follows: Primary I (1.5-2.4), Primary II (2.5-3.4), Primary III (3.5-4.4), Intermediate I (4.5-5.4), Intermediate II (5.5-6.9), Advanced (7-9.5), Task I (9-10), Task II (11-12). All levels through Advanced, measure vocabulary, reading comprehension, word study

skills, mathematics concepts, mathematics computation, mathematics application, spelling, language, social science, science, and listening comprehension. The high school levels measure reading comprehension, mathematical concepts, language.

Administration time ranges from 2 hours and 40 minutes for the Primary I Battery to 5 hours for the Advanced level. The high school battery also takes about 5 hours.

9. *Sequential Tests of Educational Progress Series II (STEP)*. Educational Testing Service, 1972. Grade range is 4-14. There are four different levels of tests including 4-6, 7-9, 10-12, and 13-14. These tests measure English expression, reading, mechanics of writing, mathematics computation, mathematics basic concepts, science, and social studies.

10. *Tests of Academic Progress*. Houghton Mifflin Company, 1972. For grades 9-12. Each of six subtests takes 45 minutes. The six tests are social studies, composition, science, reading, mathematics, and literature. This test was normed concurrently in the same school systems with the Iowa Tests of Basic Skills and the Cognitive Abilities Test. Thus, scores are comparable for grades 3-12.

G. What Are Some Examples of Individual and/or Referral Tests of Achievement?

At times, it is the teacher's responsibility to suggest that a child be referred for individual testing. This might occur when there is inconsistency in test scores over the past year or it may occur when the teacher has reason to believe that a score from a single test is not accurate. Normally, a teacher would discuss this with the principal and, if the principal concurs, arrangements will be made for further testing.

The listings in Table 11.1 are to acquaint the teacher with these diagnostic tests. In this way, the teacher will become acquainted with the test names and with what each test measures.

H. How Do You Interpret an Achievement Test?

Before attempting to interpret an achievement test, the teacher should study the test and the test manual to obtain answers to some basic questions. *What is the main purpose of the test?* That is, is it a *survey* test, a *diagnostic* test, or a *combination* of both? If it is a survey test, the emphasis will be on determining the status of the individual at the present time in basic achievement areas; a diagnostic test will indicate weak areas of achievement and will aid the teacher in determining causes of the difficulties. A combination test will attempt to serve both functions. *What is the relation of the test items to the material the teacher is teaching the pupils?* In order for the test to validly measure progress of a specific group of pupils, an analysis

TABLE 11.1

Listing of Individual Diagnostic Assessment Instruments[1]

Reading Readiness

Name of Test	Age	Time	Description	Publisher*
The Anton Brenner Developmental Gestalt Test of School Readiness	Ages 4-7	3-10 min.	This test covers number producing, number recognition, ten dot Gestalt, Sentence Gestalt, draw-a-man, school readiness evaluation, achievement-ability scale, and social emotional behavior scale. It evaluates perceptual and conceptual differentiating ability. May be employed to identify both gifted and retarded children. It can be effectively used with emotionally disturbed, culturally deprived, and non-English speaking children.	WPS
Denver Developmental Screening Test	Ages 0-6 yrs.	15-20 min.	This is a standardized screening method devised to assist in the early detection of young children with serious developmental delays. It covers four functions: gross motor, language, fine motor-adaptive, and personal-social.	LPP
First Grade Screening Test	K and beg. 1st	45 min. 30 min.	This test evaluates general knowledge, development of body image, perception of emotional motivation, visual-motor coordination, ability to follow directions, and memory.	AGS
Kindergarten Evaluation of Learning Potential	K		This instrument is designed to identify learning capacities of young children. It assesses three levels of learning: association, conceptualization, and creative self-expression.	McH
The Meeting Street School Screening Test	Grades K-1	15-20 min.	This test yields four scores in the areas of motor patterning, visual perceptual motor, and language. It is individually administered and requires no reading by the child.	CCA

1. Adapted from *Assessing the Learning Disabled: Selected Instruments* by August J. Mauser, Ed. D. (San Rafael, CA: Academic Therapy Publications, 1977).
*Index to Publishers, see listing at end of Table, page 290.

Name of Test	Age	Time	Description	Publisher*
The School Readiness Checklist	Ages 5-6	10-20 min.	This is a short questionnaire for parents containing forty-three items requiring "yes" - "no" answers. It does not require the presence of the youngster. Although no subtests are computed; items are presented in the following seven groups: growth and age, general activity related to growth, practical skills, remembering, understanding, general knowledge, and attitudes and interests. A classification table is included at the end for the approximate state of readiness for school.	RC

DIAGNOSTIC READING TESTS

Name of Test	Age	Time	Description	Publisher*
Assessment of Children's Language Comprehension: Research Edition	Ages 2-12	10-15 min.	This is an individually administered test. It is designed to assign the starting point in training for the child. It assesses core vocabulary development, comprehension of lexical items, and consistency of pattern of words missed within a sequence.	CPP
Diagnostic Reading Scales (Spache)	Grades 1-8		These scales are individually administered tests designed to identify reading deficiencies that hinder pupils from reading adequately. The scale is recommended for normal and retarded readers at the elementary, junior high and senior high levels. The test battery comprises three word recognition lists, twenty-two reading passages, and 6 supplementary phonics tests; consonant sounds, vowel sounds, consonant blends, common syllables, blends, and letter sounds. Three reading levels are yielded for each pupil.	CTB
Wisconsin Tests of Reading Skill Development: Word Attack Levels A-D	Grades K-Beg. 4th		There are four individual tests at varying levels of difficulty. The first level tests include rhyming words, shapes, letters and numbers, words and phrases, and many other language-related subtests. The highest level test includes subtests in sight vocabulary, silent letters, syllabication, accent, and possessives.	NCS

DIAGNOSTIC TESTS OF MATHEMATICS ABILITIES

Name of Test	Age	Time	Description	Publisher*
Keymath Diagnostic Arithmetic Test	Pre-School to Grade 6		This test is an individually administered test designed to provide a diagnostic assessment of skill in mathematics. The test items are divided into 14 subtests organized into 3 major areas: Content, which includes numeration, fractions, geometry, and symbols. Operations, which include addition, subtraction, multiplication, division, mental computation, and numerical reasoning. Applications which include word problems, missing elements, money measurement, and time.	AGS

SURVEY TESTS

Name of Test	Age	Time	Description	Publisher*
Wide Range Achievement Test	Grades Pre-school and up	20 min.	This instrument evaluates reading, spelling, and arithmetic skills.	GTA
Peabody Individual Achievement Test	Grades K-H.S.	30-40 min.	This test evaluates reading recognition, reading comprehension, spelling, mathematics, and general information.	AGS
Woodcock Reading Mastery Tests	Grades K-12	20-30 min.	There are five individual tests which result in separate scores as well as a total score. It is comprised of Letter Identification, Word Identification, Word Comprehension, and Passage Comprehension. It is a criterion-referenced test. There are socioeconomic adjusted norms as well as traditional total group norms.	AGS

ORAL READING TESTS

Name of Test	Age	Time	Description	Publisher*
Slosson Oral Reading Test	Grades 1-12	3 min.	This is an individual test and is based on the ability to pronounce words at different levels of difficulty.	SEP

MOTOR AND AND SENSORY ASSESSMENT TESTS

Name of Test	Age	Time	Description	Publisher*
Beery-Buktenica Visual-Motor Integration Test	Ages 2-15	10-15 min.	Form copying manual includes discussion of development of visual motor integration. The child is to reproduce various lines, shapes, and geometric forms. Separate forms for males and females are provided.	FOL
Bender Visual Motor Gestalt Test for Children	Ages 7-11	10 min.	This test provides an index of the structural and functional aspects of perceptual-motor development. It can be administered to emotionally disturbed and neurologically handicapped children.	WPS
Frostig Developmental Test of Visual Perception	Grades K-2, Nursery School	1 hr.	This test may be given in a small group or individually. The test seeks to measure five operationally defined perceptual skills (1) eye-motor coordination, (2) figure-ground, (3) constancy of shape, (4) position in space, (5) spatial relationships.	FOL
Illinois Test of Psycholinguistic Abilities	Pre-school to Intermediate grades	Varies	This test evaluates auditory decoding, visual decoding, auditory-vocal association, visual-motor association, vocal encoding, automatic-sequential ability, auditory-vocal automatic ability, auditory-vocal sequencing ability, visual-motor sequencing ability. It requires prior training in its administration.	ULP
Leavell Hand-Eye Coordinator Tests	Ages 8-14		This is an individual test which covers hand-foot preference, eye-ear preference, hand dexterity preference, visual imagery of pointed objects, incomplete objects, and moving objects.	KVC
Slingerland's Screening Test for Identifying Children With Specific Language Disability	Grade 1-4	1 hr.	This test can be given individually or in a group. It's purpose is to identify children with probable perceptual motor difficulty—visual, auditory, or kinesthetic.	EPS

AGS—American Guidance Service, Inc.
CTB—CTB/McGraw-Hill
CPP—Clinical Psychology Publishing Company
EPS—Educators Publishing Service, Inc.

FOL—Follet Educational Corporation
GTA—Guidance Testing Associates
KVC—Keystone View Company
LPP—Ladoca Project and Publishing Foundation

NSC—National Computer Systems
RC—Research Concepts
SEP—Slosson Educational Publications
ULP—University of Illinois Press
WPS—Western Psychological Services

must be made to be sure that the items are measuring the material which has been taught. *Are the test scores maximally reliable?* This requires checking the reliability section of the manual and checking the reliability coefficients. One need not be a statistical expert to figure this, but it is wise to calculate the reliability coefficients. For group tests, the coefficients should be .80 or higher. Generally, the reliability of the total test is higher than that of any of the subparts. *Are these students similar to those on whom the test was standardized?* To use the tables of norms in the manuals for interpretation, the teacher must be reasonably sure that his students are similar to those in the standardization sample.

Obviously, the above things should be checked from a sample set, if at all possible, before a test is purchased for use. Assuming that the above questions have been answered favorably, then how does one interpret a pupil's achievement test profile?

In the interpretation of an achievement profile, the key point is the study of the pattern of the plotted points. Practically all pupils will have some high points or strengths and some lower or weaker areas of achievement. What is high, average, or low? It is a relative thing, and it must be compared with some reference point or line. The author believes that three reference lines are significant in making interpretations.

1. Comparison of Each Plotted Point with the Total Battery Achievement

This comparison allows the teacher to spot immediately the points around the reference line which indicate average achievement in comparison to the total achievement; points to the right indicate higher achievement; points to the left indicate weaker areas of achievement. This comparison sets the stage for determining what these low, average, or higher points mean. Two additional reference lines are drawn through the profile to make these determinations. First, a line representing actual grade placement is drawn; and then a line representing his ability to learn (from his mental maturity test) is drawn.

2. Comparison with Actual Grade Placement

Comparing the plotted points with the actual-grade placement line enables the teacher to determine the areas in which the pupil is working at grade level, below grade level, or above grade level.

3. Comparison with Mental Age—Grade Placement

This comparison helps to determine how closely the pupil is working to his ability to learn. It is one thing to know whether a pupil is working at grade level, or above or below, and it is another thing to know how closely he is approaching his ability to achieve. Some tests use the concept of anticipated achievement or expected achievement. This concept is based on the idea that the anticipated achievement can be determined through a combination of mental age, chronological age, and actual-grade placement. These tests claim that this index is a better reference point than mental age alone in determining how close to his ability level a child is really working.

The teacher at this point can determine areas of strength, average achievement, and weakness. The next step is to determine the causes of the weak areas.

4. Determining the Causes of the Weak Areas

Achievement tests which contain the feature of diagnosis present charts for analysis of learning difficulties. The weak areas of achievement are brought to these charts, and by pinpointing the questions which were wrong or omitted, the teacher can determine the basic causes of the weak areas.

5. Making a Class Summary Chart

Most achievement batteries have a class summary sheet on which a teacher can record the individual pupil's scores, and then an analysis may be made of the results to determine strong, average, or weak areas of the group.

6. Planning a Remedial Program for the Group and for the Individual Pupils

The class analysis will aid the teacher in determining the areas in which the total group might profit in his reteaching, reviewing, and re-emphasis. It also will indicate whether the total group needs to be divided into smaller groups with common difficulties to correct. Finally, it will indicate the specific areas in which the teacher will have to work with individual pupils.

In the final analysis, the teacher instructs individual pupils. The achievement test will aid in the accomplishment of this by guiding the teacher in his assistance of the individual pupils, of small groups, and of the total class group.

I. What Are Some Uses of Achievement Tests?

As with mental ability tests, the teacher must interpret each part of the achievement test and then utilize the resultant information in teaching. Following is a listing of the principal teacher uses of achievement tests.

1. To determine the current achievement *status* of the individual student.
2. To evaluate the achievement of the pupil in relation to actual grade-placement and intellectual grade-placement.
3. To determine the strong and weak areas of individual and group achievement.

4. To analyze the causes of individual and group difficulties and then to plan remedial action.

5. To help the teacher evaluate his or her own instruction.

Some schools are now using standardized achievement tests to measure growth toward local curricular objectives in a *criterion-referenced manner.* Teachers of the various grade and subject matter areas come together and produce performance objectives. Having produced several of these for each subject and grade level, the teachers or a testing expert may identify items in a standardized achievement test which would measure growth toward each objective. A criterion level would be established for a student to pass for each set of items toward an objective. Below are some examples from various grade levels.

Performance Objectives	*Achievement Test Questions*	*Criterion Level*
	Grade One	
Word Analysis Given a word read orally, such as "bread," "store," or "rain," the student will be able to select from a set of pictured objects the object whose name rhymes with the word given him orally.	WA - 14, 15, 16, 17	2 out of 4
	Third Grade	
Study Aids—Maps Given a map showing a trail or a roadway, the student will be able to identify specific points passed in traveling the trail or roadway.	M 1, 4, 6, 10	2 out of 4
	Seventh Grade	
Comprehension-Literal Recall Given a story consisting of no more than ten paragraphs and having read the story, the student will be able to answer questions calling for memory of specific information or happenings portrayed in the story.	C 82, 94, 100, 110	2 out of 4

The student answer sheets are fed into the computer and analyzed for the specific questions identified for each objective. The analysis report will show for each pupil which objectives he has successfully passed or those he has not. At the bottom of each column depicting an objective, it can be noted what percentage of each class successfully met the criterion. Following is an *abbreviated* example with only five students.

Students   Objectives

	1	2	3	4	5
A	0	+	0	+	0
B	+	0	0	+	+
C	+	+	0	+	0
D	0	+	0	+	0
E	+	+	0	+	+
	60%	80%	0	100%	40%

Student A was successful in meeting the criterion for objectives 2 and 4 but has not yet met the criterion for 1-3-5. Whereas Student E has met the criterion for all the objectives except No. 3. The teacher can then plan diversified activities for each of his students to grow toward objectives for which objectives have not been met *at this time.*

Similarly, for group analysis, one can look at the percentage at the bottom of each objective column. Objective No. 4 is met by all students, objective No. 2 by 80%, No. 1 by 60%, No. 5 by 40%, and No. 3 by none. One will therefore need to plan activities and re-teach toward objectives in the following order of priority: Nos. 3, 5, 1, and 2.

Although this technique is used for standardized tests, the same procedure can be employed in using teacher-made tests.

An Educational Testing Service bulletin suggests eight uses for achievement tests.[2]

1. We may compare a pupil's achievement test score with the scores of other pupils in his/her school (placement).
2. We may compare a pupil's (or group's) score on a subtest with his/her (its) score on another subtest (diagnosis).
3. We may compare a pupil's (or group's) achievement test score with his/her (its) score on a previous testing (assessment).
4. We may compare a pupil's score on one achievement test with his/her score on another achievement test (prediction).
5. We may compare a school's achievement test scores with achievement test scores of a comparable group of schools (as in evaluation).
6. We may compare a pupil's (or group's) achievement test score with some fixed standard of mastery.
7. We may compare a pupil's (or group's) achievement test score with his/her (its) scores on other kinds of tests (e.g., aptitude test, interest, personality, or attitude scales).
8. We may compare a pupil's achievement test score with other data about his/her achievement (e.g., school marks, ratings).

2. From *Selecting an Achievement Test: Principles and Procedures.* Copyright © 1958, 1961, 1973 by Educational Testing Service. All rights reserved. Reprinted with permission of the publisher.

J.   What Are Some Examples of Achievement Test Profiles?

On the following pages are examples of standardization achievement test profiles of some of the more common achievement tests ranging from pre-school up through high school and adult.

1. Gates-McKillop Reading Diagnostic Tests (Figure 11.1)[3]

This battery of individually administered tests diagnoses specific deficiencies in reading performance. It is a revision of the Gates Diagnostic Tests and includes 28 scores. The tests evaluate oral reading, words, knowledge of word parts, recognizing the visual form of sounds, auditory blending. There are also supplementary tests which measure spelling, oral vocabulary, syllabication, and auditory discrimination. It is used for grades 2-6.

2. California Achievement Tests (Battery) (Figure 11.2)[4]

The 1970 edition is produced in five levels. It produces eleven or twelve scores: reading (vocabulary, comprehension, total), mathematics (computation, concepts and problems, total) language (auding, mechanics, usage and structure, total, spelling), and total battery. Derived scores include obtained grade equivalent, achievement development scale score, anticipated achievement grade equivalent, and national percentile rank.

3. Metropolitan Readiness Tests, 1976 Edition, Level I (Figure 11.3)[5]

The group-administered test measures ability in auditory memory, rhyming, letter recognition, visual matching, school language and listening, and quantitative language. The composite score is given in a percentile rank, stanine, and performance rating (low, average, high).

4. Wide-Range Achievement Test (WRAT) (Figure 11.4)[6]

The 1978 Revised Edition is appropriate for ages 5-11 (Level I) and 12 and over (Level II). It produces results in three areas: reading, spelling, and arithmetic. The scores are reported in a grade equivalent, standard score, and percentile.

3. From Arthur I. Gates and Anne S. McKillop, *Gates-McKillop Reading Diagnostic Tests.* (New York: Teachers College Press, 1962.) Reprinted by permission of the publisher.

4. From Individual Test Record, Home Report, Level 3, Form A, *California Achievement Test.* Reprinted by permission of the publisher, CTB/McGraw-Hill, Del Monte Research Park, Monterey, CA 93940. Copyright © 1970 by McGraw-Hill, Inc. All Rights Reserved. Printed in the U.S.A.

5. From Test Booklet, *Metropolitan Readiness Tests,* Level I, Form P, by Joanne Nurss and Mary E. McGauvran. Used by permission of the publisher, Harcourt Brace Jovanovich, Inc., New York. © 1976.

6. From Test Booklet, *Wide-Range Achievement Test.* Used by permission of the publisher, Jastak Assessment Systems, Wilmington, Delaware. © 1978.

FORM 1

PUPIL RECORD BOOKLET

G A T E S - M c K I L L O P
READING DIAGNOSTIC TESTS

ARTHUR I. GATES
Professor Emeritus of Education
Teachers College, Columbia University

ANNE S. McKILLOP
Professor of Education
Teachers College, Columbia University

Pupil's Name _____   School _____   Date _____

Pupil's Age _____ Birthday _____ Grade _____ Examiner _____ Teacher _____

AGE, GRADE, INTELLIGENCE	1 Raw Score	2 Grade or Other Score	3 Rating
1 Chronological Age			
2 Grade Status (A.G.)			(Date Given)
3 Binet _____ I.Q. _____ MA			
4 _____ I.Q. _____ MA			

READING AND OTHER TESTS	1 Raw Score	2 Grade or Other Score	3 Rating ( ) ( ) ( )
Date Given			
1			
2			
3			
Average Silent Reading Gr. (ASRG)			

READING DIAGNOSTIC TESTS

I. Oral Reading (OR)   ( ) ( ) ( )

Total Score

Analysis of Total Errors

a. Omissions, Words   %

b. Additions, Words   %

c. Repetitions   %

d. Mispronunciations (g through k)   %

Analysis of Mispronunciations

e. Full Reversals

f. Reversal of Parts

g. Total Wrong Order (e+f)

h. Wrong Beginnings

i. Wrong Middles

j. Wrong Endings

k. Wrong Several Parts

II. Words:
Flash Presentation   ( ) ( )

III. Words:
Untimed Presentation

IV. Phrases:
Flash Presentation

V. Knowledge of Word Parts   (OR)

1. Recognizing and Blending Common Word Parts

2. Giving Letter Sounds

3. Naming Capital Letters

4. Naming Lower-Case Letters

VI. Recognizing the Visual Form of Sounds

1. Nonsense Words

2. Initial Letters

3. Final Letters

4. Vowels

VII. Auditory Blending

VIII. Supplementary Tests   ( )

1. Spelling

2. Oral Vocabulary

3. Syllabication

4. Auditory Discrimination

5. _____

Figure 11.1 Sample Profile: Gates-McKillop Reading Diagnostic Tests (From Arthur I. Gates and Anne S. McKillop, *Gates-McKillop Reading Diagnostic Tests* (New York: Teachers College Press, 1962.) Reprinted by permission of the publisher.

Figure 11.2 Sample Profile: California Achievement Tests. (From *Individual Test Record, Home Report, Level 3, Form A, California Achievement Test.* Reprinted by permission of the publisher, CTB/McGraw-Hill, Del Monte Research Park, Monterey, CA 93940. Copyright © 1970 by McGraw-Hill, Inc. All Rights Reserved. Printed in the U.S.A.)

INDIVIDUAL TEST RECORD   HOME REPORT

Published by CTB/McGraw-Hill, Del Monte Research Park, Monterey, California 93940

LEVEL 3 FORM A

NAME ▶ JAMES AMY	TEACHER ▶ SCOTT
SCHOOL ▶ LINWOOD	GRADE ▶ 5.5
CITY ▶ ANYTOWN USA	DATE OF TESTING ▶ 02/71

BATCH ▶ 5555
GROUP ▶ 001
RUN DATE ▶ 08/23

	RAW SCORE	OGE	AAGE	DIF	NATL PCT
READING Vocabulary	19	4.3	5.2		29
READING Comprehension	29	6.8	5.5		68
TOTAL READING	48	5.2	5.3		46
MATHEMATICS Computation	45	5.8	5.8		67
MATHEMATICS Concepts & Problems	20	4.1	5.6	– 1.5	24
TOTAL MATHEMATICS	65	5.2	5.7		46
LANGUAGE Auding					
LANGUAGE Mechanics	64	9.7	6.1	+ 3.6	94
LANGUAGE Usage & Structure	20	4.3	5.7		34
TOTAL LANGUAGE	84	8.0	6.0		85
SPELLING	23	6.4	6.4		62
TOTAL BATTERY	220	5.9	5.6		62

NATIONAL · PERCENTILES

Scale: 1 2 5 10 20 30 40 50 60 70 80 90 95 98 99

TO THE PARENTS

This report gives the results of tests which your child took recently to find out which basic skills he is acquiring at satisfactory level and with which skills he needs more help. Improvement in skills comes most quickly when a student, his parents, and his teachers all have the same understanding of the areas which will require the most effort. This report does not represent... there may have been reasons why it was not the best time for him to take the tests. If you feel that this report does not represent your idea of his work or if you have questions and want further explanation, you are encouraged to see his teacher or counselor. He will help you interpret the results.

EXPLANATION OF TEST SCORES

The names of the tests in READING, MATHEMATICS, and LANGUAGE are listed on the upper left side of this sheet. The TOTAL BATTERY score includes these three areas. These headings are the key to all scores across the page. Explanations of the scores are given below, introduced by the abbreviated column heading used in the upper right hand sheet. Each of the available scores is explained. The abbreviated heading on the columns in this report will reflect which of the available scores your school has chosen.

RAW SCORE

This score always appears on this report regardless of the choice of other scores that a school may make. This tells the number of items answered correctly. It has no meaning by itself but is the key to the other scores.

OGE   OBTAINED GRADE EQUIVALENT

This shows the grade in which typical students in the nation obtained the raw score given in the first column. It indicates the grade and the month of the school year of these students. For example, if a fourth-grade student receives a score of 6.7 in the column headed OGE, it means he scored on this test like typical students in the seventh month (usually March) of Grade 6. It does not mean that he belongs in the sixth grade. Your child's grade at the time of testing is recorded at the top of this report.

ADSS   ACHIEVEMENT DEVELOPMENT SCALE SCORE

This score is sometimes chosen by schools when they desire a means of charting a student's growth over successive years of instruction with a scale which remains true regardless of the grade in which the CAT is given and regardless of which form of the CAT is given. This kind of comparison cannot be obtained from the other types of scores available.

AAGE   ANTICIPATED ACHIEVEMENT GRADE EQUIVALENT

This score shows how students in the nation who are like your child (with similar age, grade in school, sex, and academic ability) performed on this test as compared to the typical student in the nation. The comparison is made in terms of grade equivalent, the second score described above. It simply shows what grade equivalent was obtained by students like your child. This score is provided only for those students who took the test of academic aptitude in addition to the achievement test.

AASS   ANTICIPATED ACHIEVEMENT SCALE SCORE

If your school has chosen to have its students' scores reported as the Achievement Development Scale Scores, then this score, the AASS, is that scale score obtained by students like your child (with similar age, grade in school, sex, and academic ability). Again, this score is provided only for those students who took the test of academic aptitude in addition to the achievement test. As the AAGE score is compared to the OGE score, so is the AASS score compared to the ADSS score.

DIFF   DIFFERENCE

In a column headed by DIFF, there are recorded the differences between the scores described in the paragraphs above, that is, the difference between OGE and AAGE or the difference between ADSS and AASS, when these differences are large enough to be important. If, for instance, the score under the column headed OGE is significantly higher than the score under the column headed AAGE, a plus sign appears. This is to be interpreted as meaning that your child performed significantly better on this test than other students having the same age, grade in school, sex, and academic ability. A minus sign indicates that he has scored significantly lower than other students like him.

NAT PCT   NATIONAL PERCENTILE RANK
LOC PCT   LOCAL PERCENTILE RANK

This shows the percentage of students in a group that received a lower raw score than your child. For example, if a seventh-grade student scores 48 in this column, it means that 48 per cent of the seventh graders in the group received a lower raw score. A score of 50 then, is the average score for all students in the same grade as your child. Some schools may choose to have their students compared to students in a national sample. When this is done, the column will be headed by NAT PCT. Other schools may choose to have their students compared to students in the same district. When this is done, the column will be headed LOC PCT. Please do not confuse this score with the percentage of items answered correctly, which is not available on this report.

The chart at the right gives a graphic picture of your child's test scores. Because test scores are not exact measures of a student's achievement, the row of X's shows the range within which the student is most likely achieving. You will note that the score in the last column falls approximately in the middle of the row of X's on this sheet. Upon request from school districts, CTB/McGraw-Hill will report scores of students in special ways not described on this sheet. If column headings appear which are not explained in these paragraphs, they will represent special kinds of scores requested by your school district. If you desire a further interpretation of your child's test scores, you are invited to come to the school to discuss them. There is in the files of your school an analysis of the test, indicating each test item that was not answered correctly.

Metropolitan Readiness Tests

LEVEL I
Form P

Pupil's Name _____ ☐ Boy ☐ Girl Age _____
Last   First   M   Years/Months

Teacher _____ Grade _____ Date of Test _____

School _____ City _____ State _____

SUBTEST	PERFORMANCE RATING	RAW SCORE (Number Right)	SKILL AREA		
			RAW SCORE	STANINE	PERFORMANCE RATING

1. Auditory Memory   Low Average High   L A H

2. Rhyming   L A H

3. Letter Recognition   L A H   VISUAL   Low Average High   L A H

4. Visual Matching   L A H

5. School Language and Listening   L A H   LANGUAGE   L A H

6. Quantitative Language   L A H

Pre-Reading Skills Composite   RAW SCORE   PERCENTILE RANK   STANINE   PERFORMANCE RATING   L A H

8-19500

Figure 11.3 Sample Profile: Metropolitan Readiness Test, 1976 Edition. (From Test Booklet, *Metropolitan Readiness Tests,* Level I, Form P, by Joanne Nurss and Mary E. McGauvran. Used by permission of the publisher, Harcourt Brace Jovanovich, Inc., New York. © 1976.)

JASTAK
ASSESSMENT SYSTEMS

1978 EDITION **WRAT**

WIDE RANGE ACHIEVEMENT TEST

Joseph F. Jastak, Sidney W. Bijou, Sarah Jastak

Name _____	Sex: M. F.	Test Results:	Raw Score	Grade Rating	Standard Score	Percentile
Date_____ Birth Date _____ Age _____		Reading	___	___	___	___
School_____ Grade_____		Spelling	___	___	___	___
Referred by _____ Examiner _____		Arithmetic	___	___	___	___

Figure 11.4   Sample Profile: Wide-Range Achievement Test (WRAT). (Used by permission of Jastak Assessment Systems.)

Summary Statements

1. An achievement test measures the extent to which a person has achieved something, that is, acquired certain information or mastered certain skills, usually as a result of specific instructions.
2. The making of a standardized achievement test is an orderly, scientific process which involves many test experts, educators, and literally thousands of students.
3. Achievement tests are usually classified as diagnostic, single subject-matter tests, or survey batteries.
4. A diagnostic test will not only tell the teacher that a pupil is weak or deficient in a basic skill area but will also point out what parts are weak.
5. Standardized achievement tests are available for nearly every subject (agriculture to zoology) and for every grade level (K-graduate school). The single subject-matter tests are usually classified as readiness tests or tests in specific subjects.
6. Achievement test batteries consist of a group of tests in different content areas standardized on the same population so that the results of the various components may be meaningfully compared.
7. Before attempting to interpret an achievement test, the teacher should study the test and the test manual to obtain answers to some basic questions relating to the main purpose of the test, relation of the test items to the curriculum, relation of the type of student on which the test was standardized to the local students, and the reliability of the test scores.
8. One of the current uses of achievement tests is to measure growth toward local curricular objectives in a criterion-referenced manner.

Discussion Questions

1. Study the various definitions of achievement tests given at the beginning of the chapter and indicate the *common* elements which seem to come out among them.
2. Discuss the implications of an "experimental edition" of the test given to a sample of students before the final test is constructed.
3. If the school budget would allow you to use each of the three types of achievement tests, in what order would you give them in a particular grade, and why?
4. Describe the basic difference between a diagnostic test in reading and a survey test in reading.
5. In assessing a child for first grade readiness, translate the type of results you would get from the factors measured, as described in the introduction under *readiness tests,* into what useful information you would obtain.
6. Discuss the similarities and differences between a single subject-matter test built separately and one found for the same subject in an achievement battery.
7. Describe your feelings regarding the use of standardized achievement tests to measure progress toward local curricular objectives as used in the examples in Section H of this chapter.

Student Activities

1. After studying the various definitions of an achievement test given at the beginning of the chapter, devise your own definition using the common components from all of them.
2. Select a subject area on a level of your choice and build a two-way grid showing objectives on the left and subject matter content across the top. Then plot in each cell the number of items you would suggest opposite each objective and under the appropriate content. This will exhibit the plan from which a standardized test could be built. You may be asked to use this same grid in the chapter on teacher-made tests to develop test items.
3. With the help of your instructor obtain a sample set of one or more of the following as directed:
   a. A diagnostic achievement test
   b. A single-subject test
   c. A battery of achievement tests
   Using Harrington's Test Analysis Form in Chapter 9, complete the form as much as possible with the information available (use Buros' *Mental Measurements Yearbook* as an aid).

4. With the help of your instructor, select a different test for each of the categories in No. 3 and read the reviews in Buros' *Mental Measurements Yearbook*. Then write a summary of these reviews for each.

Selected Readings

Ahmann, J. Stanley, and Glock, Marvin D. *Evaluating Pupil Growth,* 5th ed. Boston: Allyn and Bacon, Inc., 1975. Chapter 11.

Aiken, Lewis R., Jr. *Readings in Psychological and Educational Testing.* Boston: Allyn and Bacon, Inc., 1973. Chapter 4.

Anastasi, Anne. *Psychological Testing,* 4th ed. New York: The Macmillan Company, 1976. Chapters 8 and 14.

Brown, Frederick G. *Principles of Educational and Psychological Testing,* 2nd ed. New York: Holt, Rinehart and Winston, 1976. Chapter 14.

Ebel, Robert L. *Essentials of Educational Measurement,* 3rd ed. Englewood Cliffs, NJ: Prentice-Hall, Inc., 1979. Chapter 16.

Gronlund, Norman E. *Measurement and Evaluation in Teaching,* 3rd ed. New York: The Macmillan Company, 1976. Chapter 12.

Hopkins, Charles D., and Antes, Richard L. *Classroom Measurement and Evaluation.* Itasca, IL: F. E. Peacock Publishers, Inc., 1978. Chapter 12.

Mehrens, William A., and Lehmann, Irvin J. *Measurement and Evaluation in Education and Psychology.* New York: Holt, Rinehart and Winston, Inc., 1973. Chapter 15.

Noll, Victor H., Scannell, Dale P., and Craig, Robert C. *Introduction to Educational Measurement,* 4th ed. Boston: Houghton Mifflin Company, 1979. Chapter 8.

Thorndike, Robert L., and Hagen, Elizabeth. *Measurement and Evaluation in Psychology and Education,* 4th ed. New York: John Wiley & Sons, Inc., 1977. Chapters 6 and 8.

Tuckman, Bruce W. *Measuring Educational Outcomes: Fundamentals of Testing.* New York: Harcourt Brace Jovanovich, Inc., 1975. Chapter 13.

Application of Measurement and Evaluation

12

Interpreting Measurement Data to Pupils and Parents

Why share measurement data with parents?

What might be accomplished in a group meeting with parents?

What are some principles to follow in interpreting data to parents in individual conferences?

Should measurement data be shared with students?

What are expectancy tables and how might they be used in test interpretation?

What is an example of current legislation on maintenance and confidentiality of student records?

A. Why Share Measurement Data with Parents?

It will be recalled that one of the basic functions of measurement and evaluation is to assist in the guidance of pupils. Modern-day philosophy of education emphasizes the importance of bringing parents in as partners in this buisiness of education. It seems logical that there will be more uniform guidance given to a pupil if both the school and the home have a common understanding of the ability and achievement exhibited by the pupil.

In addition to the philosophy that education should be a cooperative enterprise, there are at least three other reasons why teachers should share measurement data with parents: parents are curious about modern testing programs and are vitally interested in hearing any information that might concern their child; a large percentage of parents have the capacity to understand the test performance of their children and to become more effective in cooperating with the schools; and if testing programs are to be of real value, the data collected must be used rather than filed, discussed with parents and children rather than merely recorded on the cumulative record card.

If the school administration and staff can accept this point of view, it must also be noted that the type of information and the nature of the interpretation given to parents and pupils are important to discuss. Generally, the criterion in determining how far to go in interpreting psychological test information is that parents should be provided with the information they need and can understand to be more effective in helping the child develop most successfully within his capabilities. Subsequent sections will discuss both the type of information and the nature of interpretation to be provided to the parents and the pupils.

B. What Might Be Accomplished in a Group Meeting with Parents?

Some schools have found it valuable to plan a group conference which brings together a teacher or counselor and parents. On the high school level, this can be done by classes if the enrollment is not too large or by inviting a number of parents that can be adequately accommodated at one time. The title of the group conference might be "Our Evaluation Program." It is a golden opportunity to discuss with parents the broad topics relative to measurement and evaluation. It is not, however, a time to discuss individual children; that comes later.

Some of the topics that might be included in the group conference are these:

The scope of the evaluation program
Defining the measurement and evaluation process
The relation of measurement and evaluation to the objectives of instruction
The purposes of measurement and evaluation in teaching
The types of measuring devices used
Explanation of the standardized testing program
Definition of some basic terms used in test interpretation (percentiles, grade equivalents, stanines, and the like)
The specific uses to which measurement data might be applied
Limitations of measurement data

Parents can participate by simply attending to listen for information but more effectively by asking questions. The group conference should be a two-way communication.

C. What Are Some Principles to Follow in Interpreting Data to Parents in Individual Conferences?

The individual teacher-parent conference begins where other methods end. The parents bring to the conference ideas and concerns about their children's abilities and achievements from other methods of school reporting. The teacher brings an insight from evidence he has gathered about the child. The individual conference for test interpretation might be included with the normal parent conferences scheduled in the elementary school, or it may be scheduled for a separate time. On the high school level, the parents of students of certain classes may be scheduled each year. For example, if an individual conference is not deemed necessary each year, parents may be invited when their child is in the ninth and eleventh year or in the tenth and twelfth grade.

Walter Durost discusses the reporting of standardized intelligence and achievement tests to parents by teachers. He stresses the following points:[1]

1. Parents are entitled to information related to their children's progress in school, especially as it relates to future educational or vocational plans.
2. Test information given to parents must be expressed in understandable terms.
3. Test results are best revealed in terms of a single scale broadly based (percentiles or stanines).
4. The information should have uniform meaning to parent and educator and demonstrated relevance (validity) for the purpose in mind such as grouping, promotion, and guidance.

James Ricks reports two principles and one verbal technique which seem to provide a sound basis for communicating the information obtained from testing.[2]

1. *Parents have the right to know whatever the school knows about the abilities, the performance, and the problems of their children.*

    The school is the agent to which parents have delegated part of the educational process, but the responsibility has been delegated, not abdicated. Thoughtful parents do not take these responsibilities lightly. The parents' right to know, then, we regard as indisputable. But, to know what? The professional staff needs to know just what evidence there is to show that the test results deserve any consideration at all. It needs equally to know the margins and probabilities of error in prediction based on tests. If the staff doesn't know *both* what the scores *mean* and *how much confidence* may properly be placed in them, it is in trouble at the start; neither staff use of the information nor transmission of it to others will be very good.

2. *The school has the obligation to see that it communicates understandable and usable knowledge.*

    Content (what are we going to say) and *language* (how we are going to say it) are inseparable when one undertakes to tell somebody something. In giving information about test results, one

---

1. Walter Durost. "How To Tell Parents About Standardized Test Results." *Test Service Notebook, No. 26* (New York: Harcourt Brace Jovanovich, Inc., 1961). Reprinted by permission of the publisher.

2. James H. Ricks, Jr., "On Telling Parents About Test Results." *Test Service Bulletin, No. 54* (New York: The Psychological Corporation, 1959).

needs to think about the general content and language to use and also about the specific terms to use. For example, one might want to discuss both the values and the weaknesses of test scores. One excellent device for this purpose would be the expectancy table or chart discussed in a later section. Such a chart can make it clear to persons without training in statistics that test results are useful predictors *and* that the predictions will not always be precise.

Specific terms used in expressing test results vary considerably in the problems they pose. They may take the form of IQ's, grade placement, standard scores, or percentiles. A good teacher will want to be sure to know the strong and weak points of each type of derived scores. But a more fundamental question remains: *Are any numbers necessary?* Numbers probably are needed, but we are struck repeatedly by the fact that some of the very best counselors and teachers present numerical data only incidentally or not at all.

At the beginning of referring to Ricks' reference, it was stated that there was a technique as well as two principles. The technique of interpreting test scores can be stated in just a few words:

"You score like people who . . ." Or, to a parent, "Your son (or daughter) scores like students who . . ."

The sentence, of course, requires completion. The completion depends on the test or other instruments, the reason for testing, and the person to whom the report is being given. Some sample completions:

". . . students who have more than average difficulty passing in arithmetic; you (or, to a parent, he/she) may need some extra help on this in the next few years."

". . . students who are disappointed later if they don't begin a language in the ninth grade and plan to take some more math and science."

There are many other possibilities. The most important thing to note is that a satisfactory report combines two kinds of information:

1. the test results of the individual person
2. something known about the test or battery and its relationship to the subsequent performance of others who have taken it

Assuming that the school has decided to share test information with parents, the following principles are suggested for the teacher and counselor to keep in mind.

1. **Make Sure That Both You and the Person to Whom You Are Interpreting the Test Results Have a Clear, Immediate Goal in Mind Which Will Serve As a Reason for the Interpretation.**

If the test interpretation conference is a routine one in the school, the goal that might be stressed is mutual understanding of the child's abilities, achievements, interests, and the like. At times a special conference is held when a decision must be made regarding the child. Then both the teacher and the parent have a focus for which the interpretation conference is being held. Although test results will not be the only factor discussed when an important decision is to be made, they are often brought into the discussion on matters relative to retardation, acceleration, or special classes.

2. **Avoid the Use of Specific Scores Whenever Possible.**

It has already been stressed that raw scores from a test are of little value in test interpretation. These scores must be converted into interpretive scales for more uniform interpretation. Some of these scores were discussed in Chapter 8 in relation to kinds of norms. These will be mentioned again with emphasis on any advantages or limitations in interpretation to parents.

Grade and age equivalents

Simply stated, a grade or age placement score is the grade or age equivalent to which a student's raw score entitles him. These are useful primarily in interpreting a student's score in relation to his present grade or age placement. On the broader scale, they are useful in evaluating the performance of a school. By obtaining the average score earned at a certain grade level and referring to the proper table of norms, it is possible to determine whether the school is doing as well as a larger group on which the test was standardized. If age equivalents were used, the average score of all children of a specific age (for example, 8.5-9.4 for nine-year-olds) would be compared with the average for the standardization group.

Grade and age equivalents have a serious limitation if used for interpreting the scores earned by individual students. For example, a sixth-grade child may obtain a grade placement of 9.3 in arithmetic computation. The parents might believe that their child is capable of doing work at the ninth-grade level and should be accelerated. It must be pointed out immediately that the student has earned a score equal to the average score earned by children in some subsequent grade. He may have earned this score by doing exceptionally well on all the work which is at or below his grade level while the average student might have missed some of these items. The student could not work adequately at the ninth-grade level because he has not had the experiences or learnings normally taught prior to the ninth-grade level.

There is also another limitation which concerns the lack of uniformity in meaning of age and grade equivalents from the lower to the higher grades. If a child is a year below the norm in reading at the second-grade level, this might be serious; however, being a year below the norm group at the ninth-grade level might be within the limits of chance variations for this grade level.

If these limitations can be explained by the teacher or counselor and understood by the parents, then age and grade equivalents are an easy way for parents to understand the relative position of their child with others.

Percentile ranks

Percentile ranks have been one of the most popular norms by which test scores are interpreted to parents, since they are applicable to many pupil traits. It is easy for parents to see the student's relative position on a scale from 0 to 100.

The limitation of the percentile rank reporting is that it is accepted many times as being more precise than it actually is. It must be remembered that a standard error exists in percentile ranks as well as in any method of reporting. In addition, many parents might believe that the percentile scale represents equal units from low to high. Parents should understand that it takes a wide range of scores to move from one percentile rank to another at the ends of the scale, but because of the high concentration of scores around the middle of the distribution, the change of a single score in the center of the distribution may result in a change of several percentile points.

Intelligence quotients

Most educators will concur that specific IQ's should not be reported to parents because of the misinterpretation which might be made. There is a tendency for parents to accept an IQ as an absolute value rather than as an estimate, to assume that it is a permanent value without considering possibility of change due to environmental factors, and to assume that IQ scores are equivalent from one IQ test to another. Also, the IQ really is only a measure of rate of learning. It has received much more emphasis than it should. Therefore, it is better to report ability in other forms, such as those already described or in stanine form described next.

TABLE 12.1

Percentage of Cases at Each Stanine Level

Stanine	Percentage of Normal Population	Description	
9	4	Superior	(4%)
8	7		
7	12	Above average	(19%)
6	17		
5	20		
4	17	Average	(54%)
3	12		
2	7	Below average	(19%)
1	4	Poor	(4%)

Stanines

The stanine scale refers to a "standard nine-point scale." Raw scores are converted to score levels from 1 (low) to 9 (high) with 5 being exactly average. The stanine method of interpretation is used quite widely because it has several advantages. It has broader units which parents can more readily understand. Stanines can be compared from test to test or among tests if the group on which they are based remains the same and if they represent more nearly equal steps or ranges of ability or achievement than other methods.

Table 12.1 shows the percentages of cases at each stanine level.

It can be explained to parents that stanines 1, 2, and 3 together represent the same range of ability as 4, 5, and 6 or 7, 8, and 9, since this breakdown is usually used in sectioning. Normally, stanines 1, 2, and 3 represent the low group; 4, 5, and 6 the average group; and 7, 8, and 9 the high group.

3. Never Discuss the Implication of Scores in Terms of Absolute Answers.

The teacher or counselor should constantly remind himself that all scores are subject to error and no single score is precise enough to make projections in absolute terms. Never make such statements as these: "This score means you will never be successful in this field," or "This score shows you will not be admitted to college," "With these scores, you will become an excellent engineer." There have been too many exceptions to such absolute predictions. The teacher or counselor is safer to discuss scores in the following terms: "Very few students with such scores have been successful in this field," or "Most students with such scores have had difficulty with college admission," or "Most students with scores like these have been very successful as engineers."

4. Try to Concentrate on Increasing Understanding Rather Than Posing As an Expert.

A basic purpose of a test interpretation is to develop mutual understanding; therefore, this is not the time to toss technical measurement terms around. Try to use the simplest synonyms for technical terms when these must be used. Also, after making a point of interpretation, the teacher or counselor should ask the question "What does this mean to you?" This will give the parent an opportunity to place the interpretation in his own terms and, if the parent's interpretation is wrong, the teacher or counselor can correct the interpretation before proceeding further.

5. Remember, Understanding and Acceptance Are Not Synonymous Terms.

A parent may be able to express understanding of the interpretation accurately, but he or she may not accept it. If a parent leaves the interpretation conference with many doubts about the results and has not had an opportunity to discuss these, it is doubtful that the conference will help the parents understanding the child better. Then teacher or counselor should always follow the parent interpretation expression with "What do you think about it?" This will not only encourage the parents to express their true feelings, but it may suggest to the teacher other factors in the child's environment that might reinforce the interpretation or place some limitation on it.

6. Never Compare One Student with Another Particular Student.

If the teacher or counselor will remember that all test results are confidential between the school and the parent, this principle will be followed. Parents should understand this confidentiality and will respect the school for maintaining this position. This principle holds true in comparing children within the same family. Stress the idea that each child has a unique personality and comparing scores would add nothing to understanding the test interpretation for the particular child presently being discussed.

7. After the Tests Have Been Interpreted, Discussion Between You and the Student or His or Her Parents Should Be Continued.

Teachers and counselors must recognize that test interpretation is only a step in a total program of action designed to help the student. If the teacher is not prepared to follow up on a test interpretation in terms of some specific actions or suggestions which the teacher, parent, and/or student should take, it is questionable whether the test interpretation should have been done in the first place. When the school accepts responsibility for test interpretation, it also accepts responsibility for follow-up actions after the test has been interpreted. It may be as simple as the parent supervising some additional home exercises in arithmetic computation to reinforce the child's learning to suggesting further testing to validate the results obtained before any definite action is taken.

Stanley and Hopkins make the following recommendations relating to the interpretation of test scores.[3]

1. Orientation for acceptance and use of test results should precede testing.
2. Until someone is qualified to use and interpret a test, that test should not be given.
3. Tests and test scores should be released to only those persons who are qualified to use and interpret the tests.
4. Test scores should be interpreted to only appropriate individuals, e.g., students and their parents or legal guardians. In all instances, the pupils' scores should be interpreted within a setting in which unauthorized persons cannot listen in on the interpretation or see the results.
5. Inasmuch as test scores are often misinterpreted by laymen, scores should be interpreted for pupils and parents, not merely distributed to them. Furthermore, scores should be interpreted when pupils or their parents request information. Unless there is a genuine felt need for information, the odds are against an increase in self-understanding on the part of the pupil or understanding on the part of the parent or even against the acceptance by the parent of information about his child.
6. Before interpreting a test, a teacher or counselor should familiarize himself with the nontest data available on the student. During the test interpretation he also should encourage the pupil to supplement the test results with nontest data.
7. A test-interpreter should encourage student participation in interpreting test scores. To help a student recall what a test, or a part of a battery, was like, the teacher or counselor can describe it in non-technical language, and he will usually find that it is helpful to show the student sample items from the test, before encouraging the student to estimate how well he did on it. If the counselor is to do this successfully, it is obvious that he must know the student and be thoroughly familiar with the tests in order to communicate accurate information to the student.
8. The test-interpreter must be very sensitive to cues which suggest that the student does not comprehend the information which is being given him.
9. The student should be encouraged to react to the test results—to raise questions or to comment on how he feels about the way the test or tests describe him. When he feels that interpreted remarks are appropriate, he will often respond to data quite spontaneously—telling how pleased he is with some scores or how he does not like or cannot accept others. For the test-interpreter it is important that he detect these feelings and that he be able to respond to them. Helping a student examine these feelings increases the chances for helping him understand and accept himself as he is.

3. Julian C. Stanley and Kenneth Hopkins, *Educational and Psychological Measurement and Evaluation* (Englewood Cliffs, N. J.: Prentice-Hall, 1972), p. 97. Original source: M. M. Ohlsen, 1963, *Interpretation of Test Scores.* In W. G. Findley, ed., "The impact and improvement of school testing programs," *The Sixty-Second Yearbook of the National Society for the Study of Education, Part II*. Chicago: University of Chicago Press, pp. 254-294.

10. There is no justification for arguing with a student about his test scores. Moreover, little can be accomplished by either defending a test or criticizing it. What test-interpreters should do is explain how the results may be used by the student to understand himself and to make certain predictions, and with what certainty.

In a teacher's manual accompanying a series of transparencies, J. A. Barr suggests the following cautions in the use of test results.[4]

1. Any single test score has limited meaning for the learning process because of the limited sampling it can make.
2. Tests may suggest limits on expected performance, but not exact levels of performance.
3. Tests useful for group guidance may not be sufficiently valid and reliable for individual interpretation.
4. Standardized test results are comparable only when normed on the same population.
5. Because of the lack of precision of measuring instruments, any standardized test score must be described as a midpoint in a band rather than as an absolute score.
6. Similar scores on tests with similar titles may have very different meanings because of the content being measured.
7. As individuals mature, their test scores tend to become more reliable. An ability test score in the eighth grade will be more predictive of a twelfth grade score than will a score earned in the primary grades.

D. Should Measurement Data Be Shared with Students?

Students have a curiosity to know how they are achieving and have a right to know their performance on all *achievement tests whether standardized or nonstandardized.* Teachers do and, of course, should grade daily assignments, unit tests, research papers, and the like and return them to the students along with comments and information. However, when it concerns standardized achievement tests, school personnel are reluctant to share these results. The success of any testing program is determined by what happens as a result of the findings. As has been emphasized before, the results should be interpreted in a way which is meaningful to the pupils. In the elementary school, K-6, the type of interpretation should be descriptive—placed on the basis of above average, average, or below average. A third-grader could profit from such an interpretation as the following.

> In reading comprehension, Mary, you were a little low. The test indicates that you can improve if you have more practice in following directions and in using reference material accurately. We will try to work together on this.

Above the sixth-grade level, students can profit from interpretation of results in the form of quartiles, percentiles, grade and age placements,

4. J. A. Barr, *Interpreting Standardized Tests* (San Jose, California: The Lansford Publishing Co., 1973), p. 22.

stanines, expectancy tables, and the like. Again, after the derived scores are shown, descriptive information is helpful on what the scores mean. Students who do well are encouraged to continue to do well if they know they can and are expected to do above average performance. Students who may be low in certain areas are equally motivated if it is shown how they can improve. If a student feels that the teacher is on his side and places the interpretation on as positive a basis as possible, student cooperation will frequently follow.

It usually is dangerous to present the results of intelligence tests directly to pupils. Any interpretation of ability should be translated into strong and/or weak areas of ability rather than a total IQ or MA. Most students will consider it sufficient to see a profile of ability points plotted with general interpretation given for each area. Difficulty arises when the teacher attempts to interpret an ability profile in which all the points are relatively low. Here the teacher or counselor should try to help the child accept any limitations and put emphasis on what can be accomplished through consistently strong effort. The teacher should not encourage unrealistic ambitions, but the child can be helped to set more realistic goals in line with his ability. There is probably more reason to interpret ability tests to senior high school students relative to educational and vocational guidance than at any other time except when special consideration must be given for an academic or a behavior problem.

The following section will assist the teacher or counselor in translating test results into expectancies. Ultimately, this is the type of information which both pupils and parents would like to have interpreted for them.

E. What Are Expectancy Tables and How Might They Be Used in Test Interpretation?

An expectancy table is a useful device for communicating results to parents and assisting in giving meaning to test interpretation. It also assists the teacher in spotting those students who may be performing below expectancy, at expectancy, or above expectancy, or in other words, those that may be working below capacity (under-achievers), at capacity, or above capacity (over-achievers). The type of interpretation depends upon the two variables in the expectancy chart.

Figure 12.1 is an expectancy chart in its simplest form. On the left vertical is an indication of ability from 1 (low) to 5 (high). Across the top is an index of achievement from 1 to 5. By plotting ability and achievement level for each student and putting the name in the appropriate cell, we can see how each is performing (achievement) in relation to ability. A "staircase" is built from the lower left to upper right which is always one cell above and below the exact plotted point. Any student ap-

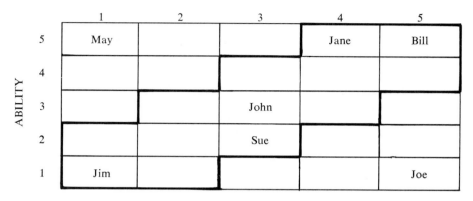

Figure 12.1 Ability-Achievement Expectancy Chart.

pearing within the "staircase" is performing at his level of ability; if the student appears to the left of the "staircase," he is achieving below his level; to the right, above his level.

In Fig. 12.1, Jim, Sue, John, Jane, and Bill are achieving at their level of ability; May is achieving at a level less than her ability; and Joe is achieving at a level above his ability. In a simple way, then, each student can be spotted as to level of performance in relation to ability.

Technically, an expectancy table shows the relationship between performance level intervals and criterion categories (arithmetic achievement test–intelligence test; ratings of students–clerical test score; midterm examination–pretest). Teachers and counselors can make expectancy tables with no special training in testing or statistics. Especially helpful would be Bulletin No. 38 of the Psychological Corporation's *Test Service Bulletins* (For address, see Appendix I). In order for the expectancy chart to be stable, it should include a large number of students and should be kept up-to-date with as much current data as possible. For use in any given year, the teacher or counselor is comparing present students with themselves or with previous students of similar age or grade and performance on the two variables under consideration. The school administration can also build expectancy tables for teachers to use for a given grade level and/or in certain subjects. These can be mimeographed and the teacher can superimpose the data for his specific class on it by writing the name of students in the correct squares.

In this way, the teacher could immediately see how many of his students are working higher or lower than expectancy (in terms of scholastic aptitude), and he can compare the distribution of scores for his class with those for the school district. Figure 12.2 illustrates a type of two-variable chart which can be used with any standardized test that has stanine scores,

Stanines on Achievement Test

	1	2	3	4	5	6	7	8	9	Total
9					Walt 1	1	Nina 1		1	4
8						1		5		6
7					Phil 2		3			5
6			Lois 2	Tom 2	Tina 4	1		1		10
5	Pete 2	1	Roy 2	Sam 4		2	1			12
4				Jo 3	Sue 1	2				6
3	Amy 1	May 1		Ann 1	Jim 1					4
2		Sara 1								1
1										0
Total	3	3	4	10	9	7	5	6	1	48

Stanines on Intelligence Test,

Names of 16 Pupils in Miss Jones' Seventh-Grade English Class, Entered on a Two-Variable Chart for All Seventh-Grades in Lodi Junior High School.

This chart is designed to show the relationship between stanine scores on an intelligence test and stanine scores on the local English test (the correlation is about .55 between these two tests). All cases with the diagonal "staircase" have the same stanine scores in both the intelligence and the English tests, or their stanines in these two tests differ by only one score. For all cases to the right of the diagonal "staircase" (in this case 10% of Lodi Junior High students), the students' English stanine exceeded his intelligence stanine by two or more points. For all cases to the left (in this case, 33%), the students' English stanine was two or more points below his intelligence test stanine.

Figure 12.2 Expectancy Chart for English Test.

for example, the Metropolitan Achievement Tests. Stanine scores represent equal units of ½ SD; moreover, stanine norms are easily developed from local data (the procedure for assigning scores to stanine levels is discussed in Harcourt, Brace Jovanovich *Test Service Notebook* No. 23: "The Characteristics, Use, and Computation of Stanines").

In this chart, the teacher could see that only one student, or less than 1% of her class appears to be over-achievers (Jim) as compared with 10% in the school. On the other hand, 8 students, or 50%, of her class appear to be under-achievers, as compared with 33% in the school. Seven students, or about 44%, of Miss Jones' class are performing at expectancy level.

Table 12.2 below and Table 12.3, on page 319, illustrate two other forms of the expectancy tables.

This summary was obtained by preparing a two-way distribution chart with Expectancy Levels at the left and IQ Levels across the top.

Expectancy for any intelligence level was set as the middle 50 percent of achievement performance for the expectancy level; below expectancy was set as the lowest 25 percent; and above expectancy was set as the highest 25 percent. The decision about what represents the expected level of achievement is a somewhat arbitrary one. With Table 12.2 available, a third-grade teacher in this school could interpret individual cases as to expectations by finding the proper IQ level first and then the appropriate grade placement. Referring to the level of expectancy column, the teacher could then be guided by the level of performance expected of the child.

Table 12.3 is based on applications of a general scholastic aptitude test (the American College Test) administered to 2479 freshmen at the University of Wisconsin-Whitewater. To interpret a student's score, the counselor or teacher need only direct attention to the row of the table corresponding

TABLE 12.2

Summary Table of Expectations for End of Third Grade on Metropolitan Reading Test According to Otis IQ

Level of Expectancy	IQ'S 120+	IQ's 110-119	IQ's 100-109	IQ's 90-99	IQ's 89 & below
Below Expectancy	3.9 & below	3.4 & below	3.4 & below	3.0 & below	2.6 & below
At Expectancy	4.0 – 5.1	3.5 – 4.8	3.5 – 4.8	3.1 – 4.3	2.7 – 3.6
Above Expectancy	5.2 & above	4.9 & above	4.9 & above	4.4 & above	3.7 & above

TABLE 12.3

Grade-Point Average Expectancy Table for
First-Semester Freshman Achievement

Composite ACT Score	Percent Expected to Earn			
Standard Score	F to D 0 - 1.0	D to C 1.0 - 2.0	C to B 2.0 - 3.0	B to A 3.0 - 4.0
32-34			25	75
29-31	1		14	84
26-28	1.5	1.5	22	75
23-25	2	4	42	52
20-22	4	6	55	35
17-19	4	13	56	27
14-16	7	17	62	15
11-13	5	25	62	8
1-10	12	35	50	3
N = 2479				

Source: Prepared for author by the Testing Office, University of Wisconsin-Whitewater, 1979.

to the correct standard score; the entries show how likely the student is to attain any particular grade-point average. This explanation is more definite and more complete than can be offered by any other system of norms. If the ACT test were administered to a high school senior and a result were available, the teacher or counselor could assist the student in considering his probable academic performance. For example, 90% of students who scored in the 20-22 standard score range would be expected to earn a 2.0 (C) or higher; 35% of this group would be expected to earn a 3.0 (B) or higher.

In interpreting the results of an expectancy table, Lyman suggests the following points be considered.[5]

1. We need to be certain we are using the same test (including the same form, level, edition, etc.).
2. The table is based on results that have been found in the past; it may or may not be relevant to the present group (or individual).
3. If the table is based on the performance of people from another office (company, school, or college), it may or may not apply to ours.
4. We can have more confidence in expectancy levels that are based on large numbers of scores (percentages are sometimes used to disguise small numbers).
5. An expectancy table may be used to spot individuals (or subgroups) that do not perform as we would expect; by noting instances in which

5. Howard B. Lyman, *Test Scores and What They Mean*, 3rd ed. (Englewood Cliffs, N.J.: Prentice-Hall, Inc., 1978), p. 61.

predictions miss, we may check back to discover possible reasons for the failure.

6. In a sense, we may think of an expectancy table as a set of norms in which one's test score is compared with the criterion performance of others who have made that same score.

F. What Is an Example of Current Legislation on Maintenance and Confidentiality of Student Records?

Several states and the federal government have passed legislation regarding the maintenance and confidentiality of student records. On the federal level, Section 438 of the General Education Provisions Act relates to the protection of the right and privacy of parents and students. In Wisconsin, Section 118.125 of the Wisconsin Statutes refers to the maintenance and confidentiality of student records.

A sample set of policies meeting the Wisconsin Law and the General Education Provisions Act follows.

Maintenance and Confidentiality of Student Records

1. Student records are maintained in the interest of the student, to assist the school in providing appropriate educational experiences.
2. Student records include all records relating to an individual student other than notes or records maintained for personal use by teachers or other certified personnel which are not available to others, and records necessary for, and available only to, persons involved in psychological treatment of a student.
   a. Progress records maintained by the school include: identifying data, a statement of courses taken by the student, the student's grades, the student's extra-curricular activities and the student's attendance record.
   b. Behavioral records maintained by the school include all student records other than progress records. They are:
      (1) Standardized achievement tests
      (2) Mental maturity tests
      (3) Personality evaluations
      (4) Evaluations for educational needs
      (5) Health records
      (6) Teacher evaluations other than grades
      (7) Statements relating to individual student behavior
3. All student records are confidential, with the following exceptions:
   a. A pupil, or a parent or guardian of a minor pupil, shall, upon request, be shown and provided with a copy of the pupil's progress records.
   b. An adult pupil, or the parent or guardian of a minor pupil, shall, upon request, be shown, in the presence of a person qualified to explain and interpret the records, the pupil's behavioral records. Such pupil or parent or guardian shall, upon request, be provided with a copy of the behavioral records.

    c. The judge of any court of this state or of the United States shall, upon order, be provided by the school district clerk with a copy of all progress records of a pupil who is the subject of any proceeding in such court.

    d. Pupil records may be made available to persons employed in the school which the pupil attends who are required by the Department of Public Instruction under s. 115.28 (7) to hold a certificate, license, or permit.

    e. Upon the written permission of an adult pupil, or the parent or guardian of a minor pupil, the school shall make available to the person named in the permission form, the pupil's progress records or such portions of his behavioral records as determined by the person authorizing the release.

    f. Pupil records shall be provided to a court in response to a subpoena by parties to an action for in camera inspection, to be used only for purposes of impeachment of any witness who has testified in the action. The court may turn said records or parts thereof over to parties in the action or their attorneys if said records would be relevant and material to a witness's credibility or competency.

    g. The School Board may provide the Department of Public Instruction or any public officer with any information required under Chapters 115 to 121.

    h. Notwithstanding their confidential status, student records may be used in suspension and expulsion proceedings and by the multi-disciplinary team under Chapter 115 of the statutes.

    i. When such information is furnished in compliance with judicial order, or pursuant to any lawfully issued subpoena, upon condition that parents and the students are notified of all such orders or subpoenas in advance of the compliance therewith by the educational institution or agency, records will be released.

4. The building principal shall have primary responsibility for maintaining the confidentiality of all student records kept at that school.

    a. All requests for inspection or for transfer to another school or school district should be directed to the building principal or director of student services, who will then determine whether inspection or transfer is permitted under this policy.

    b. The building principal or qualified counselors shall be present to interpret behavioral records when inspection is made under item (3) (b).

    c. Upon transfer of student records to the central student services office under item 5 herein, these duties shall be assumed by the director of student services.

5. While students are attending school, their records will be maintained in the school of attendance. Upon transfer of the student to another school operated by the district, the records shall be transferred to that school. When the student ceases to be enrolled in a school operated by the district his or her records will be transferred as provided in section 7 herein. Records remaining after 90 days, will be transferred to the central student services office.

6. Records which are transferred to the central student services office when the student ceases to be enrolled, shall be maintained as follows:

    a. All behavioral records will be destroyed one year after the date the student graduated from or last attended the school unless the student and his or her parent or guardian, if the student is a minor, gives permission that the records may be maintained for a longer period of time.

b. Where such written permission is received, behavioral records will be destroyed seven (7) years after the date the student graduated from, or last attended, the school.

c. Progress records will be destroyed fifty (50) years after the student ceases to be enrolled in the school district.

d. Seven years after the student ceases to be enrolled in the school system, all progress records will be maintained on microfilm. Two sets will be made, with one stored in the fireproof safe at the central student services office and the second set stored in the fireproof safe in the central administrative office.

7. Student records relating to a specific student, shall be transferred to another school or school district upon receipt of written notice from an adult student or the parent or guardian of a minor student, that the student intends to enroll in the other school or school district, or upon written notice from the other school or school district, that the student has enrolled.

8. An adult pupil, or a parent or guardian of a minor child shall have an opportunity for a hearing to challenge the content of their pupil's records, to insure that the records are not inaccurate, misleading, or otherwise in violation of the privacy or other rights of students, and to provide an opportunity for the correction or deletion of any such inaccurate, misleading, or otherwise inappropriate data contained therein.

Summary Statements

1. Parents should be brought in as partners with the school in the educational enterprise; therefore, test data should be shared with pupils and parents rather than merely recorded on the cumulative record card.

2. The criterion in determining how far to go in interpreting psychological tests data with parents is that parents should be provided with the information they need and can understand to be more effective in helping their child to develop.

3. A group meeting with parents to discuss broad topics relative to the measurement and evaluation program will assist in general understanding of the program and will serve as background information for individual conferences on test interpretation.

4. Some principles to follow in interpreting data to parents in individual conferences include the following:

a. Make sure that there is an immediate goal for the test interpretation of a student's profile.

b. Avoid the use of special scores whenever possible; the interpretation is best if it is in general and descriptive terms giving meaning to test scores.

c. Do not discuss implications of test scores in absolute terms, since every test score is subject to error.

    d. Put emphasis on increasing understanding rather than posing as an expert.

    e. Ask parents for their opinions on the interpretation of the test results, remembering that understanding and acceptance are not synonymous terms.

    f. Never compare any specific student with any other particular student.

    g. Discussion between the teacher and student and his or her parents should be continued after the tests have been interpreted.

5. Achievement test results should be interpreted to students in a meaningful manner; however, extreme care should be taken in interpreting intelligence tests. When it is done, it should be done for a particular reason and then interpreted in terms of strong and weak areas of ability. The purpose should be to assist the child to accept his or her abilities and to attempt to capitalize on any assets of ability.

6. Expectancy tables are instruments used to assist in communicating and interpreting results to pupils and parents. The tables are expressed as the probability of a student reaching a certain performance level on the basis of his or her test results compared with previous students of like results, age, and grade level.

7. Several states and the federal government have passed legislation regarding the maintenance and confidentiality of student records.

Discussion Questions

1. Describe any arguments as to why measurement data should not be shared with parents.

2. Discuss the five or six topics you believe would be of major importance to include in a program for parents entitled "Our Evaluation Program."

3. Summarize the main points relative to the principle of test interpretation: "Avoid the use of specific scores whenever possible."

4. Explain what seem to be the guidelines in sharing measurement data with pupils.

5. Discuss the steps you would use in building an expectancy table for measurement data on the grade level or subject of your major interest.

6. Discuss the implications for the school administration, counselor, and teacher to the part of student record legislation which says, "An adult pupil, or the parent or guardian of a minor pupil, shall, upon request, be shown, in the presence of a person qualified to explain and interpret the records, the pupil's behavioral records."

Student Activities

1. Assume that you have been asked to assist in drafting a letter to parents explaining the school's philosophy in sharing measurement data with them. List the basic points you would want to include in such a letter so that the parents would understand the school's position clearly and would know what to expect in terms of test interpretation.

2. For each of the following parent reactions during a test interpretation, write briefly what your position would be and how you would respond to the parents.
   a. "Test results fluctuate so much that it seems a waste of time to discuss them."
   b. "What is the IQ of my child?"
   c. "Does this mean that my son will fail in college?"
   d. "My daughter (in seventh grade) received a grade placement of 10.0 in arithmetic. Could she be promoted to tenth-grade mathematics?"
   e. "How do Mary's scores compare with her brother's?"
   f. "What happens now that we know he is having difficulty in grammar?"

3. Build a two-way expectancy chart like Figure 12.2 with ability results on the left and achievement results across the top. After tallying the scores for each of the 50 pupils, draw the staircase showing the area in which all scores have the same stanine scores in both intelligence and achievement or their stanines in these two tests differ by only one score. Then write a summary of the expectancy table, pointing out the percentage of the class in each of the three expectancy areas.

Intelligence Scores	Achievement Scores	Intelligence Scores	Achievement Scores	Intelligence Scores	Achievement Scores
9	5	6	3	5	4
9	6	6	4	5	5
9	7	6	4	5	6
9	9	6	5	5	6
8	6	6	5	5	7
8	8	6	5	4	4
8	8	6	5	4	4
8	8	6	6	4	4
8	8	6	8	4	5
8	8	5	1	4	6
7	5	5	1	4	6
7	5	5	2	3	1
7	7	5	3	3	4
7	7	5	3	3	5
7	7	5	4	2	2
6	3	5	4	2	3
				1	3
				1	3

4. In regard to student record legislation:
   a. List those agencies or persons who can view student records without the student or parental approval; and
   b. List those agencies or persons who normally use student records but who now would require student or parental approval.

Selected Readings

Ahmann, J. Stanley, and Glock, Marvin D. *Measuring and Evaluating Educational Achievement*, Boston: Allyn and Bacon, Inc., 1975. Chapter 8.

Barr, J. A. *Interpreting Standardized Tests*. San Jose, California: The Lansford Publishing Co., 1973. Page 22.

Durost, Walter. "How to Tell Parents About Standardized Test Results," *Test Service Notebook, No. 26*. New York: Harcourt Brace Jovanovich, Inc., 1961.

Gronlund, Norman E. *Measurement and Evaluation in Teaching*, 3rd ed. New York: The Macmillan Company, 1976. Chapter 15.

Noll, Victor H., Scannell, Dale P., and Craig, Robert C. *Introduction to Educational Measurement*, 4th ed. Boston: Houghton Mifflin Company, 1979. Chapter 14.

Payne, David A., and McMorris, Robert F. *Educational and Psychological Measurement*. Morristown, NJ: General Learning Press, 1974. Part IV.

Ricks, James H., Jr. "On Telling Parents About Test Results," *Test Service Bulletin, No. 54*. New York: The Psychological Corporation, 1959.

TenBrink, Terry D. *Evaluation. A Practical Guide for Teachers*. New York: McGraw-Hill Book Company, 1974. Chapter 9.

13

Grading, Marking, and Reporting Practices

What are the purposes of school marks?

What are some problems of marking?

What is the basis for scoring results obtained through measurement?

What are some methods of grading?

How are grades distributed?

How do you assign course marks?

How do you assign marks to classes having different levels of academic ability?

What are some systems of marking?

What are some examples of reporting forms?

How does one evaluate a current system of marking and reporting and/or establish a new system?

A. What Are the Purposes of School Marks?

The purposes of school marks can best be explained from the standpoint of the users—the students, parents, teachers, other school personnel, and employers.

Reporting to Students

Marks can serve a motivation function and a guidance function with students. When we speak of using marks for motivation, we mean it in the positive sense; that is, for improvement of learning. A student may be challenged to work harder and to view the mark as an improvement of learning. One must guard against overstressing the high marks, however. They should not become ends in themselves. A student might place the mark as the goal and narrowly work for that and sacrifice his creativity and imagination in the process. Likewise, some students may feel that they do not have the ability to obtain a higher mark and therefore will settle for a lesser one. But if we stress the idea of marks for improvement rather than status, all students may have an incentive to work harder.

Marks may serve as a *guidance* function for students. They may tell the student that he is good in physics and math, for example, and does less well in English and speech. With the help of a teacher or counselor, this type of information may help him to pursue educational or vocational goals more in line with his abilities. The correlation between high school marks and college marks is somewhat above .50. As a result, other information should be considered, but school marks can definitely be one factor in helping the student make educational or vocational plans.

Reporting to Parents

Marks can be one of the best communication devices between the school and the home. If school personnel have made the effort to explain to parents the nature of the marking system and what marks mean, such reports should clarify the goals of the school, indicate the student's strengths and weaknesses in learning, and provide an understanding of the student's non-intellectual growth. If the parents know what the school is trying to accomplish, they are better able to cooperate with the student. Second, if they can see the strengths and weaknesses their child is having they can better commend or encourage the child's learning. Last, by knowing non-intellectual growth as well as academic growth, parents can better obtain a picture of the total youngster and aid him or her educationally, vocationally and personally.

Use of Marks by Teachers and Other School Personnel

Marks serve as a great *informational* source for teachers, counselors, and administrators. Of course, they would be supplemented by other data from test scores, observation, and the like. Most teachers feel that they can better understand their students faster if they have some evidence of past achievement. Having this information, they can plan their instruction in a more appropriate manner. Marks can also play a *diagnostic* function for a teacher by knowing areas of strengths and weaknesses for a given pupil and, thereby, attempting to individualize instruction.

Counselors use marks for many purposes. They may help the student have a better self-concept and understanding of one's self. They could be the cause of emotional problems and, knowing this, it would help the counselor to better work with the student and teachers. In helping a student to plan his educational or vocational goals, marks certainly are one piece of evidence that the counselor will want to use.

The administrator has many uses for school marks. These include: promotion of students, graduation, distributing honors or awards, athletic eligibility, recommendation for post-secondary school entrance, and recommendation to employers.

Since marks are so important to each of the above, it is imperative that representatives from each group have input into the marking system of a school.

B. What Are Some Problems of Marking?

The problem of estimating student learning and achievement has been a persistent one on all levels of education. There seems to be constant discussion among school personnel as to the best ways to mark student progress. There is much experimentation with various systems of marking, but no one system seems to be acceptable to all. Green states seven rather persistent problems relating to the marking process.[1]

1. There is widespread misunderstanding of the meaning of the terms "scoring," "grading," and "marking."
2. Course marks often fail to reflect the real course achievement of pupils.
3. Course marks are often based on insufficient evidence of pupil achievement.
4. Many teachers lack clearly defined criteria for assigning course marks, or assign them carelessly without serious effort to assess achievement.
5. Teachers often permit such extraneous factors as the "halo effect," personality conflicts, class attendance, and discipline to influence pupils' course marks.
6. Teachers, parents, and pupils rarely share an understanding of the nature and extent of achievement represented by specific course marks.
7. Pupils frequently work for a specific course mark rather than to learn as much as possible in a course.

Most of the problems listed are self-explanatory. However, the first one is of such importance that the terms need definition. The terms "scoring," "grading," and "marking" are not interchangeable; a precise definition and correct use of the terms is a first essential step toward clarifying the misunderstanding.

Scoring means the process of correcting assignments, tests, projects, term papers or giving so many points for a performance or a product. The scores are usually in *raw score* form.

Grading goes beyond scoring in that it assigns a grade to whatever is being evaluated. It usually will be preceded by scoring, although in some cases it may not.

Marking refers to the process of assigning a composite *course grade* at the end of the marking period. This will have taken into consideration all evidence of pupil achievement during the course.

1. Reprinted by permission of Dodd, Mead & Company, Inc. from *Introduction to Measurement and Evaluation* by John A. Green. Copyright © 1970 by Dodd, Mead & Company, Inc.

C. What Is the Basis for Scoring Results Obtained Through Measurement?

It should be stressed before discussing scoring, grading, and marking procedures that it is assumed that the teacher has stated objectives for teaching and learning (Step I in the teaching process); has provided the *best* opportunities for the students to grow toward the objectives (Step II); and is now ready to evaluate student progress toward the goals of instruction (Step III).

The measuring instrument which is used must be the best one to measure growth toward the objective. Some examples of measuring instruments and how they are usually scored follows.

1. *Objective tests*—Usually one point for each correct item unless the item contains more than one response (e.g., a true-false converse test or a three-column matching test). Sometimes a guessing correction is applied. If so, the usual formula is:

$$\text{Score} = \text{rights} - \frac{\text{wrongs}}{(N-1)}$$

   (N meaning the number of choices in the recognition item.) Thus, a true-false item would simply become rights — wrongs. In a four-choice multiple-choice, it would be rights — wrongs/3 or the like.

2. *Essay tests*—The examiner usually decides the number of points an essay question is worth by the number and quality of ideas which are expected for the most complete response. It might be one point for each idea or, to give some opportunity to be more discriminating in quality of response, each idea might be worth 0, 1, or 2 points. The points are then added to obtain a score for the item.

3. *Work samplings, performances, or products*—In scoring this area, there may be standardized scoring procedures or a teacher may make up his own. In a typing class, a person's score may be based on the speed and accuracy within the typed sample. In a speech class or in a vocal performance, the teacher may base the score on a predetermined number of points. In a gymnastics meet, there is usually a maximum of ten points given for a performance. In scoring an art object, the judges may agree on the total points given or an individual teacher may decide for his own class.

A checklist or rating scale is usually used as a basis for arriving at the total score. In the case of several raters, these are usually turned in to a chief scorer who will average the scores for a total score.

In any event, the student has a right to know how a performance is going to be scored. In many cases, it is possible for the student to score his own performance if the criteria are explained and the student is given a "score card."

D.   What Are Some Methods of Grading?

As stated previously, grading goes beyond scoring in that it sets some value on the score. This value is one which might be entirely individualized in case of criterion-referenced testing (e.g., he met the criterion of passing 2 of the 4 items or he met the criterion of performance of 80%, and therefore he "passes" or moves on to the next task). Or it may be comparable in norm-referenced testing (T-score of 50, stanine of 5, percentile rank of 50, z-score of 0, a grade of C, or a numerical score of 83).

Following are some of the various types of grading.
1. Rank—arranging the scores from high to low. Then, give a rank to each score starting with 1 for the highest score and going on down. This type of grading is relative and does not take into consideration the absolute difference between scores. (See Chapter 7 for the ranking method.)
2. Percentile Rank—arrange the scores from high to low and give a rank value as above. Then, substitute in the following formula.

$$PR = 100 - \frac{(100R - 50)}{N}$$

(See Chapter 8 for more on percentile rank.)
3. Percent—sometimes teachers put all grading on a percentage system. The usual classifications are as follows:

$$
\begin{array}{ll}
93\text{-}100 = & \text{Excellent or A} \\
85\text{- }92 = & \text{Very Good or B} \\
78\text{- }84 = & \text{Good or C} \\
70\text{- }77 = & \text{Poor or D} \\
\text{Below } 70 = & \text{Failure or F}
\end{array}
$$

4. Symbols—The usual is a five-classification set of A-F. The A-F may be based on the percent system described in the previous section or there may be other definitions of it. A very common use of symbols is H - S - U meaning high or honors, satisfactory, or unsatisfactory. There is also just the S (satisfactory) or U (unsatisfactory). The P (pass) or F (fail) is another form of symbolism.
5. Standard Scores—These are all scores based on the normal curve using the mean and standard deviation as the basic components. Each of these is discussed as *derived scores* in Chapter 8.

$$z\text{-}score = \frac{X - M}{SD}$$ where M is the mean of the distribution; X is the

raw score; and SD is the standard deviation. This is mostly used as an ingredient to get at the T-score or stanine.

T-score $= 10z + 50$ in which the mean is always 50 and a standard deviation of 10. Some teachers help their students interpret these by saying 60+ might be an A; 50-60, a B; 40-50, a C; 30-40, a D; and below 30, an F.

Stanines: a nine-point scale which has the following distribution

Stanine	1	2	3	4	5	6	7	8	9
Percentage	4%	7%	12%	17%	20%	17%	12%	7%	4%

See Appendix H for the computation of stanines.

Or, using the z-score, the formula becomes:

$$\text{Stanine} = 2z + 5 \text{ (rounded to nearest whole number)}$$

E. How Are Grades Distributed?

One of the most difficult tasks facing conscientious teachers is that of distributing grades on a specific set of papers, tests, or projects. The varieties of procedures for grade distribution are probably as numerous as are teachers; however, three common approaches to this stage of evaluation appear to be (1) by normal breaks in the distribution; (2) by the "normal curve" of distribution; and (3) by the use of the mean and standard deviation.

Distribution by breaks assumes that the pupils' scores cluster around certain homogeneous points and, therefore, the pupils are entitled to the same grade. When a teacher uses the "normal curve" for distribution, he believes that all traits are distributed normally (this is hardly ever true), and therefore A's and F's B's and D's should be equal in number. A more recent plan of distribution purports to be a little more scientific; specifically, it requires using the mean and standard deviation. The mean is the average or typical middle position, and the standard deviation is a unit of distance which can be measured above and below the mean. Teachers using this method believe that one should start where the class is (typical position), and students at certain distances above and below this position are entitled to differential grades.

Table 13.2 reveals how the three methods vary using the same set of scores.

Distribution by "breaks" produced an even number of grades in each category which is quite atypical in this distribution. To develop "breaks," some teachers determine the range; divide the range by the number of categories of grades desired; subtract this quotient from the top score to determine the "A"; from that point, they subtract the quotient again to get the "B" starting point; and continue on. The "normal curve" produced an even

TABLE 13.1

Distribution of Grades Using the Mean and Standard Deviation

A = M + 1.5 SD and above

B = M + .5 SD up to 1.5 SD

C = Between ± .5 SD

D = M — .5 SD to —1.5 SD

F = M — 1.5 SD and below

distribution of A's and F's, of B's and D's, and the most in the category of C. The "normal curve" of distribution used here was 7 percent each of A's and F's, 24 percent each of B's and D's, and 38 percent of C's. This is accomplished by multiplying the specific percent times the total cases (N = 15) and then counting the result down from the top. The method of using the mean and standard deviations "shifted" with the distribution and thus produced a grading variance unique for this class. Since this method requires a somewhat more sophisticated computation, it will be explained in the next paragraph.

The mean is figured as in Chapter 7 for ungrouped data:

$$M = \frac{\Sigma fX}{N}$$

For an extremely accurate standard deviation, this can be figured as in Chapter 7. However, a short-cut method is available and can be used in this instance to obtain a fairly accurate estimate:

$$SD = \frac{\frac{\text{Sum of Top}}{\text{1/6 of Scores}} - \frac{\text{Sum of Lowest}}{\text{1/6 of Scores}}}{\frac{1}{2}N}$$

In the above analysis, the mean was 86 and the SD was 8. Table 13.1 was then used to distribute the grades.

F. How Do You Assign Course Marks?

An important principle of measurement stressed early in this book is that measurement should be varied and comprehensive, consonant with the objectives of the course. If this principle is followed, the teacher will have a number of grades or samples of performances from which a final mark can be determined.

TABLE 13.2

Distribution of Grades by Various Methods

Scores	By Breaks	By Normal Curve	By Mean and SD
98		A (1)	A (1)
96	A (3)		
95	————	B (4)	B (4)
92			
90	B (3)	————	————
89	————		
86			C (4)
85	C (3)	C (5)	
84	————		————
82		————	
81	D (3)		
80	————	D (4)	D (6)
78			
76	F (3)	————	
75		F (1)	————

$N=15$

An analysis of Table 13.2 reveals the following distribution of traditional grades:

Grades	By Breaks	"Normal" Curve	Mean and SD
A	3	1	1
B	3	4	4
C	3	5	4
D	3	4	6
F	3	1	None
	15	15	15

Three methods will be discussed first in which the boundaries of each system are defined and the variability remains relatively the same. Then, an additional method will be shown when the variability of the groups will be different.

1. Grade-point average

This is simply grading on an A-B-C-D-F system or some similar letter combination. By assigning A = 4, B = 3, C = 2, D = 1, and F = 0, one can simply add up the points and divide by the number of entries; the result is a grade-point average. For example, the following grades obtained during a marking period might be:

B on class contribution	=	3
C on daily assignments	=	2
A on the project	=	4
B on the unit test	=	3
		$\overline{12} \div 4 = 3.0$

A 3.0 is equal to a B.

Since there will be fractional amounts at times, the following ranges are suggested:

$$A = 3.5\text{-}4.0$$
$$B = 2.5\text{-}3.4$$
$$C = 1.5\text{-}2.4$$
$$D = 0.5\text{-}1.4$$
$$F = \text{Below } 0.5$$

2. Simple averages

In this method, the teacher usually uses a percent score based on 100 or some other boundaries of raw scores arbitrarily determined. The scores are merely added up and an average obtained. Suppose there were these scores.

$$90 \quad 90 \quad 80 \quad 80 \quad 40$$

The arithmetic average (mean) would be 76 or in the normal letter designation a D. Yet four of the five scores were C or better. In this case, two things could be done. *First,* take the median rather than the mean and his average is 80 or a C. *Second,* drop the extreme score and average the remainder which would be a better arithmetic average.

3. Point-score method

This is very similar to the grade-point average method except that points are given on each student's performance rather than giving a letter grade first. It may be on a 3 - 2 - 1 basis or a 5 - 4 - 3 - 2 - 1 basis whichever one chooses. Again, it is adding up the scores and finding the average.

There are times when you want to have one or more types of student performance count more than others, that is, have more weight. Or there are variances in grading practices within the various performances even if they are all to count the same. The differences in *variability* of the different sets of scores must be taken into account. The more variable a set of scores from which a grade was obtained, the greater weight that component will have. Take the following case:

	Test 1	Test 2	Composite Score
Jean	80	40	120
Joe	60	70	130
Test Range	20	30	

Since each got one top score and one bottom score, and because the weights were the same, each should have received the same composite score. However, Joe received the higher composite score since his better performance was on the test with greater variability.

The answer to this problem is to convert each score to some standard score so each would have the same variability. You will recall that some standard scores were z-scores, T-scores, stanines, among others. Since it is relatively easy to convert a set of scores to stanines, it is the suggested way.

The following twenty scores have been placed in order from high to low: 50-48-47-45-43-41-41-37-35-30-28-25-23-20-18-15-12-10-8-5
From the table in Appendix H, you find that for an N of 20, the stanines are distributed as follows:

$$1 \quad 2 \quad 3 \quad 4 \quad 5 \quad 6 \quad 7 \quad 8 \quad 9$$

Number of students receiving each score

$$(N) \ 20 = 1 \quad 1 \quad 2 \quad 4 \quad 4 \quad 4 \quad 2 \quad 1 \quad 1$$

One can then assign stanine values as follows:

50 - 9	41 - 6	28 - 5	15 - 4
48 - 8	40 - 6	25 - 5	12 - 3
47 - 7	37 - 6	23 - 4	10 - 3
45 - 7	35 - 5	20 - 4	8 - 2
43 - 6	30 - 5	18 - 4	5 - 1

Now, because the stanine distribution was the same variability, a *composite average* can be obtained. The formula is as follows:

$$C = \frac{\Sigma WS}{\Sigma W}$$

where: C = composite average
Σ = summation
W = weight for each category
S = standard score (stanine) for each category

Then, the various categories of scores can have the same weight or different weights as desired. Take the following example:

Category	Weight	Stanine
Class contribution	1	4
Daily work	1	6
Project	1	7
Unit Test	2	4

The composite average:

$$C = \frac{(1 \times 4) + (1 \times 6) + (1 \times 7) + (2 \times 4)}{1 + 1 + 1 + 2} = \frac{25}{5} = 5$$

The composite is not a true stanine, but it does give you a figure which, when compared with other students, will give a ranking on which to assign a mark.

G. How Do You Assign Marks to Classes Having Different Levels of Academic Ability?

There is much discussion among school faculties as to marking practices when there are classes of different levels of academic ability. Probably, most faculties would favor giving more high marks in classes of high ability. But, if they agree on that, they also agree, whether they realize it or not, on giving lower than average marks in some classes. There are both advantages and disadvantages in differentiating levels of marking to correspond with ability levels in various classes.

Table 13.3 presents a reference chart that one can use in distributing marks for differing levels of ability. There are four steps involved in using this table.

1. Select from the first column the ability level most appropriate for the ability level of the class.

   This could be determined in one of two ways. Notice that the last two columns in the table are headed Ability Measures. If the grade-point

TABLE 13.3

*Letters Mark Distributions for Classes at
Different Levels of Ability*

Ability Level	Lower Limits of A's	Percentage of Marks					Ability Measures	
		A	B	C	D	F	GPA	Percentile
Exceptional	0.3	34	38	22	5	0	2.80	79
Superior	0.6	28	38	26	7	1	2.60	73
Good	0.9	18	36	32	12	2	2.40	66
Fair	1.20	12	30	37	18	3	2.20	58
Average	1.50	7	24	38	24	7	2.00	50
Weak	1.80	4	18	37	31	10	1.80	42
Poor	2.1	2	12	34	36	16	1.60	34

Source: The above table was developed by the author and David J. Lien, graduate student in Astronomy, University of Illinois, Urbana, Illinois.

averages (GPA) of the class members in their previous course work are known, the mean of these GPAs indicates which ability level is appropriate for the class. For example, if the class GPA average is 2.42, the teacher would conclude that the class level designated "good" would be appropriate.

If the GPAs were not available or were undesirable to use for some other reason, average aptitude test scores might be used. Most of these scores are expressed in percentile norms. After averaging the raw score of all the class members, the average score would be entered into the percentile table and the appropriate average percentile would be obtained. If, for example, it came out to be 41, one could conclude from the last column in Table 13.3 that this class might be designated as "weak."

2. Calculate the median and the standard deviation of the scores on which the marks are to be distributed.

This information is needed for the next step to find out the lower limit of the A's and subsequently the rest of the marks. Remember that the median is the average point, on either side of which there are an equal number of scores. Apply the formula

$$\text{Mdn} = \frac{N + 1}{2} \text{ (Result Count Up)}$$

There is a short-cut method of figuring for the standard deviation which might be applied here. That is, divide the difference between the sums of the scores in the upper and lower one-sixth of the distribution of scores by one-half of the number of cases (N). The formula is

$$\frac{\text{Sum of the upper one-sixth} - \text{Sum of the lower one-sixth}}{\frac{1}{2} N}$$

For example: The sum of the top one-sixth of the scores is 120, the lower one-sixth is 60, and N = 20.

$$\frac{120 - 60}{\frac{1}{2} \, N} = \frac{60}{10} = 6.0 \text{ SD}$$

3. Determine the lower score limits of the A, B, C, and D mark intervals, using the median, the standard deviation, and the appropriate lower limit factor from Table 13.3.

   Once you have decided on the level of ability of the class, have obtained the median and standard deviation of the distribution of scores for that group, then apply the data to find the lower limit of where the A's would begin. For example, supposing you decided that your class would be considered *average*. Supposing you found out the median of the distribution of scores for that group was 60 and the SD was 10. Looking at Table 13.3, you note for an "average" class, the lower limit of the A's would begin at 1.5 SD above the median. Thus, the median, 60, plus 1.5 SD (10) equals 60 + 15. The lower limit of the A's begins at 75.

   Since the score interval that corresponds to each mark is one standard deviation in extent, once the lower limit of the A interval is obtained, the lower limits of the B, C, and D intervals can be found by successive subtractions of the standard deviation from the lower limit of the A's. Thus, in the example in the previous paragraph, 75 started the lower limit of the A's. Since the SD was 10, the B's would start at 65 (75 − 10), the C's at 55 (65 − 10), and the D's at 45 (55 − 10). The F's, of course, would be any scores less than 45.

4. Assign the designated marks to the students whose scores fall in intervals determined for each mark.

   Table 13.4 illustrates the application of this method of mark assignment to a sample problem.

   The previous data about the class indicates that the average GPA was 2.60 and the mean percentile on aptitude was 72. According to Table 13.3, this would classify the class as *Superior*. The achievement scores have a median of 91 and an SD of 12.8. To determine the distribution of A's, B's, C's, D's, and F's, the above data can be translated to the *Marks Distribution* chart in Table 13.4. The lower limit of A's for a *Superior* group is 0.6 SD above the mean. Thus, to the *median* of 91 is added 0.6 or 12.8 (SD) which would equal 98.68. Since the lower limit of each succeeding mark is 1 SD value below the lower limit of the next mark above, the B is 98.68 − 12.8 or 85.88. Succeeding marks are found in the same way. The intervals are then set up for each mark and the percentage figured for each one. Note that the percentages obtained in the sample problems were 30% A's 35% B's, 30% C's, 5% D's, and no F's. From Table 13.3, note that the theoretical percentages for the *Superior*

TABLE 13.4

Sample Problem in Mark Distribution

A. Data about the class
   1. Ability level measures
      a. Mean GPA on previous year's work = 2.60
      b. Mean percentile on aptitude test = 72
      c. Appropriate grade distribution level (from Table 13.3) = Superior
   2. Achievement Scores (N = 20)

110	100	90	80
108	98	88	78
106	96	86	76
104	94	84	74
102	92	82	72

B. Calculations from the above data

   1. Median $= \dfrac{20+1}{2} = \dfrac{21}{2} = 10.5$ (Count Up) $= 91$

   2. Standard Deviation $= \dfrac{428-300}{10} = \dfrac{128}{10} = 12.8$

   3. Distribution of Marks

Mark	Lower Limit	Intervals	Number	Percent
A	$91 + (0.6 \times 12.8) = 98.68$	99-110	6	30
B	$98.68-12.8 = 85.88$	86-98	7	35
C	$85.88-12.8 = 73.08$	73-85	6	30
D	$73.08-12.8 = 60.28$	60-72	1	5
F		Below 60	0	0

---

group would be 28, 38, 26, 7, and 1 percent respectively. The latter are the percentages if the distribution was *normally distributed*. Since the sample was not normally distributed, the percentages were slightly different.[2]

H. What Are Some Systems of Marking?

Although it would be exaggerating somewhat to say that there were as many methods or systems of marking as there are school systems, it seems that way as one views the various reporting practices discussed in the next section. It is interesting that there have been changes, but many of the old methods linger on. The main idea in each of the various systems will be summarized so that you, the reader, can then decide which method or methods you would like to see used in your school.

---

2. For further details relative to the above method, see Robert Ebel's *Essentials of Educational Measurement* (Englewood Cliffs, NJ: Prentice-Hall, Inc.) © 1972. Pp. 341-345.

1. Percentage System

Usually a classification similar to the following is established.

93-100 = A	70-77 = D
85- 92 = B	Below 70 = F
78- 84 = C	

This system assumes that everything can be put on a 100% basis and a teacher can accurately grade within this range. It assumes more preciseness than there actually can be; it reduces the range of scores from 70-100; and it says that anyone who does not get "70%" correct fails. This is not used as much as it used to be.

2. ABCDF System

This system is still probably the most predominant. It may be combined with the percentage system, as above, or it may have its own definitions as follows:

A = Very good	A = Very good; work is consistently good.
B = Above average	B = Good; work is generally good.
C = At level	C = Average; required work is acceptable.
D = Below level	D = Below average; work is not well done.
F = Total lack of effort or work	F = Unsatisfactory

Sometimes the A-F system is a combination of the child being rated with himself or herself and with others as below.

Academic Development (rated with self)

Grade-Level Standing (rated with others)

A — Pupil is doing excellent work and is working at or near capacity.

B — Pupil is doing good work and is working at or near capacity.

1 — Above grade level

C — Pupil is doing average work *OR* all that should be expected of him/her.

2 — At grade level

D — Pupil is doing much less than should be expected of him/her.

3 — Below grade level

F — Pupil is making no noticeable progress.

Another system presents a variation as follows:

Scholarship   *Application*

E — Ex.   95-100   1 — Working to best of ability
G — V. G.   87- 94   2 — Not working as hard as pupil can and
S — Satis.   79- 86   should work
P — Poor   70- 78   3 — Very poor effort
F — Fail   Bel. 70   4 — Failure due to lack of effort
                            5 — Failure due to irregular attendance

The dual system embodies many desirable factors and is therefore highly recommended. It certainly is much more adequate than other systems in meeting the informational functions; that is, it is attempting to give meaning to pupils and to parents as to the student's performance in relation to his own ability and in relation to the achievement of others. It motivates both the better and the poorer pupils. The better pupils are able to interpret the degree to which they are working to capacity. The poorer pupils generally are not doomed to failure in the strict sense of the word. It is possible for a slow learner to obtain a "C," which is acceptable to the student, the parents, and "society"; yet at the same time, the dual interpretation enables the pupil and the parents to know at what level the child is working in relation to others.

3. Other Letter Symbols

There are many combinations of symbols which are used.

H — High level of performance   S — Satisfactory
S — Satisfactory   U — Unsatisfactory
N — Needs to improve
                                  P — Pass
V — Very Good   F — Fail
S — Satisfactory
P — Poor   P — Pass
                                  N — No credit
X — Above grade level
Y — At grade level
Z — Below grade level

The last two deserve some mention because of current interest in them. The P-F system has been inaugurated in some schools to encourage students to take some elective courses they might not otherwise take if they had to compete in the A-F system. The opponents say it does not discriminate well enough and it is difficult to interpret when a person transfers or applies for post-high school admission to some institution. Some have combatted this by restricting the use of the system to 10-20% of the course work of any given student.

The P-N system says that a person either passes or gets no credit. There is no stigma of the F here and a student can take it over until he gets a P if it is a required course. For a non-required course, he will not receive credit and may have to take it again or take another course if the credit is needed.

4. Written Communication

The idea here is to write a personal letter to the parent about the child's progress. On the surface it sounds good and, if a teacher had a small number of children in class, it would be feasible. The problems are that writing a letter is very time consuming, is often written vaguely, does not come to grips with the child's problems, is often misunderstood by parents, and requires great care in grammar and written expression.

If written communications are used, some schools use the following ideas.

    a. Write them at different time intervals rather than for all students at one time

    b. Indicate strengths and weaknesses and give suggestions to overcome weakness

    c. Be optimistic and encouraging

    d. Enlist home-school cooperation in joint efforts

    e. Use common language; stress understanding

    f. Use expressions which will be accepted, that will not produce anxiety or defensiveness

5. Parent Conferences

The one method which has become rather universal, at least in grades K-6, is the parent conference. It is usually held twice a year and takes the place of the written report form for those periods. An example of a parent conference form will be shown in the next section but some principles and procedures utilized in the conference follow this paragraph. Usually, a statement such as this is sent home to the parents to obtain an idea as to what will take place in the conference and to encourage participation of the parents.

PARENT-TEACHER CONFERENCES[3]

A. WHY A PARENT-TEACHER CONFERENCE:

    The conferences are planned for the purpose of having the parents and the teacher get a better picture of the child at home and at school. In order to make the conference more meaningful, specific topics and questions have been set up that the teacher or parent might consider discussing at the meet-

---

3. From Jefferson City School System, Jefferson, Wisconsin, 1974. Used by permission.

ing. Will you please read the following pages before you meet with the teacher?

B. TIME ALLOWED FOR CONFERENCES:

Fifteen minutes will be allowed each parent for a conference. It is necessary that the time be limited to this amount in view of the fact that each teacher must keep to a schedule. Should you wish additional time, please make an appointment for another conference at a date and time convenient to you and the teacher. It is unfair to take the time of another parent in order to get answers that you may wish.

C. WHAT WILL THE TEACHER TALK ABOUT?

Following is some of the information the teacher may discuss with you about your child:

Mental Aspects:
1. Academic progress
2. Mental ability versus achievement
3. Achievement test results
4. Concentration

Social Aspects:
1. Relationship with other children
2. Responsibility at school
3. Respect for property (that of school and others)

Physical Aspects:
1. Eyesight
2. Hearing
3. Cleanliness
4. Nutrition
5. Coordination

Emotional Aspects:
1. Fears
2. Sensitiveness
3. Aggressiveness
4. Show-off attitude
5. Temper control
6. Poise
7. General disposition

D. WHAT WILL THE TEACHER ASK ABOUT?

The teacher will want to know how the child reacts in the home. Listed below are some of the questions she may ask:

1. How does the child behave at home?
2. Does he have certain responsibilities at home? Care of personal belongings?
3. Does he have certain interests? Hobbies?
4. How does he respond to discipline?
5. Does he spend much time at home alone?
6. What types of recreation does your child enjoy?
7. What are his eating habits?
8. Does he get enough rest and sleep?
9. Have you observed any unfavorable emotional responses the child might have such as fears, sensitiveness, and temper?

E. WHAT WILL THE PARENT ASK ABOUT?

Because some parents have said they did not know what questions they should ask, the following suggestions are listed for your convenience:

1. What are the strengths and weaknesses of my child?
2. What can we do to help him at school?
3. Is his schoolwork as good as it should be for him?
4. Does he seem to be worrying about anything?
5. What special problems does he face?
6. What special abilities does he have?

6. Pictures

On the kindergarten level especially, some schools have gone to simple, cartoon drawings depicting positive growth in some trait. Under each picture is a statement such as:

I follow directions
I work quietly
I finish my work
I speak clearly
I practice good manners

By each picture are two spaces, one for the first semester and one for the second semester. The symbols to place in the spaces are:

U — Usually
I — Improving
N — Not yet

If no symbol is used with the picture, it signifies that the child has not been exposed to the activity as yet.

7. Checklists and Rating Scales

One of the developments which has gained increasing popularity is the use of the checklist or rating scale. It developed when the use of behavioral objectives came into the picture. If you started to help the child grow toward certain objectives, then you should evaluate growth toward these objectives at the end. Examples of these are shown in the next section, but a few ideas about them here would seem appropriate.

They are used both for academic growth and for non-academic growth (effort, personal growth, social skills, and the like). They can be devised as simply as is the following for reading:

Reading
    Skill
    Comprehension

Or they can be as complete for reading as:

Reading
     Reads with understanding and comprehension
     Analyzes new words
     Uses a broad vocabulary
     Reads a wide variety of materials
     Selects reading material at his appropriate level
On the non-academic growth side, they can be as simple as:
     Obeys rules (followed by an M for most of the time or N for needs
       improvement)

To: Work Habits—Personal Characteristics	I	II
1. Practices good study habits	✔	
2. Listens well		✔
3. Is neat		✔
4. Cooperates in work and play	✔	

(A check mark indicates deficiency in a specific area)

8. Self-Evaluation

An area which is receiving more attention recently is the concept of self-evaluation. This text has stressed that one of the functions of measurement and evaluation is to furnish instruction to students—the idea of self-directed learning. The first thing which is necessary is to produce a classroom atmosphere which encourages self-evaluation. Sawin has suggested the following principles for helping students to grow toward good self-evaluation.[4]

   a. Set a good example in the practice of evaluation and self-evaluation.
   b. Maintain a classroom atmosphere which encourages self-evaluation.
   c. Conduct classroom activities in such a way that student efforts toward self-evaluation result in satisfying experiences.
   d. Encourage self-evaluation but do not try to force it.
   e. Give the student opportunities to practice the evaluation skills you want him to develop.
   f. Work at joint evaluation with students.
   g. Discourage the student from trying to evaluate too many things at a time.
   h. Have students maintain written records of certain goals and their progress toward them.

4. From *Evaluation and the Work of the Teacher* by Enoch I. Sawin. © 1969 by Wadsworth Publishing Company, Inc., Belmont, California 94002. Pp. 198-199. Reprinted by permission of the publisher.

i. Have class discussions for clarifying important goals and criteria for self-evaluation.

j. Have programmed textbooks, teaching machines, and exercises with answers available for supplementary use.

It should be pointed out that students' self-evaluation should not be a replacement for the marking and reporting done by the teachers. It will help the student to understand the goals he is working toward and to see how he perceives himself as growing toward those goals. Sometimes, it serves as a basis for a student-teacher conference in discussing both the student's and the teacher's perception of progress.

9. Individualized Instruction Marking Practices

a. Goal Record Cards

This consists of a separate card for each subject which a student is studying. It usually lists all the important objectives to be achieved by the student during a designated term. As a student masters a specific objective, it is checked off or is given a quality grade. The cards can be given out during parent-teacher conferences or can be sent out about twice a year. A student may keep the card, or a duplicate one, and when he feels that he is ready to be measured on an objective, he takes the card to the teacher for evaluation. Thus, it keeps the pupil informed as to where he is and what he has yet to learn.

b. Behavioral Mastery Reports

These are similar to the goal cards except that these are usually more detailed for each subject. Objectives for a subject are listed under different levels which are hierarchical in nature. After each objective are three column headings: Pre-test, Progress, Post-test.

If a pupil took the pre-test and got the answers all right or the minimum for mastery he would have an M placed in that column meaning mastered. If he received less than the minimum, the percentage which he got right would be place in the column. If, after study, he takes a second test, either an M or a percentage correct, if not sufficient for mastery, would be placed in the "Progress" column. If he did not receive an M there, but took the post-test and received enough to meet the minimum for mastery, he would receive an M there.

If, anywhere along the line, a student is making little or no progress, an R would be placed in the appropriate column connoting that remedial help is needed. A P in the post-test column would mean the student is making reasonable progress, but additional practice is recommended. An objective not taught (for some reason) would contain an X in the post-test column.

Summarizing the columns and symbols, they are as follows:

Columns	Symbols
Pre-test—Progress—Post-test	X = Not presented as yet
	R = Remedial help recommended
	P = Making reasonable progress; recommend additional practice
	M = Mastered

c. Contracts for Marks

Here, a teacher devises a list of requirements for each grade— usually A, B, C, or Pass. The student and teacher in conference agree on and "sign a contract." A student works at his own pace to complete the requirements. Quality as well as quantity is stressed. If a student falls behind in the contract, but feels he can still meet it, additional experiences are provided to help reach the goal. If a child feels that he or she has chosen a contract unwisely, it can be changed upon consultation between the child and the teacher. Where used, this system has been most successful on the junior high level and above.

I. What Are Some Examples of Reporting Forms?

Although there are many traditional reporting forms yet in use, there have been several recent changes in reporting practices. An article in an NEA Research Summary summarizes these changes.[5] See Table 13.5, p. 348.

Following is a series of figures depicting different types of reporting forms. A brief description of each is presented.

1. Kindergarten

Figure 13.1   From Kenosha Unified School District #1.[6]

This is a printed, single sheet with four carbon copies automatically made when the top form is filled out. It uses the symbols of S for Satisfactory Growth, P for Some Progress, N for Needs Improvement, and X for

5. National Education Association, *Marking and Reporting Pupil Progress.* Research Summary, 1970, pp. 5-6.

6. Progress Report for Kindergarten, Kenosha Unified School District #1, Kenosha, WI. Reprinted by permission of the School System.

TABLE 13.5

Recent Changes in Reporting Practices

Practice:	*Some change toward:*
1. Pupil evaluation conducted and reported exclusively by the teacher.	Pupil preparation of a brief written evaluation of own work.
2. Listing only broad subject fields. The pupil receives a single mark in each broad subject classification.	Explaining in terms of pupil behavior the activities that compose each subject-matter field as well as character traits. More detailed explanation of the meaning of marks on the written report card.
3. Comparing all pupils with a set standard or with their classmates.	Combined use of individual progress marks and comparative marks. Comparing each pupil's progress with his own apparent ability (especially in elementary school) or with himself as well as with others.
4. Using a single report form for the entire school.	Developing forms suited specifically to the goals of specific grades or levels.
5. Pupils receiving marks at six-week or nine-week intervals.	Less frequent reporting, e.g., twice a year.
6. Providing a line for a teacher comment, and a line for the parent's signature.	Providing space for both teacher and parent comments.
7. Central office supervisory staff, with suggestions from teachers, develop the report card.	Organizing committees of supervisors, teachers, parents, and pupils to improve reporting practices.
8. Use of only a card to report pupil progress to parents.	Combining reporting by both report cards and parent-teacher conferences, often alternating for reporting periods.
9. Using a relatively small card printed black on white.	Using a large folder in color with typographical design and explanations to parents. Pictures and cartoons on the card are often used at the primary level.
10. Including only school subjects and perhaps an item titled character or deportment.	Including numerous objectives under such titles as social adjustment, personal development, and work habits.
11. Using percentage or letter grades, which are sometimes defined in such terms as excellent, good, fair, and failure.	Developing additional symbols of statements, which reflect more understanding of child development (such as needs more time and help). Increased use of descriptive terms and interpretation.

Source: Reprinted with permission from National Education Association, *Marking and Reporting Pupil Progress,* Research Summary, 1970-S1, 1970, pp. 5-6.

KENOSHA UNIFIED SCHOOL DIST. #1
Kindergarten Progress Report

SCHOOL _____ SCHOOL YEAR 19___ 19___ STUDENT _____

PARENTS: This report is an indication of your child's achievement.

EVALUATION KEY

S Satisfactory growth
P Some progress
N Needs improvement
X Does not apply at this time

ATTENDANCE RECORD:

	Quarter			
	1	2	3	4
Days present				
Days absent				
Times tardy				

ASSIGNMENT FOR NEXT YEAR:

Assigned to grade _____

Date _____

Teacher: _____

Principal: _____

SOCIAL DEVELOPMENT	Quarter			
	1	2	3	4
Accepts rules and routine				
Plays/works well with others				
Shares/takes turns				
Shows self-control				
Shows self-confidence				
Respects property of others				
Adjusts easily to new situations				
Shows courtesy and respect to others				
Accepts responsibility for own actions				

WORK HABITS				
Listens attentively				
Follows directions				
Begins work promptly				
Works independently				
Works neatly				
Completes assignments on time				
Shows willingness to try				
Seeks help when needed				
Works without disturbing others				

FIRST QUARTER COMMENTS

SECOND QUARTER COMMENTS

READING DEVELOPMENT	Quarter			
	1	2	3	4
Recognizes own name				
Prints own name				
Shows interest in books/stories				
Tells story from picture				
Sees similarities in pictures, symbols, & words				
Recognizes alphabet				
Works from left to right				
Associates beginning sounds with letters				
Tells a story in sequence				

LANGUAGE DEVELOPMENT				
Speaks clearly				
Expresses ideas adequately				
Speaks in complete sentences				
Remembers information				
Determines answers to questions & situations				

MUSIC				
Shows enthusiasm for music				
Reproduces rhythmic patterns				
Enjoys singing				

THIRD QUARTER COMMENTS

MATH DEVELOPMENT	Quarter			
	1	2	3	4
Identifies shapes				
Counts 25 objects				
Recognizes numbers to 10				
Understands math terms				
Applies knowledge of numbers				

PHYSICAL DEVELOPMENT				
Dresses self				
Jumps, hops, skips, balances				
Uses crayons/scissors well				
Practices good health habits				
Prints symbols clearly				
Physical education participation				

ART				
Identifies colors				
Creates with art materials				
Interested in a variety of art activities				

FOURTH QUARTER COMMENTS

TEACHER _____

00-8646

Figure 13.1 Sample: Kindergarten Progress Report. (From the Kenosha Unified School District #1, Kenosha, WI. Printed by permission of the School System.)

Does Not Apply at This Time. It includes the following major headings with check-traits underneath each: Social Development, Reading Development, Math Development, Work Habits, Language Development, Physical Development, Art, and Music. There is also space for comments for each quarter report.

Figure 13.2   From the Palmyra-Eagle Area School District[7]

This is a very complete, oversize, single-sheet form. It uses the symbols of + for Superior, ✔ for Average, I for Improvement Shown, and — for Need for Improvement. The major areas, including check-traits underneath each, include Social and Emotional Development, Physical Development—Motor, Physical Development—Health, Work and Study Habits, Academic Development, Music, Reading Readiness, Math-Science Readiness, Social Studies, and Art. It also is a carbon form, producing two copies. Like most carbon sets, the last is on a stiffer type of paper or light cardboard for school filing purposes.

Figure 13.3   From Green Bay Area Public Schools.[8]

The symbols of S for Satisfactory; I for Improving, further development necessary; and U for Unsatisfactory are used in this report form. It is a carbon form making four carbons plus the original. This allows a copy for the school and for all interested parties. It is checked each quarter.

The major headings, with appropriate sub-traits, include Physical Development, Social Development, Language Development, Work Habits, Skills—Social, Skills—Reading Readiness, and Skills—Math. There is also space for the teacher to add comments for each quarter.

2. Primary

Figure 13.4   From Milwaukee Public Schools.[9]

The Student Progress Report—Primary is based on the principle of the development of the whole child; thus, the report form reports many phases of growth. Only those items which pertain to the child's growth are marked. The symbols used are: O meaning outstanding; S meaning satisfactory; N meaning needs to improve; and U meaning unsatisfactory. It includes the areas of reading, language arts, mathematics, social studies, science, expressive arts, health and physical education, study habits and assignments,

---

7. From the Palmyra-Eagle Area School District. Printed by permission of the School System, Palmyra, WI.

8. Report Card, Kindergarten. Joint School District #1, Green Bay, WI. Used by permission of the School System.

9. From Milwaukee Public Schools. Printed by permission of the Milwaukee Public Schools System, Milwaukee, WI.

KINDERGARTEN REPORT *Palmyra-Eagle Area School District* BATTLE CREEK KINDERGARTEN 701 Maple Street Palmyra, Wisconsin 53156 Telephone: 495 - 2115 - Ext. 33 PALESTINE KINDERGARTEN 138 Elkhorn Road Eagle, Wisconsin 53119 Telephone: 594 - 2323	STUDENT NAME	TEACHER NAME	GRADE	SCHOOL YEAR

ATTENDANCE	1	2	*All items may not be marked -*
Present			*only those which apply to your child.*
Absent			+ - Superior
Tardy			V - Average
HEIGHT			I - Improvement Shown
WEIGHT			— - Need for Improvement

Will report to
_____ grade in
19_____

Social and Emotional Development	1	2
Respects rightful authority		
Willing to share and take turns		
Seeks and responds to others		
Plays alone		
Asserts own rights		
Observes school rules		
Accepts reasonable limits easily		
Displays self control		
Solves own problems		
Uses materials appropriately		
Approaches new experiences with confidence		

Total School Attitude	1	2
Accepts school with a positive attitude		

Comments: _____
_____
_____
_____

Physical Development	1	2
Large muscle use/coordination		
1. Climbing		
2. One foot hopping		
3. Two foot hopping		
4. Galloping		
5. Skipping		
6. Jumping		
7. Balance beam		
8. Ball handling (catch, bounce, throw)		

Comments: _____
_____
_____
_____
_____

Small muscle use/coordination		
1. Pencil and crayon use large boundary		
small boundary		
2. Uses correct pencil/crayon grip		
3. Uses Correct scissors grip		
4. Able to cut on lines		
5. Fingerplays		
6. Dresses self		
7. Buttons		
8. Ties shoes		
9. Zips		

Comments: _____
_____
_____
_____

Physical Development-Health	1	2
Good sitting and standing posture		
Appears (a) well rested (b) energetic (c) listless		

Comments: _____
_____
_____
_____

Work and Study Habits	1	2
Usually attends to task		
Waits for/listens to directions		
Understands directions		
Follows directions		
Completes work in reasonable time		
Works to capacity		
Works without disturbing others		
Seeks needed help at appropriate times		
Solves own problems		
Uses free time constructively		
Replaces materials and cleans work or play area		

Comments: _____
_____
_____
_____
_____

Academic Development	1	2
Language Arts (Receptive and Expressive Language)		
Takes part in informal discussion		
Speaks in complete sentences		
Uses descriptive language		
Shows or retells stories or events in sequence		
Tells own age		
Tells own first and last name		
Manuscripts own first and last names		
Tells address (street, house number, or highway and box number)		
Knows parents' first and last names		
Tells own telephone number		

Comments: _____
_____
_____
_____

Music	1	2
Participates in vocal music		
Participates in rhythm activities		

Comments: _____

Reading Readiness	1	2
Recognizes name in manuscript first last		
Knows left, right		
Practices left to right progression		
Practices top to bottom progression		
Is developing letter recognition		
Is developing sound recognition		
Recognizes rhyming worls		
Recognizes rhyming word phrases		
Recognizes likenesses & differences:		
between pictures and shapes		
between letters and numbers		
between words and word phrases		
Recognizes & names 8 basic colors		
Recognizes beginning consonent sounds		

Comments: _____
_____
_____
_____
_____
_____

Math - Science Readiness	1	2
Rote counts to		
Recognizes numerals 1 to 10 in random order		
Demonstrates understanding of sets and members of sets		
Matches one-to-one		
Demonstrates one-more-than		
Recognizes spatial position: up, down, in, on, behind, above, over, beside, below, under, left, right		
Is developing scientific awareness		

Comments: _____
_____
_____
_____

Social Studies	1	2
Participates in study units		

Comments: _____
_____
_____

Art	1	2
Participates in art activities		

Comments: _____
_____
_____
_____

Form No. KRC - 3 — Supreme School Supply Co., Arcadia, WI 54612

Figure 13.2 Sample: Kindergarten Report from the Palmyra-Eagle Area School District, Eagle, WI. (Printed by permission of the School System, Palmyra, WI.)

KINDERGARTEN REPORT CARD
Green Bay Area Public Schools
Green Bay, Wisconsin

SCHOOL _____

YEAR 19 _____ to 19 _____

CHILD _____

TEACHER(S) _____

PRINCIPAL _____

S – Satisfactory I – Improving - Further development necessary U – Unsatisfactory

Blank Space – Not applicable this report period

COMMENTS:

PHYSICAL DEVELOPMENT

QUARTER #: 1 2 3 4

Large Muscle Coordination
Running, hopping, galloping
Skips
Ball handling (bouncing, catching, dribbling)
Small Muscle Coordination
Dresses self in outdoor clothing
Ties bows
Prints name
Prints numerals
Eye-Hand Coordination (Handling materials—scissors, crayons, etc.)

SOCIAL DEVELOPMENT

Is courteous and considerate
Plays well with others
Shows self-confidence
Shows self-control (self-discipline)
Assumes responsibility for learning (takes part in group activities, such as games, discussions, speaking, etc.)

LANGUAGE DEVELOPMENT

Speaks in a clear voice
Uses sentences to express self
Is attentive when others are speaking
Understands verbal discussions

No. of Days This Quarter
No. of Days Attended
Next Year's Assignment

WORK HABITS

QUARTER #: 1 2 3 4

Follows directions
Works independently
Works carefully
Completes work on time
Makes good use of free time

SKILLS—Social

Knows address
Knows telephone number
Knows days of week in sequence
Sings and expresses rhythms

SKILLS— Reading Readiness

Identifies 8 basic colors
Recognizes rhyming words
Recognizes name
Has developed left to right sequence
Identifies upper case letters at random
Identifies lower case letters at random
Identifies likenesses and differences
Recognizes beginning consonant sounds

SKILLS—Math

Identifies six basic shapes
Recognizes numerals 0-10
Understands sets 0-10
Can count to
Recognizes ordinals (first, second, third, etc.)

Figure 13.3 Sample: Kindergarten Report Card, Green Bay Area Public Schools, Green Bay, WI. (Printed by permission of the School System.)

milwaukee public schools

STUDENT PROGRESS REPORT - PRIMARY
School Year 19____ - 19____

Student _____   School _____

Teacher _____   Principal _____

	1	2	3	4
Days Absent				
Times Tardy				

Primary Year _____

Placement Next Year _____

Since we believe in the development of the whole child, we wish to report on many phases of growth. Only those items which pertain to your child's growth have been marked.

O means outstanding; S means satisfactory; N means needs to improve; U means unsatisfactory

READING   1 2 3 4

1. Shows interest and enjoyment in reading
2. Understands what is read
3. Reads well orally
4. Works out new words independently

LANGUAGE ARTS

5. Expresses ideas clearly orally
6. Expresses ideas well in written form
7. Applies spelling skills
8. Spells assigned words correctly
9. Acquiring skill in handwriting

MATHEMATICS

10. Understands meaning of numbers
11. Understands process of addition
12. Mastering addition facts
13. Understands process of subtraction
14. Mastering subtraction facts
15. Understands process of multiplication
16. Mastering multiplication facts
17. Understands process of division
18. Mastering division facts
19. Computes accurately
20. Shows growth in reasoning ability

SOCIAL STUDIES

21. Is acquiring skills
22. Is developing understandings

SCIENCE   1 2 3 4

23. Is acquiring skills
24. Is developing understandings

EXPRESSIVE ARTS

25. Responds to music experiences
26. Responds to art experiences

HEALTH AND PHYSICAL EDUCATION

27. Is developing an understanding of health practices
28. Is acquiring physical education skills

STUDY HABITS AND ASSIGNMENTS

29. Has materials ready
30. Listens and follows directions
31. Begins work promptly
32. Completes assignments on time
33. Takes pride in work done
34. Works well alone

PERSONAL AND SOCIAL GROWTH

35. Shows growth in self-control
36. Gets along well with others
37. Accepts constructive criticism
38. Assumes responsibilities
39. Follows school rules
40. Participates in class activities
41. Plays well on the playground
42. Is courteous in speech and actions.
43. Appears neat and clean

MPS Primary Reading Levels   1   2   3   4

1. Readiness
2. Charts
3. Pre-Primers
4. Primers – Easy
5. Primers – Hard
6. First – Easy
7. First – Hard
8. Second – Easy
9. Second – Hard
10. Third – Easy
11. Third – Hard
12. Independent

Mathematics Levels   1   2   3   4

Readiness
Book 1 – 1/2
Book 1 – 2/2

Book 2 – 1/2
Book 2 – 2/2

Book 3 – 1/2
Book 3 – 2/2

Figure 13.4 Sample: Student Progress Report—Primary from Milwaukee Public Schools, Milwaukee, WI. (Printed by permission of the Milwaukee Public School System, Milwaukee, WI.)

and personal and social growth. Under each heading is a checklist of appropriate traits to mark. On the bottom, the reading and mathematics book levels are indicated.

Figure 13.5 From Kenosha Unified School District #1.[10]

Each basic academic area has two grades. Achievement is based on understanding the subject as judged by tests and teacher observation. Effort indicates how hard the child worked according to his/her potential.

Symbols used are: A for Excellent, B for Above Average, C for Average, D for Below Average, and F for Very Low Achievement. The basic areas of reading and mathematics indicate the level in which the child is presently working.

Evaluation key for sub-headings are marked as follows: 1 for above average, 2 for average, 3 for needs to improve, and * for does not apply. Included are the areas of Reading, Language Arts, Mathematics, Art, Music, Physical Education, Science/Social Studies, Spelling, Work Habits, and Conduct (letter grade). There is also space for comments for each quarter.

3. Intermediate

Figure 13.6 From Milwaukee Public Schools.[11]

This intermediate student progress report is based on the achievement, interests, and efforts of the child. It is a carbon-type form with four copies made from the original; this includes a cardboard-type school file copy.

In the non-academic areas of work and study habits and personal and scoial growth, there is a checklist under each heading in which check marks may be inserted. The checks are used to indicate traits in which the child needs to improve. The academic areas include Reading, Language Arts, Social Studies, Mathematics, Science, Expressive Arts, and Health and Physical Education. Effort and achievement are marked by using the symbols of A for Exceptional, B for Above Average, C for Average, D for Below Average and U for Unsatisfactory. Under each main heading, there is a checklist of traits related to that academic area. A check mark inserted after any trait indicates need to improve.

10. Progress Report for Grades 1-2. Kenosha Unified School District #1, Kenosha, WI. Used by permission of the School System.

11. From Milwaukee Public Schools. Printed by permission of the Milwaukee Public Schools System, Milwaukee, WI.

KENOSHA UNIFIED SCHOOL DIST. #1
Progress Report for Grades 1 - 2

SCHOOL _____ GRADE _____ SCHOOL YEAR 19___ - 19___

TEACHER'S NAME _____

STUDENT'S NAME _____

Each basic academic area has two grades:

1. ACHIEVEMENT - based upon understanding of the subject as judged by tests and teacher observation.

2. EFFORT - indicates how hard your child worked according to his/her potential.

A - Excellent
B - Above Average
C - Average
D - Below Average
F - Very Low Achievement

The basic areas of reading and mathematics have the level in which your child is presently working.

Evaluation key for sub-headings are marked:

1 - Above average
2 - Average
3 - Needs to improve
∗ - Does not apply

ATTENDANCE RECORD:	Quarter			
	1	2	3	4
Days present				
Days absent				
Times tardy				

ASSIGNMENT FOR NEXT YEAR:

Assigned to grade _____ Date _____

Teacher: _____

Principal: _____

READING	Quarter			
	1	2	3	4
GRADE LEVEL				
Achievement				
Effort				
Interested in learning to read				
Developing word attack skills				
Developing vocabulary				
Reads with understanding				
Enjoys stories, poems, books				

LANGUAGE ARTS
	Achievement			
	Effort			
Expresses ideas well orally				
Expresses ideas well in writing				
Applies rules in written work				
Writes plainly and neatly				
Uses and spells words correctly in sentences and stories				

MATHEMATICS
GRADE LEVEL	Achievement			
	Effort			
Has adequate number vocabulary				
Knows, understands arithmetic facts				
Solves story problems				
Works accurately				

ART	Quarter			
	1	2	3	4
Achievement				
Effort				
Knowledge of content and subject material				
Interest and self-confidence				
Skills in handling material				

MUSIC
	Achievement			
	Effort			
Participates in music activities				
Sings in tune				
Developing rhythmic skills				

PHYSICAL EDUCATION
	Achievement			
	Effort			
Participates in activities				
Developing motor skills and coordination				
Shows sportsmanship				

SCIENCE/SOCIAL STUDIES
	Achievement			
	Effort			
Participates in discussions and activities				
Shares related experiences				

SPELLING	Quarter			
	1	2	3	4
GRADE 2	Achievement			
	Effort			
Masters assigned words				
Spells correctly in written work				

CONDUCT (letter grade)
Shows courtesy and respect to teachers and adults				
Courteous to other students				
Growing in self-discipline				
Accepts responsibility for own actions				
Respects rights and property of others				

WORK HABITS
Listens attentively				
Follows directions				
Begins work promptly				
Works independently				
Completes work neatly				
Completes class assignments on time				
Checks and proof reads carefully				
Developing good organizational habits				
Uses time wisely				
Shows willingness to try				

FIRST QUARTER COMMENTS

SECOND QUARTER COMMENTS

THIRD QUARTER COMMENTS

FOURTH QUARTER COMMENTS

00-8574

Figure 13.5 Sample: Progress Report for Grades 1-2 from Kenosha Unified School District #1, Kenosha, WI. (Printed by permission of the School System.)

milwaukee public schools

STUDENT PROGRESS REPORT — INTERMEDIATE

School Year 19_____ – 19_____

Student_____   School_____

Teacher_____   Principal_____

	1	2	3	4
Days Absent				
Times Tardy				

Present Grade Placement_____

Grade Placement Next Year_____

This report is based on the achievement, interests, and efforts of your child.

Checks are used to indicate needs to improve

WORK AND STUDY HABITS

Needs to Improve in:	1	2	3	4
Having materials ready				
Listening and following directions				
Beginning work promptly				
Completing assignments on time				
Taking pride in work done				
Working well alone				
Working well with others				

PERSONAL AND SOCIAL GROWTH

Needs to Improve in:	1	2	3	4
Self-Control				
Getting along better with others				
Accepting constructive criticism				
Assuming responsibility				
Following school rules				
Behaving on the playground				
Being courteous				

Marking: A—Exceptional   B—Above Average   C—Average   D—Below Average   U—Unsatisfactory

Checks are used to indicate needs to improve.

READING   Effort
                       Achievement

Needs to Improve in:

Showing interest in reading _____
Oral reading _____
Comprehending what is read _____
Utilizing word attack skills _____
Utilizing study skills _____

LANGUAGE ARTS   Effort
                       Achievement

Needs to Improve in:

Expressing thoughts orally _____
Expressing thoughts in writing _____
Applying spelling skills _____
Handwriting _____

SOCIAL STUDIES   Effort
                       Achievement

Needs to Improve in:

Acquisition of skills _____
Developing understandings _____

MATHEMATICS   Effort
                       Achievement

Needs to Improve in:

Knowledge of number facts _____
Working accurately _____
Solving problems _____

SCIENCE   Effort
                       Achievement

Needs to Improve in:

Acquisition of skills _____
Developing understandings _____

EXPRESSIVE ARTS

Needs to Improve in:

Response to music experiences _____
Response to art experiences _____

HEALTH AND PHYSICAL EDUCATION

Needs to Improve in:

Understanding health facts _____
Applying good health practices _____
Acquisition of physical
  education skills _____

Figure 13.6 Sample: Student Progress Report—Intermediate from Milwaukee Public Schools, Milwaukee, WI. (Printed by permission of the Milwaukee Public School System, Milwaukee, WI.)

Figure 13.7   From Eau Claire Area Schools.[12]

This elementary progress report form is for the intermediate levels of grades 4, 5, and 6. The purpose of this report card is to give the child and his parents a good understanding of the progress that the child is making in school.

Progress is measured in terms of gains in knowledge, skills, work habits, and attitudes over a period of time. Parent conferences are scheduled for the first and third quarters. This report form is used for the second and fourth quarter. The card is divided into three sections: Knowledge and Skills, Habits and Attitudes, and Levels of Achievement.

The Knowledge and Skills area includes the academic areas of Reading, Mathematics, Language, Social Studies, and Science. The symbols used to denote progress are: S for satisfactory progress, progress is satisfactory according to this pupil's ability; N for needs to improve, progress is not satisfactory according to this pupil's ability. At the end of the academic areas, there is a statement that the child participates willingly in: Art, Music, and Physical Education. It is assumed that the same S and N symbols are used here.

In the Habits and Attitudes section, the main headings, with a checklist of traits under each, are: Behavior in Group Situations, Consideration of Others, Consideration of Property, Growth in Independence, Safety Practices, and Health Practices.

In the section on Levels of Achievement, a check mark is given indicating what level the child is achieving in the areas of reading and mathematics. This is checked as Above Average, Average, or Below Average. This helps the parent understand about where the child is achieving, regardless of the grade given in the academic areas.

Figure 13.8   From Kenosha Unified School District #1[13]

This progress report form is for grades 3-6. It is similar in structure to the primary report form. Each academic area has two grades. Achievement is based on understanding of the subject as judged by tests and teacher observation. Effort indicates how hard the child worked according to his/her potential. The symbols for the above (Achievement and Effort) are A for Excellent, B for Above Average, C for Average, D for Below Average, and F for Very Low Achievement.

The basic areas of reading and mathematics have the level in which the child is presently working. There is a checklist under each main head-

---

12. Elementary Progress Report, Intermediate Level, Grades 4-6. Eau Claire Area Schools, Eau Claire, WI. Used by permission of the School System.
13. Progress Report for Grades 3-6. Kenosha Unified School District #1, Kenosha, WI. Reprinted by permission of the Kenosha School System.

EAU CLAIRE AREA SCHOOLS
Eau Claire, Wisconsin

ELEMENTARY PROGRESS REPORT

Intermediate Level
IV-V-VI

19_____ - 19_____

The purpose of this report card is to give the child and his parents a good understanding of the progress the child is making in school. Progress is measured in terms of gains in knowledge, skills, work habits, and attitudes over a period of time. Parent-teacher conferences are also scheduled to improve communication between the parent and the teacher. If you desire more information, do not hesitate to arrange for a conference with the teacher or principal. Only by these means can we be assured that we are doing the best for your child.

Marvin Lansing, Ph. D.
Superintendent of Schools

Pupil's Name _____

School _____

Teacher's Name _____

Principal _____

Rev. '75

KNOWLEDGES AND SKILLS

	Report Period			
	1	2	3	4
READING				
Uses word recognition skills				
Uses basic study skills				
Reads with understanding				
Reads widely				
Work habits				
MATHEMATICS				
Knows mathematics facts				
Applies processes of addition, subtraction, multiplication, and division				
Solves problems				
Work habits				
LANGUAGE				
Expresses ideas well orally				
Expresses ideas well in writing				
Uses language skills in writing		CONFERENCES	CONFERENCES	
Shows growth in spelling				
Writes legibly and neatly				
Work habits				
SOCIAL STUDIES				
Finds and uses suitable reference material				
Interprets maps, globes, charts				
Takes part in class discussions				
Work habits				
SCIENCE				
Understands and applies science concepts				
Work habits				
Participates willingly in:				
ART				
MUSIC				
PHYSICAL EDUCATION				

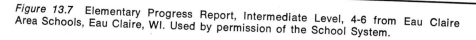

Figure 13.7 Elementary Progress Report, Intermediate Level, 4-6 from Eau Claire Area Schools, Eau Claire, WI. Used by permission of the School System.

ing; it uses the symbols of 1 for Above Average, 2 for Average, and 3 for Needs to Improve.

The various areas of academics included are: Reading, Language Arts, Spelling, Mathematics, Art, Music, Physical Education, Social Studies, and Science. In addition, there are the categories of Conduct and Work Habits. There is also space for comments for each quarter report.

Figure 13.9 *A Behavioral Reporting System for Elementary Mathematics.*[14]

Dissatisfaction with the traditional reporting system has led to the development of *behavioral mastery reports.* These usually consist of a number of objectives stated in behavioral terms and some indication of the extent to which the student has met or mastered each objective. The one illustrated is

14. From Coupeville Consolidated School District 204, Coupeville, Washington. Reprinted by permission of the Coupeville Consolidated School District 204.

EXPLANATION OF MARKS

A check (✓) indicates that the behavior described is often shown by your child. Content of the items checked is as important as the **number** of items check. Please read all items, as the unchecked ones also provide information about your child.

HABITS AND ATTITUDES

Report Period
1   2   3   4

BEHAVIOR IN GROUP SITUATIONS
Participates on his/hers own
Participates with confidence
Demonstrates self-control
Shows qualities of leadership
Shows good sportsmanship
Accepts helpful criticism

CONSIDERATION OF OTHERS
Usually shows thoughtfulness
Is growing in the recognition of the rights of others

CONSIDERATION OF PROPERTY
Shows good judgment in use and care of materials
Shows respect for property of others

GROWTH IN INDEPENDENCE
Makes good use of time
Accepts and completes responsibilities
Is able to work independently
Meets new situations well

SAFETY PRACTICES
Accepts and usually follows safety rules
Shows regard for personal safety
Shows regard for the safety of others

HEALTH PRACTICES
Appears to be rested
Appears relaxed and comfortable
Is neat and clean in appearance

(Columns 2 and 3 labeled: CONFERENCES)

IN THIS GRADE, YOUR CHILD'S ACHIEVEMENT IS AT THE LEVELS INDICATED:

IN READING
Period 2 - Above average ☐   Average ☐   Below average ☐
Period 4 - Above average ☐   Average ☐   Below average ☐

IN MATHEMATICS
Period 2 - Above average ☐   Average ☐   Below average ☐
Period 4 - Above average ☐   Average ☐   Below average ☐

Height and weight

Beginning of school year _____ inches _____ pounds

End of school year _____ inches _____ pounds

ATTENDANCE RECORD

	First half-year	Second half-year
Days absent		

PARENT'S COMMENTS _____

PARENT'S SIGNATURE

_____ (first marking period)

Your child is assigned to _____
for the next school year.   Level

_____
Teacher's signature

Additional information is enclosed if box is checked:
Period 2 ☐   Period 4 ☐

---

for an ungraded elementary school system. It includes a sample of some of the objectives at the various levels of attainment.

Each objective is measured by a pre-test to avoid having the student spend time on skills in which he can demonstrate mastery or competence. If the item is not mastered on the pre-test, an instructional strategy is planned. Generally, a student is allowed to take an examination when he believes he is capable of mastering an objective. If he is successful in meeting the criterion, an M is placed in the "Progress" column. If he does not meet the criterion, but passes 50% of the items for the objective, a 50% would be placed in the "Progress" column. If he obtains mastery on the third test, an M could be placed in the "Post-test" column. If at any point the student seems to be making little or no progress, his score on the test along with an R would indicate the teacher's belief that remedial help is required. The symbol P is reserved for the column marked "Post-test," which is a summary of the student's progress in meeting each objective throughout the school

KENOSHA UNIFIED SCHOOL DIST. #1
Progress Report for Grades 3 - 6

SCHOOL _____ GRADE _____ SCHOOL YEAR 19___ 19___   TEACHER'S NAME _____   STUDENT'S NAME _____

Each basic academic area has two grades:

1. ACHIEVEMENT - based upon understanding of the subject as judged by tests and teacher observation.

2. EFFORT - indicates how hard your child worked according to his/her potential.

A - Excellent
B - Above average
C - Average
D - Below Average
F - Very Low Achievement

The basic areas of reading and mathematics have the level in which your child is presently working.

Evaluation key for sub-headings are marked:

1 - Above average
2 - Average
3 - Needs to improve

ATTENDANCE RECORD:

	Quarter			
	1	2	3	4
Days present				
Days absent				
Times tardy				

ASSIGNMENT FOR NEXT YEAR:

Assigned to grade _____ Date _____
Teacher: _____
Principal: _____

READING

	Quarter			
	1	2	3	4
GRADE LEVEL				
Achievement				
Effort				
Reads with understanding				
Uses word attack skills				
Shows increasing vocabulary				
Reads independently				

LANGUAGE ARTS

	Achievement			
Effort				
Expresses ideas well in writing				
Expresses ideas well orally				
Uses grammar correctly				
Penmanship				

SPELLING

Achievement			
Effort			
Masters assigned words			
Spells correctly in written work			

MATHEMATICS

	Achievement			
GRADE LEVEL				
Effort				
Knows number facts				
Applies computation skills in solving problems				
Solves story problems				
Works accurately				

ART

	Quarter			
	1	2	3	4
Achievement				
Effort				
Knowledge of content and subject material				
Interest and self-confidence				
Skills in handling material				

MUSIC

Achievement			
Effort			
Participates in music activities			
Developing music skills: a. rhythm b. tonal			
Understands music concepts such as form, vocabulary, musical instruments & listening skills			

PHYSICAL EDUCATION

Achievement			
Effort			
Performs fundamental skills			
Shows physical fitness			
Shows sportsmanship			

SOCIAL STUDIES

	Quarter			
	1	2	3	4
Achievement				
Effort				
Understands essential concepts				
Uses reference materials effectively				
Uses maps skills and geographical concepts				
Contributes to group discussions				
Participates in activities				

SCIENCE

	Quarter			
	1	2	3	4
Achievement				
Effort				
Understands scientific process				
Collects, organizes and uses resources effectively				
Applies concepts learned				

CONDUCT (letter grade)

Shows courtesy and respect to teachers and adults			
Courteous to other students			
Growing in self-discipline			
Accepts responsibility for own actions			
Respects rights and property of others			

WORK HABITS

Listens attentively			
Follows directions			
Begins work promptly			
Works independently			
Completes work neatly			
Completes class assignments on time			
Checks and proof reads carefully			
Has developed good organizational habits			
Uses time wisely			
Shows willingness to try			

FIRST QUARTER COMMENTS

SECOND QUARTER COMMENTS

THIRD QUARTER COMMENTS

FOURTH QUARTER COMMENTS

00-8575

Figure 13.8 Sample: Progress Report for Grades 3-6 from Kenosha Unified School District #1, Kenosha, WI. (Reprinted by permission of the Kenosha School System.)

Code: X = Not yet presented by teacher
R = Remedial help recommended
P = Making reasonable progress toward objectives;
recommend additional practice
M = Mastered

	Pretest	Progress	Posttest
Level 1			
Counts by rote through 9			
Identifies orally numerals through 9 ___			
Writes numerals through 5 ___			
Recognizes the number for groups contained through 5 by counting members in corresponding sets ___			
Identifies and describes a set by using many collections of objects			
Arranges members of sets in order as to height and length by using objects and pictures ___			
Predicts the next object in a sequence, such as O□ O□ — —			
Level 2			
Identifies and describes equivalent and nonequivalent sets by using collections of various objects in comparing two sets ___			
Identifies and describes equal sets arranged in different patterns ___			
Identifies and describes subsets, recognizing smaller groups within a larger group, excluding the empty set ___			
Matches the numeral with the number of members in sets up to 5			
Identifies the printed word with the number of members in a set through 5 ___			
Identifies orally the penny, nickel and ¢ sign, using coins and associating symbol 1¢ with 1 penny, 5¢ with a nickel ___			
Identifies orally the numbers for groups contained through 9 by counting the numbers in corresponding sets ___			
•			
•			
•			
Level 30			
Uses proportions to find a number when the percent is known ___			
Computes percent of error in measurement problems ___			
Computes the volume of polygons using the metric system ___			
Identifies complimentary and supplementary angles by drawing and labeling each ___			
Computes the angles of polygons and intersecting lines ___			
Computes the arithmetic mean of a series of numerals ___			
Adds and subtracts positive and negative integers ___			
Multiplies and divides positive and negative integers ___			
Uses tables to determine solution for an equation in two variables			
Identifies the median in a series of numerals ___			

Figure 13.9 A Behavioral Reporting System for Elementary Mathematics. (From Coupeville Consolidated School District 204, Coupeville, Washington. Reprinted by permission of the Coupeville Consolidated School District 204.)

year. The *P* signifies that, although the student has not yet mastered the objective, he is making reasonable progress and that remedial services are not indicated; rather, additional practice is recommended. An *X* in the "Posttest" column would indicate that the objective had not been taught at this time.

4. Junior High

Figure 13.10   From Racine Unified School District.[15]

This is another computer-printed report form. There is space for academic progress, attitude and behavior, and the absence and tardiness record.

Grading for academic progress uses the normal A-F system plus a P for pass and I for incomplete. It is assumed that some courses may be taken on a P-F basis.

The Attitude and Behavior section includes rating on industry, leadership, cooperation, and responsibility. It is rated by H for high; S for satisfactory; and N for needs to improve.

A "Yes" marked after a subject in the Teacher Conference Request Column indicates that the teacher would like a parent conference.

Figure 13.11   From Green Bay Public Schools.[16]

This report form combines evaluation of academic progress, comments for improving attitudes and behavior, and an indication of grade range. The academic area lists the school subjects, teacher, the teacher's grade for each quarter, and a final grade for the year. The grade symbols include: A for Excellent; B Above Average; C for Average; D for Below Average; E for Minimum Passing; F for Failure; and I for Incomplete. The two grade range symbols include + (plus) for upper area of grade range and − (minus) for the lower area of grade range.

Also, after each subject is a space for a symbol indicating comments for improving attitudes and behavior. Explanation of numbers and symbols are on the back of the form. The symbols are numbers, each of which stands for a particular comment. These include 1 for excellent growth in attitude, self-discipline, attention, and school citizenship; 2 for satisfactory growth; 3 for making progress, needs to concentrate and work more steadily; 4 for should participate more in class activity; 5 for be more courteous, respect property and rights of others; 6 for should attend class more regularly; 7 for

15. Junior High Report Card. Racine Unified School District, Racine, WI. Used by permission of the School System.

16. Progress Report—Junior High. Joint School District #1. Green Bay, WI. Used by permission of the school district.

REPORT CARD

RACINE
UNIFIED
SCHOOL
DISTRICT

RACINE
WISCONSIN

INSTRUCTOR NAME

TEACHER CONF REQUEST

SUBJECT NAME

		PERIOD MARK			CURRENT ATTEMPTED UNITS	ATTITUDE BEHAVIOR		
1	2	3	4	FINAL		IND	LEAD	COOP	RESP

TO PARENT OR GUARDIAN

	DAYS ABSENT	TIMES TARDY	GRADE LEVEL
			HOME ROOM
			STUDENT NUMBER
			UNITS COMPLETED
			CURRENT YEAR
			DATE
1st Qtr.			
2nd Qtr.			
3rd Qtr.			
4th Qtr.			
Totals			

MARKING SYSTEM

A - SUPERIOR
B - ABOVE AVERAGE
C - AVERAGE
D - BELOW AVERAGE

F - FAILURE
P - PASS
I - INCOMPLETE

ATTITUDE AND BEHAVIOR CODE

H - HIGH
S - SATISFACTORY
N - NEEDS TO IMPROVE

SEE
OTHER
SIDE

Figure 13.10 Sample: Junior High Report Card, Racine Unified School District, Racine, WI. (Used by permission of the School System.)

363

PROGRESS REPORT
JOINT SCHOOL DISTRICT NO. 1 – GREEN BAY, ET AL.

Figure 13.11 Progress Report—Junior High from Joint School District #1, Green Bay, WI. (Used by permission of the school district.)

Figure 13.11   Continued

TO PARENT OR GUARDIAN:

The educational welfare of pupils is encouraged when cooperation and understanding exists between the school and the home. This Progress Report is prepared at the close of each nine weeks as a basis for promoting cooperation and understanding. In addition to recording student achievement, the Progress Report presents an indication of the growth needed in personal characteristics that lead to good citizenship in the school and community.

Effort, initiative, work habits, and conduct are represented in the attitude and behavior comments. We hope you will regard the recommendations for character development as important values along with the scholastic grade. You are invited to consult the teacher, guidance counselor, or administration if a conference is indicated or seems advisable. Please call the school for an appointment.

GRADE EXPLANATION	RANGE	GRADE POINTS
A EXCELLENT. Is making excellent progress; displays unusual interest, originality, and initiative; does work of excellent quality.	93-100	4
B ABOVE AVERAGE. Is making very good progress; displays above average effort; does very good work promptly and neatly; has very good study habits.	85-92	3
C AVERAGE. Is making good progress; makes a response on definitely assigned work; is developing satisfactory study habits.	77-84	2
D BELOW AVERAGE. Needs to improve; can do better work with more effort; should improve study habits and daily work; should prepare required work with more thoroughness.	70-76	1
E MINIMUM PASSING. Indicates that although a student has not met minimum achievement requirements, credit is being granted for this course because the student has tried with reasonable effort and lacks the ability to improve by repeating the course.		0
F FAILURE. Is making unsatisfactory progress; displays little effort to achieve; lacks interest; work is too poor to justify passing in this subject.		
I INCOMPLETE. Indicates assigned work has not been completed usually because of condition beyond the pupil's control. If the work is not made up within a reasonable length of time, the pupil's grade will be changed from I to F.		

W WITHDRAWAL

COMMENTS FOR IMPROVING ATTITUDES AND BEHAVIOR

1 Excellent growth. Works well with students and teachers; shows good attitude, controls temper, displays good self-control. Assumes responsibility through self-discipline. Is courteous. Respects and observes school regulations. Is attentive in class. Practices desirable school citizenship.
2 Satisfactory growth.
3 Making progress; need to concentrate and work more steadily.
4 Should participate more in class activity.
5 Be more courteous; respect property and the rights of others.
6 Should attend class more regularly.
7 Make better use of study halls; avoid careless work habits.
8 Develop a more cooperative attitude.
9 PARENT CONFERENCE DESIRED. As a matter of mutual convenience, please call the school for an appointment with the teacher.

SYMBOLS AND ABBREVIATIONS

+ Upper area of grade range (plus).
— Lower area of grade range (minus).
cmt Comments For Improving Attitudes And Behavior.

make better use of study halls, avoid careless work habits; 8 for develop a more cooperative attitude; and 9 for parent conference desired.

Figure 13.12 *From Milwaukee Public Schools.*[17]

This report card is called the middle/junior high school progress report, grade 6-8. It is a computer printed card. It includes space for the academic subjects and grades, attendance and tardiness record, and a conduct grade.

The course grades have little variation of the A-F theme. Rather, it goes A through D plus a U and an I. A means Excellent, pupil does outstanding work, shows initiative and high interest; B means Above Average, pupil makes good progress, frequently does excellent work; C means Average, pupil's progress is satisfactory, does work of good quality; D means Below Average, pupil makes fair progress, might do better with more effort and improved study habits; U means Unsatisfactory (failure), pupil's work is too poor to receive a passing grade; and I means Incomplete, this grade is given when a pupil does not complete work for a good reason and work can be made up within a reasonable time and a grade would then be given.

The conduct grade reflects the teacher's view of how well a child practices good school citizenship. The teacher observes the extent to which the pupil participates in class, respects school and classroom rules, and gets along with other pupils and teachers.

5. High School

Figure 13.13 *From Joint School District No. 1—Green Bay Area.*[18]

This is very similar to the junior high form from the Green Bay District that is shown in the previous section. This is less structured with open spaces under the subject heading in which the particular subjects a student is taking are printed. There is a place for a first and a second semester grade.

For more complete information, read the description of the junior high form of the Green Bay District.

Figure 13.14 *From Milwaukee Public Schools.*[19]

This is similar to the junior high form from Milwaukee as shown in the previous section; there are a few differences, however. The reader is referred to the description of the junior high form for the basic information.

17. From Milwaukee Public Schools. Printed by permission of the Milwaukee Public School System, Milwaukee, WI.

18. Progress Report—Senior High School. Joint School District #1, Green Bay, WI. Used by permission of the school district.

19. From Milwaukee Public Schools. Printed by permission of the Milwaukee Public Schools System, Milwaukee, WI.

In addition to the A-D, U and I, which is on the junior high form, this also has N meaning No Credit and P for passing. The No Credit differs from the Incomplete in that the N is given only in certain courses to those students who do not complete course requirements.

The report form is issued three times and would include an exam grade and final grade. There is room for a conduct grade as in the junior high form.

Figure 13.15 and 13.16   From NLT Computer Services Corporation, Beloit, Wisconsin.[20]

This is an example of a standardized computer printout form; however, a high degree of flexibility is given to the school to determine the specific information shown on the grade report. There is space on the bottom of the form to print a LEGEND explaining the symbols used. There is also room to insert the student's name and school. There is room at the right below the chart to report such things as credits attempted and grade points for the current semester, summary of credits attempted, grade points, and cumulative grade point average. There is also room for rank in class. The E and the A columns are for Effort and Attitude.

Figure 13.16 shows the computer printout form with complete pupil and school information.

Marking and Reporting Forms for Special Types of Schools

In Appendix L will be marking and reporting forms for special types of schools. These include Creatives Art School, Teacher-Pupil Learning Center, Fundamental School, Gifted and Talented School, and Open Classroom School. Each of these schools are briefly described in the appendix prior to the form being presented.

J. How Does One Evaluate a Current System of Marking and Reporting and/or Establish a New System?

In recent years there has been widespread experimentation with various types of reporting practices within school systems. In most cases, teachers, administrators, and parents or a combination of all three react sufficiently to cause a need for an evaluation of the current systems of marking and reporting.

Following are suggestions that can be used as a guide for comprehensive evaluation of the current program and for developing changes or revisions of the current program.

20. Senior High Report Forms. NLT Computer Services Corporation, Beloit, WI. Used by permission of the NLT Corporation.

milwaukee public schools

MIDDLE/JUNIOR HIGH SCHOOL
PROGRESS REPORT
GRADES 6-8

_____ (STUDENT NAME)

_____ _____ _____ (SEX) (SERIAL NO.)

SCHOOL

PRINCIPAL

(HOMEROOM) (TEACHER)

HOMEROOM: ABSENT

HOMEROOM: TARDY

CLASS GRADE

COURSE NUMBER	COURSE NAME	PER	INSTR	ROOM	CLASS GRADE						FINAL GRADE
					1	2	3	4	5	6	

	1	2	3	4	5	6	TOTAL

1	2	3	4	5	6

STUDENT COPY SEE BACK FOR EXPLANATION OF GRADING

368

TO THE PARENTS OF OUR STUDENTS:

The grades on this report represent the best professional judgment of the teachers as to the progress your son or daughter is making in school. If you have any questions about these grades, contact the school and request that the teacher or an administrator call you. Better still, arrange for a meeting with the teacher or administrator at the school.

Also included on this report is the attendance record of your daughter or son. Consistent and regular attendance has a direct effect on school achievement. I encourage you to be sure that your children are in school every day the schools are in session.

School achievement can also be improved if the communication activities in the classroom—reading, discussion, listening, analyzing—also take place in your family circle. This is the kind of "homework" in which we can all participate.

Our children benefit tremendously when the home and the school work together to prepare them for the adult world which lies ahead.

LEE R. MC MURRIN
SUPERINTENDENT OF SCHOOLS

EXPLANATION OF MARKING SYSTEM FOR SUBJECT OFFERINGS

GRADE	DESCRIPTION OF GRADE
A	**EXCELLENT**—Pupil does outstanding work; shows initiative and high interest.
B	**ABOVE AVERAGE**—Pupil makes good progress; frequently does excellent work.
C	**AVERAGE**—Pupil's progress is satisfactory; does work of good quality.
D	**BELOW AVERAGE**—Pupil makes fair progress; might do better with more effort and improved study habits.
U	**UNSATISFACTORY (Failure)**—Pupil's work is too poor to receive a passing grade.
I	**INCOMPLETE**—This grade is given when a pupil does not complete work for a good reason, such as illness. Work can be made up within a reasonable time, and a grade would then be given.

EXPLANATION OF CONDUCT GRADE

This grade reflects the teacher's view of how well a child practices good school citizenship. The teacher observes the extent to which the pupil participates in class, respects school and classroom rules, and gets along with other pupils and teachers.

Figure 13.12 Sample: Middle/Junior High School Progress Report, Grades 6-8 from Milwaukee Public School System, Milwaukee, WI. (Printed by permission of the Milwaukee Public School System, Milwaukee, WI.)

HOME ROOM _____ TEACHER _____ STUDENT _____ GRADE _____

SUBJECT	1	CMT	2	CMT	SEM GRADE	3	CMT	4	CMT	SEM GRADE	TEACHER
1											
2											
3											
4											
5											
6											
7											
8 Physical Education											
ATTENDANCE	A	T	A	T		A	T	A	T		

PARENT OR GUARDIAN _____

School _____

Principal _____

19 ___ 19 ___

PROGRESS REPORT
JOINT SCHOOL DISTRICT NO. 1 – GREEN BAY, ET AL.

Figure 13.13 Sample: Progress Report—Senior High School from Joint School District #1, Green Bay, WI. (Used by permission of the school district.)

Figure 13.13 Continued

TO PARENT OR GUARDIAN:

The educational welfare of pupils is encouraged when cooperation and understanding exists between the school and the home. This Progress Report is prepared at the close of each nine weeks as a basis for promoting cooperation and understanding. In addition to recording student achievement, the Progress Report presents an indication of the growth needed in personal characteristics that lead to good citizenship in the school and community.

Effort, initiative, work habits, and conduct are represented in the attitude and behavior comments. We hope you will regard the recommendations for character development as important values along with the scholastic grade. You are invited to consult the teacher, guidance counselor, or administration if a conference is indicated or seems advisable. Please call the school for an appointment.

	GRADE EXPLANATION	RANGE	GRADE POINTS
A	EXCELLENT. Is making excellent progress; displays unusual interest, originality, and initiative; does work of excellent quality.	93-100	4
B	ABOVE AVERAGE. Is making very good progress; displays above average effort; does very good work promptly and neatly; has very good study habits.	85-92	3
C	AVERAGE. Is making good progress; makes a response on definitely assigned work; is developing satisfactory study habits.	77-84	2
D	BELOW AVERAGE. Needs to improve; can do better work with more effort; should improve study habits and daily work; should prepare required work with more thoroughness.	70-76	1
E	MINIMUM PASSING. Indicates that although a student has not met minimum achievement requirements, credit is being granted for this course because the student has tried with reasonable effort and lacks the ability to improve by repeating the course.		0
F	FAILURE. Is making unsatisfactory progress; displays little effort to achieve; lacks interest; work is too poor to justify passing in this subject.		
I	INCOMPLETE. Indicates assigned work has not been completed usually because of condition beyond the pupil's control. If the work is not made up within a reasonable length of time, the pupil's grade will be changed from I to F.		

W WITHDRAWAL

COMMENTS FOR IMPROVING ATTITUDES AND BEHAVIOR

1 Excellent growth. Works well with students and teachers; shows good attitude, controls temper, displays good self-control. Assumes responsibility through self-discipline. Is courteous. Respects and observes school regulations. Is attentive in class. Practices desirable school citizenship.
2 Satisfactory growth.
3 Making progress; need to concentrate and work more steadily.
4 Should participate more in class activity.
5 Be more courteous; respect property and the rights of others.
6 Should attend class more regularly.
7 Make better use of study halls; avoid careless work habits.
8 Develop a more cooperative attitude.
9 PARENT CONFERENCE DESIRED. As a matter of mutual convenience, please call the school for an appointment with the teacher.

SYMBOLS AND ABBREVIATIONS

✚ Upper area of grade range (plus).
━ Lower area of grade range (minus).
cmt Comments For Improving Attitudes And Behavior.

milwaukee public schools

HIGH SCHOOL
PROGRESS REPORT
GRADES 9-12

SCHOOL

PRINCIPAL

(STUDENT NAME)   (SEX)   (SERIAL NO.)

(CLASS)   (HOMEROOM) (TEACHER)

HOMEROOM: ABSENT

HOMEROOM: TARDY

		1	2	3	TOTAL

COURSE NUMBER	COURSE NAME	PER	INSTR	ROOM	GRADE 1	GRADE 2	GRADE 3	EXAM GRADE	FINAL GRADE	UNITS EARNED

1	2	3

TO THE PARENTS OF OUR STUDENTS:

The grades on this report represent the best professional judgment of the teachers as to the progress your son or daughter is making in school. If you have any questions about these grades, contact the school and request that the teacher or an administrator call you. Better still, arrange for a meeting with the teacher or administrator at the school.

Also included on this report is the attendance record of your daughter or son. Consistent and regular attendance has a direct effect on school achievement. I encourage you to be sure that your children are in school every day the schools are in session.

School achievement can also be improved if the communication activities in the classroom—reading, discussion, listening, analyzing—also take place in your family circle. This is the kind of "homework" in which we can all participate.

Our children benefit tremendously when the home and the school work together to prepare them for the adult world which lies ahead.

LEE R. MC MURRIN
SUPERINTENDENT OF SCHOOLS

PROGRESS TOWARD GRADUATION

The requirements for graduation include earning 18 units, of which 14 must be earned in grades 10 through 12. Specific course requirements and the reading proficiency requirement must also be met. If you desire further information regarding these requirements, please contact the school your son or daughter attends.

EXPLANATION OF CLASS GRADES

A EXCELLENT—Student does outstanding work; shows initiative and high interest.

B ABOVE AVERAGE—Student makes good progress; frequently does excellent work.

C AVERAGE—Student's progress is satisfactory; does work of good quality.

D BELOW AVERAGE—Student makes fair progress; might do better with more effort and better study habits.

E BELOW AVERAGE—Same as Grade D, except that the student must complete remedial work before advancing to the next level in that subject.

U UNSATISFACTORY (Failure)—Student's work is too poor to receive a passing grade.

N NO CREDIT—This grade is given only in certain courses to those students who do not complete course requirements.

I INCOMPLETE—This grade is given when a student does not complete work for a good reason, such as illness. Work can be made up within a reasonable time, and a grade would then be given.

P PASSING—This grade is for successful completion of a course but is not computed in the grade point average. The student's work and progress could vary from excellent through fair.

EXPLANATION OF CONDUCT GRADE

This grade reflects the teacher's view of how well a student practices good school citizenship. The teacher observes the extent to which the student participates in class, respects school and classroom rules, and gets along with other students and teachers.

Figure 13.14 Sample: High School Progress Report, Grades 9-12 from Milwaukee Public Schools, Milwaukee, WI. (Printed by permission of the Milwaukee Public Schools System, Milwaukee, WI.)

NLT Computer Services Corporation
AN AFFILIATE OF NLT CORPORATION

GRADE REPORT

STUDENT NAME	STUDENT NUMBER	HOME ROOM	CLASS	SEX	SCHOOL	DATE	DELIVERY CODE

COURSE AND SECTION	COURSE NAME	INSTRUCTOR NAME	PERIOD 1				PERIOD 2				PERIOD 3				PERIOD 4				SEMESTER 1		SEMESTER 2		SEMESTER 3		FINAL GRADE
			GRADE	E	A	ABS	GRADE	E	A	ABS	GRADE	E	A	ABS	GRADE	E	A	ABS	EXAM	GRADE	EXAM	GRADE	EXAM	GRADE	
STUDENTS ALL COURSE AVERAGE →																									

ATTENDANCE SUMMARY		
PERIOD	TARDY	ABSENCE
FIRST		
SECOND		
THIRD		
FOURTH		
TOTAL		

1

Figure 13.15 Sample: Grade Report from NLT Computer Services Corporation, Beloit, WI. (Used by permission of the NLT.)

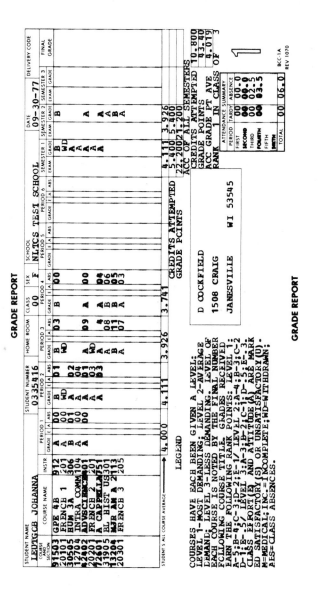

The Grade Report is prepared on a standard format used for all schools grading with NLTCS; however, a high degree of flexibility is given to the school to determine the specific information shown on the Grade Report. The information printed in the LEGEND area is optional for each school. Other options such as Rank in Class, Total Grade Points Earned, Total Credits Attempted, Total Credits Earned, and Grade Point Average are offered. Four copies of each Grade Report are prepared.

Figure 13.16 Sample: Completed (fictitious material) Grade Report from NLT Computer Services Corporation, Beloit, WI. (Used by permission of NLT Computer Services Corporation.)

1. Form a committee consisting of teachers, parents, and administrators (plus students if on secondary level).
2. Have the committee study the local program, including such items of reporting as differences at various grade levels, comparative grades and individual differences, grouping and evaluation, and types of marks.
3. Bring in some outstanding speakers on the subject to permit school personnel and parents to hear their viewpoints.
4. Prepare and distribute a questionnaire to acquire an adequate sampling of parents' opinions; it might be advisable to use a stratified random sampling technique (percentage of population by area, socioeconomic status, or other means). The following questionnaire or a similar one might be used.

Reporting Forms

a. What is your opinion of our present report form (card)?
b. Does the present report form give you a concise picture of your child's progress in school in academic achievement; in social and individual growth?
c. Do you feel that the report form should include a checklist for social and emotional growth, work habits, and health habits?
d. Which grading system do you prefer? (Give examples here for parents to check: A B C D F; numerical grades such as 90, 85, 75, 60; O-S-U; E, VG, G, F, P, among others.)

Conference Reporting

a. Do you believe parent conferences are worthwhile?
b. Do you believe parent conferences should replace report cards?
c. Do you believe both parent conferences and report cards should be used?
d. How often should report cards be issued during the school year?
e. How many parent-teacher conferences should be held?
f. When would you prefer to have these conferences held?
g. Would you prefer to have each homeroom teacher schedule parent-teacher conferences within a short period of time?
h. Do you feel that the present time allowed for conference (give present time) is adequate?
i. Do you feel that the child should be present during part of the conference?

5. Tabulate and analyze the results of the responses on the questionnaires.
6. Make a study of the various types of report forms currently in use throughout the state and the nation. The committee must consistently keep in mind that ultimately a reporting form must be "tailor-made" for its specific school system, but it can profit from the efforts and resultant findings of other school systems.

7. Agree on the grouping of grade levels for using uniform report cards. One suggested grouping could be kindergarten, primary, intermediate, junior high, and high school.
8. Have subcommittees prepare sample report forms on the various grade levels, and then have the entire committee review them for continuity and for content.
9. Produce the report forms by mimeograph for the year of trial and evaluation.
10. Prepare a brochure to be distributed at the beginning of the school year to teachers and parents explaining the new system. Plan a meeting of the PTA and of other parent groups, either individually or combined, to further discuss the reporting system and to present an opportunity for school personnel to answer the questions of the parents.
11. Toward the end of the school year, send a second questionnaire to parents with specific questions concerning the evaluation method being used. Also ask the teachers for their estimations of the method being tested.
12. When modifications have been made and it appears that the reporting form is ready for more permanent use, have it printed. Remember, the form should be generally appealing with liberal use of color, and it should be fairly compact yet complete in terms of all preferential information as revealed by the study.

Summary Statements

1. Marks can serve as a motivation and a guidance function with students. A student may be challenged to work harder and view the mark as an improvement of learning. Marks may provide data to counsel the students on strengths and weaknesses.
2. Marks can be one of the best communication devices between the school and the home.
3. Marks serve as a great informational source for teachers, counselors, and administrators. Most school personnel feel that they can better understand the students more quickly if they have some evidence of past achievement.
4. Problems of marking center around semantics, clearly defined criteria, and uniform interpretation of the results; thus, the need for a comprehensive approach to the development of a school marking system.
5. Marking depends on the use of the best measurement tools to measure how learning has met the objectives. Some of the most common tools include objective tests; essay tests; and judging work samples, performances, or products.

6. Some of the most used methods of grading include rank, percentile rank, symbols, and standard scores.
7. Grades may be distributed by the "breaks" method, normal curve of distribution, and the mean and standard deviation.
8. Assigning course marks may be by grade-point average; simple averages; and point-score method.
9. When giving different weights to performance for a final mark, the differences in variability of the different sets of scores must be taken into account.
10. There are both advantages and disadvantages in differentiating levels of marking to correspond with ability levels in various classes. Differentiating levels of marking requires uniform ability measures for the pupils in various classes.
11. Systems of marking include percentage, A-F, other letter symbols, written communication, parent conferences, checklists and rating scales, self-evaluations, and behavioral mastery reports.

Discussion Questions

1. Describe an example of how school marks may be used for the functions of motivating students, guiding students, communicating between school and home, and as an informational source for school personnel.
2. Explain in your own words the differences between scoring, grading, and marking.
3. Select the method of grading you prefer and describe its advantages.
4. Cite the advantages and limitations of each method of distributing grades—by breaks, normal curve, and the use of the mean and standard deviation.
5. Are there any particular advantages in any of the methods of assigning course marks?
6. Explain why it is necessary to consider the variability of the distribution of scores when you average scores and desire to give different weights to different performances.
7. Discuss the pros and cons in differentiating levels of marking to correspond with ability levels in various classes.
8. Which system of reporting progress appeals to you? Why?

Student Activities

1. Using the following information, describe in a page how you might guide a student in planning his future.

Ability Scores (in Percentiles)			*Marks*	
Language	—	42	English	C
Non-Language	—	84	Mathematics	A
Total	—	62	Science	B
			Social Studies	B
			Reading	C

2. The instructor will divide the class into groups and will ask some of you to role-play as a teacher, counselor, or administrator. Discuss in your group what uses the role you are playing would make of school marks. Be ready to discuss these uses with the total class.

3. Considering the seven problems associated with marking, write a 250-word essay (or be ready with a 5-minute oral report) on your experience with these problems as a recipient of marks so far in your education.

4. Figure the grade-point averages and assign a mark to each result.

a	*b*	*c*
A	A	B
A	B	C
B	B	C
C	C	D
C	C	F

5. Figure a simple average for the following list of scores.

$$95 \quad 95 \quad 85 \quad 85 \quad 80 \quad 75 \quad 50$$

Would the mean or the median be a more reliable average? Why?

6. Figure the composite average from the following information. Use the formula for the composite average when different weights are to be assigned to the different performances.

Category	*Weight*	*Stanine*
Class Contribution	1	8
Daily Work	1	6
Project	2	7
Unit Test	2	6

7. The instructor will divide the class into small groups. Each group is to think of one advantage and one limitation (if any) for the following systems of marking and reporting. Be ready to come back and contribute these to the total class discussion.

A-F	S-V	Parent Conference
H-S-N	P-F	Checklists and Rating Scales
X-Y-Z	Written	Behavioral Mastery Reports
	Communications	Percentages

Selected Readings

Ahmann, J. Stanley, and Glock, Marvin D. *Evaluating Pupil Growth,* 5th ed. Boston: Allyn and Bacon, Inc., 1975. Chapter 15.

———. *Measuring and Evaluating Educational Achievement,* 2nd ed. Boston: Allyn and Bacon, Inc., 1975. Chapter 11.

Bennion, Donald H. *Assessing Student Learning.* Dubuque, IA: Kendall-Hunt Book Co., 1977. Chapter 9.

Ebel, Robert L. *Essentials of Educational Measurement,* 3rd ed. Englewood Cliffs, NJ: Prentice-Hall, Inc., 1979. Chapter 12.

Green, John A. *Teacher-Made Tests,* 2nd ed. New York: Harper & Row, Publishers, 1975. Chapter 9.

Gronlund, Norman E. *Measurement and Evaluation in Teaching,* 3rd ed. New York: The Macmillan Company, 1976. Chapter 19.

Kirschenbaum, Howard, Simon, Sidney B., and Napier, Rodney W. *Wad-Ja-Get? The Grading Game in American Education.* New York: Hart Publishing Company, Inc., 1971.

Linneman, Richard H., and Merenda, Peter F. *Educational Measurement,* 2nd ed. Glenview, IL: Scott, Foresman and Company, 1979. Chapter 6.

Mehrens, William A., and Lehmann, Irvin J. *Measurement and Evaluation in Education and Psychology.* New York: Holt, Rinehart and Winston, 1973. Chapter 13.

Noll, Victor H., Scannell, Dale P., and Craig, Robert C. *Introduction to Educational Measurement,* 4th ed. Boston: Houghton Mifflin Company, 1979. Chapter 14.

Noll, Victor H., Scannell, Dale P., and Noll, Rachel P. *Introductory Readings in Educational Measurement.* Boston: Houghton Mifflin Company, 1972. Chapter 36.

Payne, David A. *The Assessment of Learning: Cognitive and Affective.* Lexington, Massachusetts: D. C. Heath & Co., 1974. Chapter 17.

Sax, Gilbert. *Principles of Educational Measurement and Evaluation.* Belmont, California: Wadsworth Publishing Company, Inc., 1974. Pp. 521-553.

Scannell, Dale P., and Tracy, D. B. *Testing and Measurement in the Classroom.* Boston: Houghton Mifflin Company, 1975. Chapter 9.

TenBrink, Terry D. *Evaluation. A Practical Guide for Teachers.* New York: McGraw-Hill Book Company, 1974. Chapter 9.

Thorndike, Robert L., and Hagen, Elizabeth. *Measurement and Evaluation in Psychology and Education,* 4th ed. New York: John Wiley & Sons, 1977. Chapter 15.

Wick, John W. *Educational Measurement. Where Are We Going and How Will We Know When We Get There?* Columbus, Ohio: Charles E. Merrill Publishing Company, 1973. Chapter 10.

14

Individualized Education

Individual Educational Program
Assessment in Individually Guided Education

A. Individual Educational Program

Following is a condensed summary of the paperback book, *The Individual Educational Program (IEP) Manual*. To obtain a more complete understanding of the topic, the reader is referred to: James Lynn, Dan Woltz, and William Brush, *The Individual Educational Program (IEP) Manual* (Hollister, CA: Argonaut Publications, 1977) pp. 79-88 and Appendixes A-F. Reprinted by permission of the publisher.

Public Law 94-142

1. Education for All Handicapped Children Act of 1975

On November 29, 1975, Public Law 94-142 was signed into existence. The law, which took effect in October, 1977, is a direct effort to assure all children with special needs of a free and appropriate public education designed on an individual basis to meet each child's unique needs.

The key feature of PL 94-142 is the requirement that all students with exceptional needs have a written *Individual Educational Program* (IEP) designed to meet their special needs. The program is to be written by a team consisting of "local education agency personnel, the teacher, the parent or guardian of the child, and whenever appropriate, the child himself or herself."

The IEP should include the following elements:

a. A statement of the present level of the student's educational performance.

b. A statement of the annual goals, including short-term objectives.

c. A statement of the specific educational services to be provided and the extent to which the student will be able to participate in regular programs.

d. The projected dates for initiation of such services and their anticipated duration.

e. Appropriate objective criteria, evaluation procedures, and schedules for determining whether instructional objectives have been met.

2. Three Levels of the IEP

There are three levels which comprise the IEP system for designing, implementing, and maintaining an appropriate educational program for the student with special needs. Level I, *The Comprehensive Plan,* works to formulate overall and long-term goals of the program in line with the student's prioritized needs and present level of functioning. Level II, *The Implementation Plan,* translates the goals of the first level into short-term, attainable objectives and includes suggestions on how to implement those objectives with appropriate strategies and resources. Level III, *The Evaluation,* evaluates the effectiveness of the program based on measurable criteria and, when appropriate, allows for modification and revision of the IEP for the following year.

PL 94-142 requires a re-evaluation of each IEP at least once a year by the Student Study Team. This required evaluation process, called *The Product* or *Annual Evaluation,* reviews the effectiveness of the long-term IEP goals. Most schools will also use what is called *Process Evaluation.* This continues throughout the school year and monitors the implementation of the short-term objectives.

3. Normal Areas of Assessment

Following is a list of the major areas which may be considered in the assessment of a student.

a. Educational Assessment
   This area helps to determine whether a student has made sufficient academic progress in his or her educational program.

b. Cognitive and Intellectual Assessment
   This concerns knowing or how one acquires information. Intelligence is closely related to and deals with both natural and learned ability to think and reason.

c. Language Assessment
   This will enable one to determine the level of language development that a student has for learning.

d. Physical Assessment
   This area usually includes assessment for vision and hearing, psychomotor skills, and general health.

e. Social-Emotional Behavioral Assessment
    Assessment here would evaluate such traits as honesty, self-confidence, responsible behaviors, inter-personal behaviors, and impulse control.

f. Culture Fair Assessment
    An attempt is made here to assess the cultural heritage of the student being referred. Team members need to be cognizant of any cultural bias that may be present in a particular test, assessment device, or any other situational facts that may adversely affect the student.

g. Personality Assessment
    The assessment in this area is usually the primary responsibility of the psychologist. He uses various methods to obtain specific behaviors as indicators of personality.

h. School and Family Environment Assessment
    This area of assessment includes observing and interviewing the student in the environment (classroom, playground, and the like) where the initial referral originated.

i. Career and Vocational Assessment
    Different levels in school attempt to have the student experience different areas of the world of work and then one can assess the student's understanding. From elementary grades through high school, the topics might include: Career Awareness, Career Exploration, Career Orientation and Preparation, and Vocational Education.

4. Summary of the Evaluation Phase

The evaluation of the IEP involves both a Process Evaluation and a Product Evaluation. The Process Evaluation considers the progress of the student toward the specific objectives of the implementation plan. This is a continuous activity of the Study Team throughout the student's educational program.

The Product Evaluation, or Annual Evaluation, is usually conducted only once or twice a year. This considers the long-term progress of the student toward the annual goals set in the total comprehensive plan. As a result of these evaluations, necessary changes may be made in the goals and objectives of the student's IEP. Normally, the steps in both of these evaluations include reviewing of the planning stage, collection of evaluative data, comparison of evaluative criteria to collected data, subjective evaluation and informal observation, and interpretation and decision-making.

Case Study of an IEP Evaluation Plan

D. G.: 7-year-old physically handicapped girl

Referral was made by the girl's first grade teacher who indicated that D. G. was having hearing and listening problems.

Family: D. G. is an only child with parents who are cooperative with school personnel.

Developmental History: Training skills were within the norm; somewhat hyperactive and history of ear infection with occasional hearing loss; overweight for age; somewhat uncoordinated.

Medical Information: Hearing loss confirmed by family physician. Tubes were placed in ears for drainage and this seemed to help.

Educational Assessment: Auditory memory is all right; left to right movement was weak; had difficulty tracking; copying skills letter-by-letter slow but sure; intelligence test showed M.A. of 8.5 and IQ of 126; achievement test showed grade equivalents of 1.8 in Reading, 1.7 in Spelling, and 1.9 in Arithmetic.

Social-Emotional Adjustment: Seems to have a good disposition and self-confidence; reacts well with peers and adults; appears anxious to learn.

Present Levels of Performance

D. G. appears to have poor fine and gross motor skills; slow copying skills; difficulty in encoding, classifying, and listening and paying attention to tasks.

Long-Term Goal Statements

D. G. will manifest better listening and attending skills by carrying out commands/tasks.

D. G. will demonstrate fine motor control and coordination as judged by quality of her printed letters.

D. G. will be able to manifest greater gross motor control and coordination as judged by her gait.

Suggested Response to Long-Term Goals

Only one will be given here as an example.

Long-Term Goal: D. G. will manifest better listening and attending skills by carrying out three command tasks.

Special Education Area: Placement in physically handicapped regular day-class program taught by learning-handicapped teacher. She will spend about 20% of her time in this program starting on 3/20/81 and ending on 12/15/81.

Suggested Responses to Short-Term Objectives

Again, only one will be given here as an example.

Short-Term Objective: Given three related commands as tasks, D. G. will be able to carry them out in a given order.

Teaching Tasks: Ask her to report orally two commands and then follow them in sequence.

Carries out two and then three simple related tasks or commands in order.

Use positive reinforcement consistently for specific steps in accomplishing objective or goal.

Resources and Materials for Implementation: Physically handicapped aide will assist.

Use a series of tasks in following directions.

Projected starting and stopping dates: Begin on 3/20/81 and end on 12/15/81.

Evaluation Criteria

D. G. will carry out in order three related commands.

For detailed information about The Individual Educational Program, see the *Manual* by Lynn, Woltz, and Brush as listed at the beginning of this section. Also, most State Departments of Public Instruction will have guides for the IEP.

B. Assessment in Individually Guided Education

Following is a condensed version of the paperback book, *Individually Guided Education: Assessment.* To obtain a more complete understanding of this topic, the reader is referred to: Joan Beuger, Ellen Bloomfield, Maxine Brady, Ira Kerns, *Individually Guided Education: Assessment* (Dayton, Ohio: Institute for Development of Educational Activities, Inc., 1972) 72 pages. Reprinted by permission of the publisher.

What will tomorrow hold? The world is changing at a phenomenal rate. In Alvin Toffler's book, *Future Shock*, he discusses the psychological buffeting that everyone is experiencing due to rapid changes in our environment.

Are our schools preparing students to cope with tomorrow? Educators do have a vast array of new techniques, materials, equipment, and basic concepts to use as a result of research and innovation. Teachers cannot lock themselves to a teacher's manual; their job is to make each day more effective than the last for the students.

Individually Guided Education (IGE) provides for continuous improvement daily. In schools of this type, the students and staff work together to achieve specific learning objectives. Continuous assessment provides students and staff opportunities to evaluate themselves and to determine progress. In this program, students learn how to learn. They determine what they need to do to accomplish objectives, to judge whether they have reached the objectives, and to develop alternative ways of accomplishing objectives if their first attempts fail. In this way, they learn to adapt much more easily to the world of tomorrow.

1. The Name of the Game

Assessment is the basis for Individually Guided Education (IGE). It provides data on students, is an ongoing process, is inseparable from the learning process, and it goes on at all levels within a school. There are two main areas for student assessment which must be considered. These include the student's achievement and the student's personal characteristics and learning style.

a. Assessing Student Achievement

In assessing student achievement, two approaches may be used. The first is *norm-referenced assessment.* This approach tells how the population of a given school, student group, or individual learner compares in performance with the performance average of the population on which the test was standardized. This approach has little value in the IGE program.

The second approach is called *criterion-referenced assessment.* In this method, the individual's performance is compared with the performance criterion established for a given test. In IGE, learning objectives and criteria for mastery are established, learning programs are planned with the student, and assessment is used to monitor progress in the individual learning program.

Thus, through criterion-referenced assessment, what the student has learned, how he has learned it, and what he needs to learn next are determined.

b. Assessing the Learner and His Learning Style

The teacher has to become acquainted with the learner. An attempt is made to study the family background and interests of each student and link this data to the objectives for the student. The learning style indicates how a student learns. The teacher needs to observe how the student *has and has not learned.* This information aids in developing an effective learning program.

By the same token, knowledge of the individual's characteristics, including interests, motivation, past achievement, and difficulties, will provide a sound basis for designing a suitable means of assessment for each learning objective.

c. Assessment Variables

There are five principal variables in any assessment plan. They are the assessment medium, the mode, frequency, place, and personnel. The selections to be made in each of these areas will be determined by who and what is to be assessed and how it is to be taught.

(1) The *assessment medium* refers to the kind of response the learner will be asked to make during assessment (written, oral, or visual, or any combination).

(2) The *assessment mode* refers to the size of the group being assessed. It may be *independent* (an individual learner and assessment materials); *one-to-one* (a staff member or another pupil with the individual learner and assessment materials/activities); *small group* (2 to 15 learners and assessment materials/activities, supervised or unsupervised); or *large group* (15 learners to a whole unit and assessment materials/activities, supervised or unsupervised.)

(3) The *frequency of assessment,* when to assess, is usually determined very simply. Assessment is done when information is needed. Four varying rates of assessment have been developed.

　(a) *Fixed assessment* is assessment scheduled in advance either by day or specific times (beginning, middle, end) of the learning program.

　(b) *Occasional assessment* is assessment administered whenever the staff chooses, usually to verify a teacher judgment.

　(c) *Demand assessment* is assessment that is requested by individual learners when they feel that they need it or are ready for it.

　(d) *Ongoing assessment* is assessment which monitors the learning environment in a continuous fashion, usually by work sampling and observation.

(4) The *place of assessment* can be either a regularly occupied room, part of a multi-purpose room, a desk in the hall, the library—in other words, anywhere that is appropriate and available.

(5) *Personnel,* which could include teachers, aides, and parents, must be informed of whatever role they are to play in the assessment. This can be supervision of the entire session, monitoring the learning environment, collection of materials, distribution of materials, making sure that the student comes to school with the proper attire, supplies, and the like.

2. Types of Assessment

It must be stressed that IGE assessment is an ongoing process. The types of assessment include paper-and-pencil assessment, work-sampling assessment, observation, performance assessment, and student-prepared assessment.

a. Paper-and-Pencil Assessment

This assessment is probably the most familiar to teachers, but it is not always suitable for IGE since it is not always criterion-referenced. However, certain items or parts of a test might be useful. The key is to be sure that the assessment fits the learning objectives, not vice versa.

There are some disadvantages to paper-and-pencil assessment. It is usually very structured and might take an excessive amount of time. Some children are not suited for paper-and-pencil tests; e.g., those from a non-English speaking home or those with poor reading or writing skills. Thus, due to the learner's deficiencies, a paper-and-pencil test might give invalid information about the learner's progress. At times, other assessment might be more appropriate to measure toward a specific objective. Some students get "turned off" by tests since they become repetitious and routine. Sometimes, tests create undue tension in students and the students "freeze up" during the test situation. In summary, published paper-and-pencil tests must be carefully evaluated in the IGE program; some parts of standardized tests can be used effectively if appropriate for stated objectives; teacher-made paper-and-pencil tests are also appropriate in certain cases; and prepared tests, along with their objectives, should be kept in an organized and accessible file.

b. Work-Sampling Assessment

Work-sampling assessment is the analysis of written materials and other projects produced by the learner in the course of his learning program. It is a common assessment in IGE which works relatively well. It eliminates the interruption of learning experiences and puts less emotional stress on the students. The student can determine when he is ready to show his work. Thus, it helps to make learning and testing part of school life, drawing the learning and testing into a unified, personal experience.

c. Observation

Observation is the assessment of the learner's progress by means of sensory awareness. It is very commonly used by teachers and is most suitable for IGE. This is because it does not interrupt the learning process, and it offers an opportunity to assess the whole child's feelings, attitudes, thinking processes, and skill development.

There are two types of observation. These are the *unstructured* and the *structured* observations. *Unstructured* observation is continuous with certain objectives in mind. *Structured* observation is used when the objective is to be measured over a period of time and when behavior to be measured is to be typical. It is designed as follows: State the objective to be observed; determine the behaviors indicative of achievement toward objective; determine the means of recording; and last, design the logistics, e.g., who observes, who is observed, when, where, how, and the like.

Observation lends itself readily to discovering affective attitudes and reasoning; attitudes toward peers, school in general, self, subjects, and the like. It also helps students to understand others around them through the use of the observation method.

d. Performance Assessment

In this type of assessment, the learner is asked to demonstrate achievement of an objective by means of an activity or action. The pupil is normally aware that he is being assessed. Teacher aides and para-professionals can assist in performance assessment. There is no reason that students cannot give each other certain performance tests.

There are several advantages of performance assessment over paper-and-pencil assessment. These include:
a. appropriateness for almost any learning objective
b. application-oriented, that is, can they apply what they have learned?
c. not dependent on reading or writing skills
d. provides opportunity for creativity
e. allows for the playback mirror effect; that is, it allows children to see and hear themselves.

e. Student-Prepared Assessment

In this type, the student is permitted, and encouraged, to suggest how he can demonstrate achievement of objectives. This allows for critiquing by both the individual student and the group; thus, it promotes good critical thinking habits. The whole process is learner-motivated, learner-achieved, and learner-evaluated.

3. Affective Assessment

Affective characteristics comprise an important area for assessment. Teachers are familiar with interest inventories and sociometric devices. The problem with these instruments is that they are difficult to interpret and apply. As a result, they are not used very often.

Highly structured types of assessment are generally poor ways to measure affective objectives. The student might be unsure of the objectives and might respond in the way that he sees that the teacher expects him to— as a perfect pupil. With such structured assessment, it is easy to start comparing pupils to each other or to formal standards. One might forget that the individual is not absolute or infallible.

Some of the better instruments for affective assessment include:

Open-ended questions encourage the learner to explore attitudes and values.

Performance tests may be used to get social objectives and work attitudes through individual or group conferences. Another performance test approach would be to use hypothetical situations for discussion. In general, students respond well to "what if" situations because they can let their imaginations run free.

Work sampling will also provide information on the learner's attitudes toward his work. Comparing work in different subject areas, in different media, or with other students can indicate preferences and special interests.

Observation is a primary means of assessment of affective domain. A learner's expression, his tone of voice, his pace in starting and completing a task, and what he does when given free rein, all give information to the Unit teachers.

A system of *anecdotal records* is perhaps the best way to make observations useful in affective assessment. Staff members can recognize significant behavior and record the observation in an anecdotal record while it is still fresh in mind. These records can be pulled out at the appropriate time to give the teaching team a picture of a learner in a specific area.

a. Communicating with Students

Probably the most important assessment device known is *communication*. The "informal chat" can be the key to getting the critical assessment information you need about a student to plan an effective learning program for him. Many IGE teachers say that they feel "closer" to their students because of the flow of communication from pupils to staff, from staff to pupils.

b. The Interview Approach

General probing interviews of a casual nature with a student will provide a great deal of affective information. Assessing the learner's motivation is one of the jobs that can be handled through effective communications. If you want to learn what is motivating a student, the most natural thing to do is to ask him. And then listen!

There should be regular sessions to *determine interest* assessment, but casual, ad hoc sessions with the individual can, and should, go on all the time. When you talk with pupils you can, in particular, find out their attitudes toward ways of learning, approaches to subject matter, different means of assessment, and the like.

The kind of personal student feedback you get in an interview can be used to prepare assessment alternatives. Student feedback is a great help when you have to choose among alternatives because of some reason—budget, space, or time limitations; you can't offer them all.

c. Elements for Successful Communication

There are three key elements for successful communications: *frequency, attitude, proper management of communication opportunities.* The *frequency of communication* is every bit as important as the length of a particular session. The accessibility of teachers is an important factor in the quality, as well as the quantity, of communication in the Unit. Your *attitude* is, overall, the most important factor in good and frequent exchange. If your students find that they can come to you and be heard and answered, you will discover that the task of learning what they are up to will become more meaningful and will yield more reliable results. *Good management of communication opportunities* will also help. Instead of turning down a learner who asks for an ear when yours are busy, try to postpone him a bit to your earliest free time or direct him to someone else who is available.

You should seek out other sources to corroborate and complete the information that you get from talking with learners. *Parents* are a good source who tend to have an above-average interest in the school life of their children. Special personnel in the school—*psychologist, counselor, nurse,* and the like—should be called in to interview learners whenever a need is indicated. Another source of insight into learners is the people with whom they communicate frequently: close friends, siblings, and others in school with whom they are close.

d. Using Affective Assessment

A very important point must be made; that is, the information gathered through the various means of affective assessment *must be used.* A child's learning style, feelings, or special situational problems are overlooked by many teachers. But, in the IGE school, every child is an important individual and his or her specialness must be considered in the planning of individualized learning programs and assessment. At Unit meetings, for example, every effort should be made to bring everyone's affective information to bear on the planning.

4. The Assessment Continuum

IGE assessment is a continuum flowing through all IGE learning programs, recording, organizing, managing and analyzing data, planning new assessments, and communicating current assessment information.

a. Ongoing Assessment

Most ongoing assessment is provided through the less structured assessment means of observation and work-sample techniques. When ongoing assessment indicates that a learner is ready to demonstrate his achievement, more structured assessment can be planned to determine whether the student has reached an adequate level of achievement of his/her objective(s) and to verify teacher judgment. Usually a test, performance or written, is used, although, at times, observation or work-sampling might be sufficient to indicate achievement toward the objectives(s). One should avoid testing individuals or groups for the sake of routine or convenience. Learners work at their own rate and are not expected to reach accomplishment of objectives all at the same time.

b. Using Assessment Data

Organizing assessment data is essential and it is important that all personnel are aware as to what is available about each learner and where it can be found. Rating scales, for example, record information on work habits, social behavior, and the like. Checklists concerning behaviors are very common.

There are several ways of managing data. A teacher may prepare a wall chart in which the student's names are listed down on one side and learning objectives across the top. A date is noted in the appropriate box when a student has reached that objective. The information is at once visible to the students. One must watch that the chart does not cause undue competition among the students.

Punch cards are the heart of another management system. There is a card for each student in each subject area or educational goal. When a student achieves an objective, that square on the card is punched open with a hand card punch. Cards are stored in a box. If a teacher wants to know which children have achieved a certain objective, a metal skewer is inserted into the cards and run through holes in cards in the square marking a specific learning objective.

The unpunched cards can be allowed to drop as the skewer approaches them; these indicate the students who have not yet reached the goal.

So far, computers are not feasible for most schools. However, many do have access to a central computer on a time-sharing basis. If you do have this opportunity, give your programmer all the information and cooperation that he or she needs to tailor a program to fit your needs and then be prepared to learn the few skills and concepts that it takes to effectively use the system that the programmer devises.

c. Analyzing Assessment Data

In addition to analyzing assessment data in meetings of the IGE Planning System, analysis should occur in student-teacher, parent-student-teacher, and other meetings related to student achievement. An agenda should be prepared and circulated before each Unit meeting. It should describe the assessment tasks that are going to be discussed at the meeting. These include: planning assessment procedures, analyzing results of assessment, consideration of new assessment materials, or grouping. Assignments may be made during the meeting creating certain "task force" groups of Unit members to handle any of the missions mentioned, and brainstorm new assessment means to prepare assessment results for analysis by the whole team.

d. Planning Learning Programs

The planning of learning programs includes the selection of materials, time blocks, space, and the formation of groups for learning. These decisions are always closely tied to the information gained from assessment.

Possible alternative programs for learning should be available from the beginning. Then, when the Unit meets to examine assessment results, the details of these programs can begin to be finalized.

Responsibilities for various aspects of a learning segment might be divided among the teachers in a Unit. One or two teachers might take the responsibility for examining records and assessment data on the learners and devising appropriate plans for a learning segment. These plans would then be reviewed by the other teachers. At the next meetings, coordination of the plans would take place in terms of time, space, and staff requirements. During all these meetings, each teacher can keep in mind her knowledge of assessment results and of individual learners in order to provide constructive feedback at each stage of the planning.

e. Choosing New Objectives

Assessment results show either that a learner needs more work or that he is demonstrating a suitable level of achievement of his objective. In the first case, assessment is used to show the learner's needs; a new learning program and ongoing assessment follow. The second case, achievement of one objective calls for a new objective to be chosen. There are several possible responses to this result, depending on timing and on the type of objective achieved.

f. Learner Involvement

The learners must be involved in their own learning process. Objectives should always be stated so that learners can understand them and measure their own performance or behavior against the objectives.

Use of individual folders, to which the learner has ready access, also encourages involvement with his or her own progress. The most effective way of involving learners in assessment is to enable them to assess their own performance for achievement of objectives. Student-prepared checklists can be used in areas where the same basic skill has to be applied in different areas. The student can practice independently or with peers and can record his or her own progress in other applications.

g. Communicating Assessment Information

Assessment becomes meaningful when shared with teachers, learners, and parents. Students should know assessment results and the effects that those results will have on their learning program. The teacher is responsible for sharing results with the learner. Failure should not be a punishment; it should be a shared concern. The sharing must be honest and candid. Many children do not really feel disappointed with failure until adults put the onus of shame on it.

Parents should be involved in assessment, when possible, and should be kept informed. There are several kinds of parent reports. Both written reports and scheduled parent-teacher conferences are essential parts of the parental side of assessment. Although the reports usually are divided into subject areas and sub-skills, at this point the link with traditional reporting methods ends.

The normal five or six grades of the evaluative scale are replaced by a more individualized means of reporting. A note to parents should accompany the report to explain it more fully; that is, the idea of relating a learner to his own capacity rather than to the achievement of others. The grade is often a "plus or minus," indicating a learner's performance compared to reasonable expectations for him or her. A written commentary would usually accompany the report to give more explanation to the pluses and/or minuses.

There is an imperative need for live teacher-parent communication about the child's development. Conferences should be scheduled at least twice a year. The tone of the conferences should be constructive.

As one can see, communication plays a major role in IGE assessment: communication between student and teacher, teacher and teacher, teacher and parent. The sharing of assessment information by everyone involved with the learner is essential for the learner's optimum development.

Appendixes

Appendix A

A Condensed Version of the Cognitive Domain of the Taxonomy of Educational Objectives [1]

KNOWLEDGE

1:00 KNOWLEDGE

Knowledge, as defined here, involves the recall of specifics and universals, the recall of methods and processes, or the recall of a pattern, structure, or setting. For measurement purposes, the recall situation involves little more than bringing to mind the appropriate material. Although some alteration of the material may be required, this is a relatively minor part of the task. The knowledge of objectives emphasizes most the psychological processes of remembering. The process of relating is also involved in that a knowledge test situation requires the organization and reorganization of a problem such that it will furnish the appropriate signals and cues for the information and knowledge the individual possesses. To use an analogy, if one thinks of the mind as a file, the problem in a knowledge test situation is that of finding in the problem or task the appropriate signals, cues, and clues which will most effectively bring out whatever knowledge is filed or stored.

1.10 Knowledge of Specifics

The recall of specific and isolable bits of information. The emphasis is on symbols with concrete referents. This material, which is at a very low level of abstraction, may be considered the elements from which more complex and abstract forms of knowledge are built.

1.11 Knowledge of Terminology

Knowledge of the referents for specific symbols (verbal and nonverbal). This may include knowledge of the most generally accepted symbol referent, knowledge of the variety of symbols which may be

1. From Benjamin S. Bloom (editor), Max D. Engelhart, Edward J. Furst, Walker H. Hill, and David R. Krathwohl, *Taxonomy of Educational Objectives, Handbook I:Cognitive Domain,* David McKay Company, 1956, pp. 201-207. Reprinted with permission of the publishers.

used for a single referent, or knowledge of the referent most appropriate to a given use of a symbol.

To define technical terms by giving their attributes properties or relations.

Familiarity with a large number of works in their common range of meanings.[2]

1.12   Knowledge of Specific Facts

Knowledge of dates, events, persons, places, etc. This may include very precise and specific information such as the specific date or exact magnitude of a phenomenon.

The recall of major facts about particular cultures.

The possession of a minimum knowledge about the organisms studied in the laboratory.

1.20   Knowledge of Ways and Means of Dealing with Specifics

Knowledge of the ways of organizing, studying, judging, and criticizing. This includes the methods of inquiry, the chronological sequences, and the standards of judgment within a field as well as the patterns of organization through which the areas of the fields themselves are determined and internally organized. This knowledge is at an intermediate level of abstraction between specific knowledge on the one hand and knowledge of universals on the other. It does not so much demand the activity of the student in using the materials as it does a more passive awareness of their nature.

1.21   Knowledge of Conventions

Knowledge of characteristic ways of treating and presenting ideas and phenomena. For purposes of communication and consistency, workers in a field employ usages, styles, practices, and forms which best suit their purposes and/or which appear to suit best the phenomena with which they deal. It should be recognized that although these forms and conventions are likely to be set up on arbitrary, accidental, or authoritative bases, they are retained because of the general agreement or concurrence of individuals concerned with the subject, phenomena, or problem.

Familiarity with the forms and conventions of the major types of work; e.g., verse, plays, scientific papers, etc.

To make pupils conscious of correct form and usage in speech and writing.

2. Each subcategory is followed by illustrative educational objectives selected from the literature.

1.22   Knowledge of Trends and Sequences

Knowledge of the processes, directions, and movements of phenomena with respect to time.

Understanding of the continuity and development of American culture as exemplified in American life.
Knowledge of the basic trends underlying the development of public assistance programs.

1.23   Knowledge of Classifications and Categories

Knowledge of the classes, sets, divisions, and arrangements which are regarded as fundamental for a given subject field, purpose, argument, or problem.

To recognize the area encompassed by various kinds of problems or materials.
Becoming familiar with a range of literature.

1.24   Knowledge of Criteria

Knowledge of the criteria by which facts, principles, opinions, and conduct are tested or judged.

Familiarity with criteria for judgment appropriate to the type of work and the purpose for which it is read.
Knowledge of criteria for the evaluation of recreational activities.

1.25   Knowledge of Methodology

Knowledge of the methods of inquiry, techniques, and procedures employed in a particular subject field as well as those employed in investigating particular problems and phenomena. The emphasis here is on the individual's knowledge of the method rather than his ability to use the method.

Knowledge of scientific methods of evaluating health concepts.
The student shall know the methods of attack relevant to the kinds of problems of concern to the social sciences.

1.30   Knowledge of the Universals and Abstractions in a Field

Knowledge of the major schemes and patterns by which phenomena and ideas are organized. These are the large structures, theories, and generalizations which dominate a subject field or which are quite generally used in studying phenomena or solving problems. These are at the highest levels of abstraction and complexity.

1.31   Knowledge of Principles and Generalizations

Knowledge of particular abstractions which summarize observations of phenomena. These are the abstractions which are of value in explaining, describing, predicting, or in determining the most appropriate and relevant action or direction to be taken.

Knowledge of the important principles by which our experience with biological phenomena is summarized.
The recall of major generalizations about particular cultures.

1.32 Knowledge of Theories and Structures

Knowledge of the body of principles and generalizations together with their interrelations which present a clear, rounded, and systematic view of a complex phenomenon, problem, or field. These are the most abstract formulations, and they can be used to show the interrelation and organization of a great range of specifics.

The recall of major theories about particular cultures.
Knowledge of a relatively complete formulation of the theory of evolution.

INTELLECTUAL ABILITIES AND SKILLS

Abilities and skills refer to organized modes of operation and generalized techniques for dealing with materials and problems. The materials and problems may be of such a nature that little or no specialized and technical information is required. Such information as is required can be assumed to be part of the individual's general fund of knowledge. Other problems may require specialized and technical information at a rather high level such that specific knowledge and skill in dealing with the problem and the materials are required. The abilities and skills objectives emphasize the mental processes of organizing and reorganizing material to achieve a particular purpose.

2.00 COMPREHENSION

This represents the lowest level of understanding. It refers to a type of understanding or comprehension such that the individual knows what is being communicated and can make use of the material or idea being communicated without necessarily relating it to other material or seeing its fullest implications.

2.10 Translation

Comprehension as evidenced by the care and accuracy with which the communication is paraphrased or rendered from one language or form of communication to another. Translation is judged on the basis of faithfulness and accuracy; that is, on the extent to which the material in the original communication is preserved although the form of the communication has been altered.

The ability to understand nonliteral statements (metaphor, symbolism, irony, exaggeration).

Skill in translating mathematical verbal material into symbolic statements and vice versa.

2.20   Interpretation

The explanation or summarization of a communication. Whereas translation involves an objective part-for-part rendering of a communication, interpretation involves a reordering, rearrangement, or new view of the material.

The ability to grasp the thought of the work as a whole at any desired level of generality.

The ability to interpret various types of social data.

2.30   Extrapolation

The extension of trends or tendencies beyond the given data to determine implications, consequences, corollaries, effects, etc., which are in accordance with the conditions described in the original communication.

The ability to deal with the conclusions of a work in terms of the immediate inference made from the explicit statements.

Skills in predicting continuation of trends.

3.00   APPLICATION

The use of abstractions in particular and concrete situations. The abstractions may be in the form of general ideas, rules of procedures, or generalized methods. The abstractions may also be technical principles, ideas, and theories which must be remembered and applied.

Application to the phenomena discussed in one paper of the scientific terms or concepts used in other papers.

The ability to predict the probable effect of a change in a factor on a biological situation previously at equilibrium.

4.00   ANALYSIS

The breakdown of a communication into its constituent elements or parts such that the relative hierarchy of ideas is made clear and/or the relations between the ideas expressed are made explicit. Such analyses are intended to clarify the communication, to indicate how the communication is organized, and the way in which it manages to convey its effects, as well as its basis and arrangement.

4.10   Analysis of Elements

Identification of the elements included in a communication.

The ability to recognize unstated assumptions.

Skill in distinguishing facts from hypotheses.

4.20   Analysis of Relationships

The connections and interactions between elements and parts of a communication.

> Ability to check the consistency of hypotheses with given information and assumptions.
> Skill in comprehending the interrelationships among the ideas in a passage.

4.30   Analysis of Organizational Principles

The organization, systematic arrangement, and structure which hold the communication together. This includes the "explicit" as well as "implicit" structure. It includes the bases, necessary arrangement, and mechanics which make the communication a unit.

> The ability to recognize form and pattern in literary or artistic works as a means of understanding their meaning.
> Ability to recognize the general techniques used in persuasive materials, such as advertising, propaganda, etc.

5.00   SYNTHESIS

The putting together of elements and parts so as to form a whole. This involves the process of working with pieces, parts, elements, etc., and arranging and combining them in such a way as to constitute a pattern or structure not clearly there before.

5.10   Production of a Unique Communication

The development of a communication in which the writer or speaker attempts to convey ideas, feelings, and/or experiences to others.

> Skill in writing, using an excellent organization of ideas and statements.
> Ability to tell a personal experience effectively.

5.20   Production of a Plan, or Proposed Set of Operations

The development of a plan of work or the proposal of a plan of operations. The plan should satisfy requirements of the task which may be given to the student or which he may develop for himself.

> Ability to propose ways of testing hypotheses.
> Ability to plan a unit of instruction for a particular teaching situation.

5.30   Derivation of a Set of Abstract Relations

The development of a set of abstract relations either to classify or explain particular data or phenomena, or the deduction of propositions and relations from a set of basic propositions or symbolic representations.

Ability to formulate appropriate hypotheses based upon an analysis of factors involved, and to modify such hypotheses in the light of new factors and considerations.

Ability to make mathematical discoveries and generalizations.

6.00   EVALUATION

Judgments about the value of material and methods for given purposes. Quantitative and qualitative judgments about the extent to which material and methods satisfy criteria. Use of a standard of appraisal. The criteria may be those determined by the student or those which are given to him.

6.10   Judgments in Terms of Internal Evidence

Evaluation of the accuracy of a communication from such evidence as logical accuracy, consistency, and other internal criteria.

Judging by internal standards, the ability to assess general probability of accuracy in reporting facts from the care given to exactness of statement, documentation, proof, etc.

The ability to indicate logical fallacies in arguments.

6.20   Judgments in Terms of External Criteria

Evaluations of material with reference to selected or remembered criteria.

The comparison of major theories, generalizations, and facts about particular cultures.

Judging by external standards, the ability to compare a work with the highest known standards in its field—especially with other works of recognized excellence.

Appendix B

A Condensed Version of the Affective Domain of the Taxonomy of Educational Objectives[1]

1.0 RECEIVING (ATTENDING)

At this level we are concerned that the learner be sensitized to the existence of certain phenomena and stimuli; that is, that he be willing to receive or to attend them. This is clearly the first and crucial step if the learner is to be properly oriented to learn what the teacher intends that he will. To indicate that this is the bottom rung of the ladder, however, is not at all to imply that the teacher is starting *de novo*. Because of previous experience (formal or informal), the student brings to each situation a point of view or set which may facilitate or hinder his recognition of the phenomena to which the teacher is trying to sensitize him.

1.1 Awareness

Awareness is almost a cognitive behavior. But unlike *Knowledge,* the lowest level of the cognitive domain, we are not so much concerned with a memory of, or ability to recall, an item or fact as we are that, given appropriate opportunity, the learner will merely be conscious of something—that he take into account a situation, phenomenon, object, or state of affairs. Like *Knowledge* it does not imply an assessment of the qualities or nature of the stimulus, but unlike *Knowledge* it does not necessarily imply attention. There can be simple awareness without specific discrimination or recognition of the objective characteristics of the object, even though these characteristics must be deemed to have an effect. The individual may not be able to verbalize the aspects of the stimulus which cause the awareness.

1. From David R. Krathwohl, Benjamin S. Bloom, and Bertram B. Masia, *Taxonomy of Educational Objectives, Handbook II: Affective Domain,* David McKay Company, 1964, pp. 176-185. Reprinted with permission of the publishers.

Develops awareness of aesthetic factors in dress, furnishings, architecture, city design, good art, and the like.

Develops some consciousness of color, form, arrangement, and design in the objects and structures around him and in descriptive or symbolic representations of people, things, and situations.[2]

1.2   Willingness to Receive

In this category we have come a step up the ladder but are still dealing with what appears to be cognitive behavior. At a minimum level, we are here describing the behavior of being willing to tolerate a given stimulus, not to avoid it. Like *Awareness*, it involves a neutrality or suspended judgment toward the stimulus. At this level of the continuum the teacher is not concerned that the student seek it out, nor even, perhaps, that in an environment crowded with many other stimuli, the learner will necessarily attend to the stimulus. Rather, at worst, given the opportunity to attend in a field with relatively few competing stimuli, the learner is not actively seeking to avoid it. At best, he is willing to take notice of the phenomenon and give it his attention.

Attends (carefully) when others speak—in direct conversation, on the telephone, in audiences.

Appreciation (tolerance) of cultural patterns, exhibited by individuals from other groups—religious, social, political, economic, national, etc.

Increase in sensitivity to human need and pressing social problems.

1.3   Controlled or Selected Attention

At a somewhat higher level we are concerned with a new phenomenon, the differentiation of a given stimulus into figure and ground at a conscious or perhaps semiconscious level—the differentiation of aspects of a stimulus which is perceived as clearly marked off from adjacent impressions. The perception is still without tension or assessment, and the student may not know the technical terms or symbols with which to describe it correctly or precisely to others. In some instances it may refer not so much to the selectivity of attention as to the control of attention, so that when certain stimuli are present they will be attended to. There is an element of the learner's controlling the attention here, so that the favored stimulus is selected and attended to despite competing and distracting stimuli.

Listens to music with some discrimination as to its mood and meaning and with some recognition of the contributions of various musical elements and instruments to the total effect.

Alertness toward human values and judgments on life as they are recorded in literature.

---

2. Illustrative objectives selected from the literature follow the description of each subcategory.

2.0 RESPONDING

At this level we are concerned with responses which go beyond merely attending to the phenomenon. The student is sufficiently motivated that he is not just 1.2 *Willing to receive,* but perhaps it is correct to say that he is actively attending. As a first stage in a "learning by doing" process the student is committing himself in some small measure to the phenomena involved. This is a very low level of commitment, and we would not say at this level that this was "a value of his" or that he had "such and such an attitude." These terms belong to the next higher level that we describe. But we could say that he is doing something with or about the phenomenon besides merely perceiving it, as would be true at the next level below this of 1.3 *Controlled or selected attention.*

This is the category that many teachers will find best describes their "interest" objectives. Most commonly we use the term to indicate the desire that a child become sufficiently involved in or committed to a subject phenomenon, or activity that he will seek it out and gain satisfaction from working with it or engaging in it.

2.1 Acquiescence in Responding

We might use the word "obedience" or "compliance" to describe this behavior. As both of these terms indicate, there is a passiveness so far as the initiation of the behavior is concerned, and the stimulus calling for this behavior is not subtle. Compliance is perhaps a better term than obedience. since there is more of the element of reaction to a suggestion and less of the implication of resistance or yielding unwillingly. The student makes the responses, but he has not fully accepted the necessity for doing so.

> Willingness to comply with health regulations.
> Obeys playground regulations.

2.2 Willingness to Respond

The key to this level is in the term "willingness," with its implication of capacity for voluntary activity. There is the implication that the learner is sufficiently committed to exhibiting the behavior that he does so not just because of a fear of punishment, but "on his own" or voluntarily. It may help to note that the element of resistance or of yielding unwillingly, which is possibly present at the previous level, is here replaced with consent or proceeding from one's own choice.

> Acquaints himself with significant current issues in international, political, social, and economic affairs through voluntary reading and discussion.
> Acceptance of responsibility for his own health and for the protection of the health of others.

2.3   Satisfaction in Response

The additional element in the step beyond the *Willingness to respond* level, the consent, the assent to responding, or the voluntary response, is that the behavior is accompanied by a feeling of satisfaction, an emotional response, generally of pleasure, zest, or enjoyment. The location of this category in the hierarchy has given us a great deal of difficulty. Just where in the process of internalization the attachment of an emotional response, kick, or thrill to a behavior occurs has been hard to determine. For that matter there is some uncertainty as to whether the level of internalization at which it occurs may not depend on the particular behavior. We have even questioned whether it should be a category. If your structure is to be a hierarchy, then each category should include the behavior in the next level below it. The emotional component appears gradually through the range of internalization categories. The attempt to specify a given position in the hierarchy as the one at which the emotional component is added is doomed to failure.

The category is arbitrarily placed at this point in the hierarchy where it seems to appear most frequently and where it is cited as or appears to be an important component of the objectives at this level on the continuum. The category's inclusion at this point serves the pragmatic purpose of reminding us of the presence of the emotional component and its value in the building of affective behaviors. But it should not be thought of as appearing and occurring at this one point in the continuum and thus destroying the hierarchy which we are attempting to build.

> Enjoyment of self-expression in music and in arts and crafts as another means of personal enrichment.
>
> Finds pleasure in reading for recreation.
>
> Finds pleasure in conversing with many different kinds of people.

3.0   VALUING

This is the only category headed by a term which is in common use in the expression of objectives by teachers. Further, it is employed in its usual sense: that a thing, phenomenon, or behavior has worth. This abstract concept of worth is in part a result of the individual's own valuing or assessment, but it is much more a social product that has been slowly internalized or accepted and has come to be used by the student as his own criterion of worth.

Behavior categorized at this level is sufficiently consistent and stable to have taken on the characteristics of a belief or an attitude. The learner displays this behavior with sufficient consistency in appropriate situations that he comes to be perceived as holding a value. At this level, we are not concerned with the relationships among values but rather with the internalization of a set of specified, ideal values. Viewed from another standpoint, the objectives classified here are the prime stuff from which the conscience of the individual is developed into active control of behavior.

This category will be found appropriate for many objectives that use the term "attitude" (as well as, of course, "value").

An important element of behavior characterized by *valuing* is that it is motivated, not by the desire to comply or obey, but by the individual's commitment to the underlying value guiding the behavior.

3.1 Acceptance of a Value

At this level we are concerned with the ascribing of worth to a phenomenon, behavior, object, etc. The term "belief," which is defined as "the emotional acceptance of a proposition or doctrine upon what one implicitly considers adequate ground" (English and English, 1958, p. 64), describes quite well what may be thought of as the dominant characteristic here. Beliefs have varying degrees of certitude. At this lowest level of *valuing* we are concerned with the lowest levels of certainty; that is, there is more of a readiness to re-evaluate one's position than at the higher levels. It is a position that is somewhat tentative.

One of the distinguishing characteristics of this behavior is consistency of response to the class of objects, phenomena, etc., with which the belief or attitude is identified. It is consistent enough so that the person is perceived by others as holding the belief or value. At the level we are describing here, he is both sufficiently consistent that others can identify the value, and sufficiently committed that he is willing to be so identified.

> Continuing desire to develop the ability to speak and write effectively.
> Grows in his sense of kinship with human beings of all nations.

3.2 Preference for a Value

The provision for this subdivision arose out of a feeling that there were objectives that expressed a level of internalization between the mere acceptance of a value and commitment of conviction in the usual connotation of a deep involvement in an area. Behavior at this level implies not just the acceptance of a value to the point of being willing to be identified with it, but the individual is sufficiently committed to the value to pursue it, to seek it out, to want it.

> Assumes responsibility for drawing reticent members of a group into conversation.
> Deliberately examines a variety of viewpoints on a controversial issue with a view to forming opinions about them.
> Actively participates in arranging for the showing of contemporary artistic efforts.

3.3   Commitment

Belief at this level involves a high degree of certainty. The ideas of "conviction" and "certainty beyond a shadow of doubt" help to convey further the level of behavior intended. In some instances this may border on faith, in the sense of its being a firm emotional acceptance of a belief upon admittedly non-rational grounds. Loyalty to a position, group, or cause would also be classified here.

The person who displays behavior at this level is clearly perceived as holding the value. He acts to further the thing valued in some way, to extend the possibility of his developing it, to deepen his involvement with it and with the things representing it. He tries to convince others and seeks converts to his cause. There is a tension here which needs to be satisfied; action is the result of an aroused need or drive. There is a real motivation to act out the behavior.

> Devotion to those ideas and ideals which are the foundations of democracy.
> Faith in the power of reason and in methods of experiment and discussion.

4.0   ORGANIZATION

As the learner successively internalizes values, he encounters situations for which more than one value is relevant. Thus necessity arises for (a) the organization of the values into a system, (b) the determination of the interrelationships among them, and (c) the establishment of the dominant and pervasive ones. Such a system is built gradually, subject to change as new values are incorporated. This category is intended as the proper classification for objectives which describe the beginnings of the building of a value system. It is subdivided into two levels, since a prerequisite to interrelating is the conceptualization of the value in a form which permits organization. *Conceptualization* forms the first subdivision in the organization process; *Organization of a value system* the second.

While the order of the two subcategories seems appropriate enough with reference to one another, it is not so certain that 4.1 *Conceptualization of a value* is properly placed as the next level above 3.3 *Commitment.* Conceptualization undoubtedly begins at an earlier level for some objectives. Like 2.3 *Satisfaction in response,* it is doubtful that a single completely satisfactory location for this category can be found. Positioning it before 4.2 *Organization of a value system* appropriately indicates a prerequisite of such a system. It also calls attention to a component of affective growth that occurs at least by this point on the continuum but may begin earlier.

4.1   Conceptualization of a Value

In the previous category, 3.0 *Valuing,* we noted that consistency and stability are integral characteristics of the particular value or belief. At this level (4.1) the quality of abstraction or conceptualization is added. This permits the individual to see how the value relates to those that he already holds or to new ones that he is coming to hold.

Conceptualization will be abstract, and in this sense it will be symbolic. But the symbols need not be verbal symbols. Whether conceptualization first appears at this point on the affective continuum is a moot point, as noted above.

> Attempts to identify the characteristics of an art object which he admires.
>
> Forms judgments as to the responsibility of society for conserving human and material sources.

4.2   Organization of a Value System

Objectives properly classified here are those which require the learner to bring together a complex of values, possibly disparate values, and to bring these into an ordered relationship with one another. Ideally, the ordered relationship will be one which is harmonious and internally consistent. This is, of course, the goal of such objectives, which seek to have the student formulate a philosophy of life. In actuality, the integration may be something less than entirely harmonious. More likely the relationship is better described as a kind of dynamic equilibrium which is, in part, dependent upon those portions of the environment which are salient at any point in time. In many instances the organization of values may result in their synthesis into a new value or value complex of a high order.

> Weighs alternative social policies and practices against the standards of the public welfare rather than the advantage of specialized and narrow interest groups.
>
> Develops a plan for regulating his rest in accordance with the demands of his activities.

5.0   CHARACTERIZATION BY A VALUE OR VALUE COMPLEX

At this level of internalization the values already have a place in the individual's value hierarchy, are organized into some kind of internally consistent system, have controlled the behavior of the individual for a sufficient time that he has adapted to behaving this way; and an evocation of the behavior no longer arouses emotion or affect except when the individual is threatened or challenged.

The individual acts consistently in accordance with the values he has internalized at this level, and our concern is to indicate two things: (a) the generalization of this control to so much of the individual's behavior that he is described and characterized as a person by these pervasive controlling tendencies, and (b) the intergration of these beliefs, ideas, and attitudes into a total philosophy or world view. These two aspects constitute the sub-categories.

5.1   Generalized Set

The generalized set is that which gives an internal consistency to the system of attitudes and values at any particular moment. It is selective responding at a very high level. It is sometimes spoken of as a determining tendency, an orientation toward phenomena, or a predisposition to act in a certain way. The generalized set is a response to highly generalized phenomena. It is a persistent and consistent response to a family of related situations or objects. It may often be an unconscious set which guides action without conscious forethought. The generalized set may be thought of as closely related to the idea of an attitude cluster, where the commonality is based on behavioral characteristics rather than the subject or object of the attitude. A generalized set is a basic orientation which enables the individual to reduce and order the complex world about him and to act consistently and effectively in it.

> Readiness to revise judgments and to change behavior in the light of evidence.
> Judges problems and issues in terms of situations, issues, purposes, and consequences involved rather than in terms of fixed, dogmatic precepts of emotionally wishful thinking.

5.2   Characterization

This, the peak of internalization process, includes those objectives which are broadest with respect both to the phenomena covered and to the range of behavior which they comprise. Thus, here are found those objectives which concern one's view of the universe, one's philosophy of life, one's *Weltanschauung*—a value system having as its object the whole of what is known or knowable.

Objectives categorized here are more than generalized sets in the sense that they involve a greater inclusiveness and, within the group of attitudes, behaviors, beliefs, or ideas, an emphasis on internal consistency. Though the internal consistency may not always be exhibited behaviorally by the students toward whom the objective is directed, since we are categorizing teachers' objectives this consistency feature will always be a component of *Characterization* objectives.

As the title of the category implies, these objectives are so encompass-ing that they tend to characterize the individual almost completely.

> Develops for regulation of one's personal and civic life a code of be-havior based on ethical principles consistent with democratic ideas.
> Develops a consistent philosophy of life.

Appendix C

Illustrative Verbs[1]

Illustrative Verbs for Stating General Instructional Objectives

Analyze	Compute	Interpret	Perform	Translate
Apply	Create	Know	Recognize	Understand
Appreciate	Demonstrate	Listen	Speak	Use
Comprehend	Evaluate	Locate	Think	Write

Illustrative Verbs for Stating Specific Learning Outcomes

"Creative" Behaviors

Alter	Paraphrase	Reconstruct	Rephrase	Rewrite
Ask	Predict	Regroup	Restate	Simplify
Change	Question	Rename	Restructure	Synthesize
Design	Rearrange	Reorder	Retell	Systematize
Generalize	Recombine	Reorganize	Revise	Vary
Modify				

Complex, Logical, Judgmental Behaviors

Analyze	Conclude	Deduce	Formulate	Plan
Appraise	Contrast	Defend	Generate	Structure
Combine	Criticize	Evaluate	Induce	Substitute
Compare	Decide	Explain	Infer	

1. National College Verb List, developed by Calvin K. Claus, Psychology Department, National College of Education, Evanston, Ill. From a paper presented at the annual meeting of the National Council on Measurement in Education, Chicago, February, 1968. Printed by permission of C. K. Claus.

General Discriminative Behaviors

Choose	Detect	Identify	Match	Place
Collect	Differentiate	Indicate	Omit	Point
Define	Discriminate	Isolate	Order	Select
Describe	Distinguish	List	Pick	Separate

Social Behaviors

Accept	Communicate	Discuss	Invite	Praise
Agree	Compliment	Excuse	Join	React
Aid	Contribute	Forgive	Laugh	Smile
Allow	Cooperate	Greet	Meet	Talk
Answer	Dance	Help	Participate	Thank
Argue	Disagree	Interact	Permit	Volunteer

Language Behaviors

Abbreviate	Edit	Punctuate	Speak	Tell
Accent	Hyphenate	Read	Spell	Translate
Alphabetize	Indent	Recite	State	Verbalize
Articulate	Outline	Say	Summarize	Whisper
Call	Print	Sign	Syllabify	Write
Capitalize	Pronounce			

"Study" Behaviors

Arrange	Compile	Itemize	Mark	Record
Categorize	Copy	Label	Name	Reproduce
Chart	Diagram	Locate	Note	Search
Cite	Find	Look	Organize	Sort
Circle	Follow	Map	Quote	Underline

Music Behaviors

Blow	Compose	Hum	Pluck	Strum
Bow	Finger	Mute	Practice	Tap
Clap	Harmonize	Play	Sing	Whistle

Physical Behaviors

Arch	Face	Jump	Push	Step
Bat	Float	Kick	Run	Stretch
Bend	Grab	Knock	Skate	Swim
Carry	Grasp	Lift	Ski	Swing
Catch	Grip	March	Skip	Toss
Chase	Hit	Pitch	Somersault	Throw
Climb	Hop	Pull	Stand	Walk

Arts Behaviors

Assemble	Dot	Illustrate	Press	Stamp
Blend	Draw	Melt	Roll	Stick
Brush	Drill	Mix	Rub	Stir
Build	Fold	Mold	Sand	Trace
Carve	Form	Nail	Saw	Trim
Color	Frame	Paint	Sculpt	Varnish
Construct	Hammer	Paste	Shake	Wipe
Cut	Handle	Pat	Sketch	Wrap
Dab	Heat	Pour	Smooth	

Drama Behaviors

Act	Display	Express	Pass	Show
Clasp	Emit	Leave	Perform	Sit
Cross	Enter	Move	Proceed	Start
Direct	Exit	Pantomime	Respond	Turn

Mathematical Behaviors

Add	Derive	Group	Number	Square
Bisect	Divide	Integrate	Plot	Subtract
Calculate	Estimate	Interpolate	Prove	Tabulate
Check	Extrapolate	Measure	Reduce	Tally
Compute	Extract	Multiply	Solve	Verify
Count	Graph			

Laboratory Science Behaviors

Apply	Demonstrate	Keep	Prepare	Specify
Calibrate	Dissect	Lengthen	Remove	Straighten
Conduct	Feed	Limit	Replace	Time
Connect	Grow	Manipulate	Report	Transfer
Convert	Increase	Operate	Reset	Weigh
Decrease	Insert	Plant	Set	

General Appearance, Health, and Safety Behaviors

Button	Dress	Fasten	Taste	Unzip
Clean	Drink	Fill	Tie	Wait
Clear	Eat	Go	Unbutton	Wash
Close	Eliminate	Lace	Uncover	Wear
Comb	Empty	Stop	Untie	Zip
Cover				

Miscellaneous

Aim	Erase	Lead	Relate	Stake
Attempt	Expand	Lend	Repeat	Start
Attend	Extend	Let	Return	Stock
Begin	Feel	Light	Ride	Store
Bring	Finish	Make	Rip	Strike
Buy	Fit	Mend	Save	Suggest
Come	Fix	Miss	Scratch	Supply
Complete	Flip	Offer	Send	Support
Consider	Get	Open	Serve	Switch
Correct	Give	Pack	Sew	Take
Crease	Grind	Pay	Share	Tear
Crush	Guide	Peel	Sharpen	Touch
Designate	Hand	Pin	Shoot	Try
Determine	Hang	Position	Shorten	Twist
Develop	Hold	Present	Shovel	Type
Discover	Hook	Produce	Shut	Use
Distribute	Hunt	Propose	Signify	Vote
Do	Include	Provide	Slip	Watch
Drop	Inform	Put	Slide	Weave
End	Lay	Raise	Spread	Work

Appendix D

Computation of the Pearson-Product-Moment Coefficient of Correlation

In Chapter 3, the technique of correlation was explained and a co-efficient computed by the rank-difference method (rho). The rho formula is the simplest method of obtaining a coeffcient but is best suited to computation involving a small number of cases, say 10-30. The product-moment correlation index, r, is usually more accurate than the ρ(rho) coefficient since it takes into account the absolute size of the scores and not merely their rank order. This method is illustrated with ungrouped data in the following table.

TABLE D-1

Product-Moment Correlation

Pupil	X	Y	x	y	x^2	y^2	xy (+)	xy (−)
1	29	25	4	5	16	25	20	
2	26	21	1	1	1	1	1	
3	25	20	0	0	0	0	0	
4	21	17	−4	−3	16	9	12	
5	27	18	2	−2	4	4		4
6	24	19	−1	−1	1	1	1	
7	28	23	3	3	9	9	9	
8	23	22	−2	2	4	4		4
9	22	15	−3	−5	9	25	15	
10	25	20	0	0	0	0		
							(58)	(−8)

$N=10$ $\overline{X}=25$ $\overline{Y}=20$ $\Sigma x^2=60$ $\Sigma y^2=78$

$\Sigma xy = 50$ (algebraic)

$$r = \frac{\Sigma xy}{\sqrt{\Sigma x^2 \cdot \Sigma y^2}}$$

$$= \frac{50}{\sqrt{60 \cdot 78}}$$

$$= \frac{50}{\sqrt{4680}}$$

$$= \frac{50}{68.41}$$

$$= .73$$

Appendix E

Statistical Symbols and Formulas Commonly Used in Measurement

Most of the following symbols and abbreviations pertain to and define the unexplained symbols for the formulas which follow. However, a few popular symbols and abbreviations are included although they may not relate to the specific formulas here.

cfb	Cumulative frequency of cases below lower limit of interval
d	Deviation of score from an arbitrary origin
D	Difference in ranks
$\overline{D}$	Mean of the differences between X and Y scores
f	Frequency of cases
$G.A.$	Guessed average
H	High score in a series of scores
i	Length of the interval
L	Low score in a series of scores
LL	Lower limit of a class interval
$\overline{X}$ or M	Arithmetic mean
$Mdn.$	Median
$Mo.$	Mode
N or n	Number of cases
n_x and n_y	Number of cases in each sample
pN	Percentage of distribution desired
P_p	The desired percentile
PR or P_x	Percentile rank of score X
ρ	Rho — the coefficient of correlation calculated from the rank-difference method
Q	Quartile deviation or semi-interquartile range
Q_1	The first or lower quartile; same as the 25th percentile
Q_2	The second quartile, or median
Q_3	The third or upper quartile; the 75th percentile

r	Coefficient of correlation by Pearson product-moment method
R	Range of scores (variability) or rank of a score
RCU	Result count up into the distribution
s	The standard deviation of a particular sample distribution
$S.D.$ or σ	The standard deviation of a population distribution
SE_D	Standard error of the difference between means
$SE\ est.$	Standard error of estimate
SE_M	Standard error of the mean
$\sigma x \cdot y$	The standard error of estimate of X from Y
$\sigma y \cdot x$	The standard error of estimate of Y from X
Σ	Sum of; summation
Σx^2	Sum of the squared deviations in X from M_x
Σy^2	Sum of the squared deviations in Y from M_y
Σxy	Sum of the products of deviations x and y
t	t-ratio. The ratio of any normally distributed variate to its estimated standard error
T	T-score. A standard score with a mean of 50 and an SD of 10
x	The deviation of a score from the mean of its distribution or of a series
X	Each of a series of individual measurements or scores
z	A deviation from the mean of a distribution expressed as a multiple of the standard deviation

The following formulas are frequently used in both elementary and advanced statistics. Definitions of the symbols and abbreviations used may be found above.

1. The mean

For ungrouped data: M or $\overline{X} = \dfrac{\Sigma X}{N}$ or $\dfrac{\Sigma fX}{N}$

For grouped data: M or $\overline{X} = G.A. + \left(\dfrac{\Sigma fd}{N}\right) i$

2. The median

For ungrouped data: $Mdn = \dfrac{N+1}{2}$

For grouped data: $LL + \left(\dfrac{N/2 - cfb}{f}\right) i$

3. The mode
   The score that occurs most frequently (the definition is its formula)
4. The range
   $R = H - L$
5. Quartile deviation (Q) or semi-interquartile range

$$Q = \frac{Q_3 - Q_1}{2}$$

6. Standard deviation

   For ungrouped data: $S.D.$ or $\sigma = \sqrt{\dfrac{\Sigma x^2}{N}}$ or $\sqrt{\dfrac{\Sigma f d^2}{N}}$

   For grouped data: $S.D.$ or $\sigma = i \sqrt{\dfrac{\Sigma f d^2}{N} - \left(\dfrac{\Sigma f d^2}{N}\right)^2}$

   The symbol s is used instead of σ for a particular sample standard deviation.
7. Percentiles

   For ungrouped data: $P = p_x$ of N (Count Up)

   For grouped data: $P_P = LL + i\left(\dfrac{pN - cfb}{f}\right)$

8. Percentile rank

   For ungrouped ranked data: $PR = 100 - \left(\dfrac{100R - 50}{N}\right)$

   For grouped data: $P_x = 100 \left[\dfrac{i\,(cfb) + f\,(X\text{-}LL)}{iN}\right]$

9. Standard score (z) $z = \dfrac{x}{\sigma} = \dfrac{X - M}{\sigma}$

10. T-score $50 + 10 \dfrac{(X - \bar{X})}{\sigma}$ or $10z + 50$

11. Stanine $= 2z + 5$

12. Deviation IQ $= 15z + 100$

13. Rank-difference coefficient of correlation (rho)

$$r = 1.00 - \left(\frac{6\,\Sigma D^2}{N(N^2-1)}\right)$$

14. Pearson product-moment coefficient of correlation
From original score values:

$$r_{XY} = \cfrac{\Sigma XY - \cfrac{(\Sigma X)\ (\Sigma Y)}{N}}{\sqrt{\Sigma X^2 - \cfrac{(\Sigma X)^2}{N}}\ \ \sqrt{\Sigma Y^2 - \cfrac{(\Sigma Y)^2}{N}}}$$

From deviation scores: $r = \cfrac{\Sigma xy}{\sqrt{\Sigma x^2 \cdot \Sigma y^2}}$

15. Standard error of estimate *(SE est.)*

$$\sigma x \cdot y = \sigma y\ \sqrt{1 - r^2_{xy}} \quad \text{or} \quad \sigma y \cdot x = \sigma x\ \sqrt{1 - r^2_{yx}}$$

16. Standard error of measurement

$$SEM = S_X\ \sqrt{1 - r_{XX}}$$

Appendix F

How to Compute
the Square Root of a Number

1. Point off by twos to the left and the right of the decimal point (if whole number, place decimal and point off). Add two zeroes after the decimal for each place to which you desire to report the answer.

$$349.42 = \sqrt{3'49.42'00'}$$

2. Find the largest number whose square will go into the first bracket (3) and place it as the first number in the root.

$$\begin{array}{c} 1 \\ \overline{\sqrt{3'49.42'00'}} \end{array}$$

3. Place this number also under the first bracket and subtract. Bring down the next bracket of two numbers.

$$\begin{array}{c} 1 \\ \overline{\sqrt{3'49.42'00'}} \\ \underline{1} \\ 2\ 49 \end{array}$$

4. Multiply the first number in the root (1) by two and add a zero. Place this product as the trial divisor to the left of the new dividend.

$$\begin{array}{c} 1 \\ \overline{\sqrt{3'49.42'00'}} \\ \underline{1} \\ 20\ \overline{)2\ 49} \end{array}$$

5. Decide how many times the trial divisor will go into the new dividend. Write this figure above the appropriate bracket and also in place of the zero in the trial divisor.

$$
\begin{array}{r}
1\ 8 \\
\sqrt{3'49.42'00'} \\
1 \\
28\ /\overline{2\ 49}
\end{array}
$$

6. Multiply the divisor by the new number in the root. Place the product under the current dividend, subtract, bring down the next two numbers, and continue the process until square root is obtained to the desired number of places.

$$
\begin{array}{r}
1\ 8.\ 6\ 9 \\
\sqrt{3'49.42'00'} \\
1 \\
28\ /\overline{2\ 49} \\
2\ 24 \\
366\ /\overline{25\ 42} \\
21\ 96 \\
346\quad 00 \\
3729\ /\overline{335\quad 61}
\end{array}
$$

7. The square root of 349.42 = 18.69.

Appendix G

Tables of Squares
and Square Roots

N	N^2	N	N^2	N	N^2
1	1	51	2601	101	10201
2	4	52	2704	102	10404
3	9	53	2809	103	10609
4	16	54	2916	104	10816
5	25	55	3025	105	11025
6	36	56	3136	106	11236
7	49	57	3249	107	11449
8	64	58	3364	108	11664
9	81	59	3481	109	11881
10	100	60	3600	110	12100
11	121	61	3721	111	12321
12	144	62	3844	112	12544
13	169	63	3969	113	12769
14	196	64	4096	114	12996
15	225	65	4225	115	13225
16	256	66	4356	116	13456
17	289	67	4489	117	13689
18	324	68	4624	118	13924
19	361	69	4761	119	14161
20	400	70	4900	120	14400
21	441	71	5041	121	14641
22	484	72	5184	122	14884
23	529	73	5329	123	15129
24	576	74	5476	124	15376
25	625	75	5625	125	15625
26	676	76	5776	126	15876
27	729	77	5929	127	16129
28	784	78	6084	128	16384
29	841	79	6241	129	16641
30	900	80	6400	130	16900
31	961	81	6561	131	17161
32	1024	82	6724	132	17424
33	1089	83	6889	133	17689
34	1156	84	7056	134	17956
35	1225	85	7225	135	18225
36	1296	86	7396	136	18496
37	1369	87	7569	137	18769
38	1444	88	7744	138	19044
39	1521	89	7921	139	19321
40	1600	90	8100	140	19600
41	1681	91	8281	141	19881
42	1764	92	8464	142	20164
43	1849	93	8649	143	20449
44	1936	94	8836	144	20736
45	2025	95	9025	145	21025
46	2116	96	9216	146	21316
47	2209	97	9409	147	21609
48	2304	98	9604	148	21904
49	2401	99	9801	149	22201
50	2500	100	10000	150	22500

N	$\sqrt{N}$	N	$\sqrt{N}$	N	$\sqrt{N}$
1	1.000	51	7.141	101	10.050
2	1.414	52	7.211	102	10.100
3	1.732	53	7.280	103	10.149
4	2.000	54	7.348	104	10.198
5	2.236	55	7.416	105	10.247
6	2.449	56	7.483	106	10.296
7	2.646	57	7.550	107	10.344
8	2.828	58	7.616	108	10.392
9	3.000	59	7.681	109	10.440
10	3.162	60	7.746	110	10.488
11	3.317	61	7.810	111	10.536
12	3.464	62	7.874	112	10.583
13	3.606	63	7.937	113	10.630
14	3.742	64	8.000	114	10.677
15	3.873	65	8.062	115	10.724
16	4.000	66	8.124	116	10.770
17	4.123	67	8.185	117	10.817
18	4.243	68	8.246	118	10.863
19	4.359	69	8.307	119	10.909
20	4.472	70	8.367	120	10.954
21	4.583	71	8.426	121	11.000
22	4.690	72	8.485	122	11.045
23	4.796	73	8.544	123	11.091
24	4.899	74	8.602	124	11.136
25	5.000	75	8.660	125	11.180
26	5.099	76	8.718	126	11.225
27	5.196	77	8.775	127	11.269
28	5.292	78	8.832	128	11.314
29	5.385	79	8.888	129	11.358
30	5.477	80	8.944	130	11.402
31	5.568	81	9.000	131	11.446
32	5.657	82	9.055	132	11.489
33	5.745	83	9.110	133	11.533
34	5.831	84	9.165	134	11.576
35	5.916	85	9.220	135	11.619
36	6.000	86	9.274	136	11.662
37	6.083	87	9.327	137	11.705
38	6.164	88	9.381	138	11.747
39	6.245	89	9.434	139	11.790
40	6.325	90	9.487	140	11.832
41	6.403	91	9.539	141	11.874
42	6.481	92	9.592	142	11.916
43	6.557	93	9.644	143	11.958
44	6.633	94	9.695	144	12.000
45	6.708	95	9.747	145	12.042
46	6.782	96	9.798	146	12.083
47	6.856	97	9.849	147	12.124
48	6.928	98	9.899	148	12.166
49	7.000	99	9.950	149	12.207
50	7.071	100	10.000	150	12.247

N	$\sqrt{N}$	N	$\sqrt{N}$	N	$\sqrt{N}$	N	$\sqrt{N}$	N	$\sqrt{N}$	N	$\sqrt{N}$
151	12.288	201	14.177	251	15.843	301	17.349	351	18.735	401	20.025
152	12.329	202	14.213	252	15.875	302	17.378	352	18.762	402	20.050
153	12.369	203	14.248	253	15.906	303	17.407	353	18.788	403	20.075
154	12.410	204	14.283	254	15.937	304	17.436	354	18.815	404	20.100
155	12.450	205	14.318	255	15.969	305	17.464	355	18.841	405	20.125
156	12.490	206	14.353	256	16.000	306	17.493	356	18.868	406	20.149
157	12.530	207	14.387	257	16.031	307	17.521	357	18.894	407	20.174
158	12.570	208	14.422	258	16.062	308	17.550	358	18.921	408	20.199
159	12.610	209	14.457	259	16.093	309	17.578	359	18.947	409	20.224
160	12.649	210	14.491	260	16.125	310	17.607	360	18.974	410	20.248
161	12.689	211	14.526	261	16.155	311	17.635	361	19.000	411	20.273
162	12.728	212	14.560	262	16.186	312	17.664	362	19.026	412	20.298
163	12.767	213	14.595	263	16.217	313	17.692	363	19.053	413	20.322
164	12.806	214	14.629	264	16.248	314	17.720	364	19.079	414	20.347
165	12.845	215	14.663	265	16.279	315	17.748	365	19.105	415	20.372
166	12.884	216	14.697	266	16.310	316	17.776	366	19.131	416	20.396
167	12.923	217	14.731	267	16.340	317	17.804	367	19.157	417	20.421
168	12.961	218	14.765	268	16.371	318	17.833	368	19.183	418	20.445
169	13.000	219	14.799	269	16.401	319	17.861	369	19.209	419	20.469
170	13.038	220	14.832	270	16.432	320	17.889	370	19.235	420	20.494
171	13.077	221	14.866	271	16.462	321	17.916	371	19.261	421	20.518
172	13.115	222	14.900	272	16.492	322	17.944	372	19.287	422	20.543
173	13.153	223	14.933	273	16.523	323	17.972	373	19.313	423	20.567
174	13.191	224	14.967	274	16.553	324	18.000	374	19.339	424	20.591
175	13.229	225	15.000	275	16.583	325	18.028	375	19.365	425	20.616
176	13.266	226	15.033	276	16.613	326	18.055	376	19.391	426	20.640
177	13.304	227	15.067	277	16.643	327	18.083	377	19.416	427	20.664
178	13.342	228	15.100	278	16.673	328	18.111	378	19.442	428	20.688
179	13.379	229	15.133	279	16.703	329	18.138	379	19.468	429	20.712
180	13.416	230	15.166	280	16.733	330	18.166	380	19.494	430	20.736
181	13.454	231	15.199	281	16.763	331	18.193	381	19.519	431	20.761
182	13.491	232	15.232	282	16.793	332	18.221	382	19.545	432	20.785
183	13.528	233	15.264	283	16.823	333	18.248	383	19.570	433	20.809
184	13.565	234	15.297	284	16.852	334	18.276	384	19.596	434	20.833
185	13.601	235	15.330	285	16.882	335	18.303	385	19.621	435	20.857
186	13.638	236	15.362	286	16.912	336	18.330	386	19.647	436	20.881
187	13.675	237	15.395	287	16.941	337	18.358	387	19.672	437	20.905
188	13.711	238	15.427	288	16.971	338	18.385	388	19.698	438	20.928
189	13.748	239	15.460	289	17.000	339	18.412	389	19.723	439	20.952
190	13.784	240	15.492	290	17.029	340	18.439	390	19.748	440	20.976
191	13.820	241	15.524	291	17.059	341	18.466	391	19.774	441	21.000
192	13.856	242	15.556	292	17.088	342	18.493	392	19.799	442	21.024
193	13.892	243	15.588	293	17.117	343	18.520	393	19.824	443	21.048
194	13.928	244	15.620	294	17.146	344	18.547	394	19.849	444	21.071
195	13.964	245	15.652	295	17.176	345	18.574	395	19.875	445	21.095
196	14.000	246	15.684	296	17.205	346	18.601	396	19.900	446	21.119
197	14.036	247	15.716	297	17.234	347	18.628	397	19.925	447	21.142
198	14.071	248	15.748	298	17.263	348	18.655	398	19.950	448	21.166
199	14.107	249	15.780	299	17.292	349	18.682	399	19.975	449	21.190
200	14.142	250	15.811	300	17.321	350	18.708	400	20.000	450	21.213

N	$\sqrt{N}$	N	$\sqrt{N}$	N	$\sqrt{N}$	N	$\sqrt{N}$	N	$\sqrt{N}$	N	$\sqrt{N}$
451	21.237	501	22.383	551	23.473	601	24.515	651	25.515	701	26.476
452	21.260	502	22.405	552	23.495	602	24.536	652	25.534	702	26.495
453	21.284	503	22.428	553	23.516	603	24.556	653	25.554	703	26.514
454	21.307	504	22.450	554	23.537	604	24.576	654	25.573	704	26.533
455	21.331	505	22.472	555	23.558	605	24.597	655	25.593	705	26.552
456	21.354	506	22.494	556	23.580	606	24.617	656	25.612	706	26.571
457	21.378	507	22.517	557	23.601	607	24.637	657	25.632	707	26.589
458	21.401	508	22.539	558	23.622	608	24.658	658	25.652	708	26.608
459	21.424	509	22.561	559	23.643	609	24.678	659	25.671	709	26.627
460	21.448	510	22.583	560	23.664	610	24.698	660	25.690	710	26.646
461	21.471	511	22.605	561	23.685	611	24.718	661	25.710	711	26.665
462	21.494	512	22.627	562	23.707	612	24.739	662	25.729	712	26.683
463	21.517	513	22.650	563	23.728	613	24.759	663	25.749	713	26.702
464	21.541	514	22.672	564	23.749	614	24.779	664	25.768	714	26.721
465	21.564	515	22.694	565	23.770	615	24.799	665	25.788	715	26.739
466	21.587	516	22.716	566	23.791	616	24.819	666	25.807	716	26.758
467	21.610	517	22.738	567	23.812	617	24.839	667	25.826	717	26.777
468	21.633	518	22.760	568	23.833	618	24.860	668	25.846	718	26.796
469	21.656	519	22.782	569	23.854	619	24.880	669	25.865	719	26.814
470	21.679	520	22.804	570	23.875	620	24.900	670	25.884	720	26.833
471	21.703	521	22.825	571	23.896	621	24.920	671	25.904	721	26.851
472	21.726	522	22.847	572	23.917	622	24.940	672	25.923	722	26.870
473	21.749	523	22.869	573	23.937	623	24.960	673	25.942	723	26.889
474	21.772	524	22.891	574	23.958	624	24.980	674	25.962	724	26.907
475	21.794	525	22.913	575	23.979	625	25.000	675	25.981	725	26.926
476	21.817	526	22.935	576	24.000	626	25.020	676	26.000	726	26.944
477	21.840	527	22.956	577	24.021	627	25.040	677	26.019	727	26.963
478	21.863	528	22.978	578	24.042	628	25.060	678	26.038	728	26.981
479	21.886	529	23.000	579	24.062	629	25.080	679	26.058	729	27.000
480	21.909	530	23.022	580	24.083	630	25.100	680	26.077	730	27.019
481	21.932	531	23.043	581	24.104	631	25.120	681	26.096	731	27.037
482	21.954	532	23.065	582	24.125	632	25.140	682	26.115	732	27.055
483	21.977	533	23.087	583	24.145	633	25.159	683	26.134	733	27.074
484	22.000	534	23.108	584	24.166	634	25.179	684	26.153	734	27.092
485	22.023	535	23.130	585	24.187	635	25.199	685	26.173	735	27.111
486	22.045	536	23.152	586	24.207	636	25.219	686	26.192	736	27.129
487	22.068	537	23.173	587	24.228	637	25.239	687	26.211	737	27.148
488	22.091	538	23.195	588	24.249	638	25.259	688	26.230	738	27.166
489	22.113	539	23.216	589	24.269	639	25.278	689	26.249	739	27.185
490	22.136	540	23.238	590	24.290	640	25.298	690	26.268	740	27.203
491	22.159	541	23.259	591	24.310	641	25.318	691	26.287	741	27.221
492	22.181	542	23.281	592	24.331	642	25.338	692	26.306	742	27.240
493	22.204	543	23.302	593	24.352	643	25.357	693	26.325	743	27.258
494	22.226	544	23.324	594	24.372	644	25.377	694	26.344	744	27.276
495	22.249	545	23.345	595	24.393	645	25.397	695	26.363	745	27.295
496	22.271	546	23.367	596	24.413	646	25.417	696	26.382	746	27.313
497	22.293	547	23.388	597	24.434	647	25.436	697	26.401	747	27.331
498	22.316	548	23.409	598	24.454	648	25.456	698	26.420	748	27.350
499	22.338	549	23.431	599	24.474	649	25.475	699	26.439	749	27.368
500	22.361	550	23.452	600	24.495	650	25.495	700	26.458	750	27.386

N	$\sqrt{N}$	N	$\sqrt{N}$	N	$\sqrt{N}$	N	$\sqrt{N}$	N	$\sqrt{N}$	N	$\sqrt{N}$
751	27.404	801	28.302	851	29.172	901	30.017	951	30.838	1001	31.639
752	27.423	802	28.320	852	29.189	902	30.033	952	30.854	1002	31.654
753	27.441	803	28.337	853	29.206	903	30.050	953	30.871	1003	31.670
754	27.459	804	28.355	854	29.223	904	30.067	954	30.887	1004	31.686
755	27.477	805	28.373	855	29.240	905	30.083	955	30.903	1005	31.702
756	27.495	806	28.390	856	29.257	906	30.100	956	30.919	1006	31.718
757	27.514	807	28.408	857	29.275	907	30.116	957	30.935	1007	31.733
758	27.532	808	28.425	858	29.292	908	30.133	958	30.952	1008	31.749
759	27.550	809	28.443	859	29.309	909	30.150	959	30.968	1009	31.765
760	27.568	810	28.460	860	29.326	910	30.166	960	30.984	1010	31.780
761	27.586	811	28.478	861	29.343	911	30.183	961	31.000	1011	31.796
762	27.604	812	28.496	862	29.360	912	30.199	962	31.016	1012	31.812
763	27.622	813	28.513	863	29.377	913	30.216	963	31.032	1013	31.828
764	27.641	814	28.531	864	29.394	914	30.232	964	31.048	1014	31.843
765	27.659	815	28.548	865	29.411	915	30.249	965	31.064	1015	31.859
766	27.677	816	28.566	866	29.428	916	30.265	966	31.081	1016	31.875
767	27.695	817	28.583	867	29.445	917	30.282	967	31.097	1017	31.890
768	27.713	818	28.601	868	29.462	918	30.299	968	31.113	1018	31.906
769	27.731	819	28.618	869	29.479	919	30.315	969	31.129	1019	31.922
770	27.749	820	28.636	870	29.496	920	30.332	970	31.145	1020	31.937
771	27.767	821	28.653	871	29.513	921	30.348	971	31.161	1021	31.953
772	27.785	822	28.671	872	29.530	922	30.364	972	31.177	1022	31.969
773	27.803	823	28.688	873	29.547	923	30.381	973	31.193	1023	31.984
774	27.821	824	28.705	874	29.563	924	30.397	974	31.209	1024	32.000
775	27.839	825	28.723	875	29.580	925	30.414	975	31.225	1025	32.016
776	27.857	826	28.740	876	29.597	926	30.430	976	31.241	1026	32.031
777	27.875	827	28.758	877	29.614	927	30.447	977	31.257	1027	32.047
778	27.893	828	28.775	878	29.631	928	30.463	978	31.273	1028	32.062
779	27.911	829	28.792	879	29.648	929	30.480	979	31.289	1029	32.078
780	27.928	830	28.810	880	29.665	930	30.496	980	31.305	1030	32.094
781	27.946	831	28.827	881	29.682	931	30.512	981	31.321	1031	32.109
782	27.964	832	28.844	882	29.698	932	30.529	982	31.337	1032	32.125
783	27.982	833	28.862	883	29.715	933	30.545	983	31.353	1033	32.140
784	28.000	834	28.879	884	29.732	934	30.561	984	31.369	1034	32.156
785	28.018	835	28.896	885	29.749	935	30.578	985	31.385	1035	32.171
786	28.036	836	28.914	886	29.766	936	30.594	986	31.401	1036	32.187
787	28.054	837	28.931	887	29.783	937	30.610	987	31.417	1037	32.202
788	28.071	838	28.948	888	29.799	938	30.627	988	31.432	1038	32.218
789	28.089	839	28.965	889	29.816	939	30.643	989	31.448	1039	32.234
790	28.107	840	28.983	890	29.833	940	30.659	990	31.464	1040	32.249
791	28.125	841	29.000	891	29.850	941	30.676	991	31.480	1041	32.265
792	28.142	842	29.017	892	29.866	942	30.692	992	31.496	1042	32.280
793	28.160	843	29.034	893	29.883	943	30.708	993	31.512	1043	32.296
794	28.178	844	29.052	894	29.900	944	30.725	994	31.528	1044	32.311
795	28.196	845	29.069	895	29.916	945	30.741	995	31.544	1045	32.326
796	28.213	846	29.086	896	29.933	946	30.757	996	31.559	1046	32.342
797	28.231	847	29.103	897	29.950	947	30.773	997	31.575	1047	32.357
798	28.249	848	29.120	898	29.967	948	30.790	998	31.591	1048	32.373
799	28.267	849	29.138	899	29.983	949	30.806	999	31.607	1049	32.388
800	28.284	850	29.155	900	30.000	950	30.822	1000	31.623	1050	32.404

Appendix H

Computation of Stanines [1]

The stanine scale is a simple nine-point scale of standard scores. In this scale, raw scores are converted to scores which range from One (low) to Nine (high) with a mean of Five and a standard deviation of Two. Stanines can be used wherever it is possible to arrange data in rank order; that is, from the highest to the lowest. Thus, they can be used to transform ranks, raw test scores, or almost any other kinds of information that will serve to serialize or order the performances of individuals within a particular group. It is only necessary that the assumption of normality of distribution not be unreasonable.

Possible applications of the stanine method of score transformation are as follows: Establishing local norms, maintaining progress records, counseling and guiding students, and reporting pupil progress. It is important to remember a limiting factor of this or any other system of transformed scores: *such scores are comparable from test to test only when the group upon which the transformed scores are based is the same for all tests.*

Frequently it is necessary for the teacher to assign a score to some such product as a drawing, an essay, or a tie rack. The problem in each case is to arrange the products in rank order so that they may be assigned stanines. The following suggested steps indicate how this may be done.

1. Write the words "Excellent," "Very Good," "Good," "Fair," and "Poor" on slips of paper or cards. Place these far enough apart so that the products or papers to be arranged can be laid in piles below each of the headings. Tentatively assign each product to one of these categories.
2. When all of the products have been similarly categorized, arrange the products *within* the middle group (bearing the heading "Good") in order of judged excellence, from the best to the poorest. A product may be moved up or down from the category to which it has been previously

1. *The Characteristics, Use, and Computation of Stanines* by Walter N. Durost. Test Service Notebook No. 23, © 1961 by Harcourt Brace Jovanovich, Inc., NY. Reproduced by permission.

assigned. There is no restriction on the number of cases that may be put in any one category.

3. Continue this process until the products within each of the categories have been arranged from best to poorest. This will result in a total rank order comprising all of the products from the very best, in the group headed "Excellent," to the very poorest, in the group headed "Poor."

4. After serializing or ranking all of the products in this way, it is simple to determine the number of cases at each stanine level by referring to the Stanine Table. Since the products are arranged in rank order, the number of cases will coincide precisely with the numbers in the table.

It has been pointed out consistently that data from many different sources are required for a sound program of evaluation. These data, however, are often expressed in a variety of ways. The need for a system that would quantify all such information—that would make it comparable—is therefore a very real one. The stanine system does this; it provides a convenient and uncomplicated technique for deriving valid and meaningful composites.

TABLE H.1

Stanine Table

Stanine Table, showing number of cases falling at each level of a 9-point normalized standard score scale when the mean equals 5 and the standard deviation equals 2.

Directions: Under N, find the number corresponding to number of cases in the group. Entries in columns 1 to 9 give the number of cases which should receive the stanine score indicated at the top of the columns. These figures are computed by multiplying the total number of cases in the group by the percentage of cases at each level. The figures are rounded off values to give a symmetrical distribution of cases for any value of N given in the table.

Number of cases	Percentage of cases at each level								
	4%	7%	12%	17%	20%	17%	12%	7%	4%
	STANINES								
N	1	2	3	4	5	6	7	8	9
20	1	1	2	4	4	4	2	1	1
21	1	1	2	4	5	4	2	1	1
22	1	2	2	4	4	4	2	2	1
23	1	2	2	4	5	4	2	2	1
24	1	2	3	4	4	4	3	2	1
25	1	2	3	4	5	4	3	2	1
26	1	2	3	4	6	4	3	2	1
27	1	2	3	5	5	5	3	2	1
28	1	2	3	5	6	5	3	2	1
29	1	2	4	5	5	5	4	2	1
30	1	2	4	5	6	5	4	2	1
31	1	2	4	5	7	5	4	2	1
32	1	2	4	6	6	6	4	2	1
33	1	2	4	6	7	6	4	2	1
34	1	3	4	6	6	6	4	3	1

TABLE H.1   *Continued*

Number of cases	Percentage of cases at each level								
	4%	7%	12%	17%	20%	17%	12%	7%	4%
					STANINES				
N	1	2	3	4	5	6	7	8	9
35	1	3	4	6	7	6	4	3	1
36	1	3	4	6	8	6	4	3	1
37	2	3	4	6	7	6	4	3	2
38	1	3	5	6	8	6	5	3	1
39	1	3	5	7	7	7	5	3	1
40	1	3	5	7	8	7	5	3	1
41	1	3	5	7	9	7	5	3	1
42	2	3	5	7	8	7	5	3	2
43	2	3	5	7	9	7	5	3	2
44	2	3	5	8	8	8	5	3	2
45	2	3	5	8	9	8	5	3	2
46	2	3	5	8	10	8	5	3	2
47	2	3	6	8	9	8	6	3	2
48	2	3	6	8	10	8	6	3	2
49	2	4	6	8	9	8	6	4	2
50	2	3	6	9	10	9	6	3	2
51	2	3	6	9	11	9	6	3	2
52	2	4	6	9	10	9	6	4	2
53	2	4	6	9	11	9	6	4	2
54	2	4	7	9	10	9	7	4	2
55	2	4	7	9	11	9	7	4	2
56	2	4	7	9	12	9	7	4	2
57	2	4	7	10	11	10	7	4	2
58	2	4	7	10	12	10	7	4	2
59	3	4	7	10	11	10	7	4	3
60	3	4	7	10	12	10	7	4	3
61	3	4	7	10	13	10	7	4	3
62	3	4	7	11	12	11	7	4	3
63	3	4	7	11	13	11	7	4	3
64	3	4	8	11	12	11	8	4	3
65	3	4	8	11	13	11	8	4	3
66	3	4	8	11	14	11	8	4	3
67	3	5	8	11	13	11	8	5	3
68	3	5	8	11	14	11	8	5	3
69	3	5	8	12	13	12	8	5	3
70	3	5	8	12	14	12	8	5	3
71	3	5	8	12	15	12	8	5	3
72	3	5	9	12	14	12	9	5	3
73	3	5	9	12	15	12	9	5	3
74	3	5	9	13	14	13	9	5	3
75	3	5	9	13	15	13	9	5	3
76	3	5	9	13	16	13	9	5	3
77	3	6	9	13	15	13	9	6	3
78	3	6	9	13	16	13	9	6	3
79	3	6	10	13	15	13	10	6	3
80	3	6	9	14	16	14	9	6	3
81	3	6	9	14	17	14	9	6	3
82	3	6	10	14	16	14	10	6	3
83	3	6	10	14	17	14	10	6	3
84	4	6	10	14	16	14	10	6	4

TABLE H.1   *Continued*

Number of cases	Percentage of cases at each level								
	4%	7%	12%	17%	20%	17%	12%	7%	4%
				STANINES					
N	1	2	3	4	5	6	7	8	9
85	3	6	10	15	17	15	10	6	3
86	3	6	10	15	18	15	10	6	3
87	4	6	10	15	17	15	10	6	4
88	3	6	11	15	18	15	11	6	3
89	4	6	11	15	17	15	11	6	4
90	4	6	11	15	18	15	11	6	4
91	4	6	11	15	19	15	11	6	4
92	4	6	11	16	18	16	11	6	4
93	4	6	11	16	19	16	11	6	4
94	4	7	11	16	18	16	11	7	4
95	4	7	11	16	19	16	11	7	4
96	4	7	11	16	20	16	11	7	4
97	4	7	12	16	19	16	12	7	4
98	4	7	12	16	20	16	12	7	4
99	4	7	12	17	19	17	12	7	4
100	4	7	12	17	20	17	12	7	4

DIRECTIONS FOR TALLY SHEET

1. Arrange test papers or answer sheets in rank order from high to low. On a separate piece of paper list every score in a column from the highest obtained to the lowest, Column A. Opposite each score write the number of individuals who obtained that score. This may be done by counting the papers or answer sheets having the same score, or it may be done by tallying the scores in the manner shown in Column B.
2. Add the frequencies (C) and write the total at the bottom of the column (D). This is shown to be 90.
3. Beginning at the bottom, count up (cumulate) to one-half the total number of scores, in this case 45 (one-half of 90). This falls opposite the score of 34 (E), which is the median to the nearest whole number.
4. In the column at the extreme left of the Stanine Table, look up the total number of cases (90). In this row are the theoretical frequencies of cases at each stanine level for 90 cases. In the middle of this row you will find the number of cases (18) to which a stanine of 5 should be assigned. Starting with the median in the Tally Sheet, lay off as nearly this number (18) of scores as you can. Here it is 20.

Stanine	A Score Interval	B Tallies	C Fre- quencies	Grouping	
				Actual	Theo- retical
	58	/	1		
	57	—	—	4	4
9	56	/	1		
	55	//	2		
	54		—		
	53		—		
	52		—		
	51	/	1	7	6
8	50	/	1		
	49	//	2		
	48		—		
	47	///	3		
	46	/	1		
	45	///	3		
7	44	//	2	12	11
	43		—		
	42	///// /	6		
	41	//	2		
	40	//	2		
6	39	//	2	12	15
	38	/	1		
	37	////	5		
	36	////	5		
	35	//	2		
5	34 E	//// //	7	20	18
	33	///	3		
	32	///	3		
	31	////	5		
	30	/	1		
4	29	///	3	14	15
	28	///	3		
	27	//	2		
	26	////	4		
3	25	//// /	6	13	11
	24	///	3		
	23	/	1		
2	22	/	1	4	6
	21	//	2		
	20	/	1		
1	19	—	—	4	4
	18	/	1		
	17	//	2		

90 D

Figure H.1 Tally Sheet for Distribution of Scores.

5. Working upward and downward from scores falling in stanine 5, assign scores to stanine levels so as to give the closest approximation possible to the theoretical values. It is helpful to separate these scores in the manner shown in Column A.

After having made a tentative assignment, make any adjustments necessary to bring the actual frequencies at each level into the closest possible agreement with the theoretical values. Remember, however, that all equal scores must be assigned the same stanines.

Appendix I

Selected Test Publishers Directory

Other publishers not listed here are in Buros' *Eighth Mental Measurements Yearbook.*

American Association on Mental Deficiency, 5201 Connecticut Avenue N.W., Washington, DC 20015

American College Testing Program, P.O. Box 168, Iowa City, IA 52240

American Guidance Service, Inc., Publishers' Building, Circle Pines, MN 55014

American Printing House for the Blind, 1139 Frankfort Ave., Louisville, KY 40206

Behavioral Publications, Inc., 2852 Broadway, New York, NY 10025

Behavioral Sciences, Inc., 3000 Sand Hill Road, Menlo Park, CA 94025

Bobbs-Merrill Company, Inc., 4300 W. 62nd St., Indianapolis, IN 46268

Bureau of Educational Measurements, Emporia Kansas State College, Emporia, KS 66801

Bureau of Educational Research and Service, University of Iowa, Iowa City, IA 52242

College Entrance Examination Board, 888 Seventh Ave., New York, NY 10019

Committee on Diagnostic Reading Tests, Inc., Mountain Home, NC 28758

Consulting Psychologists Press, Inc., 577 College Ave., Palo Alto, CA 94306

Cooperative Tests and Services, 2725 Sand Hill Road, Menlo Park, CA 94025

Counselor Recordings and Tests, Box 6184, Acklen Station, Nashville, TN 37212

CTB/McGraw-Hill, Del Monte Research Park, Monterey, CA 93940

Educational and Industrial Testing Service, P. O. Box 7234, San Diego, CA 92107

Educational Testing Service, Princeton, NJ 08540

General Educational Development Testing Service, American Council on Education, 12 DuPont Circle, Washington, DC 20036

Guidance Associates of Delaware, Inc., 1526 Gilpin Avenue, Wilmington, DE 19806

Harcourt Brace Jovanovich, Inc., 757 Third Avenue, New York, NY 10017

Houghton Mifflin Company, One Beacon St., Boston, MA 02107

Institute for Personality and Ability Testing, 1602 Coronado Drive, Champaign, IL 61820

Instructional Objectives Exchange Distribution Center, P. O. Box 24095, Los Angeles, CA 90024

NCS Interpretive Scoring System, 4401 West 76th Street, Minneapolis, MN 55435

The Psychological Corporation, 757 Third Avenue, New York, N.Y. 10017.

Psychological Test Specialists, P. O. Box 9229, Missoula, MT 59801

Psychologists and Educators Press, 211 West State Street, Jacksonville, IL 62650

Psychometric Affiliates, Box 3167, Munster, IN 46321

Rand McNally & Company, P.O. Box 7600, Chicago, IL 60680

Scholastic Testing Services, Inc., 480 Meyer Road, Bensenville, IL 60106

Science Research Associates, Inc., 155 N. Wacker Drive, Chicago, IL 60606

Scott, Foresman & Company, 1900 East Lake Avenue, Glenview, IL 60025

Slosson Educational Publications, 140 Pine Street, East Aurora, NY 14052

Stoelting Company, 1350 S. Kostner Avenue, Chicago, IL 60623

Teachers' College Press, 1234 Amsterdam Avenue, New York, NY 10027

Western Psychological Services, 12031 Wilshire Boulevard, Los Angeles, CA 90025

Appendix J

Examples of Profiles of Early Childhood Tests

Following are some examples of various types of profiles used for standardized tests that are frequently administered to children of the early childhood age group.

Figure J.1 Frostig Developmental Test of Visual Perception[1]

The third edition of this test is used for ages 3-8. It produces seven scores: eye-motor coordination, figure-ground discrimination, form constancy, position in space, spatial relations, total, and perceptual quotient, Results are expressed in age equivalents, scaled scores, and perceptual quotient for the total.

Figure J.2 Developmental Profile[2]

Designed as a replacement for the Vineland Social Maturity Scale, the Developmental Profile uses parent interview to estimate developmental level in five functional areas: physical skill, self-help, social competence, academic skills, and communicative ability. Test ages are semi-annually through the first four years and yearly thereafter to a ceiling of 10-12 years, depending on the subscale. Scores to be used as a developmental profile are displayed as developmental ages in each functional area, and a ratio IQ equivalency score (IQE) is determined from the age equivalent of the academic scale. The test is designed for ages birth to 12.

1. Profile is from test booklet, *Developmental Test of Visual Perception*, Third Edition, devised by Marianne Frostig. Used by permission of the publisher, Consulting Psychologist Press, Inc., Palo Alto, CA. Copyright 1966.

2. From *Developmental Profile, Scoring and Report Form*, devised by Gerald D. Alpern and Thomas J. Boll. Used by permission of publisher, Psychological Developmental Publications, Aspen, CO. Copyright 1972.

NOTES AND COMMENTS

MARIANNE FROSTIG

DEVELOPMENTAL TEST OF VISUAL PERCEPTION

CHILD'S NAME ....

PARENT'S NAME ....

ADDRESS ....TELEPHONE ....

YEAR   MONTH   DAY

DATE OF TEST _____ _____ _____

BIRTH DATE _____ _____ _____

CHRONOLOGICAL AGE _____ _____ _____

I.Q. ....HANDEDNESS ....GRADE ....

SOCIAL ADJUSTMENT ....

READING ACHIEVEMENT ....

MEDICAL DIAGNOSIS IF AVAILABLE ....

DIAGNOSING PHYSICIAN AND AGENCY ....

....TELEPHONE ....

EXAMINER ....

SUBTESTS	I	II	III	IV	V	TOTAL
RAW SCORES						
AGE EQUIVALENTS						
SCALED SCORES						

PERCEPTUAL QUOTIENT	

I	II	III a	III b	IV	V
1	1	1	1	1	1
2	2	2	2	2	2
3	3	3	3	3	3
4	4	4	4	4	4
5	5	5	5	5	5
6	6	6	6	6	6
7	7	7	7	7	7
8	8	8	8	8	8
9		9	9		
10		10	10		
11		11	11		
12		12	12		
13		13	13		
14		14	14		
15		15	15		
16			16		
			17		
			18		

I	II	III	IV	V

Total

Figure J.1 Sample Profile: Frostig Developmental Test of Visual Perception. From *Developmental Test of Visual Perception*, Third Edition, devised by Marianne Frostig. Used by permission of the publisher, Consulting Psychologist Press, Inc., Palo Alto, CA. Copyright 1966.)

DEVELOPMENTAL PROFILE

SCORING & REPORT FORM

PSYCHOLOGICAL DEVELOPMENT PUBLICATIONS
P.O. Box 3198
Aspen, Colorado 81611

Copyright 1972
Gerald D. Alpern, Ph. D.
Thomas J. Boll, Ph. D.

Child's Name: _____ *School Placement:* _____ *Date:* _____

Rater: _____ *Birthdate:* _____

Interviewee: _____ *Relationship to Child:* _____ *Chronological Age:* _____

DEVELOPMENTAL SKILL AGE PROFILE

COMMENTS AND CONCLUSIONS

Physical Age _____ yrs.-mos.

Self-Help Age _____ yrs.-mos.

Social Age _____ yrs.-mos.

Academic Age _____ yrs.-mos.

Communication Age _____ yrs.-mos.

I. Q. Equivalency Score _____

Figure J.2 Sample Profile: Developmental Profile. (From *Developmental Profile, Scoring and Report Form*, devised by Gerald D. Alpern and Thomas J. Boll. Used by permission of publisher, Psychological Developmental Publications, Aspen, CO. Copyright 1972.)

Figure J.3 Goldman-Fristoe-Woodcock Test of Auditory Discrimination[3]

This test, for ages four and over, is designed to identify and assess the ability to distinguish among speech sounds. It can help to identify and assess discrimination deficits for those subjects who cannot be given standard tests because of age or communication problems. It produces speech-sound discrimination scores under two conditions: quiet and background noise. It gives total errors and pauses under each condition and gives a percentile rank.

Figure J.4 Animal Crackers: A Test of Motivation to Achieve, Research Edition[4]

This test is for K-1. Devised in 1973, it produces six scores: School enjoyment, self confidence, purposiveness, instrumental activity, self-evaluation, and total. Scores are reported in percentile form. The test is designed to measure achievement motivation, particularly academic achievement, in pre-school, kindergarten, and first grade children.

Figure J.5 Denver Developmental Screening Test[5]

This standard test, for ages two weeks to six years, detects children with serious developmental delays. It covers four functions: gross-motor, language, fine-motor-adaptive, and personal-social. It produces a profile which may be interpreted as normal, questionable, or abnormal.

3. From *Examiner's Manual, Goldman-Fristoe-Woodcock Test of Auditory Discrimination* devised by Ronald Goldman, Macalyne Fristoe, and Richard W. Woodcock. Reproduced by special permission of American Guidance Service, Circle Pines, MN. Copyright © 1970.

4. From Individual Performance Record of *Animal Crackers: A Test of Motivation to Achieve*, devised by Dorothy C. Adkins and Bonnie L. Ballif. Reprinted by permission of the publisher, CTB/McGraw-Hill, Del Monte Research Park, Monterey, CA 93940. Copyright © 1973 by McGraw-Hill, Inc. All Rights Reserved. Printed in the U.S.A.

5. From Individual Profile Sheet of the *Denver Developmental Screening Test*, devised by William K. Frankenburg, M.D., and Josiah B. Dodds, Ph.D. Used by permission of the authors. © 1969, University of Colorado Health Science Center.

GOLDMAN - FRISTOE - WOODCOCK
TEST OF AUDITORY DISCRIMINATION

By Ronald Goldman, Ph.D.; Macalyne Fristoe, M.S.; and Richard W. Woodcock, Ed.D.

AGS

NAME _____ AGE _____ GRADE _____ SCHOOL _____

TEACHER _____ DATE _____ EXAMINER _____

COMMENTS _____

Tape Player: Make _____ Model _____ Earphones Used: ☐ Yes ☐ No   Pretraining with Large Training Plates: ☐ Yes ☐ No

TRAINING PROCEDURE
Words Failed to Train

TOTAL WORDS _____
TEST WORDS(*) _____

QUIET SUBTEST

TOTAL ERRORS _____
PERCENTILE RANK _____
PAUSES _____

NOISE SUBTEST

TOTAL ERRORS _____
PERCENTILE RANK _____
PAUSES _____

TRAINING PROCEDURE

Indicate correct responses by a (+), incorrect responses by a zero (0). Blank spaces indicate trial not administered.

Plate	Stimulus Word	Trial 1	Trial 2	Trial 3		Plate	Stimulus Word	Trial 1	Trial 2	Trial 3
1:	chair			*		1:	coal			*
	she						mail			
2:	light			*		2:	veil			*
	tack						key			
3:	see			*		3:	rail			*
	cash						pat			
4:	cab			*		4:	back			*
	comb						bee			
5:	core			*		5:	pea			*
	bear						patch			
6:	shack			*		6:	cone			*
	fat						tear			
7:	path			*		7:	sat			*
	bite						wake			
8:	core			*		8:	knee			*
	hair						tail			
9:	fair			*		9:	shack			*
	write						pig			
10:	lake			*		10:	pear			*
	nail						tea			
11:	pack			*		11:	sign			*
	sail						cat			
12:	vine			*		12:	wig			*
	night						pail			
13:	shine			*		13:	whale			*
	dig						cap			
14:	line			*		14:	big			*
	hat						calf			
15:	cab			*		15:	Jack			*
	me						rake			
16:	make			*		16:	we			*
	sack						catch			

Return to Plate 1 and present the second trial of stimulus words.

A zero in Trial 3 indicates failure to learn a word-picture associa- tion (failure to train).

Return to any failed items, giving a second trial. Repeat for Trial 3.

Words coded * are Test Words.

QUIET SUBTEST

Record the number of the subject's response for each plate. If necessary to stop the test procedure due to slow subject response, place a check (✓) under "Pause."

Plate	Test Word	Subj's Resp.	Correct Resp.	Pause		Plate	Test Word	Subj's Resp.	Correct Resp.	Pause
17:	cash	(3)	■			32:	cap	(2)	▲	
18:	wake	(1)	●			33:	bear	(1)	★	
19:	dig	(3)	★			34:	lake	(3)	●	
20:	me	(3)	●			35:	we	(1)	♦	
21:	fair	(4)	■			36:	sign	(2)	■	
22:	catch	(4)	▲			37:	coal	(4)	♦	
23:	tack	(2)	▲			38:	mail	(1)	●	
24:	rake	(3)	♦			39:	pack	(3)	■	
25:	knee	(1)	●			40:	sail	(4)	▲	
26:	Jack	(3)	★			41:	bee	(1)	●	
27:	big	(1)	♦			42:	shack	(2)	★	
28:	vine	(2)	♦			43:	tea	(4)	▲	
29:	night	(3)	●			44:	make	(4)	●	
30:	cone	(4)	●			45:	back	(4)	♦	
31:	pail	(4)	▲			46:	hair	(3)	■	

To score errors, make a slash through the number printed in the "Correct Response" column.

ERROR ANALYSIS

	PLOSIVES	CONTINUANTS	NASALS
VOICED	★	♦	■
UNVOICED	●	▲	

TOTAL PLOSIVES _____ TOTAL CONTINUANTS _____ TOTAL NASALS _____
TOTAL VOICED _____ TOTAL UNVOICED _____

NOISE SUBTEST

Record the number of the subject's response for each plate. If necessary to stop the test procedure due to slow subject response, place a check (✓) under "Pause."

Plate	Test Word	Subj's Resp.	Correct Resp.	Pause		Plate	Test Word	Subj's Resp.	Correct Resp.	Pause
	Practice Items:					62:	vine	(2)	♦	
47:	light	(1)	●			63:	night	(1)	●	
48:	see	(4)	▲			64:	cone	(4)	●	
49:	comb	(3)	♦			65:	pail	(4)	▲	
						66:	cap	(2)	▲	
	Test Items:					67:	shack	(3)	★	
50:	bear	(2)	★			68:	tea	(3)	▲	
51:	we	(4)	♦			69:	make	(2)	●	
52:	lake	(3)	●			70:	back	(3)	♦	
53:	coal	(4)	♦			71:	hair	(1)	■	
54:	sign	(1)	■			72:	cash	(3)	■	
55:	mail	(3)	●			73:	wake	(1)	●	
56:	pack	(4)	■			74:	dig	(3)	★	
57:	sail	(4)	▲			75:	me	(4)	●	
58:	bee	(2)	●			76:	fair	(2)	■	
59:	Jack	(3)	★			77:	catch	(3)	▲	
60:	knee	(4)	●			78:	tack	(4)	▲	
61:	big	(2)	♦			79:	rake	(1)	★	

To score errors, make a slash through the number printed in the "Correct Response" column.

ERROR ANALYSIS

	PLOSIVES	CONTINUANTS	NASALS
VOICED	★	♦	■
UNVOICED	●	▲	

TOTAL PLOSIVES _____ TOTAL CONTINUANTS _____ TOTAL NASALS _____
TOTAL VOICED _____ TOTAL UNVOICED _____

Published by
AMERICAN GUIDANCE SERVICE, INC. · Publishers' Building, Circle Pines, Minn. 55014

Copyright © 1970 American Guidance Service, Inc.

Figure J.3 Goldman–Fristoe–Woodcock Test of Auditory Discrimination. (From *Examiner's Manual, Goldman–Fristoe–Woodcock Test of Auditory Discrimination* devised by Ronald Goldman, Macalyne Fristoe, and Richard W. Woodcock. Reproduced by special permission of American Guidance Service, Circle Pines, MN. Copyright © 1970.)

INDIVIDUAL PERFORMANCE RECORD

ANIMAL CRACKERS
A Test of Motivation to Achieve
Research Edition

Dorothy C. Adkins, Ph.D.
Bonnie L. Ballif, Ph.D.

NAME _____ GRADE _____ SEX _____ TEST DATE _____
year   month   day

TEACHER _____ SCHOOL _____ BIRTH DATE _____
year   month   day

EXAMINER _____ TESTING TIME _____ AGE _____ = _____ months

CONSISTENCY CHECK

Sample		
A	I	C
B	I	C
C	I	C
D	I	C

The Consistency Check is part of the scoring record for an individually administered test. For each sample item, check the I if the child's stated preference and his item response are inconsistent; check the C if preference and response are consistent.

	Raw Score	Percentile
School Enjoyment	___	___
Self-Confidence	___	___
Purposiveness	___	___
Instrumental Activity	___	___
Self-Evaluation	___	___
TOTAL TEST	___	___

Responses are indicated by L for the animal in the left-hand position in the test booklet and R for the animal in the right-hand position in the test booklet. The keyed response for each item is the shaded letter. Check the L or the R opposite the item number to show the child's response to each item. Item groupings by motivation components are: School Enjoyment, Self-Confidence, Purposiveness, Instrumental Activity, and Self-Evaluation. The raw score for a component is the number of responses marked in the shaded areas in the columns for that component; the total test raw score is the sum of the component raw scores.

Figure J.4 Sample Profile: Animal Crackers: A Test of Motivation to Achieve, Research Edition. (From Individual Performance Record of *Animal Crackers: A Test of Motivation to Achieve*, devised by Dorothy C. Adkins and Bonnie L. Ballif. Reprinted by permission of the publisher, CTB/McGraw-Hill, Del Monte Research Park, Monterey, CA 93940. Copyright © 1973 by McGraw-Hill, Inc. All Rights Reserved. Printed in the U.S.A.)

443

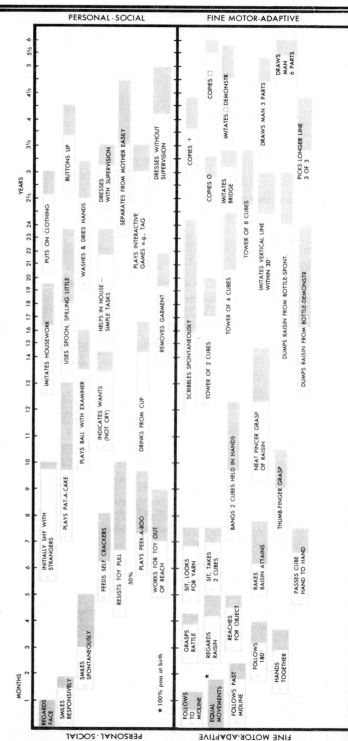

DENVER DEVELOPMENTAL SCREENING TEST

STO.=STOMACH
SIT=SITTING

PERCENT OF CHILDREN PASSING
25 50 75 90

May pass by report ——→
Footnote No. ——→
see back of form
Test Item

444

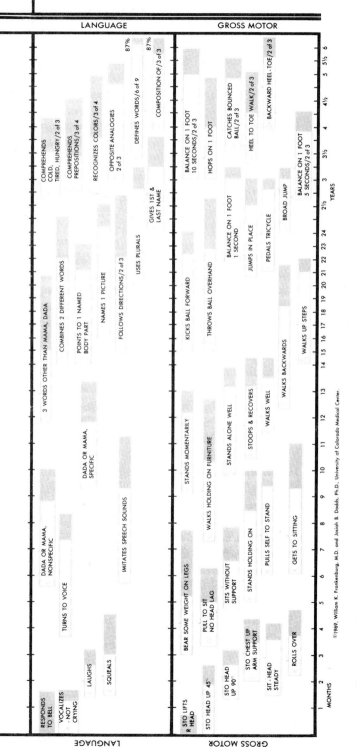

Figure J.5 Sample Profile: Denver Developmental Screening Test. (From Individual Profile Sheet of the *Denver Developmental Screening Test*, devised by William K. Frankenburg, M.D., and Josiah B. Dodds, Ph.D. Used by permission of the authors. © 1969, University of Colorado Health Science Center.)

Appendix K

Percent of Cases Falling Below Selected Values on the Normal Curve

Deviation in Standard Deviation Units	Percent of Cases Falling Below	Deviation in Standard Deviation Units	Percent of Cases Falling Below
+3.0	99.9	0.5	69.1
2.9	99.8	0.4	65.6
2.8	99.7	0.3	61.8
2.7	99.6	0.2	57.9
2.6	99.5	0.1	54.0
2.5	99.4	0.0	50.0
2.4	99.2	—0.1	46.0
2.3	98.9	—0.2	42.1
2.2	98.6	—0.3	38.2
2.1	98.2	—0.4	34.4
2.0	97.7	—0.5	30.9
1.9	97.1	—0.6	27.4
1.8	96.4	—0.7	24.2
1.7	95.5	—0.8	21.2
1.6	94.5	—0.9	18.4
1.5	93.3	—1.0	15.9
1.4	91.9	—1.1	13.6
1.3	90.3	—1.2	11.5
1.2	88.5	—1.3	9.7
1.1	86.4	—1.4	8.1
1.0	84.1	—1.5	6.7
0.9	81.6	—1.6	5.5
0.8	78.8	—1.7	4.5
0.7	75.8	—1.8	3.6
0.6	72.6		

Deviation in Standard Deviation Units	Percent of Cases Falling Below	Deviation in Standard Deviation Units	Percent of Cases Falling Below
—1.9	2.9	—2.5	0.6
—2.0	2.3	—2.6	0.5
—2.1	1.8	—2.7	0.4
—2.2	1.4	—2.8	0.3
—2.3	1.1	—2.9	0.2
—2.4	0.8	—3.0	0.1

Appendix L

Marking and Reporting Forms Used in Special Types of Schools

All of the following forms are from the Milwaukee Public Schools, Milwaukee, Wisconsin. These specialty schools were started in 1975 and give the Milwaukee parents an opportunity to choose from a variety of educational opportunities for their children. Although these forms are illustrative of the elementary level, specialty schools are available for the high school level also.

The forms reprinted in this section represent the following types of specialty schools:

Creative Arts School
Teacher-Pupil Learning Center
Fundamental School
Gifted and Talented
Open Classroom School

The Milwaukee Public School System has kindly allowed me to reprint these forms.

Figure L.1 Creative Arts School (4-year-old Kindergarten to Grade 6)[1]
The goal of this school is to use art experiences as a vital part of the educational program. The Creative Arts School follows the general curriculum guidelines for all Milwaukee Public elementary schools. There is instruction in mathematics, language arts, reading, science, and social studies as well as in art, music, drama, and physical education. This school encourages creativity and self-expression in a variety of ways—through art, music, dance, drama, and creative writing.

1. From the Milwaukee Public Schools. Printed by permission of the Milwaukee Public Schools System, Milwaukee, Wisconsin.

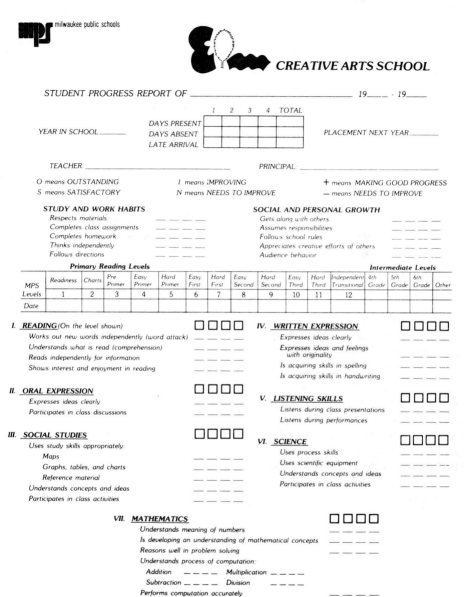

Figure L.1 Sample: Student Progress Report Form—Creative Arts School. (Printed by permission of the Milwaukee Public Schools System, Milwaukee, Wisconsin.)

Figure L.2   Teacher-Pupil Learning Center (4-year-old Kindergarten-Grade 6)[2]

The Teacher-Pupil Learning Center matches a child's learning style with appropriate instructional methods and materials. This is carried out through an individualized approach to learning using a diagnosis of pupil's strengths and weaknesses and making a prescription and program for each child. Instructional materials and equipment provide for differences in children's learning rates and styles.

Figure L.3   Fundamental School (5-year-old Kindergarten-Grade 6)[3]

There are seven attendance area specialty schools distributed throughout the Milwaukee district. The Fundamental School is one of these schools. It emphasizes basic skills and subjects, homework, dress codes, and academic progress. The report is based on the achievement and efforts of the child. At the beginning, a basis for determining grades is given for better parental understanding.

Figure L.4   Gifted and Talented School (Now named the Golda Meier School, formerly called the Fourth Street School) (Upper Primary-Grade 5)[4]

This entire school is designed for the gifted and talented children in upper primary, fourth grade, and fifth grade. The pupils are selected on the basis of their ability, achievement, study skills, self-confidence, creative talents, and leadership qualities. The difference in the curriculum of this school from the others is the depth in which the subjects are explored and the special opportunities available to help pupils develop other interests.

Figure L.5   Open Classroom School (Grades 6-8)[5]

The Open Education program provides an informal multi-age setting. The basic belief common to both elementary and middle school open education programs is that school is most productive when students make choices for learning activities which are related to their personal interests and real-life experiences. The activity sheets completed daily by each student include plans for what is to be accomplished and the approximate amount of time that person will spend on each activity. The students then evaluate the benefit of their activities each day. While some restrictions assure inclusion of basic subjects, there is ever-increasing freedom for students to make decisions and to become responsible learners.

2. From the Milwaukee Public Schools. Printed by permission of the Milwaukee Public Schools System, Milwaukee, Wisconsin.

3. From the Milwaukee Public Schools. Printed by permission of the Milwaukee Public Schools System, Milwaukee, Wisconsin.

4. From the Milwaukee Public Schools. Printed by permission of the Milwaukee Public School System, Milwaukee, Wisconsin.

5. From the Milwaukee Public Schools. Printed by permission of the Milwaukee Public Schools System, Milwaukee, Wisconsin.

mps milwaukee public schools

Teacher-Pupil Learning Center
City-Wide Specialty School
STUDENT PROGRESS REPORT - PRIMARY
School Year 19____ - 19____

Student _____   School _____

Teacher _____   Principal _____

Placement Next Year _____

	1	2	3	4
Days Absent				
Times Tardy				

This evaluation is intended to serve as a supplement to parent-teacher conferences. We recommend that you confer with the teacher in order to gain a more complete understanding of your child's progress within his/her prescriptive program.

GRADING CODE

(1) Child is making excellent progress

(2) Child is making progress

(3) Child needs help.

(NA) Skill does not apply

WORK AND STUDY HABITS

	1	2	3	4
Follows directions				
Completes tasks				
Works independently				
Works with others				
Completes homework				

SOCIAL DEVELOPMENT

	1	2	3	4
Gets along with others				
Accepts responsibility				
Respects rules and authority				

READING

Readiness Skills:

	1	2	3	4
Auditory process skills				
Visual process skills				
Uses both auditory and visual processes to learn				

There are twelve primary reading levels. At this time your child

is on level ____ ____ ____ ____

There are three intermediate reading levels. At this time your child

is on level ____ ____ ____

At this reading level your child:

Uses word attack skills at level:

____ ____ ____ ____

	1	2	3	4
Applies word attack skills				
Reads with understanding				
Reads independently				
Reads well orally				

SPELLING LEVELS - CHECK

Level 1___ Level 2___ Level 3___

Level 4___ Level 5___ Level 6___

Shows mastery in spelling lessons				
Applies spelling skills in written work				

LANGUAGE

Uses listening skills				
Uses speaking skills				
Uses grammar skills				
Uses written language skills				
Does creative writing				

HANDWRITING

Shows skill in manuscript				
Shows skill in cursive writing				

MATHEMATICS

PRIMARY LEVELS - CHECK

Level 1___ Level 2___ Level 3___

Enrichment progress____

Understands process:

	1	2	3	4
Understands meaning of numbers				
Addition				
Subtraction				
Multiplication				
Division				
Time and measurement				
Shows mastery in computation				
Reasons in problem solving				
Applies related study skills				

SOCIAL STUDIES

Participates in activities after field trips				
Is developing understandings				
Applies related study skills				

SCIENCE

Participates in activities related to units				
Is developing understandings				
Applies related study skills				

EXPRESSIVE ARTS

Responds to music activities				
Responds to art activities				

PHYSICAL EDUCATION

Responds to physical education activities				

4th QUARTER

Figure L.2 Sample: Student Progess Report—Primary, Teacher-Pupil Learning Center. (Printed by permission of the Milwaukee Public Schools System, Milwaukee, Wisconsin.)

mps milwaukee public schools

FUNDAMENTAL SCHOOL
STUDENT PROGRESS REPORT

School Year 19 _____ - _____

Pupil _____

Teacher _____

	1	2	3	4
Days Absent				
Times Tardy				

School _____

Principal _____

Present Grade Placement _____

Grade Placement Next Year _____

This report is based on the achievement and efforts of your child.
Basis for determining grades:

1. Completion and quality of daily class work.
2. Contributions to class discussions and class work.
3. Completion and quality of assigned homework.
4. Test Scores

Marking code for academic subjects:

A 90-100   **B** 80-89   **C** 70-79   **D** 60-69   **F** Below 60 (Failure)

Period	1	2	3	4	Average
READING Achievement					
Effort					
MATHEMATICS Achievement					
Effort					
ENGLISH Achievement					
Effort					
SPELLING Achievement					
Effort					
HANDWRITING Achievement					
Effort					
SCIENCE Achievement					
Effort					
SOCIAL STUDIES Achievement					
Effort					
HEALTH Achievement					
Effort					
MUSIC Effort					
ART Effort					
PHYSICAL EDUCATION Effort					

Marking code for conduct and work habits.

A Outstanding   **B** Very Good   **C** Satisfactory
D Fair   **F** Unsatisfactory

Check (✓) means improvement needed.

CONDUCT

Needs to:

Follow school rules
Follow room rules
Respect authority
Respect rights of others
Respect property
Be courteous
Show self-control

WORK HABITS

Needs to:

Complete classwork on time
Complete homework on time
Arrange work properly
Work neatly
Listen and follow directions
Organize desk and materials
Complete necessary corrections

Comments:

READING LEVEL

Latest date indicates level at which your child is reading.

Kindergarten
_____ 1. Readiness

First Grade
_____ 2. Charts
_____ 3. Pre-Primer
_____ 4. Primer - easy
_____ 5. Primer - hard
_____ 6. First reader - easy

Second Grade
_____ 7. First reader - hard
_____ 8. Second reader - easy
_____ 9. Second reader - hard

Third Grade
_____ 10. Third reader - easy
_____ 11. Third reader - hard
_____ 12. Transition

Fourth Grade
_____ Fourth reader

Fifth Grade
_____ Fifth reader

Sixth Grade
_____ Sixth reader
_____ Above sixth grade

Figure L.3 Sample: Student Progress Report, Fundamental School. (Printed by permission of the Milwaukee Public Schools System, Milwaukee, Wisconsin.)

Dear Parents and Students,

The staff of the Fourth Street School for Gifted and Talented presents this report. These grades represent the teachers' professional judgment of the progress your child is making in school. In evaluating your child's progress, attention has been given to both achievement and effort. Letter grades with the following descriptors and point values have been used in this evaluation. The "performance score" is the result of averaging all grades found on the report.

A	Excellent	4 Points
B	Very Good	3 Points
C	Good	2 Points
D	Fair	1 Point
U	Unsatisfactory	0 Points

Special areas are reserved for comment by parent, student and teacher and are intended to enhance and further personalize the progress report. Please review this report. Good communication among student, parent and school strengthens the process of education. Your comments are welcome.

Sincerely,

The Fourth Street School Staff

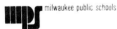 milwaukee public schools

Figure L.4   Sample: Pupil Progress Report, Gifted and Talented School (Golda Meier School). (Printed by permission of the Milwaukee Public Schools System, Milwaukee, Wisconsin.)

Figure 4.L   Continued

milwaukee public schools

4th st. SCHOOL

PUPIL PROGRESS REPORT

STUDENT NAME	NUMBER

QUARTER	SCHOOL YEAR

GRADE LEVEL		ROOM	

INSTRUCTOR/COURSE	ACHIEVEMENT				EFFORT				COMMENTS
	1	2	3	4	1	2	3	4	

STUDENT COPY

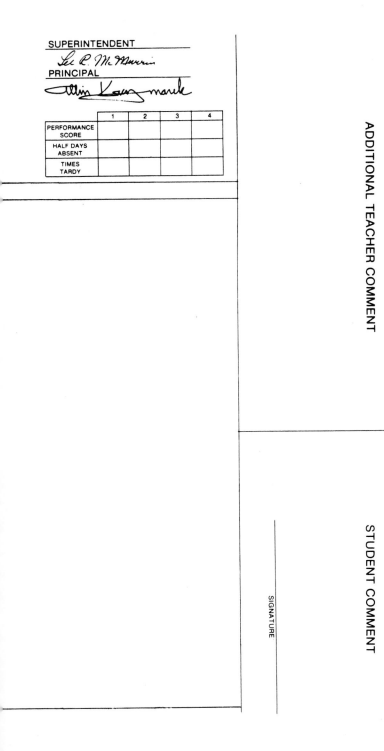

SUPERINTENDENT

PRINCIPAL

	1	2	3	4
PERFORMANCE SCORE				
HALF DAYS ABSENT				
TIMES TARDY				

ADDITIONAL TEACHER COMMENT

PARENT COMMENT

Please detach and return this portion to your child's teacher.

SIGNATURE

STUDENT COMMENT

SIGNATURE

milwaukee public schools

ROBINSON OPEN CLASSROOM SCHOOL
STUDENT PROGRESS REPORT TO PARENTS

STUDENT'S NAME _____
(Last)   (First)

DATE _____ CENTER _____ DAYS ABSENT _____

Your child is participating in an open classroom experience. Emphasis is placed on developing skills and attitudes for independent learning. The following observations reflect an opinion of your child's response to this experience at this time.

1. No observable growth   3. Maintains high level   5. *See written comments

2. Substantial growth   4. Not applicable

	1st		2nd	3rd	4th	5th
	YES	NO				
1. Ability to direct own learning						
2. Ability to select and begin a task						
3. Ability to complete a project or activity						
4. Confidence in own abilities						
5. Respect for peers and adults and their rights and needs						
6. Reading skills						
7. Uses reading for pleasure and to inform						
8. Development of mathematical concepts						
9. Uses resources independently						
10. Ability to set own goals						
11. Ability to evaluate own progress						
12. Uses time responsibly (not interfering with rights of others)						
13. Uses time productively						
14. Ability to function within guidelines						

STUDENT'S NAME _____
(Last)   (First)

TEACHER COMMENTS:

STUDENT COMMENTS:

PRINCIPAL _____ TEACHER _____

Figure L.5 Sample: Student Progress Report to Parents, Open Classroom School. (Printed by permission of the Milwaukee Public Schools System, Milwaukee, Wisconsin.)

Appendix M

Selected Test Scoring Services

American College Testing Program
  P. O. Box 168
  Iowa City, IA 52240

California Test Bureau
  Del Monte Research Park
  Monterey, CA 93940

Educational Testing Service
  Princeton, NJ 08540
    College Entrance
    Examination Board

Harcourt Brace Jovanovich, Inc.
(Psychological Corporation)
  Test Department
  757 Third Avenue
  New York, NY 10017

Houghton Mifflin Scoring Service
  Box 30
  Iowa City, IA 52240

Measurement Research Center
(MRC)
  321 Market Street
  Iowa City, IA 52240

National Computer Systems, Inc.
  1015 South Sixth Street
  Minneapolis, MN 55404

Science Research Associates, Inc.
  Electronic Scoring Service
  259 East Erie Street
  Chicago, IL 60611

Testscor
  2312 Snelling Avenue
  Minneapolis, MN 55404

Appendix N

A Glossary of Common Measurement Terms*

Academic Aptitude—The combination of native and acquired abilities that is needed for school work; likelihood of success in mastering academic work, as estimated from measures of the necessary abilities. (Also called scholastic aptitude.)

Achievement Age—The age for which a given achievement test score is the real or estimated average. (Also called educational age or subject age.) If the achievement age corresponding to a score of 36 on a reading test is 10 years, 7 months (10-7), this means that pupils 10 years, 7 months achieve, on the average, a score of 36 on that test.

Achievement Test—A test that measures the extent to which a person has "achieved" something—acquired certain information or mastered certain skills, usually as a result of specific instruction.

Age Equivalent—The age for which a given score is the real or estimated average score.

Age Norms—Values representing typical or average performance for persons of various age groups.

Alternate-Form Reliability—The closeness of correspondence, or correlation, between results on alternate (equivalent or parallel) forms of a test; thus a measure of the extent to which the two forms are consistent or reliable in measuring whatever they do measure, assuming that the examinees themselves do not change in the abilities measured between the two testings. See **Reliability, Reliability Coefficient, Standard Error.**

---

*This glossary includes the more common terms in test manuals and the literature of measurement. It has been taken, with some revision, from *A Glossary of 100 Measurement Term*, by Roger T. Lennon (Test Service Notebook, No. 13, Copyright 1954 by Harcourt Brace Jovanovich, New York) and *A Glossary of Measurement Terms*, Monteerey, California: CTB/McGraw-Hill; reproduced by permission of the publishers.

Aptitude—A combination of abilities and other characteristics, whether native or acquired, known or believed to be indicative of an individual's ability to learn in some particular area.

Arithmetic Mean—The sum of a set of scores divided by the number of scores. (Commonly called average, mean.)

Average—A general term applied to measures of central tendency. The three most widely used averages are the arithmetic mean, the median, and the mode.

Battery—A group of several tests standardized on the same population, so that results on the several tests are comparable. Sometimes loosely applied to any group of tests administered together, even though not standardized on the same subjects.

Ceiling—The upper limit of ability measured by a test.

Coefficient of Correlation—A measure of the degree of relationship, or "going-togetherness," between two sets of measures for the same group of individuals.

Completion Item—A test calling for the completion (filling in) of a phrase, sentence, etc., from which one or more parts have been omitted.

Correction for Guessing—A reduction in score for wrong answers, sometimes applied in scoring true-false or multiple-choice questions. Many question the validity or usefulness of this device, which is intended to discourage guessing and to yield more accurate rankings of examinees in terms of their true knowledge. Scores to which such corrections have been applied—e.g., rights minus wrongs, or rights minus some fraction of wrongs—are often spoken of as "corrected for guessing" or "corrected for chance."

Correlation—Relationship or "going-togetherness" between two scores or measures; tendency of one score to vary concomitantly with the other, as the tendency of students of high IQ to be above average in reading ability. The existence of a strong relationship—*i.e.*, a high correlation—between two variables does not necessarily indicate that one has any causal influence on the other. See **Coefficient of Correlation.**

Criterion—A standard by which a test may be judged or evaluated; a set of scores, ratings, etc., that a test is designed to predict or to correlate with. See **Validity.**

Decile—Any one of the nine percentile points (scores) in a distribution that divide the distribution into ten equal parts; every tenth percentile. The first decile is the 10th percentile, the 9th decile is the 90th percentile, etc.

Derived Score—A score that has been converted from a qualitative or quantitative mark on one scale into the units of another scale.

1. Grade Placement Equivalent
2. Chronological Age Equivalent
3. Chronological Age-Grade Placement
4. Educational Age
5. Intelligence Quotient (IQ)
6. Intelligence (MA) Grade Placement
7. Mental Age
8. Percentile Rank
9. Standard Score (sigma-score, *T*-score, *z*-score)
10. Anticipated Achievement Grade Placement

Deviation—The amount by which a score differs from some reference value, such as the mean, the norm, or the score on some other test.

Deviation IQ—See **Intelligence Quotient.**

Diagnostic Test—A test used to "diagnose," that is, to locate specific areas of weakness or strength, and to determine the nature of weaknesses or deficiencies; it yields measures of the components or subparts of some larger body of information or skill. Diagnostic achievement tests are most commonly prepared for the skill subjects—reading, arithmetic, spelling.

Discriminating Power—The ability of a test item to differentiate between persons possessing much of some trait and those possessing little.

Distribution (frequency distribution)—A tabulation of scores from high to low, or low to high, showing the number of individuals that obtain each score or fall in each score interval.

Equivalent Form—Any of two or more forms of a test that are closely parallel with respect to the nature of the content and the difficulty of the items included, and that will yield very similar average scores and measures of variability for a given group.

Error of Measurement—See **Standard Error.**

Expectancy Norms—Any of various methods for adjusting achievement test norms with respect to mental ability and chronological age and/or other characteristics of the person or persons to whom the tests are given.

Expected Grade Placement—A computed score representing the achievement test performance of an individual based on a regression technique which is a function of both mental age and chronological age and expressed in grade placement units.

Extrapolation—A process of estimating values of a function beyond the range of available data.

Face Validity—Refers to the acceptability of the test and test situation by the examinee or user, in terms of apparent uses to which the test is to be put. A test has face validity when it appears to measure the variable to be tested.

Factor Analysis—A method (centroid, grouping, principal components) of analyzing the intercorrelations among a set of variables such as test scores. Factor analysis attempts to account for the interrelationships in terms of some underlying "factors," preferably fewer than the original variables. It reveals how much of the variation in each of the original measures arises from or is associated with each of the hypothetical factors.

Frequency Distribution—See **Distribution.**

Grade Equivalent—The grade level for which a given score is the real or estimated average.

Grade Norm—The average score obtained by pupils of given grade placement. See **Norms.**

Intellectual Status Index—A statistically derived index number which indicates the extent to which the chronological age and mental ability of a pupil differ from the chronological age and mental ability characteristics of the basic norming sample for the grade involved. An Intellectual Status Index of 100 indicates that a pupil's chronological age and mental ability characteristics are equivalent to those of the basic norming sample. Values above and below 100 indicate superior and inferior characteristics respectively in an individual pupil as compared with the basic norming sample.

Intelligence Quotient (IQ)—Originally, the ratio of a person's mental age to his/her chronological age (MA/CA) or, more precisely, especially for older persons, the ratio of mental age to the mental age normal for chronological age in both cases multiplied by 100 to eliminate the decimal). More generally, IQ is a measure of brightness that takes into account both the score on an intelligence test and age. A deviation IQ is such a measure of brightness, based on the difference or deviation between a person's obtained score and the score that is normal for the person's age. The following table shows the classification of IQ's offered by Terman and Merrill for the Stanford-Binet test, indicating the percentage of persons in a normal population who fall in each classification. This table is roughly applicable to tests yielding IQ's having standard deviations of about 16 points (not all do). It is important to bear in mind that any such table is arbitrary, for there are no inflexible lines of demarcation between "feeble-minded" and "borderline," etc.

Classification	IQ	Percentages of All Persons
Near genius or genius	140 and above	1
Very superior	130-139	2.5
Superior	120-129	8
Above average	110-119	16
Normal or average	90-109	45
Below average	80-89	16
Dull or borderline	70-79	8
Feeble-minded: moron	60-69	2.5
Feeble-minded: imbecile, idiot	59 and below	1

Interpolation—In general, any process of estimating intermediate values between two known points. As applied to test norms, it refers to the procedure used in assigning interpreted values (*e.g.*, grade or age equivalents) to scores between the successive average scores actually obtained in the standardization process. In reading norm tables, it is necessary at times to interpolate to obtain a norm value for a score between scores given in the table.

Item Analysis—The process of evaluating single test items by any of several methods. It usually involves determining the difficulty value and the discriminating power of the item and often its correlation with some criterion.

Kuder-Richardson Formulas—Formulas for estimating the reliability of a test from information about the individual items in the test, or from the mean score, standard deviation, and the number of items in the test. Because the Kuder-Richardson formulas permit estimation of reliability from a single administration of a test, without the labor involved in dividing the test into halves, their use has become common in test development. The Kuder-Richardson formulas are not appropriate for estimating the reliability of speeded tests.

Matching Item—A test item calling for the correct association of each entry in one list with an entry in a second list.

Mean—See **Arithmetic Mean.**

Median—The middle score in a distribution; the 50th percentile; the point that divides the group into two equal parts. Half of the group of scores fall below the median and half above it.

Mental Age (MA)—The age for which a given score on an intelligence test is average or normal. If a score of 55 on an intelligence test corresponds to a mental age of 6 years, 10 months, then 55 is presumably the average score that would be made by an unselected group of children 6 years, 10 months of age.

Mode—The score or value that occurs most frequently in a distribution.

Multiple-Choice Item—A test item in which the examinee's task is to choose the correct or best answer from several given answers or options.

Multiple-Response Item—A special type of multiple-choice item in which two or more of the given choices may be correct.

N—The symbol commonly used to represent the number of cases in a distribution, study, etc.

Normal Distribution—A distribution of scores or measures that in graphic form has a distinctive bell-shaped appearance. In a normal distribution, scores or measures are distributed symmetrically about the mean, with as many cases at various distances above the mean as at equal distances below it, with cases concentrated near the average and decreasing in frequency the further one departs from the average, according to a precise mathematical equation. The assumption that mental and psychological characteristics are distributed normally has been very useful in much test development work.

Norm Line—A smooth curve drawn through the mean or median scores of successive age or grade groups or through percentile points for a single group.

Norms—Statistics that describe the test performance of specified groups, such as pupils of various ages or grades in the standardization group for a test. Norms are often assumed to be representative of some large population, as of pupils in the country as a whole. Norms are descriptive of average, typical, or mediocre performance; they are not to be regarded as standards or as desirable levels of attainment. Grade, age, and percentile are the most common types of norms.

Objective Test—A test in the scoring of which there is no possibility of difference of opinion among scorers as to whether responses are to be scored right or wrong. It is contrasted with a "subjective" test—*e.g.*, the usual essay examination to which different scorers may assign different scores, ratings, or grades.

Omnibus Test—A test (1) in which items measuring a variety of mental operations are all combined into a single sequence rather than being grouped together by type of operation and (2) from which only a single score is derived, rather than separate scores for each operation or function. Omnibus tests make for simplicity of administration: one set of directions and one overall time limit usually suffice.

Percentile (P)—A point (score) in a distribution below which falls the percent of cases indicated by the given percentile. Thus the 15th percentile denotes the score or point below which 15% of the scores fall. "Percentile" has nothing to do with the percentage of correct answers an examinee has on a test.

Percentile Rank—The percent of scores in a distribution equal to or lower than the score corresponding to the given rank.

Performance Test—As contrasted with paper-and-pencil test, a test requiring motor or manual response on the examinee's part, generally but not always involving manipulation of concrete equipment or materials. Cornell-Coxe Performance Ability Scale, Arthur Point Scale of Performance Tests, and Bennett Hand-Tool Dexterity Test are performance tests, in this sense. "Performance Test" is also used in another sense, to denote a test that is actually a work-sample, and in this sense, it may include paper-and-pencil tests, as, for example, a test in accountancy, or in taking shorthand, or in proofreading, where no materials other than paper and pencil may be required, but where the test response is identical with the behavior about which information is desired.

Personality Test—A test intended to measure one or more of the non-intellective aspects of an individual's mental or psychological make-up.

Power Test—A test intended to measure level of performance rather than speed of response; hence one in which there is either no time limit or a very generous one.

Practice Effect—The influence of previous experience with a test on a later administration of the same test or a similar test; usually, an increase in the score on the second testing, attributed to increased familiarity with the directions, kinds of questions, etc. Practice effect is greatest when the interval between testings is small, when the materials in the two tests are very similar, and when the initial test-taking represents a relatively novel experience for the subjects.

Product-Moment Coefficient—See **Coefficient of Correlation**

Profile—A graphic representation of the results on several tests, for either an individual or a group, when the results have been expressed in some uniform or comparable terms.

Prognosis(Prognostic) Test—A test used to predict future success or failure in a specific subject or field.

Projective Technique (Projective Method)—A method of personality study in which the subject responds as he chooses to a series of stimuli such as ink blots, pictures, unfinished sentences, etc. So-called because of the assumption that under this free-response condition the subject "projects" into his/her responses manifestations of personality characteristics and organization that can, by suitable methods, be scored and interpreted to yield a description of his basic personality structure. The Rorschach (ink-blot) Technique and the Murray Thematic Apperception Test (TAT) are the most commonly used projective methods.

Quartile—One of three points that divide the cases in a distribution into four equal groups. The lowest quartile, or 25th percentile, sets off the lowest fourth of the group; the middle quartile is the same as the 50th percentile, or median; the third quartile, or 75th percentile, marks off the highest fourth.

r—See **Coefficient of Correlation.**

Random Sample—A sample of the members of a population drawn in such a way that every member of the population has an equal chance of being included—that is, drawn in a way that precludes the operation of bias or selection.

Range—The difference between the lowest and highest scores obtained on a test by some group.

Raw Score—The first quantitative result obtained in a scoring test. Usually the number of right answers, number right minus some fraction of number worng, time required for performance, number of errors, or similar direct, unconverted, uninterpreted measure.

Readiness Test—A test that measures the extent to which an individual has achieved a degree of maturity or acquired certain skills or information needed for undertaking successfully some new learning activity. Thus a reading readiness test indicates the extent to which a child has reached a developmental stage where he/she may profitably begin a formal instructional program in reading.

Recall Item—An item that requires the examinee to supply the correct answer from his/her own memory or recollection, as contrasted with a recognition item, in which he/she need only identify the correct answer.

Recognition Item—An item requiring the examinee to recognize or select the correct answer from among two or more given answers.

Reliability—The extent to which a test is consistent in measuring whatever it does measure; dependability, stability, relative freedom from errors of measurement. Reliability is usually estimated by some form of reliability coefficient or by the standard error of measurement.

Reliability Coefficient—The coefficient of correlation between two forms of a test, between scores on repeated administrations of the same test, or between halves of a test, properly corrected. These three coefficients measure somewhat different aspects of reliability but all are properly spoken of as reliability coefficients. See **Alternate-Form Reliability, Kuder-Richardson Formulas, Split-Half Coefficient, Test-Retest Coefficient.**

Representative Sample—A sample that corresponds to or matches the population of which it is a sample with respect to characteristics important for the purposes under investigation—e.g., in an achievement test norm sample, proportion of pupils from each state, from various regions, etc.

Scholastic Aptitude—See **Academic Aptitude.**

Sigma—Designation for **Standard Error** and most frequently applied to **Standard Deviation.**

Skewness—The tendency of a distribution to depart from symmetry or balance around the mean.

Sociometry—Measurement of the interpersonal relationships prevailing among the members of a group. By means of sociometric devices, *e.g.*, the sociogram, an attempt is made to discover the patterns of choice and rejection among the individuals making up the group—which ones are chosen most often as friends or leaders ("stars"), which are rejected by others ("isolates"), how the group subdivides into clusters or cliques, etc.

Spearman-Brown Formula—A formula giving the relationship between the reliability of a test and its length. The formula permits estimation of the reliability of a test lengthened or shortened by any amount, from the known reliability of a test of specified length. Its most common application is in the estimation of reliability of an entire test from the correlation between two halves of the test (split-half reliability).

Split-Half Coefficient—A coefficient of reliability obtained by correlating scores on one half of a test with scores on the other half. Generally, but not necessarily, the two halves consist of the odd-numbered and the even-numbered items.

Standard Deviation (SD)—A measure of the variability or dispersion of a set of scores. The more the scores cluster around the mean, the smaller the standard deviation.

Standard Error (SE)—An estimate of the magnitude of the "error of measurement" in a score—that is, the amount by which an obtained score differs from a hypothetical true score. The standard error is an amount such that in about two-thirds of the cases the obtained score would not differ by more than one standard error from the true score.

Standard Score—A general term referring to any of a variety of "transformed" scores, in terms of which raw scores may be expressed for reasons of convenience, comparability, ease of interpretation, etc.

Standardized Test (Standard Test)—A systematic sample of performance obtained under prescribed conditions, scored according to definite rules, and capable of evaluation by reference to normative information. Some writers restrict the term to tests having the above properties, whose items have been experimentally evaluated, and/or for which evidences of validity and reliability are provided.

Stanine—One of the steps in a nine-point scale of normalized standard scores. The stanine (short for standard-nine) scale has values from 1 to 9, with a mean of 5 and a standard deviation of 2.

Stratified Sample—A sample in which cases are selected by the use of certain controls, such as geographical region, community size, grade, age, sex.

Survey Test—A test that measures general achievement in a given subject or area, usually with the connotation that the test is intended to measure group status, rather than to yield precise measures of individuals.

***T*-Score**—A derived score based upon the equivalence of percentile values to standard scores, thus avoiding the effects of skewed distributions, and usually having a mean equated to 50 and a standard deviation equated to 10.

Test-Retest Coefficient—A type of reliability coefficient obtained by administering the same test a second time after a short interval and correlating the two sets of scores.

True-False Item—A test question or exercise in which the examinee's task is to indicate whether a given statement is true or false.

True Score—A score entirely free of errors of measurement. True scores are hypothetical values never obtained by testing, which always involves some measurement error. A true score is sometimes defined as the average score of an infinite series of measurements with the same or exactly equivalent tests, assuming no practice effect or change in the examinee during the testings.

Validity—The extent to which a test does the job for which it is used. Validity, thus defined, has different connotations for various kinds of tests and, accordingly, different kinds of validity evidence are appropriate for them. For example:

1. The validity of an achievement test is the extent to which the content of the test represents a balanced and adequate sampling of the outcomes (knowledge, skills, etc.) of the course or instructional program it is intended to cover (content, face, or curricular validity). It is best evidenced by a comparison of the test content with courses of study, instructional materials, and statements of instructional goals, and by critical analysis of the processes required in responding to the items.

2. The validity of an aptitude, prognostic, or readiness test is the extent to which it accurately indicates future learning success in the area for which it is used as a predictor (predictive validity). It is evidenced by correlations between test scores and measures of later success.

3. The validity of a personality test is the extent to which the test yields an accurate description of an individual's personality traits or personality organization (status validity). It may be evidenced by agreement between test results and other types of evaluation, such as ratings or clinical classifications, but only to the extent that such criteria are themselves valid.

   The traditional definition of validity as "the extent to which a test measures what it is supposed to measure," seems less satisfactory than the above, since it fails to emphasize that the validity of a test is always specific to the purposes for which the test is used and that different kinds of evidence are appropriate for appraising the validity of various types of tests.

Validity of a test item refers to the discriminating power of the item—its ability to distinguish between persons having much and those having little of some characteristic.

Variability—The spread or dispersion of scores, usually indicated by quartile deviations, standard deviations, range of 90-10 percentile scores, etc.

Index

Tests Index